An Introduction to Modern One-Act Plays

Marshall Cassady

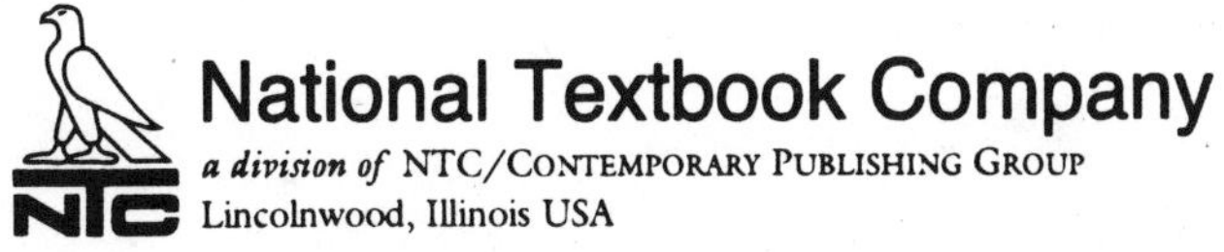
National Textbook Company
a division of NTC/Contemporary Publishing Group
Lincolnwood, Illinois USA

Author acknowledgment

I thank James D. Kitchen for his help in the mechanics of preparing this book and Ann-Marie Dobbs for her help in preparing the Instructor's Guide.

Dedication

Far echoes, my shadow,
and my elephant farm in Calcutta:
in memory of Charles Rector

Cover design
Jeanette Wojtyla

Text design
Arlene Sheer

Published by National Textbook Company, a division of NTC Publishing Group.

Library of Congress Catalog Card Number: 90-61971
Manufactured in the United States of America.

8 9 VP 9 8 7 6 5

Contents

Acknowledgments

Foreword

In *An Introduction to Modern One-Act Plays* you will find a variety of contemporary dramas, chosen to illustrate a range of genres and styles. The plays range from a farcical comedy by Anton Chekhov to the absurdity of Ionesco; from the near hopelessness of Lou Rivers's drama of the depression era to the tragedy of the innocent victims of Nazism.

The plays are classified by genre, although the classifications are not airtight. The Yeats play, for example, might be considered by some as experimental drama. Similarly, the Kaufman play might be considered comedy. The categories are not absolute but are simply a useful way to group plays that have much in common.

An introduction to each play provides a better understanding of who the playwrights are and why they wrote as they did.

Finally, at the end of each play are discussion questions designed to stimulate thinking and understanding. Some of the questions require specific answers, such as indicating the particular comic devices a playwright has used, but others deal with the play's interpretation. Conceivably, one person could interpret a play in a way completely different from that of another person. This is as it should be, so long as the interpretations can be justified, so long as they can be backed up by pointing to specific lines in the play that bear out what the interpreter believes.

History

Although it is often thought that the one-act play is a development of the modern theatre, the form has been around for centuries. In medieval times, the Japanese Noh drama had a highly condensed plot that fit the one-act form's length. At the same time, Miracle and Mystery plays were generally just one act long, as were early English comedies, such as John Heywood's *The Four P's*, written in the sixteenth century. During that same century, the *commedia dell'arte*, a type of improvisational farce, developed in Italy and most often was presented in a one-act form.

The one-act play gained prominence in various European countries during the eighteenth century. The most popular type was *Le Grand Guignol*, which developed in Paris during the latter part of the nineteenth century. Following this tradition, entire theatres were devoted entirely to producing one-act plays, all of a sensational nature.

The one-act form attracted both American and European writers in the 1890s. Most of the plays were presented in vaudeville theatres in the United States and as curtain raisers in England. Those performed in America often were short versions of successful plays starring well-known actors. Curtain raisers were presented to keep an audience entertained while latecomers were seated.

Until well into the second decade of the twentieth century, the one-act plays presented in America were generally inconsequential. Rather than dealing with important themes and characters, most were built around contrived incidents. There were exceptions, however. William Gillette, for instance, wrote realistic melodramas that created the illusion of real life, and William Dean Howells introduced a literary note into the form.

From this beginning there developed a market for amateur productions of short plays that catered to family entertainment and uncomplicated production.

In 1911 the Irish Players from the Abbey Theatre in Dublin toured the United States presenting well-developed one-acters written by such people as John Millington Synge and William Butler Yeats. At about the same time, James Barrie in England began writing a series of one-acters that were grouped together for a single performance.

Then in 1915 the Washington Square Players began presenting a series of one-act plays at the Bandbox Theatre in New York. In three years they presented sixty plays, including one-acters by such well-known writers as Susan Glaspell.

In 1916 the Provincetown Players presented Eugene O'Neill's first produced play, *Bound East for Cardiff*. This, along with his other one-acters, used realistic characters in situations the audiences understood and with whom they identified. Since O'Neill wrote largely from experience, he brought to the one-act form both a truthfulness and an insight into the human condition that most often had been missing up to this point. His plays were largely responsible for ushering in an era of one-acters dealing with important themes and subjects.

Just after World War I, so-called art theatres became popular. They encouraged experimentation with the one-act form and the presentation of provocative ideas.

Then, for a time, interest in the form lagged. In the 1960s there was a resurgence of one-acters written by such playwrights as Peter Shaffer, Jean Claude van Italie, and Neil Simon. Often, these were a series of interrelated plays, centering around a particular theme.

Again, in the 1980s, there was a renewed interest, with one-acters being presented across the United States—from the Ensemble Studio Theatre in Manhattan to the One-Act Theatre Ensemble in Los Angeles. In recent years one-acters have been presented on Broadway, off-Broadway, and off-off-Broadway, winning such awards as Tonys and Pulitzer Prizes.

Structure

The one-act play is to the full-length play as the short story is to the novel. The one-act play, like the short story, is not an inferior form. It is simply different.

There are a number of ways in which the one-act play is unique. First, of course, is its brevity. Although there are exceptions, modern one-acters usually have a playing time of forty minutes to an hour. This means that the play must get to the point immediately.

There often is not as much exposition as in a longer play. Only those facts absolutely necessary for the audience's understanding of the situation and the characters are presented.

In most instances, there are fewer characters, usually no more than two to five, all of whom are essential to the basic action.

The plot of the one-acter is usually simple. In a longer play, there often are a series of events and complications. The one-acter usually deals with only one major event involving one complication. The climax, or turning point, occurs within the last few minutes, and there is little time for the denouement, events following the climax. In a three-act play, the climax often occurs near the middle of the third act, allowing more time for the denouement.

Yet the one-acter often has the same focus as a full-length play. It can deal with the same problems and themes.

It has been said that the one-act play is to the theatre as the lyric poem is to literature. More specifically, the one-acter is like a haiku. Because of its length, it often presents ideas more objectively and more concisely, allowing the audience to draw its own conclusions to round out the experience.

The plays in this book differ greatly in the way they are written as well as in their subject matter. One reason for that is that the one-act play has for years been a vehicle for experimentation. The Theatre of the Absurd, for instance, began with one-acters and only later moved to the longer form.

As you read the plays in this book, keep this in mind: Drama is meant to be performed. Reading a play is not the same as seeing one. Whereas the short story is meant to be read, drama is meant to be acted. The experience of drama on the printed page is almost as remote from the stage as a musical score is from a performance in a concert hall. To read these plays for their full effect, you need to read imaginatively. You need to assume the roles of actor, director, designer in your mind.

Tragedy

Aristotle said that tragedy "is an imitation of an action that is serious, complete, and of a certain magnitude; in language embellished with each kind of artistic ornament, the several kinds being found in separate parts of the play; in the form of action, not narrative; through pity and fear effecting the proper purgation of these emotions."

Many theatre theorists believe that all tragedy must follow this definition, that it has to deal with highly serious and profound problems. Often, it deals with human nature at its most basic—the struggle of good versus evil. Tragic protagonists battle either a flaw in themselves or evil in others, forces always more powerful than they. But through defeat, they remain noble and in this respect are triumphant.

The purpose of tragedy is to make the audience experience emotion by identifying with the tragic hero and his or her struggles. Because of tragedy's elevated spirit, the language is generally elevated as well. Also, to be effective, according to Aristotle, a tragedy must be presented in the form of action. Only if we see what the tragic hero does can we identify with that person. Then we can feel compassion and share in the suffering. We can grieve at the tragic hero's defeat, which is what Aristotle meant by pity. The *fear* is the anxiety aroused by viewing the play, and it then should carry over in our concern for others.

The *purgation of emotions* means a release of emotional tension, a catharsis, that leaves us at peace. We have identified with a noble character, a human being like ourselves. Therefore, we must to a degree possess that character's nobility and positive traits. When the protagonist pursues a goal to the end, we feel the same strength and persistence in ourselves. If the character is good, we, too, have the capacity for goodness, reaffirmed by the protagonist's noble battle. We suffer with the character but can also feel superior. The protagonist has suffered a defeat whereas we are safe and have not been defeated, yet. Above all, tragedy reaffirms our faith in ourselves as part of the human race. Even when tragic characters die, their heroism lives. Not their deaths but what the playwright says about life is important.

The workings of the protagonist's mind are the most important aspect of a tragedy. The ways in which the character reacts create the tragedy, so the writer has to be a skilled analyst of human behavior. The playwright makes us feel we are experiencing the struggle and death of someone close to us. Although good, tragic heroes are imperfect. Because of their weaknesses, we can relate to them.

Even though we suffer with the tragic hero, we find aesthetic beauty in the drama with its grandeur of character, theme, and action. The playwright tries to show life as it is, except perhaps for the grandeur and loftiness. Tragic heroes face the consequences of their actions and realize that they will be defeated. But along the way, they experience new insights into their characters as the audience members experience insights into themselves.

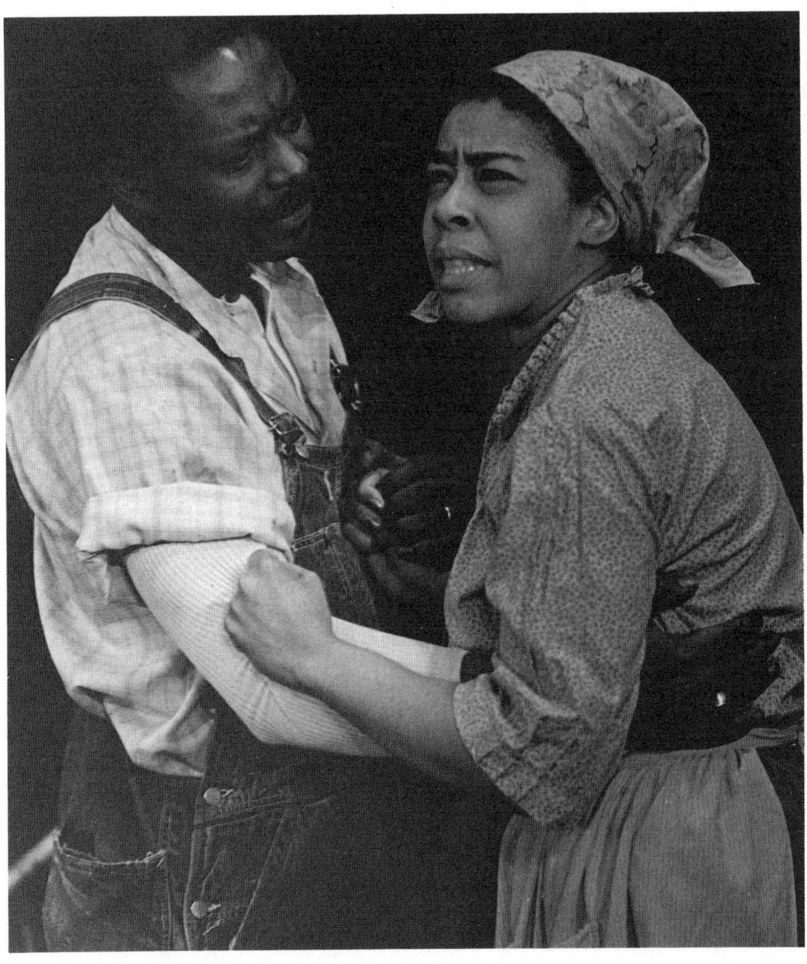

In a scene from This Piece of Land *by Lou Rivers, Perry tries to comfort Rosa in her distress. (A Douglas E. Hunnikin photo, courtesy of Lou Rivers, from a production by the American Theatre Company, New York City)*

LOU RIVERS

This Piece of Land

LOU RIVERS was born in Savannah, Georgia, in 1922. After college he taught language arts and organized a black community theatre that produced some of his plays. He later earned an M.A. degree and a Ph.D. degree and became a college professor.

Since then he has managed to combine two careers: teaching and playwriting.

THIS PIECE OF LAND defies strict classification. Even though the protagonist is dying, she has no tragic flaw that has brought about her defeat. Rather, circumstances cause the hardships the characters have to endure.

Yet the play is close to tragedy in that it makes a powerful statement about the triumph of the human spirit over powerful oppression.

This Piece of Land Lou Rivers

Characters:

THE SINGER
ROSA
PERRY
SISTER WATERS
THE DEACON
MISS NANCY
LEROY
MR. CHARLIE
MR. MORGAN

All characters are Black except one, Mr. Charlie.

Setting:

Time: 1932. One summer day. Place: A small farm in South Carolina.

Center left is a one-story wooden shack obliquely facing downstage. The shack is above the yard and contains several steps leading from the yard up to its long porch and center door flanked by two windows. The porch holds many potted plants, a bench for sitting, and other household items. Upstage, a curved skydrop runs the full length of the stage giving the scene depth and providing right and left exits. A tree down right helps to define the acting area in front of the house and makes for a third exit to the road beyond the scene. There's an element of mysticism about the scene, the grounds not being clearly defined as separate from the sky.

The curtain rises on a quiet scene, just before dawn. The SINGER*'s silhouette slowly fades in across the sky. He sings and plays his guitar to the night fading into dawn.*

SINGER: *(Slow and lamenting)*

"Mornin comes afore the noon.
. . . Then evenin comes . . .
And night's too soon . . .
Spring of year is like the morn . . .
. . . And so life goes . . .
When a man is born.

Autumn comes,
And winter chills.
The baby laughs . . .
The young man thrills.
Day starts low;
The noon runs high.

Seasons begin
And seasons die . . ."

*(*SINGER *makes a horizontal crossing against the sky and disappears beyond the house. A lamp light appears in one of the windows and moves across to the next window. Soon* ROSA *enters from the house. She stands on the porch looking up and about her when* PERRY, *carrying a farming tool, enters from the house; he stands on the porch beside* ROSA. *Presently he crosses and exits up stage beyond the skydrop.* ROSA *waves to him, stands there thinking, returns into the house. Soon the light moves from the window to the next; increases in intensity; shimmers; then goes out. The lights fade up to late morning. The* DEACON, MISS NANCY, *and* SISTER WATERS, *fanning herself, enter slowly and heavily, bringing a vase, quilts, and other items.* ROSA *comes to the porch.)*

SISTER WATERS: Good morning, Sister Rosa.

*(*ROSA *returns greetings as* SISTER WATERS *puts her vase on the top step. Sympathetically.)*

I tried to sell your things, but nobody was able to buy them.

MISS NANCY: *(Putting her items down on the top step.)* And I tried every house on Main Street, Sister. Folks ain't got no use for them now.

THE DEACON: *(He puts his items on the top step.)* I even tried the white folks' churches, Sister. But Sister, as Nancy said there's so little money stirrin nowadays. We did our best. ROSA *looks down on the items then looks searchingly towards the horizon.)*

ROSA: M-m-m-m-m. *(Presently.)* Thank you all for tryin. *(Picks up the vase, studies it.)* I remember Misses Walker wanted to buy this.

MISS NANCY: I especially asked Misses Walker.

ROSA: Once she offered me one hundred dollars for this vase . . . said it was genuine antique.

MISS NANCY: She said she'd bought herself another one. *(*ROSA *fondles the quilt.)*

THE DEACON: We did our best, Sister.

ROSA: I'm sure you all did.

THE DEACON: And as you know, we couldn't begin to pay what you is askin for them.

ROSA: *(Nods.)* I understand. Thank you all for tryin.

MISS NANCY: We wish we could do more to help.

ROSA: Just pray, dear friends, that I don't falter. I've put my trust in Jesus and—well, thank you all for what you all tried to do.

SISTER WATERS: *(Crosses to* ROSA.*)* I pray for you. *(*ROSA *squeezes her hand.)*

ROSA: God bless you. Just remember—I don't want Perry to learn a word about this. *(They nod.)* Now don't let me keep you. I know you all have your own chores to do.

(They nod in agreement and slowly and heavily exit. ROSA *studies the articles then takes them into the house. When she comes back to the porch she hears* LEROY, *who is off, singing: "O Mary Don't You Weep." He enters from the opposite direction carrying his coat thrown across his arm.)*

LEROY: Hey, Mamma!

ROSA: *(Without exuberance.)* Hey, Leroy.

LEROY: *(Sits on top step. Silence, as he looks about him.)* Phew! It must be at least ninety in the shade today. *(Takes his polka dot handkerchief from his hip pocket and wipes his brow.)* We sure nuff could use some rain, huh?

ROSA: Guess the Lord seen no reason yet to give it. *(Sits on the bench and takes her pipe and tobacco from her apron pocket. She fills her pipe.* LEROY *obliquely studies her.)*

LEROY: I know one thing for sure though, if this dry spell don't end off soon, not nary a farmer around here is gonna git a thing to yield this year but tomatoes.

ROSA: It haint been too bad. . . I guess. . . for the tomatoes. Perry says we ought to get a right good yield.

LEROY: Maybe so! But it sure aint much good when the market is already over-run with tomatoes, and George Junior says he heard Mr. Medina aint giving but thirty cents now.

ROSA: Thirty cents.

LEROY: Yes, mam, thirty cents!

ROSA: Lord, hush! Perry mightyn as well feed his tomatoes to the swine! What's they offerin in the big market?

LEROY: I don't know for sure, Mamma, but George Junior told Clarence Brown they is all offerin thirty cents.

ROSA: M-m-m-m. *(Lights her pipe and smokes.)*

LEROY: *(Mops his brow.)* Phew! This sure is a hot one, huh? Where's papa?

ROSA: Out on the farm—pickin the last of the tomatoes. . . He'll be headin in toreckly for something to eat!

(Silence.)

LEROY: You feelin all right, Mamma?

ROSA: No worse then usual.

(Silence.)

LEROY: Sadie told me you all finally heard from Carmen! . . . We thought we oughta write them and ask them to help out a bit.

ROSA: Taint no use to write them.

LEROY: I reckon not. Sadie said Carmen wrote she still wish it was some way she could come back home for a while.

ROSA: *(Smoking her pipe.)* That's what she writ. . . For a while at least she said. Said Thomas hadn't yet got no steady work.

LEROY: Can't say that sound too good, do it? He's been outta work for a long time.

ROSA: Perry said that, too—Both me and him has heared everywheres is as mean as hit can be—It's the depression they calls it.

LEROY: Is papa gonna send for them to come home?

ROSA: What for? . . . And with what? . . . Aint no money here. Might as well starve out there as to comin back home to starve down here. *(Silence.)* How's your younguns?

LEROY: All right. Booker Washington was kinda puny for a day or so—cuttin his teeth. I reckon—he's all right now, huh? Sadie said you sent a message you wanted to see me.

ROSA: I do! It's on business . . . I want when you go to town this afternoon to fetch Mr. Morgan out here to see me.

LEROY: You mean Mr. J.P. Morgan on West Bread Street?

ROSA: I do!

LEROY: *(Anxious.)* Now, what for, Mamma? Didn't you just go to town last week to see Mr. Morgan?

ROSA: I did! Yes, I did. And I went the week before, and he knows it's for business.

LEROY: But, Mamma, why? Why you wanta—

ROSA: *(Puffing on her pipe.)* I wants to see the man on business, Leroy. That's all I'm sayin.

LEROY: Mr. Morgan is a busy man—

ROSA: You just go fetch him and leave the rest to me and him.

(Silence.)

LEROY: *(Troubled.)* Lord knows, Sadie and me tried everything we knowed to get hold of some money.

ROSA: Payment on the mortgage is due this month. Them bank folks done writ the second letter they don't aim to wait no longer.

LEROY: Mamma, now twont it be better if you and papa just give up all this strugglin and go on and let Mr. Charlie pay off the mortgage—

ROSA: No! It can't never be better!

LEROY: He did it for the others, Mamma!

ROSA: This piece of land is Perry's. Hit can't never mean to Mr. Charlie what it means to Perry. And I don't mind tellin you, Leroy, the whole notion of him losing it is about to heave the heart out of his chest.

LEROY: It aint like you and papa was givin up the land for keeps. Mr. Charlie could pay off the mortgage like he did for Alex and the others, and each year you and papa could pay back a little of whatever you could. I don't see no harm in it.

ROSA: Twon't but a fool who thinks Alex and them others is ever gonna own their lands again.

LEROY: I don't know about that, Mamma—Alex said—

ROSA: Well, I do! Every year Alex, Bo-Sam, and them others don't pay nothing back but the interest on their lands, and the main loans keeps waitin right there for them to pay hit off, and they'll never be able to pay it off. Poor old Mr. Maxwell died and his widow and poor six children had to move offern that farm less in a month, the old lady being too weak to sharecrop—

LEROY: Well, I sure don't see how you and papa aim to beat that mortgage!

ROSA: We'll beat it. I got a plan.

LEROY: *(Studies his mother.)* Got somethin to do with Mr. Morgan?

ROSA: Never you mind! You jest fetch Mr. Morgan. After all, Perry mortgaged this farm for gettin me to doctors—and to the hospital—

LEROY: Papa don't grudge you nothin he's done for you—

ROSA: —And I don't aim to see him lose this land after all the hard work he done put in it—not on my account—especially when all the doctors and hospital aint done me no good!

LEROY: You's doing all right, Mamma! The doctors told you—It takes time. Don't expect to get well as quick as you want to! There's time for everything, Mamma!

ROSA: Hush, boy! Hush, Leroy! Now you know papa wouldn't like to hear you talk like that, huh? He's done everything—

LEROY: *(Concerned.)* Mamma—

ROSA: Do you hear me, Leroy?

LEROY: *(Nods.)* Yes, mam!

ROSA: If God chose it to be this way—then it'll have to be, I guess—But I don't aim for Perry to lose both me and the land, not at the same time. *(Rises.)* Here comes Perry now—drippin with sweat, poor man!

PERRY: *(Entering.)* Thought I saw Mr. Charlie's car headin this way! *(Looks to the road.)* Musta made a stop! Hey, boy! What's brung you over here afore eatin time? *(Chuckles.)* Lookin for a handout, eh?

LEROY: No, Papa! Mamma told Sadie last night she wanted to see me.

ROSA: *(Crosses on porch to fetch a towel; throws towel to* PERRY.*)* Want him to run an errand in town for me.

PERRY: *(Sits. Sighs, mops his brow.)* This sure is a hot one, eh?

LEROY: I told mamma it must be at least ninety degees under the shade.

PERRY: One of them mean critters is down there at the furnace all right. *(Bites a piece of tobacco.)* How's my grandboys?

LEROY: All right. Booker Washington is cuttin his bottom teeth now—and is gittin harder for Sadie to handle.

PERRY: *(Chuckles.)* Little rascal! *(Spits.)* Saw Al Ehlers at prayer meetin last night and he says the mens is meetin over at his place tomorrow night—about men's day in the church—and about that idea of the co-operative the preacher spoke about last Sunday—Wants to be sure you git over there.

LEROY: Yeah, I know. I seen Al in town day afore yesterday, and he told me then about the meetin. You aimin to go?

PERRY: Depends on how Rosa here is feelin—

ROSA: I'll be all right. Don't stay here and watch over me. Go on over there and figure out when you all can get to puttin them steps up on the church. Sure don't look good—all these months the church has went without steps. *(Deliberately.)* I don't know how you all would manage to take a deceased body into the church. *(The two men react quietly.)* I spoke to Al about that myself.

LEROY: Stop by for me, and we'll go together.

PERRY: I'll head over there after supper.

MR. CHARLIE: *(Off. Calling in the distance.)* Hey there, Perry! Perry—

PERRY: I knowed I saw his car headin this way. *(Rises and calls.)* Come on up, Mr. Charlie! Mr. Charlie, come on up!

ROSA: *(Straining to see.)* Lord, look at that man! He's go come up here wid all his lies! Sure as I'm born, that man is gonna hang up in hell by the point of his tongue.

PERRY: I told the misses and boy here I thought I seed your car comin up the road.

MR. CHARLIE: *(Off.)* Stopped off at Buddy's place!

ROSA: Don't you talk too long, Perry. I got your vittles in there nice and hot! *(*MR. CHARLIE *enters. He wears a soiled white linen suit. He mops his brow.)*

MR. CHARLIE: I'm willin to bet you all anything old Mayor Jenkins is down there firin the furnace today. This is a mean one, and you've gotta have a mean critter at the furnace.

PERRY: As hot as it is, Mr. Charlie, that furnace must be gittin help from the devil hisself. *(Both* MR. CHARLIE *and* PERRY *laugh.)*

MR. CHARLIE: We's got to git some rain soon or we is gonna parch away like them magnolia leaves. *(He points to a tree.)*

PERRY: Sit down, Mr. Charlie.

MR. CHARLIE: *(Sitting.)* Phew! *(Mops his brow.)* Rosa, how's that overall misery of yours?

ROSA: *(Sits.)* I don't complain none, Mr. Charlie. The good Lord knows how much I can bear.

MR. CHARLIE: Now aint that said jest like a Christian? Rosa, I tell you, I do believe the good Lord is purifyin you for his kingdom. I tell my wife all the time if there's a true-true Christian anywheres around these parts, it's you.

ROSA: I tries to be, Mr. Charlie. I tries my level best.

MR. CHARLIE: And by golly you do succeed. I wouldn't want you prayin agin me, by golly, I'll tell you that!

ROSA: You needn't worry about that. If I can't pray for you, Mr. Charlie, I won't pray against you.

MR. CHARLIE: *(Laughs.)* That ought to put any mind at ease, eh, Perry? *(PERRY laughs.)* I sure don't want you people prayin agin me like you all got to prayin agin Mayor Jenkins.

LEROY: *(Chuckles.)* Mayor Jenkins was a wicked man, Mr. Charlie.

MR. CHARLIE: Maybe so . . . but twon't natcherel . . . the way he hauled off and went . . . when you all got to prayin! Twon't natcherel. *(Licks his cigar.)* Well, Perry, you ready to do business wid me?

PERRY: What business, Mr. Charlie?

MR. CHARLIE: About this here farm. Now you know what I mean—You and me don't aim to start playin cat and mouse wid each other at this late date, do we? You might as well do business wid me. I saw Leonard over at the bank this mornin and he said taint no question about foreclosin on you.

PERRY: They can't foreclose if I make my payments, Mr. Charlie?

MR. CHARLIE: *(Still licking his cigar.)* That's all dependin, aint it, if you's able to make them payments? You aint made none in two months accordin to Leonard. I'm saying, let me make them for you like I did for the other boys. They aint regrettin it none, is they? At least I aint heard no complaints. You'd have a much longer time payin it off to me than you'd have payin it off to the bank. *(Strikes a match to light his cigar.)*

PERRY: I told Mr. Leonard last week I'll make up the payment at the end of the month.

MR. CHARLIE: That's what he said you said, but then I asked him—how is it you gonna do it? Seeing as the dry season didn't yield you people out here nothin. *(Strikes another match.)*

ROSA: We got enough tomatoes to make the payments, Mr. Charlie.

PERRY: That's right! We got quite a good yield. I reckon with them at sixty-five cents a bushel, we'll be able to pay the bank up to three months on that loan—at least.

MR. CHARLIE: That's only three months! Right after, the fourth and the fifth is coming up. What you aim to do about them?

PERRY: Until I start farmin again, I was thinkin of gittin a job in town like my boy here to sort of help out.

MR. CHARLIE: *(Lights his cigar and puffs at it rapidly.)* Perry, I didn't reckon to hear you talk no foolery. There aint no jobs in town, boy, and I'm here to tell you. Why there's more men hangin around town trying to git a job—then there is flies on Lyon's Bakershop's screen door. I don't know whether you people know it or not, but we is having one hell of a depression in the country.

PERRY: Mr. Charlie, I can always make it if I have to.

MR. CHARLIE: You's a farmer, and you aint good at nothin else but farming—Aint Alex and the others told you yet—the big market aint givin but fifteen cents for tomatoes now?

PERRY: Mr. Medina told me sixty-five cents a bushel when I spoke with him the last time.

MR. CHARLIE: That was two weeks ago; the market is overrun now with tomatoes. They aint givin but fifteen cents a bushel to nobody! The white farmers as well as you people out here is gettin the *same* thing.

PERRY: Fifteen cents?

ROSA: We'll give em to the hogs before we sell em for that! *(*MR. CHARLIE *and* ROSA *stare at each other.)*

MR. CHARLIE: *(Presently.)* I know how you people out here feel. I feel the same way myself. It's a damn shame that, after all, I'm stuck with over one-hundred bushels of tomatoes. I paid my croppers sixty-five cents a bushel each last one of them, and now I gotta sell em for much less in the market. Taint no profit in doin that kind of business. Is there? Besides that, hit don't say nothin about the haulin cost from here to Charleston.

PERRY: If I can't get at least sixty-five cents a bushel for my tomatoes, I don't see how I can raise the money for the bank.

MR. CHARLIE: That's why I'm makin you my offer! You a good man, Perry!

(Silence.)

LEROY: Mr. Charlie, if papa was to sign up with you—

ROSA: Perry never said he was signin up with nobody, Leroy!

LEROY: I was only—

ROSA: —With nobody, Leroy!!

MR. CHARLIE: *(Presently.)* Leroy, what was you gonna ask me?

LEROY: I was gonna ask you, sir, how much would you give papa for his tomatoes?

MR. CHARLIE: Well—now—Leroy—I'll have to see. *(Takes his pad and pencil from his pocket.)*

LEROY: The same as you gave the others—sixty-five cents a bushel?

MR. CHARLIE: Well, now that all depends! *(Begins figuring.)*

LEROY: *(Strains to see* MR. CHARLIE*'s figuring.)* Depends on what, Mr. Charlie?

MR. CHARLIE: On how many bushels I could take from your pa! I've got more tomatoes now than I know what to do with! Perry, I tell you what I'll do. For at least fifty bushels, I'll give you sixty-five cents a bushel and pay you cash. How's that? For the remaindin bushels, I'll give you credit at thirty cents a bushel. You can't beat that nowheres around here.

LEROY: Seems fair enough to me, Papa!

MR. CHARLIE: Damn sight better than what the bank would do! Besides I oughta git a little somethin out of the deal myself—at least gas money for haulin. I'll keep the innerest the same as the bank's now got it!

Perry, what you say to that? Come on, boy, I aint got all day. *(*PERRY *looks to* ROSA *who shakes her head.* MR. CHARLIE *sees it.)*

PERRY: I can't make up my mind right yet, Mr. Charlie—

MR. CHARLIE: *(Annoyed.)* Whatcha got to make up your mind about? *(*PERRY *looks to* ROSA.*)*

PERRY: *(Presently.)* I'll have to let you know.

MR. CHARLIE: Sharecroppin aint the worse thing could happen to *you.* I'm good to my croppers! Ask Alex or any of the other boys.

PERRY: I aint sayin you aint, Mr. Charlie—It's just that—*(He looks to* ROSA *again. Turns to* MR. CHARLIE.*)* I've got to have more time to think through what I've gotta do.

MR. CHARLIE: More time! Jesus Christ—Man—You mean to tell me you aim to let a deal like this go by in search of a buyer? Where's your business sense, Perry? Time keeps movin, boy, and opportunity knocks at a new door each new second.

ROSA: Even God Himself allows us time, Mr. Charlie—

MR. CHARLIE: I'll be damn! *(Looks from* PERRY *to* ROSA, *who stares him down.)* All right, Perry! Take as long as you like—but don't let me get off to Charleston before you make up your mind—and I aim to roll my trucks startin next week.

PERRY: All right, Mr. Charlie! I'll let you know by then!

MR. CHARLIE: Good! *(Wipes his neck. Takes a fresh cigar and begins to lick it.)* You all take care of Rosa, here, and Rosa, you pray Perry do the right thing by us all. *(*ROSA *nods.)* Oh, by the way, I hear you fellows are havin a church meetin tomorrow night over at Al Ehler's house. Well, I'm sendin you all a case of Amy's home brew over there. I already told Al about it, and I paid Amy for it, and she'll keep it cool in the well till time you all's meetin. I want all of you fellows over there to think right good of me—and when you all pray, don't pray agin me!

PERRY: *(Chuckles.)* We don't aim to do much prayin over there, Mr. Charlie—just talk about our men's day program at the church.

MR. CHARLIE: All right, Perry—but just in case you all do, take care! So long, Rosa! You pray good for all of us! *(Starts, but returns.)* By the way, Perry, I heard some of you boys been talkin about formin a cooperative—It taint none of my business, but I guess you all know that's communist talk—and against our American government way of life. . . A few men in town got to whisperin about it. *(A pause.)* Just thought I'd tell you. Your preacher mightn of knowed it when he suggested it. Well, until you all make up your minds, I'll mosey on along. Gotta lots of chores fore sunset. *(He exits.)*

(Silence.)

LEROY: Papa, if I was you—

ROSA: You aint your papa! *(More silence.)* Perry, aint you ready for your vittles?

PERRY: Yeah—Rosa. Go on in and fix it.

ROSA: *(Rises.)* You stayin, Leroy?

LEROY: No, Mamma. Sadie and the boys is waitin for me.

ROSA: Tell the boys I send love to em.

LEROY: All right. . . I guess Mr. Charlie sure nuff believes we all got together and prayed against Mayor Jenkins.

ROSA: That man is scared cause he knows he's a devil! And as sure as I was born a woman, he aims to git a holt of this land, but he won't do it. I swear on my life he won't git this piece of land!

PERRY: Go on! Don't get yourself fretful!

ROSA: Hit don't need nobody prayin for or against him and his kind. They all done made homes for themselves in hell a long time ago right next to Mayor Jenkins—

PERRY: Fix me somethin to eat.

ROSA: Leroy! You don't forget to do what I told you.

LEROY: No, Mama, I won't.

ROSA: And when you see Cousin Julia and Gus in town, you tell them I said they oughta come out to see me soon if they aim to.

LEROY: All right, Mamma, I'll tell em!

*(*ROSA *exits into the house. Presently* LEROY *rises and stretches lazily. He studies* PERRY.*)*

LEROY: You all right, Papa?

PERRY: *(Nods.)* It's poor Rosa! It's so hard keepin the truth from her.

LEROY: Papa, she ain't worried about herself. She's worried about you losin this land. *(*PERRY *raises his hand to silence* LEROY. *They both look towards the door.)*

PERRY: You mosey on along. I'm all right, son.

LEROY: See you, Papa!

PERRY: Yeah, boy! I'll eat and then take some time out to stroll over to Clarence and the others. See what's happenin about these tomatoes.

LEROY: Yeah, Papa, do that! And if I was you, I'd give some real hard thinkin on what Mr. Charlie is offerin you. After all, mamma don't understand everything. *(After a pause, he exits.)*

*(*PERRY *sits there thinking. He rises, looks up to the skies.* ROSA *calls him. He wearily exits into the house. The* SINGER*'s silhouette appears on the horizon as a bent farmer hoeing the ground. He sings:)*

SINGER: "This is the land promised to me—
Forty acres to set me free.
This is the land—

This is the land—
This piece of land
Belongs to me!

Work hard, my children, eat the dust.
Work long, my children, and you must—
Break ground, my children with your hand—
But hold on—Hold on to your land!"

(The light fades into an hour later. PERRY *enters from the house picking his teeth. He crosses and stands looking up at the sky. The* SINGER*'s silhouette becomes* PERRY*'s shadow reaching across the sky. He sings:)*

SINGER: "Mornin comes afore the noon...
...Then evenin comes...
And night's too soon...
End of morn is when he's born,
And so death comes
With the sun at morn.
Laughter cries...
And weepin fills the empty quest
A black man makes
Of him that's low
And God on high,
Reasons for why...
He was born to die." *(Exits.)*

*(*PERRY *bites a piece of tobacco and crosses to exit by the way of the road. The lights fade down to a sunset.* ROSA *enters from the house with a small pail of water to wet her potted plants as the* SINGER *appears on the horizon. When she comes to a dying plant, she pulls it from the soil and turns it over in her hand and clutches it hard against her bosom. She looks to the horizon to see the silhouette of the* SINGER *who watches. Finally she throws the plant to the ground and exits into the house. The* SINGER *moves slowly across the horizon.* LEROY *and* MR. MORGAN *enter from the road.* MR. MORGAN *fans himself with a paper-card fan. He stands at the foot of the steps while* LEROY *enters upon the porch and calls.)*

LEROY: *(Knocking and calling.)* Mamma! Mamma, it's me, Leroy with Mr. Morgan.

ROSA: *(From the house.)* Comin!

LEROY: Come on up, Mr. Morgan. Have a seat.

MR. MORGAN: In a minute, Mr. Tucker! I get a whiff of cool breeze right here.

LEROY: *(Knocking.)* Mamma, come on. You know, Mr. Morgan is a busy man.

ROSA: Yes, I'm coming *(Enters.* LEROY *senses something is wrong.)*

LEROY: What's wrong, Mamma?

MR. MORGAN: Hydo, Misses Tucker?

ROSA: Right fair in the middlin, Mr. Morgan, thank you. How is Misses Morgan, and your offsprings?

MR. MORGAN: They're all fine, thank you.

ROSA: That's a blessin, I'm sure. Come up, Mr. Morgan, and have a seat. I believe it's cooler here on the porch.

MR. MORGAN: No, Misses Tucker, if you don't mind I rather stand right here. I don't know where that breeze is comin from, but right along here I'm gettin a real coolin-off feelin.

ROSA: Well, then, now you just stay right there, and Leroy will fetch you a chair from the house. Go on, Leroy, get Mr. Morgan a chair.

LEROY: *(Concerned.)* Mamma, your eyes is wet from cryin. What you been cryin about, huh?

ROSA: Go on, and do as your ma tells you. (LEROY *goes into the house.)* I hear tell the folks in town is havin it mighty hard—just as hard as we is out here on the farms.

MR. MORGAN: It's the depression, Misses Tucker. The worse one this country's ever had—and accordin to the newspapers, it's headin even for worser times.

ROSA: *(Sighs.)* Lord, I jest don't understand it.

LEROY: *(Returning with chair.)* You don't understand what, Mamma?

ROSA: Well, I don't understand for one thing how this country of ours got itself into this mess in the first place. I jes don't understand why there is so much hungriness and misery about us when there is so much food you can't even sell.

MR. MORGAN: Misses Tucker, that's the way it goes with economics. And like the newspapers point it out—in this country one time we have a boom, and the next time we have a bust. You see, at this time, we're havin a bust.

LEROY: Mamma—

ROSA: Leroy, give Mr. Morgan the chair. (LEROY *crosses down to give the chair to* MR. MORGAN.*)*

MR. MORGAN: Thank you kindly, Misses Tucker. *(He sits.* LEROY *returns to the steps below* ROSA.*)*

LEROY: Mamma, if you is painin at all, tell me the truth!

ROSA: *(Looks down at* LEROY *affectionately.)* Son, Mamma is painin every blessed hour of the day.

LEROY: Mamma, do papa know it? Have you told papa? Is that why you've been cryin cause you's painin?

ROSA: *(Touches his head.)* Mamma is all right!

LEROY: But you've been cryin, Mamma. . . and that's not like you!

ROSA: After a while, you get used to livin with pains. It's the questions, son, that keeps turnin over in your mind you jest can't seem to get no answer to.

LEROY: What's the question, Mamma? Ask me the question! I'll answer the question, Mamma! What's the question you keep turnin over in your mind? Is that why you sent for Mr. Morgan?

ROSA: *(She gently places her hand across* LEROY*'s mouth.)* Only God knows the answer, son. *(She moves away from* LEROY.*)*

MR. MORGAN: Misses Tucker, I don't *think* it's our Christian place to ever ask some kinds of questions. We then come mighty close to blasphemy.

ROSA: The good Book says God's got a reason of some kind for *everything* . . . a reason for all of us being here . . . a reason for some of us being white, and some of us being black . . .

LEROY: Mamma, stop talkin like that! You aint yourself! You want me to call the doctor?

ROSA: Why don't He see fit to let the reasons be made clear to us. Hit don't make no sense—Me being born, you, Perry, Leroy here . . . all of us strugglin to live, strugglin to hold on to a little somethin we can call our very own—and then without havin nary a word to say about it, we have to give it up and go away and be jedged.

LEROY: Mamma, you want me to call papa?—I'm goin—You don't sound right to me.

ROSA: No! *(Stops* LEROY.*)* Aint no doctor can do me no good except Doctor Jesus! *(To the alarmed* LEROY.*)* Oh, you gotta ask if you is a honest woman. Why, God Almighty, did you see fittin to put hatred and malice in the hearts of your children . . . to put this livin things within me . . . *(Holds her abdomen.)* that don't serve no aim but to sap the usefulness outta me!

LEROY: *(More alarmed.)* Mamma, what you talkin about?

ROSA: *(To God.)* Why, God, *why? (To* LEROY.*)* Hit don't make no sense! And all the pushin and shovin and folks starvin and tearin the hearts out of one another. Why?! Didn't Jesus die on the cross to put an end to it all?

(Long silence. She looks down at the frightened LEROY *and to the uncomfortable* MR. MORGAN.*)*

MR. MORGAN: Them's mighty powerful and frightenin questions you is askin of God, Misses Tucker!

ROSA: Mighty powerful questions, but you gotta ask them if you is honest, Mr. Morgan.

LEROY: Mamma, I'm gonna call papa!

ROSA: He aint on the place, Leroy! He went over to see Clarence and the others about what they aim to do with their tomatoes. He oughta be gettin back soon. You set down there and hush a while whilst I talk business with Mr. Morgan. *(She goes down to the ground to look over the land.)*

*(*LEROY *sits on the top step anxious about* ROSA. MR. MORGAN *rises when* ROSA *comes down.* ROSA *finally takes a deep sigh and turns to* MR. MORGAN.*)*

ROSA: Sit down, Mr. Morgan. *(He sits.)* Did you figure out the full amount as I told you to?

MR. MORGAN: Misses Tucker, there's plenty of time for us to figure out these things. Aint no sense in hurryin them on.

ROSA: I told you I wanted all that information figured out by the time I sent for you.

LEROY: *(Rises.)* Mamma—

ROSA: *(Waves* LEROY *quiet.)* How much you gonna charge me for that gray casket?

MR. MORGAN: *(Takes his paper from his pocket.)* Now, Misses Tucker, you—

ROSA: I mean the one with the golden stars. And the family cars? I figured it would take at least three to hold all of my relatives and closest of friends.

LEROY: By God, it aint natcherel, Mamma! It aint natcherel for us to go plannin our own burial.

ROSA: I guess it aint—when you don't know it's comin—you might look like you's hurryin it on—*(Silence.)* but when you know, Leroy, I don't see why it haint the natcherelest thing on God's earth to do.

MR. MORGAN: The sickest aint always the nearest to the grave, Misses Tucker.

ROSA: How much, Mr. Morgan?

MR. MORGAN: Well—now—you realize you picked one of the best caskets in the house. That casket by itself at least cost five hundred dollars.

ROSA: That's too much!

MR. MORGAN: But I'm gonna let you have it at three hundred dollars though.

ROSA: And the cars?

MR. MORGAN: Each car—let's see—well, it should cost you—say thirty dollars a car—all together ninety dollars.

ROSA: That's three hundred and ninety dollars. What's for the chimes on the hearst?

MR. MORGAN: Well, now—let me see—the chimes ought to be an additional thirty dollars. But, being it's you, I'll say twenty-five dollars. Now let's see twenty-five dollars for the chimes, plus ninety dollars for the cars, plus three hundred dollars—all total four hundred and fifteen dollars.

ROSA: Make it a round four hundred dollars, Mr. Morgan! Oh, my God! Here comes Perry. Now let's all make out like we was just talkin. You all set and keep quiet.

(PERRY *enters. He immediately senses something is wrong.* MR. MORGAN *rises.)*

PERRY: Howdy everybody?!

MR. MORGAN: Hydo, Mr. Tucker?

PERRY: Howdy, Mr. Morgan? *(Looks from* LEROY *to* ROSA.*)* What's Mr. Morgan doin out here wid his pad and pencil? *(*LEROY *turns away.)*

LEROY: Mamma wouldn't let me fetch you!

PERRY: *(Turns to* ROSA, *who walks away. Turns to* MR. MORGAN, *who lowers his head.)* Aint somebody's gonna tell me what the buryin man's doin out here on my place? *(Goes to* ROSA.*)*

ROSA: Perry, I sent for him to come here!

PERRY: Is you shuttin me out on something, Rosa? Why? What you want to see Mr. Morgan about?

ROSA: Perry, can't a woman who knows she's gonna die, make the arrangements for her own funeral?

PERRY: Who's dyin?

ROSA: *I'm* dyin! Perry, I'm dyin.

PERRY: Who said anything about you dyin? *(Turns to* LEROY.*)* Boy, did you tell your ma—

LEROY: Not me, Papa! By God, I never mentioned a word!

PERRY: *(To* ROSA.*)* Who told you such an audacious lie, Rosa? Who in heaven's name—

ROSA: Taint no lie, Perry, and if anybody told me, it was you! *(Reads his eyes.)* The deep down hurt inside you told me. You told me in everything you did, in everything you said to me—

PERRY: Oh, Good God, have mercy. *(Walks away.)*

ROSA: *(Follows him.)* Don't you know when you hurt deep you can't hide it from me—Perry, this is Rosa! You's been tryin to hold the truth back ever since the doctor told you months ago.

PERRY: Doctors have been wrong before, Rosa, you know that.

ROSA: This time, the doctors aint wrong! And I know that. You've did your best. You sent me to the hospital and they couldn't do no good! So before I go Perry, I wants to arrange things the way I want them to be. . . I went down last week and picked out the casket I like. I figured with the family we got, we could get by with the three cars. Other church members, I reckon, will donate their wagons and buggies to accommodate those others who wants to follow me to the buryin ground.

(LEROY *takes his handkerchief and weeps quietly.)*

PERRY: Rosa, don't bust my heart wide open! Don't you bust my heart, woman!

ROSA: Leroy, you stop that! Now don't you do that to Perry. *(Goes to* LEROY.*)* This is the time, boy, to give him your strength, not your weakness.

LEROY: Mamma, please—

ROSA: Taint no tears, no nothing's gonna change what's gonna happen—so we might as well build ourselves to bear the truth. *(Crosses to Perry.)* You come, Perry, sit down over here. *(She leads Perry to the step.)*

*(*LEROY *puts an affectionate arm about his father and sits beside him weeping quietly.)*

ROSA: Now, let's see Mr. Morgan, where was we?

MR. MORGAN: We figured the total to be four hundred and fifteen dollars, Misses Tucker.

ROSA: We said four hundred dollars even, Mr. Morgan.

MR. MORGAN: Yes, that's right, four hundred dollars.

ROSA: That's gonna be the cost of my funeral, not a cent over!

MR. MORGAN: If you say!

ROSA: That's what I say! *(She pulls her apron. For a brief silence she watches* PERRY *and* LEROY.*)*

MR. MORGAN: No floral pieces?

ROSA: Don't worry about the flowers. The Sisters and Brothers of the church will see to that. *(Takes policies from her apron pocket.)*Now, Mr. Morgan, here is all my life insurance paid up to full. Here's the policy for the Pilgrim's Life, the Metropolitan Life Policy, policy for the Freedom Life—all paid up to full: they should total to two thousand and four hundred dollars.

MR. MORGAN: Yes, um!

ROSA: I'm gonna ask you to make a deal with me. If you don't want to do it, you just say so. I don't want no hemmin and hawin about it, if you can't then I'm gonna send for Mr. Kraft at the Sunshine Undertakers—and I'll make the deal with him!

PERRY: No—

ROSA: My God, Perry don't fight me! *(Above* PERRY.*)* Is it a deal, Mr. Morgan?

MR. MORGAN: *(Flustered.)* Well, now—Misses Tucker—I don't—

ROSA: *(Sharply.)* I don't want no hemmin and hawin, Mr. Morgan! Is it a deal or aint it?

MR. MORGAN: *(More flustered.)* Well, I never had no deal like this before. I don't even know if it's legal.

PERRY: It aint legal! It's a sin before God!!! *(Points the way.)* You get off my place, Mr. Morgan! *(He starts for* MR. MORGAN. ROSA *and* LEROY *struggle to stop him.)*

ROSA: Perry, it aint no sin!. . .

(Stops MR. MORGAN *who has been edging away. She breaks into tears but aborts them.)*

And it's legal all right!

MR. MORGAN: How do you know, Misses Tucker? How can you tell?

ROSA: Because it's my life, Mr. Morgan. That's all it's worth. I'm givin it to you in order to save the land!

MR. MORGAN: Misses Tucker, should a piece of land mean so much to you?

PERRY: Mr. Charlie can have this damn land! I don't want it!!

(A silence. Overcome by tears, he walks abruptly away from LEROY *who tries to console him, giving the others his back. The others watch his back, seeing him finally gain control.)*

ROSA: *(Quietly.)* Is it a deal?

MR. MORGAN: *(Finally and quietly.)* It's a deal if that's—what you want.

ROSA: Very well then. You go down tomorrow and settle the business with the bank and bring the final papers and the remainders of nine hundred dollars to me—*(They hesitate.)* Thank you, Mr. Morgan! You's a good man! *(She shakes his hand and starts for the house. Stops to observe* PERRY *and* LEROY.*)* Leroy, you go home to Sadie and the younguns! Me and Perry wants to be alone. . . for a while.

MR. MORGAN: I'll drop you off, Mr. Tucker!

LEROY: Mamma—*(*ROSA *moves swiftly and exits into the house.)*

LEROY: *(After a moment.)* Papa, we shoulda known we could *never* keep her from knowing. *(He slowly moves towards the exit.)* (MR. MORGAN *crosses to* PERRY.*)*

MR. MORGAN: You being the man, Mr. Tucker, tell me what to do.

PERRY: *(Lowers his head.)* I wish I knowed. . . *(Looks into the sky.)* I wish I knowed what to tell you. . .

LEROY: Coming, Mr. Morgan?

PERRY: *(More to himself then to* MR. MORGAN.*)* I wish I knowed.

MR. MORGAN: Mr. Tucker, God help you. I'll go down to the bank first thing in the morning.

(MR. MORGAN *exits.* LEROY *follows.* PERRY *crosses to sit on the step with his head in his hands. The sun sets more. Soon* ROSA *enters. She's smoking her pipe. She stands there watching* PERRY.*)*

ROSA: Perry?

PERRY: Yes, Rosa?

ROSA: You vex with me? *(PERRY shakes his head.)* Don't be.

PERRY: I'm losing you, Rosa... What good is the land without you?

ROSA: Well, Perry... *(Sits next to him.)* for one thing, you won't lose the land to Mr. Charlie! *(Silence.)* I reckon—with all the work we put into this land, we have just about paid for it three or more times over... and to lose it for a little of nothin—you love this land—you love it like some men love a second woman— *(Silence as the two look over the land.)* We've got the grandchildren... they ought to have some home place they can return to—there's Carmen and Thomas wantin to come home for a visit... and Leroy and his younguns—This land will be a remembrance—We always said every man oughta have a little piece of land to call his own.

PERRY: But, Rosa, to take your life insurance money—

ROSA: This land is our pride... *(Puts her arm around his shoulder.)* Since I was a little girl, each week we paid on them policies. Before I did, my pa did; and since they air called life insurances they ought to go for helpin life! Don't make no sense that all I'm worth should be put into the ground behind me. *(Silence as she studies PERRY.)*

PERRY: *(Alarmed.)* What's the matter?

ROSA: Perry, do you believe in the hereafter?

PERRY: I do!

ROSA: Do you believe that heaven is as light and coolin as a rain shower on a hot summer day?

PERRY: Yes, Rosa, I believe it.

ROSA: And, do you believe hell is there at the end of eternity in all its bleakness and ugliness for wicked men?

PERRY: What you gittin at, Rosa?

ROSA: Oh, Perry, pray for me! I jest can't git it out of my head and heart—Is God any more fairer to us than the white man?

PERRY: Rosa!

ROSA: Perry, I'm falterin.

PERRY: Now don't talk no more like that!

ROSA: Perry, God mustn't be white—God mustn't be white!

PERRY: God aint got no color at all. God is the spirit of love. Jesus lived and was crucified to teach us to love one another, and he was a white man. *(He holds on to her hands.)*

ROSA: Perry, God mustn't be white. *(Holds tightly to PERRY. Presently.)* I'm feelin all right now, Perry... Look at the sun... The day's almost gone... Tomorrow, a new day, a new life... another beginning... *(After a long silence she rises.)* Come on in, and I'll rub your back for you.

PERRY: I'll come.
ROSA: All right. *(Touches him tenderly.)* Don't fret none. I'm all right now.

(She lingers to look off into the sky then exits into the house. The SINGER *in silhouette, appears on the horizon.)*

SINGER: *(As he sings, the light appears in the window.* PERRY *slowly rises and exits into the house.)*

"Mornin comes afore the noon...
...Then evenin comes...
And night's too soon...
Spring of year is like the morn...
...And so life goes...
When a man is born.

Autumn comes,
And winter chills.
The baby laughs...
The young man thrills.
Day starts low;
The noon runs high.
Seasons begin
And seasons die..."

(The light in the window goes out. The SINGER *continues to sing as he slowly moves across the horizon to completely enshroud the stage.)*

Curtain.

Questions

1. Identify the antagonist in this play and justify your choice.
2. Are there any villains in the play? Explain.
3. What is the significance of the Singer?
4. Why is the land so important to Rosa?

5. What did you think of Rosa's scheme for paying off the mortgage on the land?
6. What kind of person is Rosa? Perry? Leroy?
7. What is the play's central idea? Why do you think so?
8. Do you find the play believable? Why or why not?

WILLIAM BUTLER YEATS

At the Hawk's Well

WILLIAM BUTLER YEATS is usually considered one of the greatest twentieth-century poets. Because of this, his accomplishments as a playwright often receive less attention. Yet Yeats, who lived from 1865 to 1939, wrote more than thirty plays, blending the poetic with the dramatic.

Born near Dublin, Ireland, Yeats and another playwright, Lady Gregory, started the Irish dramatic movement in 1899, which was the real beginning of Irish theatrical tradition.

Yeats's later plays contain some of the best poetry written in the English language.

AT THE HAWK'S WELL is characteristic of Yeats's later plays in that it is brief and concise, making strict demands on the audience's imagination and intelligence. The play is highly symbolic with stark, bare language. The first of *Four Plays for Dancers*, it was originally presented in a private home, using a patterned screen for a set and with the folding and unfolding of the cloth replacing the curtain.

Based on Irish mythology, the play's central character is Cuchulain, the major hero in the Ulster Cycle of Irish heroic myth. *At the Hawk's Well* presents an episode from his early life. Although not a tragedy in the strictest sense of the word (because the hero does not die), the continuing mood is one of defeat and disillusionment.

The play contains three other references to Irish mythology. The Sidhe (pronounced *shee*) is the name of an ancient and divine race that had once owned Ireland. After being conquered by other gods, they became invisible. Sualtim, a warrior, was believed to be Cuchulain's mortal father, though Cuchulain claimed to be the son of Lugh, the Sun God. Aoife was a warrior queen, defeated in battle by Cuchulain. After Cuchulain's departure, Aoife bore him a son, Conlaoch. The boy was later unwittingly killed in combat by his father.

At The Hawk's Well William Butler Yeats

Characters

THREE MUSICIANS *(their faces made up to resemble masks)*
THE GUARDIAN OF THE WELL *(with face made up to resemble a mask)*
AN OLD MAN *(wearing a mask)*
A YOUNG MAN *(wearing a mask)*

Setting:

The Irish Heroic Age.

The stage is any bare space before a wall against which stands a patterned screen. A drum and a gong and a zither have been laid close to the screen before the play begins. If necessary, they can be carried in, after the audience is seated, by the FIRST MUSICIAN, *who also can attend to the lights if there is any special lighting. We had two lanterns upon posts—designed by Mr. Dulac—at the outer corners of the stage, but they did not give enough light, and we found it better to play by the light of a large chandelier. Indeed, I think, so far as my present experience goes, that the most effective lighting is the lighting we are most accustomed to in our rooms. These masked players seem stranger when there is no mechanical means of separating them from us. The* FIRST MUSICIAN *carries with him a folded black cloth and goes to the centre of the stage towards the front and stands motionless, the folded cloth hanging from between his hands. The two other* MUSICIANS *enter and, after standing a moment at either side of the stage, go towards him and slowly unfold the cloth, singing as they do so:*

I call to the eye of the mind
A well long choked up and dry
And boughs long stripped by the wind,
And I call to the mind's eye
Pallor of an ivory face,
Its lofty dissolute air,
A man climbing up to a place
The salt sea wind has swept bare.

As they unfold the cloth, they go backward a little so that the stretched cloth and the wall make a triangle with the FIRST MUSICIAN *at the apex supporting the centre of the cloth. On the black cloth is a gold pattern suggesting a hawk. The* SECOND *and* THIRD MUSICIANS *now slowly fold up the cloth again, pacing with a rhythmic movement of the arms towards the* FIRST MUSICIAN *and singing:*

What were his life soon done!
Would he lose by that or win?
A mother that saw her son
Doubled over a speckled shin,

Cross-grained with ninety years,
Would cry, "How little worth
Were all my hopes and fears
And the hard pain of his birth!"

The words "a speckled shin" are familiar to readers of Irish legendary stories in descriptions of old men bent double over the fire. While the cloth has been spread out, the GUARDIAN OF THE WELL *has entered and is now crouching upon the ground. She is entirely covered by a black cloak; beside her lies a square blue cloth to represent a well. The three* MUSICIANS *have taken their places against the wall beside their instruments of music; they will accompany the movements of the players with gong or drum or zither.*

FIRST MUSICIAN: *(Singing)*
The boughs of the hazel shake,
The sun goes down in the west.
SECOND MUSICIAN: *(Singing)*
The heart would be always awake,
The heart would turn to its rest.

(They now go to one side of the stage rolling up the cloth)

FIRST MUSICIAN: *(Speaking.)* Night falls;
The mountain-side grows dark;
The withered leaves of the hazel
Half choke the dry bed of the well;
The guardian of the well is sitting
Upon the old grey stone at its side,
Worn out from raking its dry bed,
Worn out from gathering up the leaves.
Her heavy eyes
Know nothing, or but look upon stone.
The wind that blows out of the sea
Turns over the heaped-up leaves at her side;
They rustle and diminish.
SECOND MUSICIAN: I am afraid of this place.
BOTH MUSICIANS: *(Singing.)*
"Why should I sleep?" the heart cries,
"For the wind, the salt wind, the sea wind,
Is beating a cloud through the skies;
I would wander always like the wind."

(An OLD MAN *enters through the audience.)*

FIRST MUSICIAN: *(Speaking.)* That old man climbs up hither,
Who has been watching by his well

These fifty years.
He is all doubled up with age;
The old thorn-trees are doubled so
Among the rocks where he is climbing.

(The OLD MAN *stands for a moment motionless by the side of the stage with bowed head. He lifts his head at the sound of a drumtap. He goes toward the front of the stage moving to the taps of the drum. He crouches and moves his hands as if making a fire. His movements, like those of the other persons of the play, suggest a marionette.)*

FIRST MUSICIAN: *(Speaking.)* He has made a little heap of leaves;
He lays the dry sticks on the leaves
And, shivering with cold, he has taken up
The fire-stick and socket from its hole.
He whirls it round to get a flame;
And now the dry sticks take the fire,
And now the fire leaps up and shines
Upon the hazels and the empty well.
MUSICIANS: *(Singing.)*
"O wind, O salt wind, O sea wind!"
Cries the heart, "it is time to sleep;
Why wander and nothing to find?
Better grow old and sleep."
OLD MAN: *(Speaking.)* Why don't you speak to me? Why don't you say:
"Are you not weary gathering those sticks?
Are not your fingers cold?" You have not one word,
While yesterday you spoke three times. You said:
"The well is full of hazel leaves." You said:
"The wind is from the west." And after that:
"If there is rain it's likely there'll be mud."
To-day you are as stupid as a fish,
No, worse, worse, being less lively and as dumb.

(He goes nearer.)

Your eyes are dazed and heavy. If the Sidhe
Must have a guardian to clean out the well
And drive the cattle off, they might choose somebody
That can be pleasant and companionable
Once in the day. Why do you stare like that?
You had that glassy look about the eyes
Last time it happened. Do you know anything?
It is enough to drive an old man crazy
To look all day upon these broken rocks,

And ragged thorns, and that one stupid face,
And speak and get no answer.
YOUNG MAN: *(Who has entered through the audience during the last speech.)*
Then speak to me,
For youth is not more patient than old age;
And though I have trod the rocks for half a day
I cannot find what I am looking for.
OLD MAN: Who speaks?
Who comes so suddenly into this place
Where nothing thrives? If I may judge by the gold
On head and feet and glittering in your coat,
You are not of those who hate the living world.
YOUNG MAN: I am named Cuchulain, I am Sualtim's son.
OLD MAN: I have never heard that name.
YOUNG MAN: It is not unknown.
I have an ancient house beyond the sea.
OLD MAN: What mischief brings you hither?—you are like those
Who are crazy for the shedding of men's blood,
And for the love of women.
YOUNG MAN: A rumour has led me,
A story told over the wine towards dawn.
I rose from table, found a boat, spread sail,
And with a lucky wind under the sail
Crossed waves that have seemed charmed, and found this shore.
OLD MAN: There is no house to sack among these hills
Nor beautiful woman to be carried off.
YOUNG MAN: You should be native here, for that rough tongue
Matches the barbarous spot. You can, it may be,
Lead me to what I seek, a well wherein
Three hazels drop their nuts and withered leaves,
And where a solitary girl keeps watch
Among grey boulders. He who drinks, they say,
Of that miraculous water lives for ever.
OLD MAN: And are there not before your eyes at the instant
Grey boulders and a solitary girl
And three stripped hazels?
YOUNG MAN: But there is no well.
OLD MAN: Can you see nothing yonder?
YOUNG MAN: I but see
A hollow among stones half-full of leaves.
OLD MAN: And do you think so great a gift is found
By no more toil than spreading out a sail,
And climbing a steep hill? O, folly of youth,
Why should that hollow place fill up for you,

That will not fill for me? I have lain in wait
For more than fifty years, to find it empty,
Or but to find the stupid wind of the sea
Drive round the perishable leaves.
YOUNG MAN: So it seems
There is some moment when the water fills it.
OLD MAN: A secret moment that the holy shades[1]
That dance upon the desolate mountain know,
And not a living man, and when it comes
The water has scarce plashed[2] before it is gone.
YOUNG MAN: I will stand here and wait. Why should the luck
Of Sualtim's son desert him now? For never
Have I had long to wait for anything.
OLD MAN: No! Go from this accursed place! This place
Belongs to me, that girl there, and those others,
Deceivers of men.
YOUNG MAN: And who are you who rail
Upon those dancers that all others bless?
OLD MAN: One whom the dancers cheat. I came like you
When young in body and in mind, and blown
By what had seemed to me a lucky sail.
The well was dry, I sat upon its edge,
I waited the miraculous flood, I waited
While the years passed and withered me away.
I have snared the birds for food and eaten grass
And drunk the rain, and neither in dark nor shine
Wandered too far away to have heard the plash,
And yet the dancers have deceived me. Thrice
I have awakened from a sudden sleep
To find the stones were wet.
YOUNG MAN: My luck is strong,
It will not leave me waiting, nor will they
That dance among the stones put me asleep;
If I grow drowsy I can pierce my foot.
OLD MAN: No, do not pierce it, for the foot is tender.
It feels pain much.
But find your sail again
And leave the well to me, for it belongs
To all that's old and withered.
YOUNG MAN: No, I stay.

1. Ghosts.
2. Gently splashed.

(The GUARDIAN OF THE WELL *gives the cry of the hawk.)*

There is that bird again.
OLD MAN: There is no bird.
YOUNG MAN: It sounded like the sudden cry of a hawk,
But there's no wing in sight. As I came hither
A great grey hawk swept down out of the sky,
And though I have good hawks, the best in the world
I had fancied, I have not seen its like. It flew
As though it would have torn me with its beak,
Or blinded me, smiting with that great wing.
I had to draw my sword to drive it off,
And after that it flew from rock to rock.
I pelted it with stones, a good half-hour,
And just before I had turned the big rock there
And seen this place, it seemed to vanish away.
Could I but find a means to bring it down
I'd hood it.
OLD MAN: The Woman of the Sidhe herself,
The mountain witch, the unappeasable shadow.
She is always flitting upon this mountain-side,
To allure or to destroy. When she has shown
Herself to the fierce women of the hills
Under that shape they offer sacrifice
And arm for battle. There falls a curse
On all who have gazed in her unmoistened eyes;
So get you gone while you have that proud step
And confident voice, for not a man alive
Has so much luck that he can play with it.
Those that have long to live should fear her most,
The old are cursed already. That curse may be
Never to win a woman's love and keep it;
Or always to mix hatred in the love;
Or it may be that she will kill your children,
That you will find them, their throats torn and bloody,
Or you will be so maddened that you kill them
With your own hand.
YOUNG MAN: Have you been set down there
To threaten all who come, and scare them off?
You seem as dried up as the leaves and sticks,
As though you had no part in life.

(The GUARDIAN OF THE WELL *gives hawk cry again.)*

That cry!

There is that cry again. That woman made it,
But why does she cry out as the hawk cries?

OLD MAN: It was her mouth, and yet not she, that cried.
It was that shadow cried behind her mouth;
And now I know why she has been so stupid
All the day through, and had such heavy eyes.
Look at her shivering now, the terrible life
Is slipping through her veins. She is possessed.
Who knows whom she will murder or betray
Before she awakes in ignorance of it all,
And gathers up the leaves? But they'll be wet;
The water will have come and gone again;
That shivering is the sign. O, get you gone,
At any moment now I shall hear it bubble.
If you are good you will leave it. I am old,
And if I do not drink it now, will never;
I have been watching all my life and maybe
Only a little cupful will bubble up.

YOUNG MAN: I'll take it in my hands. We shall both drink,
And even if there are but a few drops,
Share them.

OLD MAN: But swear that I may drink the first;
The young are greedy, and if you drink the first
You'll drink it all. Ah, you have looked at her;
She has felt your gaze and turned her eyes on us;
I cannot bear her eyes, they are not of this world,
Nor moist, nor faltering; they are no girl's eyes.

(He covers his head. The GUARDIAN OF THE WELL *throws off her cloak and rises. Her dress under the cloak suggests a hawk.)*

YOUNG MAN: Why do you fix those eyes of a hawk upon me?
I am not afraid of you, bird, woman, or witch.

(He goes to the side of the well, which the GUARDIAN OF THE WELL *has left.)*

Do what you will, I shall not leave this place
Till I have grown immortal like yourself.

(He has sat down; the GUARDIAN OF THE WELL *has begun to dance, moving like a hawk. The* Old Man *sleeps. The dance goes on for some time.)*

FIRST MUSICIAN: *(Singing or half-singing.)*
O God, protect me
From a horrible deathless body
Sliding through the veins of a sudden.

(The dance goes on for some time. The YOUNG MAN *rises slowly.)*

FIRST MUSICIAN: *(Speaking.)* The madness has laid hold upon him now,
For he grows pale and staggers to his feet.

(The dance goes on.)

YOUNG MAN: Run where you will,
Grey bird, you shall be perched upon my wrist.
Some were called queens and yet have been perched there.

(The dance goes on.)

FIRST MUSICIAN: *(Speaking.)* I have heard water plash; it comes, it comes;
Look where it glitters. He has heard the plash;
Look, he has turned his head.

(The GUARDIAN OF THE WELL *has gone out. The* YOUNG MAN *drops his spear as if in a dream and goes out.)*

MUSICIANS: *(Singing.)*
He has lost what may not be found
Till men heap his burial-mound
And all the history ends.
He might have lived at his ease,
An old dog's head on his knees,
Among his children and friends.

(The OLD MAN *creeps up to the well.)*

OLD MAN: The accursed shadows have deluded me,
The stones are dark and yet the well is empty;
The water flowed and emptied while I slept.
You have deluded me my whole life through,
Accursed dancers, you have stolen my life.
That there should be such evil in a shadow!
YOUNG MAN: *(Entering.)* She has fled from me and hidden in the rocks.
OLD MAN: She has but led you from the fountain. Look!
Though stones and leaves are dark where it has flowed,
There's not a drop to drink.

(The MUSICIANS *cry "Aoife!" "Aoife!" and strike gong.)*

YOUNG MAN: What are those cries?
What is that sound that runs along the hill?
Who are they that beat a sword upon a shield?
OLD MAN: She has roused up the fierce women of the hills,
Aoife, and all her troop, to take your life,
And never till you are lying in the earth
Can you know rest.

YOUNG MAN: The clash of arms again!
OLD MAN: O, do not go! The mountain is accursed;
Stay with me, I have nothing more to lose,
I do not now deceive you.
YOUNG MAN: I will face them.

(He goes out, no longer as if in a dream, but shouldering his spear and calling.)

He comes! Cuchulain, son of Sualtim, comes!

(The MUSICIANS *stand up; one goes to centre with folded cloth. The others unfold it. While they do so they sing. During the singing, and while hidden by the cloth, the* OLD MAN *goes out. When the play is performed with Mr. Dulac's music, the* MUSICIANS *do not rise or unfold the cloth till after they have sung the words "*a bitter life.*")*

(Songs for the unfolding and folding of the cloth.)

Come to me, human faces,
Familiar memories;
I have found hateful eyes
Among the desolate places,
Unfaltering, unmoistened eyes.

Folly alone I cherish,
I choose it for my share;
Being but a mouthful of air,
I am content to perish;
I am but a mouthful of sweet air.

O lamentable shadows,
Obscurity of strife!
I choose a pleasant life
Among indolent meadows;
Wisdom must live a bitter life.

(They then fold up the cloth, singing.)

"The man that I praise,"
Cries out the empty well,
"Lives all his days
Where a hand on the bell
Can call the milch cows
To the comfortable door of his house.
Who but an idiot would praise
Dry stones in a well?"

"The man that I praise,"
Cries out the leafless tree,

"Has married and stays
By an old hearth, and he
On naught has set store
But children and dogs on the floor.
Who but an idiot would praise
A withered tree?"

(They go out.)

Curtain.

Questions

1. Do you agree that this play illustrates the futility of Cuchulain's quest? Explain.
2. Each of the characters is symbolic. What does the Old Man symbolize? Cuchulain? The Guardian of the Well? Explain.
3. Why do you suppose Yeats wanted the play to be performed with actors wearing masks?
4. It has been said that Yeats's plays are universal, that is, they have meaning for everyone. What meaning does this play have for you?
5. The play's climax is the dance rather than any dialogue. Does this seem to you to be a good idea? Why or why not?
6. In a paragraph or two, describe the play's storyline—the progression of dramatic action.

CHARLES KRAY

A Thing of Beauty

CHARLES KRAY is an actor and director as well as a playwright. He has acted on the legitimate stage, on television, and in films. Winner of the 1987 Theatre Press award for best play *(Irish Stew and Yorkshire Pudding)*, Kray was story editor for Marlon Brando's Pennebaker Productions, and a staff writer and director with Universal Studios.

His work has been produced on public television as well as at a variety of theatres throughout the United States.

A THING OF BEAUTY is based on fact, the Nazi persecution of Jews before and during World War II. But the story is much more than that, as it presents two characters who are intelligent individuals rather than the stereotypes they could easily become. Sister Benedicta, although a Carmelite nun, is by no means perfect. Rather, she exhibits the doubts and concerns natural to anyone. Despite her fears, she confronts the Colonel and argues philosophy and the nature of humanity with him.

Neither is the Colonel entirely evil. He embraces Nazism, even to the extent of saying he "wrote" the primer for it. Yet he is much more open-minded and feeling than he at first allows anyone to believe.

The story, although concerned with the larger problem of Nazi domination and persecution, focuses on the smaller situation of two people interacting, two people caught up in events of the time, two people learning to see beyond each other's exterior. The ending, of course, is a tragic irony. Viewed in its context of time and place, *A Thing of Beauty* is certainly illustrative of the tragedy of the Holocaust.

A Thing of Beauty Charles Kray

Characters:

PRIORESS
COLONEL
BENEDICTA

Setting:

The scene is the receiving room of a convent in Germany. The time is the late 1930s. It is dusk. An elderly nun, the PRIORESS *of the convent, is pacing about the room. There is a knock at the door and she hurries to open it. A Nazi* COLONEL *enters. He is about forty. The* PRIORESS *is visibly agitated and through the ensuing formalities is impatient. The* COLONEL *is ill at ease in her presence.*

PRIORESS: Come in, Eric.
COLONEL: Thank you, Reverend Mother.
PRIORESS: Please sit down.
COLONEL: Thank you. *(She sits and he does also.)* It's been a long time, Sister.
PRIORESS: Yes, time passes much too quickly.
COLONEL: You haven't changed much.
PRIORESS: You have. I've read about you.
COLONEL: *(Ignores the remark but his manner becomes harder.)* What can I do for you, madam?
PRIORESS: I received news of my sisters.
COLONEL: I expected you would.
PRIORESS: It is true then?
COLONEL: I'm afraid so.
PRIORESS: But why?
COLONEL: We both know why, Sister.
PRIORESS: No, I don't. I don't understand why nineteen innocent nuns are taken off a train like criminals and sent to a concentration camp. We are Germans. We have done nothing to be treated this way.
COLONEL: Sister, you have been warned, as has every Carmelite convent in this area that we mean to have Edith Stein. If you are Germans, then give her up to us.
PRIORESS: There is no Edith Stein here.
COLONEL: Perhaps not. But we know that she is in Germany, hiding in a Carmelite convent. Your nuns are being held as hostage. If we do not apprehend Edith Stein, the nuns will suffer the consequences. Nineteen for one. That's not a bad trade.
PRIORESS: Why is she so important?
COLONEL: She is a Jew.
PRIORESS: Is this a crime to be a Jew?

COLONEL: It will be.

PRIORESS: You've become a cruel and vengeful man, Eric.

COLONEL: On the contrary, Sister, I'm merely a practical soldier doing his job.

PRIORESS: I remember in my eighth grade class a puzzled boy with curious blue eyes who used to dream of building bridges and buildings. Who used to serve early mass on Sunday mornings. What great promise he showed.

COLONEL: And I, sister, remember a God who taught that man had infinite capacity for love for his fellow. What great promise he showed. We've both been disappointed, Sister.

PRIORESS: Are you so disillusioned that you've turned murderer, Eric?

COLONEL: Goddammit, Sister. You are not talking to a starry-eyed eighth grade boy now. You're talking to a man. An officer of the Third Reich. You have no special privileges other than what your habit allows. I am the interrogator here. Speak civilly to me or you'll join the rest of the penguins at the concentration camp.

PRIORESS: And may God damn you, Colonel. I'm too old to be intimidated or frightened. And if you haven't progressed beyond the eighth grade except for turning into a vicious bully, you'll be treated as such. I want my nuns.

COLONEL: And I want Edith Stein. Is she a member of your convent?

PRIORESS: To admit a Jewess into our order would not only be contrary to the Carmelite temperament but a violation of the law. I told you we are Germans.

COLONEL: Sister, it is not necessary to acquaint me with German law; nor confuse me with vague terms like Carmelite temperament. Merely answer my question.

PRIORESS: Edith Stein is not a member of our convent.

COLONEL: You are sure?

PRIORESS: Yes.

COLONEL: Very well. But I promise you, I will find her.

PRIORESS: But why her? There are other Jews still walking around freely. Why her?

COLONEL: Because she is dangerous.

PRIORESS: Dangerous? The woman is the most sensitive philosopher of our time and you call her dangerous. To whom is she dangerous?

COLONEL: She is dangerous to us, to the government. It is this philosophy that makes her dangerous.

PRIORESS: She represents everything that is good and beautiful, Eric. Don't you see. She preaches God's word. A world of harmony and peace. The path to a oneness of man. White and Black. Jew and Christian. Is this dangerous?

COLONEL: It is to us. There is no oneness in man. There is oneness in strength. There is oneness in power. And those who believe in her make us weak. She must be destroyed.

PRIORESS: Then you would destroy everything good?

COLONEL: If need be. When there is no more good, the bad will become good.

PRIORESS: What a terrible, terrible day that would be.

COLONEL: No more than if the good destroyed all the bad, then the good would become bad.

PRIORESS: You sound like something out of a Nazi primer.

COLONEL: Why not? I'm helping to write that primer. And when it is finished, it will devastate the philosophy of Edith Stein just as surely as I will devastate Edith Stein herself.

PRIORESS: Eric, I knew you too well once to believe this is state policy talking. Those are the words of a personal vendetta. You're not looking for a Jew or philosopher. You're looking for someone who represents something that you once loved. That you destroyed. And now you must wipe out every other beautiful thing so that there'll be no reminder to torture you. Oh, what an unhappy man you must be.

COLONEL: There is no beauty left. It is false. Edith Stein is false. I don't want your sympathy. I want Edith Stein and I want her now. Where is she.

PRIORESS: I gave you my answer.

COLONEL: *(He goes to phone.)* Major, call Camp #83. Tell the commandant that we have not been able to find Edith Stein. Tell him that at the next stroke of the hour, I want the execution of the nineteen Carmelite nuns to begin. One every hour on the hour until the Stein woman is found. Beginning with the youngest first. Relay that message by wire to every Carmelite convent in Germany. It is now 7:25. The first execution will take place in thirty-five minutes. *(He hangs up.)*Now, Sister, where is Edith Stein?

PRIORESS: Oh, my God.

COLONEL: *(Shouts.)* Is Edith Stein in this convent? *(She does not answer.)*

COLONEL: Very well, give me your roster. *(She goes to filing cabinet.)* Do you know what the executions are like at Camp 83?

PRIORESS: Stop it.

COLONEL: Aren't you ashamed, you Carmelites, hiding a Jew? The whole countryside is aghast at this preposterous rumour. A Jew becoming a Carmelite nun. Have you no shame?

PRIORESS: You dare ask me that question?

COLONEL: I dare anything. I want Edith Stein.

PRIORESS: Oh, my poor babies.

COLONEL: Is Edith Stein a member of your convent?

PRIORESS: If she were, do you think I could pass judgment on her? I refuse to wield the power of life and death over anyone.

COLONEL: You wield that power over the nuns at Cologne.

PRIORESS: Oh, my babes.

COLONEL: You have thirty-three minutes Sister.

PRIORESS: Stop it.

COLONEL: Is Edith Stein a member of your convent?

PRIORESS: No, no.

COLONEL: You are sure.

PRIORESS: Yes, please leave me alone.

COLONEL: *(He is looking at roster.)* Very well. You have a new nun here. Her name has not been registered yet at the voting polls. A Sister Terezia Benedicta. I wish to see her.

PRIORESS: *(Has not been listening, she is still in a somewhat shocked state.)* What?

COLONEL: I wish to see Sister Benedicta.

PRIORESS: No.

COLONEL: What? Did you say no, Sister?

PRIORESS: No. I meant, no, not my poor children.

COLONEL: I see. How long has Sister Benedicta been here?

PRIORESS: I'm not sure, less than a year.

COLONEL: I wish to see her.

PRIORESS: Of course. *(She gets up somewhat dazedly and starts to exit.)*

COLONEL: Oh, Sister.

PRIORESS: Yes.

COLONEL: Very well, Sister. Thirty minutes. *(She runs from the room.)*

(He takes a few notes and begins to look at the folder. Sister BENEDICTA *enters. She is in her forties. Yet her face exudes a feeling of youth and innocence. She is an extremely composed woman. There is a sense of peace about her. Not so much in what she says or how she speaks, but her quiet persuasive manner exerts a calming influence which is immediately felt by all who come in contact with her. As she stands momentarily in the doorway, the* COLONEL *does not see her immediately, yet senses her presence. He stands, faces her, and just stares for a long moment.)*

COLONEL: Sister Benedicta?

BENEDICTA: Yes, colonel.

COLONEL: A pleasure. Won't you sit down?

BENEDICTA: Colonel, what is going to happen to our nuns at Cologne?

COLONEL: If you don't mind, Sister, I'll ask the questions.

BENEDICTA: How can you torture us like this? Reverend mother is frantic with worry.

COLONEL: I assure you, as I have assured her, they are well for the moment.

BENEDICTA: For the moment? What is going to happen to them?

COLONEL: That depends perhaps on what happens here.

BENEDICTA: I don't understand?

COLONEL: You will. Now please sit down. *(She does.)* You are a beautiful woman.

BENEDICTA: Thank you.

COLONEL: It seems awkward somehow, to compliment a nun. Is it proper?

BENEDICTA: We are women. All women enjoy flattery.

COLONEL: You make me feel like a boor. I was being sincere.

BENEDICTA: Not at all. Flattery can be sincere.

COLONEL: Of course. Somehow I could never associate nun and woman until now. Now I can understand the men in town when they talk of the beautiful women in the convent.

BENEDICTA: They are boors!

COLONEL: Some of these men have been without a woman for a long time and to them a pretty face is a pretty face. Physical appeal is not completely hidden by a nun's habit.

BENEDICTA: That is sacrilegious.

COLONEL: There is no such word in my vocabulary, Sister.

BENEDICTA: Of course, there is nothing sacred to you.

COLONEL: Only the supremacy of the individual. This is sacred to me. This is what makes man godly.

BENEDICTA: And beastly.

COLONEL: The two are synonymous, Sister.

BENEDICTA: You are like a parrot, Colonel. You spew the party line faithfully.

COLONEL: And you are quite outspoken, Sister. But what you say is neither fair nor true. Which is less intelligent, the parrot, a bird which repeats a phrase, or in this case a doctrine, or any other bird which says nothing, has nothing to say, is incapable of saying anything.

BENEDICTA: That is a weak analogy.

COLONEL: Perhaps. But so is your allusion to me as a parrot. If I embrace a philosophy, it is because this philosophy is original with me. I conceived it. I am the creator.

BENEDICTA: I imagine Herr Hitler would give you quite an argument on that point.

COLONEL: I suppose. But I am not here to discuss Herr Hitler or myself.

BENEDICTA: Why are you here, Colonel?

COLONEL: I was looking for someone. But now I want to prove something to myself.

BENEDICTA: What, Colonel?

COLONEL: In due time, Sister. Meanwhile I will ask the questions.

BENEDICTA: As you wish.

COLONEL: Tell me, Sister. How do you feel about the Catholic religion?

BENEDICTA: That seems a strange question.

COLONEL: I suppose. But in my field I sometimes get the clearest answers from strange questions.

BENEDICTA: Just what is your field, Colonel?

COLONEL: I'm an intelligence officer, Sister.

BENEDICTA: That sounds rather ostentatious.

COLONEL: Not really, Sister. Intelligence indicates a branch of service, not a man's description.

BENEDICTA: I see.

COLONEL: Now would you mind answering my strange question?

BENEDICTA: How I feel about the Catholic religion?

COLONEL: Yes.

BENEDICTA: I embrace it.

COLONEL: Is that all?

BENEDICTA: I embrace it with every fibre of my being. With my entire capacity to love. It is my solace, my joy, my comfort. It is my life.

COLONEL: Is this a required attitude for a Carmelite or your own personal conception?

BENEDICTA: My own. My feeling.

COLONEL: Feeling? Is this the Carmelite feeling?

BENEDICTA: Perhaps.

COLONEL: Then it is a required attitude.

BENEDICTA: No. Only duties are required. An attitude is developed.

COLONEL: I see. Sister, how long have you been a Carmelite?

BENEDICTA: A year.

COLONEL: Only a year? That seems odd.

BENEDICTA: Odd?

COLONEL: Well, I wouldn't classify you as a young nun.

BENEDICTA: I was a postulant for some time before that.

COLONEL: A postulant?

BENEDICTA: A novice preparing to take the vows.

COLONEL: Is that like medical internship . . . taking seven or eight years?

BENEDICTA: No, Colonel.

COLONEL: How long, then?

BENEDICTA: It depends upon the individual. The time can vary from six months to two years.

COLONEL: And how long were you a . . . posturer, is it?

BENEDICTA: Postulant, Colonel.

COLONEL: Yes, postulant. How long were you a postulant?

BENEDICTA: Six months.

COLONEL: Would you mind telling me your age, Sister?

BENEDICTA: Not at all, Colonel. I am 40.

COLONEL: And you have been a nun for one year only? What was the reason for the delay? Why didn't you become a nun sooner?

BENEDICTA: I was a teacher and my superiors felt I was needed more in the schools.

COLONEL: What about as a young girl? Did you, how do you Catholics put it, receive the call then?

BENEDICTA: No, I did not.

COLONEL: When did you receive it?

BENEDICTA: Colonel, is all this information necessary?

COLONEL: I'm afraid it is, when did you receive the call?

BENEDICTA: About five years ago.

COLONEL: Wasn't that rather late?

BENEDICTA: Not for me.

COLONEL: I don't understand.

BENEDICTA: I became a Catholic six years ago.

COLONEL: Really! This becomes more and more interesting. What were you before?

BENEDICTA: I followed the philosophy of Edmund Husserl.

COLONEL: Husserl? Germany's soap-box phenomenologist.[1] I'm surprised. I thought he was for immature college freshmen.

BENEDICTA: Perhaps. Perhaps you are not far wrong in that description, Colonel. Perhaps he opens the doors of learning for immature college freshmen.

COLONEL: And did his philosophy open any doors for you?

BENEDICTA: To study any philosophy is to walk on the edge of an abyss.

COLONEL: And you fell into the abyss of Catholicism.

BENEDICTA: Colonel, you have a distinct gift for shading a statement of fact to make it fit your own conclusions.

COLONEL: An old trick of my trade, Sister. Never allow the enemy the indulgence of accepting a positive statement.

BENEDICTA: Am I your enemy, Colonel?

COLONEL: I don't know, Sister. I hope to find out.

BENEDICTA: Then I am guilty until proven innocent?

COLONEL: Guilty? Of what, Sister?

BENEDICTA: I don't know Colonel, *I* hope to find out.

(They both laugh.)

COLONEL: Very good, Sister. You've won the point, but I've won my bet.

BENEDICTA: Bet, Colonel?

COLONEL: Yes. You know Field Major Wollman, your military governor?

1. A scientist who studies the development of the human consciousness.

BENEDICTA: Only by sight. He has been here visiting.

COLONEL: Well, he knows you. When he found I was coming here, he said "Watch that Benedicta, the brooding one, she never smiles."

BENEDICTA: He wasn't very gallant.

COLONEL: I defended you, Sister. I defended womankind. I said there wasn't a woman alive who never smiles. So we bet on it.

BENEDICTA: And you won.

COLONEL: Didn't I?

BENEDICTA: Colonel, I find you most amazing. You are a high officer investigating our convent for some seemingly important reason and you spend the time making small talk. I find it most pleasant, but I'm sure we both have more important things to do.

COLONEL: You never let your guard down for a moment, do you Sister? *(She doesn't answer.)* Very well. Sister, phenomonology is not a common religion handed down from parent to child. Were you always an advocate of Husserl?

BENEDICTA: Before I studied Edmund Husserl's philosophy I was an atheist.

COLONEL: Were your parents atheists?

BENEDICTA: I was an orphan. Colonel, I am aware that you have a file of biographical material concerning me. Are you trying to get me to make a mistake and give you information which differs from that in my file?

COLONEL: No, Sister. As a matter of fact, the reason for my questioning is for the lack of information in your file. There seems to be very little of anything concerning your life prior to your entering this convent. This is quite unusual. Of course all the information you give me will be checked. Therefore, I should caution you to be accurate as well as truthful. *(He reads from file.)* You were an orphan in the town of Augsburg, raised by Grandparents who are now deceased. Other school records were destroyed in a fire in that community some ten years ago. If you were a criminal, that would be a very convenient set of circumstances.

BENEDICTA: My background was checked by the papal authorities when I became a nun.

COLONEL: And very well, I should imagine. I understand their Gestapo is as effective as ours.

BENEDICTA: Colonel, I find your sense of humor lacking in both sense and humor.

COLONEL: I'm sorry, Sister. But I can't resist the temptation of poking at something seemingly so impregnable and formidable as the Catholic religion.

BENEDICTA: Why don't you try Naziism?

COLONEL: Believe me, Sister, I have. I don't know why I said that. I suppose it's because I know that if this room had a microphone in it, I would have been the one to put it there. But you're much too sensitive, Sister. You find my sense of humor lacking. I find you lacking a sense of humor.

BENEDICTA: Colonel, what started as an interrogation, has seemingly turned into a social visit. Are you trying to be disarming, Colonel?

COLONEL: Not at all, Sister. Not at all. Sister, you make me feel like a recalcitrant student. I haven't felt like that in years, and I'm enjoying the feeling. If I weren't, Sister, I could have you thrown in jail just for the disdain in your voice when you speak of the German state.

BENEDICTA: Should I be thankful, Colonel?

COLONEL: No, Sister. In a sense, I should be. It's refreshing. *(Pause.)* Sister, before you became an atheist, what religion did you *embrace? (He smiles.)*

BENEDICTA: Colonel, I find your choice of words as wanting as your sense of humor. *(He laughs.)* My grandfather was a man of the earth. He believed in a God, but this God communicated with my Grandfather through the soil. The wonder of this phenomena was religion enough for my grandfather so we did not belong to any formal religion.

COLONEL: I should think such a simple philosophy would have impressed you. Yet you seem to have flitted from one religion to another until at a very late age you became imbued with the Catholic faith and after this incomprehensive conversion, you commit an even more astounding act by taking the vows of a Carmelite nun at the very late age of 40.

BENEDICTA: You find this difficult to understand?

COLONEL: Impossible. I would not like to be your biographer.

BENEDICTA: Nor would I care to have you be.

COLONEL: At least we agree on something. But you haven't told me anything which makes your actions less difficult to understand.

BENEDICTA: Like all of us, I was searching, Colonel.

COLONEL: Oh, my God, Sister. I certainly expected more of you. Searching? For what? Truth? Meaning of life? The essence of man? Leave the triteness to the academicians, Sister, they thrive on it. I'm sure you're capable of making better sense. We're all searching, you say? What am I searching for, Sister?

BENEDICTA: Strength, Colonel.

COLONEL: What?

BENEDICTA: Strength.

COLONEL: Sister, if I didn't consider you an intelligent woman, I would think that a most preposterous answer. Are you aware of the power I have? The power of life and death, over you, over people in Germany, over people in Europe. Is there a greater strength?

BENEDICTA: You are being evasive, Colonel, and now I'm surprised.

COLONEL: *(He pauses for a moment, puzzled, stares at her.)* You are disturbingly astute, Sister. What am I evading?

BENEDICTA: You refuse to admit that you seek strength because you fear that such an admission would belie strength; would be weakness.

COLONEL: I will admit to your analysis somewhat, but I will not admit to your usage of the word, strength. What I seek, Sister, is idyllic. I have heard the vague terms: honor, integrity, sense of purpose, without compromise. I would like to see these terms embodied in a philosophy, or more important in an individual. I'm like your doubting Thomas. Show me. Show me these things that your religions spout about. Goodness, benevolence, oneness with your fellow man, brotherly love, Samaritans, turn the other cheek, show me. Just one, Sister, show me. And I will bow.

BENEDICTA: You have read of Jesus.

COLONEL: He is unreal to me. Just as unreal as Zeus, or Thor, or Neptune. Show me today, now, on earth, this thing I seek. This thing you call strength.

BENEDICTA: You are a bitter man.

COLONEL: Indeed. And in my bitterness is my strength. It makes *me* impregnable. It makes *me* formidable. It gives *me* power. It is *my* strength.

BENEDICTA: And are you free from compromise?

COLONEL: I don't pretend to be. I am not bound by ethics, because I cannot find any ethics which can bind me.

BENEDICTA: And so you would destroy what is good and beautiful in this life.

COLONEL: Yes. Because there is no place for the good and the beautiful. If it cannot survive, it is hypocritical, it is weak.

BENEDICTA: No. You must destroy it because beauty and goodness reflect and in this reflection you see the brutality and ugliness of your world become more ugly and more brutal, and you are shamed. And out of your shame rise the five monsters of man's mind, fear, envy, jealousy, hate, and greed. And these monsters will degenerate you and destroy you.

COLONEL: Sister, *you* are preaching fear. Do you think you can intimidate me? We are masters at this type of strategy.

BENEDICTA: Yes. It is wrong for me to try and reach you through fear. But it is also impossible to reach you through goodness. Through the teachings of Matthew.

COLONEL: Sister, the Golden Rule is a harmless piece of nonsense for schoolchildren.

BENEDICTA: Is it?

COLONEL: Show me a man who lives by it and I will see a fool.

BENEDICTA: If I show you a man who lives by it, you will see the strength you seek. And if I show you a man who dies by it, you will be shamed.

COLONEL: Show me, Sister. Where is He?

BENEDICTA: In your concentration camps.

COLONEL: What?

BENEDICTA: Yes. He is there by the thousands, now.

COLONEL: The Jew?

BENEDICTA: For the most part. But he is gentile as well.

COLONEL: The Jew. The grasping, gluttonous, avaricious Jew. He is the example you set for me, Sister? How naive you suddenly seem. Would you like to visit a camp some time and see how this paragon of brotherly love you hold before me informs on his fellow-man? Ingratiates himself for a modicum of extra comfort at the expense of his fellow man? You would tell me that he is without compromise? That he is noble?

BENEDICTA: The monsters are not selective about where they work. Even in your camps, or especially in your camps where a piece of bread may mean survival for an extra day do the monsters run rampant. You see *this,* because this is what you want to see. What you are striving for. The degradation of the human being. But you are wrong. For every single victim of the monsters, there are a thousand Matthews who live and die in the strength of their God. And they will rise. And they will destroy you. This is your curse. Not the Jew. This is what maddens you. That you can deprive them of everything, even their wills, but not their faith, not their strength.

COLONEL: Your knowledge of our camps seems more than academic Sister, as does your knowledge of the Jew. Are you very familiar with either?

BENEDICTA: The rumors about the camps are common, and I had many Jewish friends.

COLONEL: I see. For a moment I thought that Judaism might have been one of the religions you flitted to in your early years. You were never a Jew by any chance, were you?

BENEDICTA: That is hardly a requirement of a Carmelite nun.

COLONEL: Of course not. Are you familiar with Judaism, though?

BENEDICTA: I have a reading knowledge of most of the religions of the world.

COLONEL: Then you are perhaps familiar with the Talmud, and its parallel with the Babylonian law. Do you know of the lex talionis, the law of an eye for an eye, a tooth for a tooth. Is this in keeping with Matthew?

BENEDICTA: Colonel, if you're going to select platitudes which are convenient, the Talmud also says, Thou shalt love thy neighbor as thyself.

COLONEL: Sister, you know we are searching for the woman, Edith Stein.

BENEDICTA: Yes.

COLONEL: Do you know of her?

BENEDICTA: I've read some of her works.

COLONEL: She is a Jewess who, according to our information, has become a Catholic.

BENEDICTA: Oh.

COLONEL: Do you find that surprising?

BENEDICTA: I suppose it would depend on the circumstances. People have their own reasons for converting.

COLONEL: As you had, no doubt?

BENEDICTA: As I had.

COLONEL: I suppose so. Still it does seem strange for an orthodox Jewess, a scholar, no less, to take such a radical step as to become a Catholic.

BENEDICTA: No more strange than if she became a Lutheran or Calvinist, or Baptist. It is as simple as making a discovery of something which has more importance to the individual. Judaism is a moderate belief. The central truth of its teaching is that the final aim of its religion is morality. Conduct in everyday life is more important than the right belief. According to the Talmud, every good man is assured of Heaven. In Hinduism, ritual perfection is the ultimate; and in Catholicism, the faith is the most important factor in guiding man's destiny. Salvation is dependent on grace rather than merit. There should be no standard of comparison, no competition. The only standard can be what is essentially right for a person's soul. Or what he feels is right.

COLONEL: That's a very liberal attitude for a Catholic nun. Maybe you should be the one to worry about microphones.

BENEDICTA: I have my moments of indecision and question, Colonel. It is then that I seek my God. It is then that he reassures me. It is then that he justifies my love.

COLONEL: I wish I had your capacity for totalness with an emotion, Sister. For loving.

BENEDICTA: I'm sorry for you.

COLONEL: Sorry for me?

BENEDICTA: I'm sorry for anyone who has lost the capacity to love.

COLONEL: You're sorry for me. It's been a long time since anyone has said that to me. Thank you.

BENEDICTA: Do you not have a family?

COLONEL: Yes.

BENEDICTA: And with them?

COLONEL: I feel nothing. Except perhaps obligation.

BENEDICTA: That is sad. Not to know love.

COLONEL: Yet if one does not know it, he does not miss it, so it is not sad.

BENEDICTA: Do you believe that?

COLONEL: No.

BENEDICTA: To love, one must be able to give.

COLONEL: I think so. Yet there are many ways to love.

BENEDICTA: There is only one way to give in love. Give of yourself.

COLONEL: That is an easy thing to say, Sister. But for many, a difficult thing to achieve. To what extent does one give of himself? Part to love, part to business, part to religion, part to philosophy, there's nothing left for himself.

BENEDICTA: Love is selfish. Love demands much. And love rewards in kind. With love.

COLONEL: Perhaps Sister. But I find it difficult to be total in any emotion, even hate.

BENEDICTA: You are unique for a Nazi soldier.

COLONEL: And you Sister are very frank and open. An admirable quality, but in our time an essentially dangerous one. I wonder, Sister, if you are ever tortured by doubts.

BENEDICTA: No one is infallible. My doubts and weaknesses are a great cause of distress to me.

COLONEL: That's another thing we have in common.

BENEDICTA: You are distressed?

COLONEL: Continually.

BENEDICTA: I wish I could help you.

COLONEL: Now that is a strange thing for you to say.

BENEDICTA: Not really.

COLONEL: You know Sister, I came here to find Edith Stein. We were led to believe that Edith Stein has become a Carmelite nun and is cloistered in a convent, possibly this one.

BENEDICTA: *(She does not answer.)*

COLONEL: This does not surprise you?

BENEDICTA: I am surprised.

COLONEL: At what I've told you or at the fact that I know?

BENEDICTA: *(She does not answer this question.)* Have you found her yet, this Edith Stein?

COLONEL: There are many nuns in this convent, Sister. At this point I have spoken to only Sister Terezia Benedicta. You may go, Sister.

BENEDICTA: What about the nuns interned at Cologne?

COLONEL: They will be released, Sister.

BENEDICTA: Thank you, Colonel.

COLONEL: You may go, Sister.

BENEDICTA: Colonel . . .

COLONEL: You may go, Sister! *(She starts to go.)* Oh, Sister. *(She stops.)* I shall go on searching.

BENEDICTA: Goodbye, Colonel.

COLONEL: Goodbye. *(He walks to the desk and writes a comment on her file. He then picks up the phone.)* Gestapo Headquarters, extension 711. Major, send word to Camp #83 . . . *(The door bursts open and the* PRIORESS *rushes in.)*

PRIORESS: Colonel!

COLONEL: *(Into phone.)* Just a minute. Yes, Rev. Mother.

PRIORESS: Colonel, I must speak to you.

COLONEL: Sister, I'm busy now.

PRIORESS: I must speak to you now.

COLONEL: *(Into phone.)* I'll call you back. *(Hangs up.)* What is it?

PRIORESS: I cannot have the deaths of those children on my conscience.

COLONEL: I beg your pardon.

PRIORESS: My nuns, interned at Cologne. I can't bear the thought of them.

COLONEL: I'm sorry, Reverend Mother, but . . .

PRIORESS: No, let me finish. I've thought this over many times in the past short while. I hoped you would find out for yourself. I prayed you would. Now I must tell you. I must tell you the information regarding Edith Stein.

COLONEL: Sister, before you speak . . .

PRIORESS: Don't stop me or I'll be unable to. Oh, God, oh my god, Sister Benedicta and Edith Stein are the same person. *(She sits dazedly in the chair, crying. The* COLONEL *stands motionless for a long time. He walks slowly to a chair and sits.)*

COLONEL: *(To himself.)* A thing of goodness and beauty must be destroyed. It reflects and in its reflection, ugliness and brutality become more ugly and more brutal and they must destroy it. It cannot survive.

PRIORESS: What?

COLONEL: Nothing, Sister, nothing of any importance at all. *(He picks up phone.)* Gestapo headquarters. Extension 711. Major? Yes, it is I. Yes, I found her. She is at the convent. Send a car down. Yes, I will wait. *(He begins to walk around the room slowly.)*

PRIORESS: What I have done, what you have forced me to do, is despicable. *(He doesn't answer.)* I have a responsibility to my convent. I could not risk the lives of all those sisters.

COLONEL: I understand, Sister.

PRIORESS: How terrible this will be for Sister Benedicta.
COLONEL: Yes. This will be most terrible for Sister Benedicta.
PRIORESS: What will happen to her?
COLONEL: She will be sent to Auschwitz.
PRIORESS: May God forgive us.
COLONEL: No Sister. May we forgive God.

Curtain, as he prepares to leave.

Questions

1. The Colonel says that the "supremacy of the individual" is all that is sacred to him. "It makes men godly." Do you think he really believes this? Support your answer through dialogue in the play.
2. Trace the development of the relationship between the Colonel and Sister Benedicta. At what point does his attitude toward her begin to change?
3. What is the play's central idea? How do you know?
4. Do you believe this play is a tragedy? Why or why not?
5. Would Hitler consider the Colonel a "good" Nazi? Why or why not?
6. Point out instances of Sister Benedicta's evasiveness in answering the Colonel's questions. Why do you suppose he does not pursue the questions further?
7. What is the significance of the discussion of love?
8. What is the significance of the ending? How does it affect you?

Comedy

The opposite of tragedy is comedy. It has the purpose of making us laugh. Most often we are asked to laugh at ourselves and our institutions—to take ourselves less seriously.

Whereas tragedy is a fairly narrow form, comedy has the greatest variety of any dramatic genre. It can be slapstick or gentle. It most often shows a deviation from the norm of everyday life, even though it often is concerned with the mundane and the pettiness of day-to-day living.

Comedy has a variety of purposes in making us laugh, and they differ from play to play. At times the writer may want to have us take ourselves less seriously or to free us from tension, even if just for a couple of hours. Many times the writer of comedy reminds us of our own frailties but tells us they aren't so serious as we sometimes think. Another purpose of comedy may be to correct social injustice. If we can laugh at social and character flaws, maybe we will be more inclined to correct them. Comedy also keeps us from gaining too high an opinion of ourselves. In this way, it is corrective.

The humor in a comedy can come from the treatment of character or situation. It forces us to view any deviation objectively. Any subject matter can be treated in a humorous light. When the deviation from the norm becomes too painful or too severe, however, the comedy suffers and ceases to be funny. It would be cruel and unfunny, for example, to treat physical deformities or handicaps as sources of comedy. More often, it is circumstances over which we have control or our views of uncontrollable forces that comprise the subject matter.

Eccentricities of character can be humorous, as in Molière's treatment of Harpagon's greed in *The Miser*. Other character traits that might be the basis of comedy are hypocrisy, laziness, or overwhelming ambition. Humorous treatment of situations also can be the basis of comedy. Protagonists may become involved in situations with which they are unable to cope or that are outside their knowledge and experience. An example would be a plumber posing as a brain surgeon. In effect, comedy ridicules our tendency to be what we are not or to place too much importance on our achievements and our goals.

Unlike tragedy, comedy must end happily. The protagonist has to win. If he or she were to be defeated, the audience would feel guilt or shame for having laughed at the character. It is important, therefore, to develop a comic frame of reference. If audience members aren't given this frame of reference, they may not know how to respond. The spectators should know that what they are seeing isn't to be taken too seriously, and that they aren't expected to identify either with the character or the situation, unless the playwright wishes them to laugh with instead of at the protagonist.

Certain devices can help establish a comic frame of reference: derision, incongruity, exaggeration, repetition, surprise, and character inconsistency.

Derision means laughing at people or institutions by poking fun at them. Its object is to deflate egos or cause discomfort. It can be effective but often runs the risk of seeming too bitter, in which case the audience may identify with the intended victim.

Incongruity involves placing opposites or different elements together in a deviation from the norm. An example is a tall woman with a short man.

Exaggeration means enlargement through overstatement. For example, most people are not as greedy as Molière's character, Harpagon. Exaggeration often encompasses the other comic devices by heightening them.

Repetition includes the verbal or visual gag that is done over and over, for an example, a character's tripping over a stool each time he or she enters or exits.

Surprise simply is the unexpected. We know every joke will have a punch line, which we anticipate. But even though we know it's coming, its contents are unexpected. Surprise includes the pun, the insult, or other verbal wit in a play.

Character inconsistency means a personality trait that doesn't seem to fit with the others, for example, a murderer helping old women across the street.

Closely related to derision but often considered a subgenre of comedy is satire, which ridicules for the purpose of reform but is gentler.

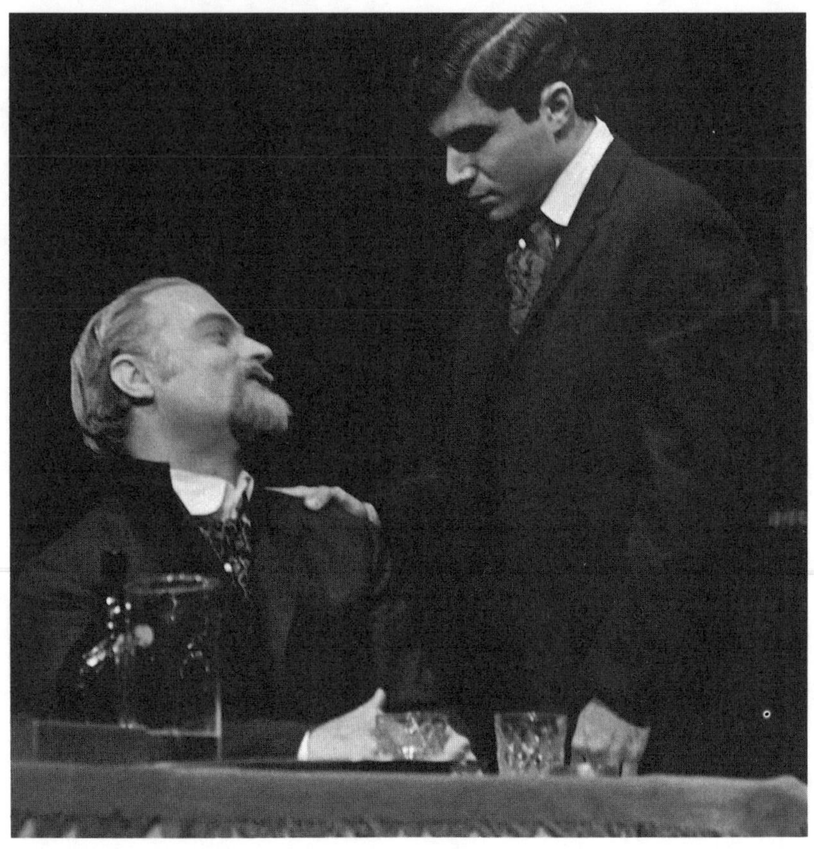

In this opening scene from A Marriage Proposal, *Lomov asks Tschubukov for his daughter's hand in marriage. (A Gleason photo, courtesy of Kent State University, Ohio)*

ANTON CHEKHOV

A Marriage Proposal

ANTON CHEKHOV originally studied medicine and received his degree from Moscow University in 1884. Throughout his student days he wrote short stories and plays. He was influenced by vaudeville and French farce, as can be seen from plays like *The Marriage Proposal* and *The Bear*.

His first full-length plays were not successful during their premieres, and he would have given up playwriting except that he was persuaded to allow the newly founded Moscow Art Theatre to revive *The Seagull*. The play was given a more realistic interpretation than previously and so was more successful.

Chekhov's earlier plays failed because he tried to break new ground in getting away from the currently popular melodrama.

Although Chekhov wrote at the end of the nineteenth century and the first few years of the twentieth, his plays were not generally familiar to American audiences until well into the 1920s.

A MARRIAGE PROPOSAL was written in the latter part of the nineteenth century but was not professionally produced in America until years later.

A comedy, the play has farcical elements in that it takes little intellectual effort to follow the contrived plot, and the characters are one-dimensional.

Most of the humor comes from the three characters' arguments, which directly conflicts with the purpose of Lomov's visit—to propose marriage. Despite the arguing, all three characters want the marriage to take place.

A Marriage Proposal Anton Chekhov

English Version by Hilmar Baukhage and Barrett H. Clark

Characters:

STEPAN STEPANOVITCH TSCHUBUKOV, *a country farmer*
NATALIA STEPANOVNA, *his daughter (aged 25)*
IVAN VASSILIYITCH LOMOV, *Tschubukov's neighbor*

Setting:

Reception room in TSCHUBUKOV*'s country home, Russia. Time: The present.* TSCHUBUKOV *discovered as the curtain rises. Enter* LOMOV*, wearing a dress-suit.*

TSCHUB: *(Going toward him and greeting him.)* Who is this I see? My dear fellow! Ivan Vassiliyitch! I'm so glad to see you! *(Shakes hands.)* But this is a surprise! How are you?

LOMOV: Thank you! And how are you?

TSCHUB: Oh, so-so, my friend. Please sit down. It isn't right to forget one's neighbor. But tell me, why all this ceremony? Dress clothes, white gloves and all? Are you on your way to some engagement, my good fellow?

LOMOV: No, I have no engagement except with you, Stepan Stepanovitch.

TSCHUB: But why in evening clothes, my friend? This isn't New Year's!

LOMOV: You see, it's simply this, that —*(Composing himself.)* I have come to you, Stepan Stepanovitch, to trouble you with a request. It is not the first time I have had the honor of turning to you for assistance, and you have always, that is—I beg your pardon, I am a bit excited! I'll take a drink of water first, dear Stepan Stepanovitch. *(He drinks.)*

TSCHUB: *(Aside.)* He's come to borrow money! I won't give him any! *(To Lomov.)* What is it, then, dear Lomov?

LOMOV: You see—dear—Stepanovitch, pardon me, Stepan—Stepan—dearvitch—I mean—I am terribly nervous, as you will be so good as to see—! What I mean to say—you are the only one who can help me, though I don't deserve it, and—and I have no right whatever to make this request of you.

TSCHUB: Oh, don't beat about the bush, my dear fellow. Tell me!

LOMOV: Immediately—in a moment. Here it is, then: I have come to ask for the hand of your daughter, Natalia Stepanovna.

TSCHUB: *(Joyfully.)* Angel! Ivan Vassiliyitch! Say that once again! I didn't quite hear it!

LOMOV: I have the honor to beg—

TSCHUB: *(Interrupting.)* My dear, dear man! I am so happy that everything is so—everything! *(Embraces and kisses him.)* I have wanted this to happen for so long. It has been my dearest wish! *(He represses a tear.)*

And I have always loved you, my dear fellow, as my own son! May God give you His blessings and His grace and—I always wanted it to happen. But why am I standing here like a blockhead? I am completely dumbfounded with pleasure, completely dumbfounded. My whole being—I'll call Natalia—

LOMOV: Dear Stepan Stepanovitch, what do you think? May I hope for Natalia Stepanovna's acceptance?

TSCHUB: Really! A fine boy like you—and you think she won't accept on the minute? Lovesick as a cat and all that—! *(He goes out, right.)*

LOMOV: I'm cold. My whole body is trembling as though I was going to take my examination! But the chief thing is to settle matters! If a person meditates too much, or hesitates, or talks about it, waits for an ideal or for true love, he never gets it. Brrr! It's cold! Natalia is an excellent housekeeper, not at all bad-looking, well educated—what more could I ask? I'm so excited my ears are roaring! *(He drinks water.)* And not to marry, that won't do! In the first place, I'm thirty-five—a critical age, you might say. In the second place, I must live a well-regulated life. I have a weak heart, continual palpitation, and I am very sensitive and always getting excited. My lips begin to tremble and the pulse in my right temple throbs terribly. But the worst of all is sleep! I hardly lie down and begin to doze before something in my left side begins to pull and tug, and something begins to hammer in my left shoulder—and in my head, too! I jump up like a madman, walk about a little, lie down again, but the moment I fall asleep I have a terrible cramp in the side. And so it is all night long! *(Enter* NATALIA STEPANOVNA.)

NATALIA: Ah! It's you. Papa said to go in: there was a dealer in there who'd come to buy something. Good afternoon, Ivan Vassiliyitch.

LOMOV: Good day, my dear Natalia Stepanovna.

NATALIA: You must pardon me for wearing my apron and this old dress: we are working today. Why haven't you come to see us oftener? You've not been here for so long! Sit down. *(They sit down.)* Won't you have something to eat?

LOMOV: Thank you, I have just had lunch.

NATALIA: Smoke, do, there are the matches. Today it is beautiful and only yesterday it rained so hard that the workmen couldn't do a stroke of work. How many bricks have you cut? Think of it! I was so anxious that I had the whole field mowed, and now I'm sorry I did it, because I'm afraid the hay will rot. It would have been better if I had waited. But what on earth is this? You are in evening clothes! The latest cut! Are you on your way to a ball? And you seem to be looking better, too—really. Why are you dressed up so gorgeously?

LOMOV: *(Excited.)* You see, my dear Natalia Stepanovna—it's simply this: I have decided to ask you to listen to me—of course it will be a surprise, and indeed you'll be angry, but I—*(Aside)*. How fearfully cold it is!

NATALIA: What is it? *(A pause.)* Well?

LOMOV: I'll try to be brief. My dear Natalia Stepanovna, as you know, for many years, since my childhood, I have had the honor to know your family. My poor aunt and her husband, from whom, as you know, I inherited the estate, always had the greatest respect for your father and your poor mother. The Lomovs and the Tschubukovs have been for decades on the friendliest, indeed the closest, terms with each other, and furthermore my property, as you know, adjoins your own. If you will be so good as to remember, my meadows touch your birch woods.

NATALIA: Pardon the interruption. You said "my meadows"—but are they yours?

LOMOV: Yes, they belong to me.

NATALIA: What nonsense! The meadows belong to us—not to you!

LOMOV: No, to me! Now, my dear Natalia Stepanovna!

NATALIA: Well, that is certainly news to me. How do they belong to you?

LOMOV: How? I am speaking of the meadows lying between your birch woods and my brick-earth.

NATALIA: Yes, exactly. They belong to us.

LOMOV: No, you are mistaken, my dear Natalia Stepanovna, they belong to me.

NATALIA: Try to remember exactly, Ivan Vassiliyitch. Is it so long ago that you inherited them?

LOMOV: Long ago! As far back as I can remember they have always belonged to us.

NATALIA: But that isn't true! You'll pardon my saying so.

LOMOV: It is all a matter of record, my dear Natalia Stepanovna. It is true that at one time the title to the meadows was disputed, but now everyone knows they belong to me. There is no room for discussion. Be so good as to listen: my aunt's grandmother put these meadows, free from all costs, into the hands of your father's grandfather's peasants for a certain time while they were making bricks for my grandmother. These people used the meadows free of cost for about forty years, living there as they would on their own property. Later, however, when—

NATALIA: There's not a word of truth in that! My grandfather, and my great-grandfather, too, knew that their estate reached back to the swamp, so that the meadows belong to us. What further discussion can there be? I can't understand it. It is really most annoying.

LOMOV: I'll show you the papers, Natalia Stepanovna.

NATALIA: No, either you are joking, or trying to lead me into a discussion. That's not at all nice! We have owned this property for nearly three hundred years, and now all at once we hear that it doesn't belong to us. Ivan Vassiliyitch, you will pardon me, but I really can't believe my ears. So far as I am concerned, the meadows are worth very little. In all they don't contain more than five acres and they are worth only a few hundred roubles, say three hundred, but the injustice of the thing is what affects me. Say what you will, I can't bear injustice.

LOMOV: Only listen until I have finished, please! The peasants of your respected father's grandfather, as I have already had the honor to tell you, baked bricks for my grandmother. My aunt's grandmother wished to do them a favor—

NATALIA: Grandfather! Grandmother! Aunt! I know nothing about them. All I know is that the meadows belong to us, and that ends the matter.

LOMOV: No, they belong to me!

NATALIA: And if you keep on explaining it for two days, and put on five suits of evening clothes, the meadows are still ours, ours, ours! I don't want to take your property, but I refuse to give up what belongs to us!

LOMOV: Natalia Stepanovna, I don't need the meadows, I am only concerned with the principle. If you are agreeable, I beg of you, accept them as a gift from me!

NATALIA: But I can give them to you, because they belong to me! That is very peculiar, Ivan Vassiliyitch! Until now we have considered you as a good neighbor and a good friend; only last year we lent you our threshing machine so that we couldn't thresh until November, and now you treat us like thieves! You offer to give me my own land. Excuse me, but neighbors don't treat each other that way. In my opinion, it's a very low trick—to speak frankly—

LOMOV: According to you I'm a usurper, then, am I? My dear lady, I have never appropriated other people's property, and I shall permit no one to accuse me of such a thing! *(He goes quickly to the bottle and drinks water.)* The meadows are mine!

NATALIA: That's not the truth! They are mine!

LOMOV: Mine!

NATALIA: Eh? I'll prove it to you! This afternoon I'll send my reapers into the meadows.

LOMOV: W-h-a-t?

NATALIA: My reapers will be there today!

LOMOV: And I'll chase them off!

NATALIA: If you dare!

LOMOV: The meadows are mine, you understand? Mine!

NATALIA: Really, you needn't scream so! If you want to scream and snort and rage you may do it at home, but here please keep yourself within the limits of common decency.

LOMOV: My dear lady, if it weren't that I were suffering from palpitation of the heart and hammering of the arteries in my temples, I would deal with you very differently! *(In a loud voice.)* The meadows belong to me!

NATALIA: Us!

LOMOV: Me! *(Enter* TSCHUBUKOV, *right.)*

TSCHUB: What's going on here? What is he yelling about?

NATALIA: Papa, please tell this gentleman to whom the meadows belong, to us or to him?

TSCHUB: *(To* LOMOV.*)* My dear fellow, the meadows are ours.

LOMOV: But, merciful heavens, Stepan Stepanovitch, how do you make that out? You at least might be reasonable. My aunt's grandmother gave the use of the meadows free of cost to your grandfather's peasants; the peasants lived on the land for forty years and used it as their own, but later when—

TSCHUB: Permit me, my dear friend. You forget that your grandmother's peasants never paid, because there had been a lawsuit over the meadows, and everyone knows that the meadows belong to us. You haven't looked at the map.

LOMOV: I'll prove to you that they belong to me!

TSCHUB: Don't try to prove it, my dear fellow.

LOMOV: I will!

TSCHUB: My good fellow, what are you shrieking about? You can't prove anything by yelling, you know. I don't ask for anything that belongs to you, nor do I intend to give up anything of my own. Why should I? If it has gone so far, my dear man, that you really intend to claim the meadows, I'd rather give them to the peasants than you, and I certainly shall!

LOMOV: I can't believe it! By what right can you give away property that doesn't belong to you?

TSCHUB: Really, you must allow me to decide what I am to do with my own land! I'm not accustomed, young man, to have people address me in that tone of voice. I, young man, am twice your age, and I beg you to address me respectfully.

LOMOV: No! No! You think I'm a fool! You're making fun of me! You call my property yours and then expect me to stand quietly by and talk to you like a human being. That isn't the way a good neighbor behaves, Stepan Stepanovitch! You are no neighbor, you're no better than a landgrabber. That's what you are!

TSCHUB: Wh-at? What did he say?

NATALIA: Papa, send the reapers into the meadows this minute!

TSCHUB: *(To LOMOV.)* What was that you said, sir?

NATALIA: The meadows belong to us and I won't give them up! I won't give them up! I won't give them up!

LOMOV: We'll see about that! I'll prove in court that they belong to me.

TSCHUB: In court! You may sue in court, sir, if you like! Oh, I know you, you are only waiting to find an excuse to go to law! You're an intriguer,[1] that's what you are! Your whole family were always looking for quarrels. The whole lot!

LOMOV: Kindly refrain from insulting my family. The entire race of Lomov has always been honorable! And never has one been brought to trial for embezzlement, as your dear uncle was!

TSCHUB: And the whole Lomov family were insane!

NATALIA: Every one of them!

TSCHUB: Your grandmother was a dipsomaniac,[2] and the younger aunt, Nastasia Michailovna, ran off with an architect.

LOMOV: And your mother limped. *(He puts his hand over his heart.)* Oh, my side pains! My temples are bursting! Lord in Heaven! Water!

TSCHUB: And your dear father was a gambler—and a glutton!

NATALIA: And your aunt was a gossip like few others!

LOMOV: And you are an intriguer. Oh, my heart! And it's an open secret that you cheated at the elections—my eyes are blurred! Where is my hat?

NATALIA: Oh, how low! Liar! Disgusting thing!

LOMOV: Where's the hat—? My heart! Where shall I go? Where is the door—? Oh—it seems—as though I were dying! I can't—my legs won't hold me—*(Goes to the door.)*

TSCHUB: *(Following him.)* May you never darken my door again!

NATALIA: Bring your suit to court! We'll see! *(LOMOV staggers out, center.)*

TSCHUB: *(Angrily.)* The devil!

NATALIA: Such a good-for-nothing! And then they talk about being good neighbors!

TSCHUB: Loafer! Scarecrow! Monster!

NATALIA: A swindler like that takes over a piece of property that doesn't belong to him and then dares to argue about it!

TSCHUB: And to think that this fool dares to make a proposal of marriage!

NATALIA: What? A proposal of marriage?

TSCHUB: Why, yes! He came here to make you a proposal of marriage.

NATALIA: Why didn't you tell me that before?

TSCHUB: That's why he had on his evening clothes! The poor fool!

1. Crafty plotter.

2. A person with an irresistible craving for alcohol.

NATALIA: Proposal for me? Oh! *(Falls into an armchair and groans.)* Bring him back! Bring him back!

TSCHUB: Bring whom back?

NATALIA: Faster, faster, I'm sinking! Bring him back! *(She becomes hysterical.)*

TSCHUB: What is it? What's wrong with you? *(His hands to his head.)* I'm cursed with bad luck! I'll shoot myself! I'll hang myself!

NATALIA: I'm dying! Bring him back!

TSCHUB: Bah! In a minute! Don't bawl! *(He rushes out, center.)*

NATALIA: *(Groaning.)* What have they done to me? Bring him back! Bring him back!

TSCHUB: *(Comes running in.)* He's coming at once! The devil take him! Ugh! Talk to him yourself, I can't.

NATALIA: *(Groaning.)* Bring him back!

TSCHUB: He's coming, I tell you! "Oh, Lord! What a task it is to be the father of a grown daughter!" I'll cut my throat! I really will cut my throat! We've argued with the fellow, insulted him, and now we've thrown him out!—and you did it all, you!

NATALIA: No, you! You haven't any manners, you are brutal! If it weren't for you, he wouldn't have gone!

TSCHUB: Oh, yes, I'm to blame! If I shoot or hang myself, remember *you'll* be to blame. You forced me to it! You! *(*LOMOV *appears in the doorway.)* There, talk to him yourself! *(He goes out.)*

LOMOV: Terrible palpitation!—My leg is lamed! My side hurts me—

NATALIA: Pardon us, we were angry, Ivan Vassiliyitch. I remember now—the meadows really belong to you.

LOMOV: My heart is beating terribly! My meadows—my eyelids tremble—*(They sit down.)* We were wrong. It was only the principle of the thing—the property isn't worth much to me, but the principle is worth a great deal.

NATALIA: Exactly, the principle! Let us talk about something else.

LOMOV: Because I have proofs that my aunt's grandmother had, with the peasants of your good father—

NATALIA: Enough, enough. *(Aside.)* I don't know how to begin. *(To* LOMOV.*)* Are you going hunting soon?

LOMOV: Yes, heath-cock shooting, respected Natalia Stepanovna. I expect to begin after the harvest. Oh, did you hear? My dog, Ugadi, you know him—limps!

NATALIA: What a shame! How did that happen?

LOMOV: I don't know. Perhaps it's a dislocation, or maybe he was bitten by some other dog. *(He sighs.)* The best dog I ever had—to say nothing of his price! I paid Mironov a hundred and twenty-five roubles for him.

NATALIA: That was too much to pay, Ivan Vassiliyitch.

LOMOV: In my opinion it was very cheap. A wonderful dog!

NATALIA: Papa paid eighty-five roubles for his Otkatai, and Otkatai is much better than your Ugadi.

LOMOV: Really? Otkatai is better than Ugadi? What an idea! *(He laughs.)* Otkatai better than Ugadi!

NATALIA: Of course he is better. It is true Otkatai is still young; he isn't full-grown yet, but in the pack or on the leash with two or three, there is no better than he, even—

LOMOV: I really beg your pardon, Natalia Stepanovna, but you quite overlooked the fact that he has a short lower jaw, and a dog with a short lower jaw can't snap.

NATALIA: Short lower jaw? That's the first time I ever heard that!

LOMOV: I assure you, his lower jaw is shorter than the upper.

NATALIA: Have you measured it?

LOMOV: I have measured it. He is good at running, though.

NATALIA: In the first place, our Otkatai is pure-bred, a full-blooded son of Sapragavas and Stameskis, and as for your mongrel, nobody could ever figure out his pedigree; he's old and ugly, and as skinny as an old hag.

LOMOV: Old, certainly! I wouldn't take five of your Otkatais for him! Ugadi is a dog and Otkatai is—it is laughable to argue about it! Dogs like your Otkatai can be found by the dozens at any dog dealer's, a whole pound-full!

NATALIA: Ivan Vassiliyitch, you are very contrary today. First our meadows belong to you and then Ugadi is better than Otkatai. I don't like it when a person doesn't say what he really thinks. You know perfectly well that Otkatai is a hundred times better than your silly Ugadi. What makes you keep on saying he isn't?

LOMOV: I can see, Natalia Stepanovna, that you consider me either a blindman or a fool. But at least you may as well admit that Otkatai has a short lower jaw!

NATALIA: It isn't so!

LOMOV: Yes, a short lower jaw!

NATALIA: *(Loudly.)* It's not so!

LOMOV: What makes you scream, my dear lady?

NATALIA: What makes you talk such nonsense? It's disgusting! It is high time that Ugadi was shot, and yet you compare him with Otkatai!

LOMOV: Pardon me, but I can't carry on this argument any longer. I have palpitation of the heart!

NATALIA: I have always noticed that the hunters who do the most talking know the least about hunting.

LOMOV: My dear lady, I beg of you to be still. My heart is bursting! *(He shouts.)* Be still!

NATALIA: I won't be still until you admit that Otkatai is better! *(Enter* TSCHUBUKOV.*)*

TSCHUB: Well, has it begun again?

NATALIA: Papa, say frankly, on your honor, which dog is better: Otkatai or Ugadi?

LOMOV: Stepan Stepanovitch, I beg of you, just answer this: has your dog a short lower jaw or not? Yes or no?

TSCHUB: And what if he has? Is it of such importance? There is no better dog in the whole country.

LOMOV: My Ugadi is better. Tell the truth, now!

TSCHUB: Don't get so excited, my dear fellow! Permit me. Your Ugadi certainly has his good points. He is from a good breed, has a good stride, strong haunches, and so forth. But the dog, if you really want to know it, has two faults; he is old and he has a short lower jaw.

LOMOV: Pardon me, I have palpitation of the heart!—Let us keep to facts—just remember in Maruskins's meadows, my Ugadi kept ear to ear with the Count Rasvachai and your dog.

TSCHUB: He was behind, because the Count struck him with his whip.

LOMOV: Quite right. All the other dogs were on the fox's scent, but Otkatai found it necessary to bite a sheep.

TSCHUB: That isn't so!—I am sensitive about that and beg you to stop this argument. He struck him because everybody looks on a strange dog of good blood with envy. Even you, sir, aren't free from the sin. No sooner do you find a dog better than Ugadi than you begin to—this, that—his, mine—and so forth! I remember distinctly.

LOMOV: I remember something, too!

TSCHUB: *(Mimicking him.)* I remember something, too! What do you remember?

LOMOV: Palpitation! My leg is lame—I can't—

NATALIA: Palpitation! What kind of hunter are you? You ought to stay in the kitchen by the stove and wrestle with the potato peelings, and not go fox hunting! Palpitation!

TSCHUB: And what kind of hunter are you? A man with your diseases ought to stay at home and not jolt around in the saddle. If you were a hunter—! But you only ride round in order to find out about other people's dogs, and make trouble for everyone. I am sensitive! Let's drop the subject. Besides, you're no hunter.

LOMOV: You only ride around to flatter the Count!—My heart! You intriguer! Swindler!

TSCHUB: And what of it? *(Shouting.)* Be still!

LOMOV: Intriguer!

TSCHUB: Baby! Puppy! Walking drugstore!

LOMOV: Old rat! Jesuit! Oh, I know you!

TSCHUB: Be still! Or I'll shoot you—with my worst gun, like a partridge! Fool! Loafer!

LOMOV: Everyone knows that—oh, my heart!—that your poor late wife beat you. My leg—my temples—Heavens—I'm dying—I—

TSCHUB: And your housekeeper wears the trousers in your house!

LOMOV: Here—here—there—there—my heart has burst! My shoulder is torn apart. Where is my shoulder? I'm dying! *(He falls into a chair.)* The doctor! *(Faints.)*

TSCHUB: Baby! Halfbaked clam! Fool!

NATALIA: Nice sort of hunter you are! You can't even sit on a horse. *(To* TSCHUB.*)* Papa, what's the matter with him? *(She screams.)* Ivan Vassiliyitch! He is dead!

LOMOV: I'm ill! I can't breathe! Air!

NATALIA: He is dead! *(She shakes* LOMOV *in the chair.)* Ivan Vassiliyitch! What have we done! He is dead! *(She sinks into a chair.)* The doctor—doctor! *(She goes into hysterics.)*

TSCHUB: Ahh! What is it? What's the matter with you?

NATALIA: *(Groaning.)* He's dead!—Dead!

TSCHUB: Who is dead? Who? *(Looking at* LOMOV.*)* Yes, he is dead! Good God! Water! The doctor! *(Holding the glass to* LOMOV*'s lips.)* Drink! No, he won't drink! He's dead! What a terrible situation! Why didn't I shoot myself? Why have I never cut my throat? What am I waiting for now? Only give me a knife! Give me a pistol! *(*LOMOV *moves.)* He's coming to! Drink some water—there!

LOMOV: Sparks! Mists! Where am I?

TSCHUB: Get married! Quick, and then go to the devil! She's willing! *(He joins the hands of* LOMOV *and* NATALIA.*)* She's agreed! Only leave me in peace!

LOMOV: Wh—what? *(Getting up.)* Whom?

TSCHUB: She's willing! Well? Kiss each other and—the devil take you both!

NATALIA: *(groans.)* He lives! Yes, yes, I'm willing!

TSCHUB: Kiss each other!

LOMOV: Eh? Whom? *(*NATALIA *and* LOMOV *kiss.)* Very nice—! Pardon me, but what is this for? Oh, yes, I understand! My heart—sparks—I am happy, Natalia Stepanovna. *(He kisses her hand.)* My leg is lame!

NATALIA: I'm happy, too!

TSCHUB: Ahh! A load off my shoulders! Ahh!

NATALIA: And now at least you'll admit that Ugadi is worse than Otkatai!

LOMOV: Better!

NATALIA: Worse!

TSCHUB: Now the domestic joys have begun.—Champagne!

LOMOV: Better!

NATALIA: Worse, worse, worse!

TSCHUB: *(Trying to drown them out.)* Champagne, champagne!

Curtain.

Copies of this play, in individual paper covered acting editions, are available from Samuel French, Inc., 25 W. 45th St., New York, N.Y. 10036 or 7623 Sunset Blvd., Hollywood, Calif. 90046 or in Canada Samuel French, (Canada) Ltd., 80 Richmond Street East, Toronto M5C 1P1, Canada.

Questions

1. Do you think Lomov would make a good husband? Natalia a good wife? Why or why not?
2. Discounting the exaggeration, do you think a situation such as the one presented here is realistic?
3. Explain the role exaggeration plays in *A Marriage Proposal.*
4. Why do you think Chekhov made Lomov such a hypochondriac? Is this effective in the framework of the play?
5. What is the play's central idea? How do you know?
6. Why did you either like or dislike this play?

JAMES M. BARRIE

The Twelve-Pound Look

JAMES M. BARRIE was born in Scotland in 1860. Equally well known as a playwright and novelist, he probably is best remembered for *Peter Pan,* which he dramatized in 1904. His other successful plays include *The Admirable Crichton, What Every Woman Knows, The Old Lady Shows Her Medals,* and *Dear Brutus.* Although Barrie died in 1937, his plays still are produced, particularly by community theatres.

THE TWELVE-POUND LOOK is a comedy that deals with pretensions and pomposity. Despite evidence to the contrary, the central character fails to recognize that in many ways the world is not as he would like it to be. His egotism blinds him to the feelings and attitudes of others. The play, then, is a look at self-importance carried to an extreme.

The Twelve-Pound Look James M. Barrie

Characters:

SIR HARRY SIMS
LADY SIMS
TOMBES
KATE

Setting:

If quite convenient (as they say about cheques) you are to conceive that the scene is laid in your own house, and that HARRY SIMS *is you. Perhaps the ornamentation of the house is a trifle ostentatious, but if you cavil*[1] *at that we are willing to re-decorate: you don't get out of being* HARRY SIMS *on a mere matter of plush and dados. It pleases us to make him a city man, but (rather than lose you) he can be turned with a scrape of the pen into a K.C,*[2] *fashionable doctor, Secretary of State, or what you will. We conceive him of a pleasant rotundity with a thick red neck, but we shall waive that point if you know him to be thin.*

It is that day in your career when everything went wrong just when everything seemed to be superlatively right.

In HARRY'S *case it was a woman who did the mischief. She came to him in his great hour and told him she did not admire him. Of course he turned her out of the house and was soon himself again, but it spoilt the morning for him. This is the subject of the play, and quite enough too.*

HARRY *is to receive the honor of knighthood in a few days, and we discover him in the sumptuous "snuggery" of his home in Kensington (or is it Westminster?), rehearsing the ceremony with his wife. They have been at it all the morning, a pleasing occupation.* MRS. SIMS *(as we may call her for the last time, as it were, and strictly as a good-natured joke) is wearing her presentation gown, and personates the august one who is about to dub her* HARRY *knight. She is seated regally. Her jeweled shoulders proclaim aloud her husband's generosity. She must be an extraordinarily proud and happy woman, yet she has a drawn face and shrinking ways as if there were someone near her of whom she is afraid. She claps her hands, as the signal to* HARRY. *He enters bowing, and with a graceful swerve of the leg. He is only partly in costume, the sword and the real stockings not having arrived yet. With a gliding motion that is only delayed while one leg makes up on the other, he reaches his wife, and, going on one knee, raises her hand superbly to his lips. She taps him on the shoulder with a paper-knife and says huskily, "Rise, Sir Harry." He rises, bows, and glides about the room, going on his knees to various articles of furniture, and rises from each a knight. It is a radiant domestic scene, and* HARRY *is as dignified as if he knew that royalty was rehearsing it at the other end.*

1. To raise trivial and irritating objections.

2. King's Counsel.

SIR HARRY: *(Complacently.)* Did that seem all right, eh?

LADY SIMS: *(Much relieved.)* I think perfect.

SIR HARRY: But was it dignified?

LADY SIMS: Oh, very. And it will be still more so when you have the sword.

SIR HARRY: The sword will lend it an air. There are really the five moments—*(Suiting the action to the word.)*—the glide—the dip—the kiss—the tap—and you back out a knight. It's short, but it's a very beautiful ceremony. *(Kindly.)* Anything you can suggest?

LADY SIMS: No—oh no. *(Nervously, seeing him pause to kiss the tassel of a cushion.)* You don't think you have practised till you know what to do almost too well? *(He has been in a blissful temper, but such niggling criticism would try any man.)*

SIR HARRY: I do not. Don't talk nonsense. Wait till your opinion is asked for.

LADY SIMS: *(Abashed.)* I'm sorry, Harry. *(A perfect butler appears and presents a card.)* "The Flora Type-Writing Agency."

SIR HARRY: Ah, yes. I telephoned them to send someone. A woman, I suppose, Tombes?

TOMBES: Yes, Sir Harry.

SIR HARRY: Show her in here. *(He has very lately become a stickler for etiquette.)* And, Tombes, strictly speaking, you know, I am not Sir Harry till Thursday.

TOMBES: Beg pardon, sir, but it is such a satisfaction to us.

SIR HARRY: *(Good-naturedly.)* Ah, they like it downstairs, do they?

TOMBES: *(Unbending.)* Especially the females, Sir Harry.

SIR HARRY: Exactly. You can show her in, Tombes. *(The butler departs on his mighty task.)* You can tell the woman what she is wanted for, Emmy, while I change.

(He is too modest to boast about himself, and prefers to keep a wife in the house for that purpose.)

You can tell her the sort of things about me that will come better from you. *(Smiling happily.)* You heard what Tombes said, "Especially the females." And he is right. Success! The women like it even better than the men. And rightly. For they share. *You* share, *Lady* Sims. Not a woman will see that gown without being sick with envy of it. I know them. Have all our lady friends in to see it. It will make them ill for a week.

(These sentiments carry him off lightheartedly, and presently the disturbing element is shown in. She is a mere typist, dressed in uncommonly good taste, but at contemptibly small expense, and she is carrying her typewriter in a friendly way rather than as a badge of slavery, as of course it is. Her eye is clear; and in odd contrast to LADY SIMS, *she is self-reliant and serene.)*

KATE: *(Respectfully, but she should have waited to be spoken to.)* Good morning, madam.

LADY SIMS: *(In her nervous way, and scarcely noticing that the typist is a little too ready with her tongue.)* Good morning.

(As a first impression she rather likes the woman, and the woman, though it is scarcely worth mentioning, rather likes her. LADY SIMS *has a maid for buttoning and unbuttoning her, and probably another for waiting on the maid, and she gazes with a little envy perhaps at a woman who does things for herself.)*

Is that the type-writing machine?

KATE: *(Who is getting it ready for use.)* Yes. *(Not "Yes, madam," as it ought to be.)* I suppose if I am to work here I may take this off. I get on better without it. *(She is referring to her hat.)*

LADY SIMS: Certainly. *(But the hat is already off.)* I ought to apologize for my gown. I am to be presented this week, and I was trying it on.

(Her tone is not really apologetic. She is rather clinging to the glory of her gown, wistfully, as if not absolutely certain, you know, that it is a glory.)

KATE: It is beautiful, if I may presume to say so.

(She frankly admires it. She probably has a best, and a second best of her own: that sort of thing.)

LADY SIMS *(with a flush of pride in the gown)*: Yes, it is very beautiful. *(The beauty of it gives her courage.)* Sit down, please.

KATE *(the sort of woman who would have sat down in any case)*: I suppose it is some copying you want done? I got no particulars. I was told to come to this address, but that was all.

LADY SIMS *(almost with the humility of a servant)*: Oh, it is not work for me, it is for my husband, and what he needs is not exactly copying. *(Swelling, for she is proud of* HARRY.*)* He wants a number of letters answered—hundreds of them—letters and telegrams of congratulation.

KATE *(as if it were all in the day's work)*: Yes?

LADY SIMS *(remembering that* HARRY *expects every wife to do her duty)*: My husband is a remarkable man. He is about to be knighted. *(Pause, but* KATE *does not fall to the floor.)* He is to be knighted for his services to— *(On reflection.)*—for his services. *(She is conscious that she is not doing* HARRY *justice.)* He can explain it so much better than I can.

KATE *(in her business-like way)*: And I am to answer the congratulations?

LADY SIMS *(afraid that it will be a hard task)*: Yes.

KATE *(blithely)*: It is work I have had some experience of. *(She proceeds to type.)*

LADY SIMS: But you can't begin till you know what he wants to say.

KATE: Only a specimen letter. Won't it be the usual thing?

LADY SIMS *(to whom this is a new idea)*: Is there a usual thing?

KATE: Oh, yes.

(She continues to type, and LADY SIMS, *half-mesmerized, gazes at her nimble fingers. The useless woman watches the useful one, and she sighs, she could not tell why.)*

LADY SIMS: How quickly you do it! It must be delightful to be able to do something, and to do it well.

KATE *(thankfully)*: Yes, it is delightful.

LADY SIMS *(again remembering the source of all her greatness)*: But, excuse me, I don't think that will be any use. My husband wants me to explain to you that his is an exceptional case. He did not try to get this honor in any way. It was a complete surprise to him—

KATE *(who is a practical* KATE *and no dealer in sarcasm)*: That is what I have written.

LADY SIMS *(in whom sarcasm would meet a dead wall)*: But how could you know?

KATE: I only guessed.

LADY SIMS: Is that the usual thing?

KATE: Oh, yes.

LADY SIMS: They don't try to get it?

KATE: I don't know. That is what we are told to say in the letters.

(To her at present the only important thing about the letters is that they are ten shillings the hundred.)

LADY SIMS *(returning to surer ground)*: I should explain that my husband is not a man who cares for honors. So long as he does his duty—

KATE: Yes, I have been putting that in.

LADY SIMS: Have you? But he particularly wants it to be known that he would have declined a title were it not—

KATE: I have got it here.

LADY SIMS: What have you got?

KATE *(reading)*: "Indeed, I would have asked to be allowed to decline had it not been that I want to please my wife."

LADY SIMS *(heavily)*: But how could you know it was that?

KATE: Is it?

LADY SIMS *(who after all is the one with the right to ask questions)*: Do they all accept it for that reason?

KATE: That is what we are told to say in the letters.

LADY SIMS *(thoughtlessly)*: It is quite as if you knew my husband.

KATE: I assure you, I don't even know his name.

LADY SIMS *(suddenly showing that she knows him)*: Oh, he wouldn't like that!

(And it is here that HARRY *re-enters in his city garments, looking so gay, feeling so jolly that we bleed for him. However, the annoying* KATHERINE *is to get a shock also.)*

LADY SIMS: This is the lady, Harry.
SIR HARRY *(shooting his cuffs)*: Yes, yes. Good morning, my dear.

(Then they see each other, and their mouths open, but not for words. After the first surprise KATE *seems to find some humor in the situation, but* HARRY *glowers like a thundercloud.)*

LADY SIMS *(who has seen nothing)*: I have been trying to explain to her—
SIR HARRY: Eh—what? *(He controls himself.)* Leave it to me, Emmy; I'll attend to her.

*(*LADY SIMS *goes, with a dread fear that somehow she has vexed her lord, and then* HARRY *attends to the intruder.)*

SIR HARRY *(with concentrated scorn)*: You!
KATE *(as if agreeing with him)*: Yes, it's funny.
SIR HARRY: The shamelessness of your daring to come here.
KATE: Believe me, it is not less a surprise to me than it is to you. I was sent here in the ordinary way of business. I was given only the number of the house. I was not told the name.
SIR HARRY *(withering her)*: The ordinary way of business! This is what you have fallen to—a typist!
KATE *(unwithered)*: Think of it!
SIR HARRY: After going through worse straits, I'll be bound.
KATE *(with some grim memories)*: Much worse straits.
SIR HARRY *(alas, laughing coarsely)*: My congratulations!
KATE: Thank you, Harry.
SIR HARRY *(who is annoyed, as any man would be, not to find her abject)*: Eh? What was that you called me, madam?
KATE: Isn't it Harry? On my soul, I almost forget.
SIR HARRY: It isn't Harry to you. My name is Sims, if you please.
KATE: Yes, I had not forgotten that. It was my name, too, you see.
SIR HARRY *(in his best manner)*: It was your name till you forfeited the right to bear it.
KATE: Exactly.
SIR HARRY *(gloating)*: I was furious to find you here, but on second thoughts it pleases me. *(From the depths of his moral nature.)* There is a grim justice in this.
KATE *(sympathetically)*: Tell me?
SIR HARRY: Do you know what you were brought here to do?
KATE: I have just been learning. You have been made a knight, and I was summoned to answer the messages of congratulation.

SIR HARRY: That's it, that's it. You come on this day as my servant!

KATE: I, who might have been Lady Sims.

SIR HARRY: And you are her typist instead. And she has four men-servants. Oh, I am glad you saw her in her presentation gown.

KATE: I wonder if she would let me do her washing, Sir Harry? *(Her want of taste disgusts him.)*

SIR HARRY *(with dignity)*: You can go. The mere thought that only a few flights of stairs separates such as you from my innocent children—*(He will never know why a new light has come into her face.)*

KATE *(slowly)*: You have children?

SIR HARRY *(inflated)*: Two. *(He wonders why she is so long in answering.)*

KATE *(resorting to impertinence)*: Such a nice number.

SIR HARRY: *(with an extra turn of the screw)*: Both boys.

KATE: Successful in everything. Are they like you, Sir Harry?

SIR HARRY *(expanding)*: They are very like me.

KATE: That's nice. *(Even on such a subject as this she can be ribald.)*

SIR HARRY: Will you please to go.

KATE: Heigho! What shall I say to my employer?

SIR HARRY: That is no affair of mine.

KATE: What will you say to Lady Sims?

SIR HARRY: I flatter myself that whatever I say, Lady Sims will accept without comment. *(She smiles, heaven knows why, unless her next remark explains it.)*

KATE: Still the same Harry.

SIR HARRY: What do you mean?

KATE: Only that you have the old confidence in your profound knowledge of the sex.

SIR HARRY *(beginning to think as little of her intellect as of her morals)*: I suppose I know my wife.

KATE *(hopelessly dense)*: I suppose so. I was only remembering that you used to think you knew her in the days when I was the lady.

(He is merely wasting his time on her, and he indicates the door. She is not sufficiently the lady to retire worsted.)

Well, good-bye, Sir Harry. Won't you ring, and the four men-servants will show me out? *(But he hesitates.)*

SIR HARRY *(in spite of himself)*: As you are here, there is something I want to get out of you. *(Wishing he could ask it less eagerly.)* Tell me, who was the man?

(The strange woman—it is evident now that she has always been strange to him—smiles tolerantly.)

KATE: You never found out?

SIR HARRY: I could never be sure.

KATE *(reflectively)*: I thought that would worry you.

SIR HARRY *(sneering)*: It's plain that he soon left you.

KATE: Very soon.

SIR HARRY: As I could have told you. *(But still she surveys him with the smile of Mona Lisa. The badgered man has to entreat.)* Who was he? It was fourteen years ago, and cannot matter to any of us now. Kate, tell me who he was?

(It is his first youthful moment, and perhaps because of that she does not wish to hurt him.)

KATE *(shaking a motherly head)*: Better not ask.

SIR HARRY: I do ask. Tell me.

KATE: It is kinder not to tell you.

SIR HARRY *(violently)*: Then, by James, it was one of my own pals. Was it Bernard Roche? *(She shakes her head.)* It may have been some one who comes to my house still.

KATE: I think not. *(Reflecting.)* Fourteen years! You found my letter that night when you went home?

SIR HARRY *(impatient)*: Yes.

KATE: I propped it against the decanters. I thought you would be sure to see it there. It was a room not unlike this, and the furniture was arranged in the same attractive way. How it all comes back to me. Don't you see me, Harry, in hat and cloak, putting the letter there, taking a last look round, and then stealing out into the night to meet—

SIR HARRY: Whom?

KATE: Him. Hours pass, no sound in the room but the tick-tack of the clock, and then about midnight you return alone. You take—

SIR HARRY *(gruffly)*: I wasn't alone.

KATE *(the picture spoilt)*: No? oh. *(Plaintively.)* Here have I all these years been conceiving it wrongly. *(She studies his face.)* I believe something interesting happened?

SIR HARRY *(growling)*: Something confoundedly annoying.

KATE *(coaxing)*: Do tell me.

SIR HARRY: We won't go into that. Who was the man? Surely a husband has a right to know with whom his wife bolted.

KATE *(who is detestably ready with her tongue)*: Surely the wife has a right to know how he took it. *(The woman's love of bargaining comes to her aid.)* A fair exchange. You tell me what happened, and I will tell you who he was.

SIR HARRY: You will? Very well.

(It is the first point on which they have agreed, and, forgetting himself, he takes a place beside her on the fireseat. He is thinking only of what he is to tell her, but she, womanlike, is conscious of their proximity.)

KATE *(tastelessly)*: Quite like old times. *(He moves away from her indignantly.)* Go on Harry.

SIR HARRY *(who has a manful shrinking from saying anything that is to his disadvantage)*: Well, as you know, I was dining at the club that night.

KATE: Yes.

SIR HARRY: Jack Lamb drove me home. Mabbett Green was with us, and I asked them to come in for a few minutes.

KATE: Jack Lamb, Mabbett Green. I think I remember them. Jack was in Parliament.

SIR HARRY: No, that was Mabbett. They came into the house with me and—*(With sudden horror.)*—was it him?

KATE *(bewildered)*: Who?

SIR HARRY: Mabbett?

KATE: What?

SIR HARRY: The man?

KATE: What man? *(Understanding.)* Oh no. I thought you said he came into the house with you.

SIR HARRY: It might have been a blind.

KATE: Well, it wasn't. Go on.

SIR HARRY: They came in to finish a talk we had been having at the club.

KATE: An interesting talk, evidently.

SIR HARRY: The papers had been full that evening of the elopement of some countess woman with a fiddler. What was her name?

KATE: Does it matter?

SIR HARRY: No. *(Thus ends the countess.)* We had been discussing the thing and—*(He pulls a wry face.)*—and I had been rather warm—

KATE *(with horrid relish):* I begin to see. You had been saying it served the husband right, that the man who could not look after his wife deserved to lose her. It was one of your favorite subjects. Oh, Harry, say it was that!

SIR HARRY *(sourly)*: It may have been something like that.

KATE: And all the time the letter was there, waiting; and none of you knew except the clock. Harry, it is sweet of you to tell me. *(His face is not sweet. The illiterate woman has used the wrong adjective.)* I forget what I said precisely in the letter.

SIR HARRY *(pulverizing her)*: So do I. But I have it still.

KATE *(not pulverized)*: Do let me see it again. *(She has observed his eye wandering to the desk.)*

SIR HARRY: You are welcome to it as a gift. *(The fateful letter, a poor little dead thing, is brought to light from a locked drawer.)*

KATE *(taking it)*: Yes, this is it. Harry, how you did crumble it! *(She reads, not without curiosity.)* "Dear husband—I call you that for the last time—I am off. I am what you call making a bolt of it. I won't try to excuse myself nor to explain, for you would not accept the excuses nor understand the explanation. It will be a little shock to you, but only to your pride; what will astound you is that any woman could be such a fool as to leave such a man as you. I am taking nothing with me that belongs to you. May you be very happy.—Your ungrateful Kate. *P.S.*—You need not try to find out who he is. You will try, but you won't succeed." *(She folds the nasty little thing up.)* I may really have it for my very own?

SIR HARRY: You really may.

KATE *(impudently)*: If you would care for a typed copy—?

SIR HARRY *(in a voice with which he used to frighten his grandmother)*: None of your sauce! *(Wincing.)* I had to let them see it in the end.

KATE: I can picture Jack Lamb eating it.

SIR HARRY: A penniless parson's daughter.

KATE: That is all I was.

SIR HARRY: We searched for the two of you high and low.

KATE: Private detectives?

SIR HARRY: They couldn't get on the track of you.

KATE *(smiling)*: No?

SIR HARRY: But at last the courts let me serve the papers by advertisement on a man unknown, and I got my freedom.

KATE: So I saw. It was the last I heard of you.

SIR HARRY *(each word a blow for her)*: And I married again just as soon as ever I could.

KATE: They say that is always a compliment to the first wife.

SIR HARRY *(violently)*: I showed them.

KATE: You soon let them see that if one woman was a fool, you still had the pick of the basket to choose from.

SIR HARRY: By James, I did.

KATE *(bringing him to earth again)*: But still, you wondered who he was.

SIR HARRY: I suspected everybody—even my pals. I felt like jumping at their throats and crying, "It's you!"

KATE: You had been so admirable to me, an instinct told you that I was sure to choose another of the same.

SIR HARRY: I thought, it can't be money, so it must be looks. Some dolly face. *(He stares at her in perplexity.)* He must have had something wonderful about him to make you willing to give up all that you had with me.

KATE *(as if he was the stupid one)*: Poor Harry.

SIR HARRY: And it couldn't have been going on for long, for I would have noticed the change in you.

KATE: Would you?

SIR HARRY: I knew you so well.

KATE: You amazing man.

SIR HARRY: So who was he? Out with it.

KATE: You are determined to know?

SIR HARRY: Your promise. You gave your word.

KATE: If I must—

(She is the villain of the piece, but it must be conceded that in this matter she is reluctant to pain him.)

I am sorry I promised. *(Looking at him steadily.)* There was no one, Harry; no one at all.

SIR HARRY *(rising)*: If you think you can play with me—

KATE: I told you that you wouldn't like it.

SIR HARRY *(rasping)*: It is unbelievable.

KATE: I suppose it is; but it is true.

SIR HARRY: Your letter itself gives you the lie.

KATE: That was intentional. I saw that if the truth were known you might have a difficulty in getting your freedom; and as I was getting mine it seemed fair that you should have yours also. So I wrote my good-bye in words that would be taken to mean what you thought they meant, and I knew the law would back you in your opinion. For the law, like you, Harry, has a profound understanding of women.

SIR HARRY *(trying to straighten himself)*: I don't believe you yet.

KATE *(looking not unkindly into the soul of this man)*: Perhaps that is the best way to take it. It is less unflattering than the truth. But you were the only one. *(Summing up her life.)* You sufficed.

SIR HARRY: Then what mad impulse—

KATE: It was no impulse, Harry. I had thought it out for a year.

SIR HARRY: A year? *(Dazed.)* One would think to hear you that I hadn't been a good husband to you.

KATE *(with a sad smile)*: You were a good husband according to your lights.

SIR HARRY *(stoutly)*: *I* think so.

KATE: And a moral man, and chatty, and quite the philanthropist.

SIR HARRY *(on sure ground)*: All women envied you.

KATE: How you loved me to be envied.

SIR HARRY: I swaddled you in luxury.

KATE *(making her great revelation)*: That was it.

SIR HARRY *(blankly)*: What?

KATE *(who can be serene because it is all over)*: How you beamed at me when I sat at the head of your fat dinners in my fat jewelry, surrounded by our fat friends.

SIR HARRY *(aggrieved)*: They weren't so fat.

KATE *(a side issue)*: All except those who were so thin. Have you ever noticed, Harry, that many jewels make women either incredibly fat or incredibly thin?

SIR HARRY *(shouting)*: I have not. *(Is it worth while to argue with her any longer?)* We had all the most interesting society of the day. It wasn't only businessmen. There were politicians, painters, writers—

KATE: Only the glorious, dazzling successes. Oh, the fat talk while we ate too much—about who had made a hit and who was slipping back, and what the noo house cost and the noo motor and the gold soup-plates, and who was to be the noo knight.

SIR HARRY *(who it will be observed is unanswerable from first to last)*: Was anybody getting on better than me, and consequently you?

KATE: Consequently me! Oh, Harry, you and your sublime religion.

SIR HARRY *(honest heart)*: My religion? I never was one to talk about religion, but—

KATE: Pooh, Harry, you don't even know what your religion was and is and will be till the day of your expensive funeral. *(And here is the lesson that life has taught her.)* One's religion is whatever he is most interested in, and yours is Success.

SIR HARRY *(quoting from his morning paper)*: Ambition—it is the last infirmity of noble minds.

KATE: Noble minds!

SIR HARRY *(at last grasping what she is talking about)*: You are not saying that you left me because of my success?

KATE: Yes, that was it. *(And now she stands revealed to him.)* I couldn't endure it. If a failure had come now and then—but your success was suffocating me. *(She is rigid with emotion.)* The passionate craving I had to be done with it, to find myself among people who had not got on.

SIR HARRY *(with proper spirit)*: There are plenty of them.

KATE: There were none in our set. When they began to go down-hill they rolled out of our sight.

SIR HARRY *(clinching it)*: I tell you I am worth a quarter of a million.

KATE *(unabashed)*: That is what you are worth to yourself. I'll tell you what you are worth to me: exactly twelve pounds. For I made up my mind that I could launch myself on the world alone if I first proved my mettle by earning twelve pounds; and as soon as I had earned it I left you.

SIR HARRY *(in the scales)*: Twelve pounds!

KATE: That is your value to a woman. If she can't make it she has to stick to you.

SIR HARRY *(remembering perhaps a rectory garden)*: You valued me at more than that when you married me.

KATE *(seeing it also)*: Ah, I didn't know you then. If only you had been a man, Harry.

SIR HARRY: A man? What do you mean by a man?

KATE *(leaving the garden)*: Haven't you heard of them? They are something fine; and every woman is loathe to admit to herself that her husband is not one. When she marries, even though she has been a very trivial person, there is in her some vague stirring toward a worthy life, as well as a fear of her capacity for evil. She knows her chance lies in him. If there is something good in him, what is good in her finds it, and they join forces against the baser parts. So I didn't give you up willingly, Harry. I invented all sorts of theories to explain you. Your hardness—I said it was a fine want of maukishness. Your coarseness—I said it goes with strength. Your contempt for the weak—I called it virility. Your want of ideals was clear-sightedness. Your ignoble views of women—I tried to think them funny. Oh, I clung to you to save myself. But I had to let go; you had only the one quality, Harry, success; you had it so strong that it swallowed all the others.

SIR HARRY *(not to be diverted from the main issue)*: How did you earn that twelve pounds?

KATE: It took me nearly six months; but I earned it fairly.

(She presses her hand on the typewriter as lovingly as many a woman has pressed a rose.)

I learned this. I hired it and taught myself. I got some work through a friend, and with my first twelve pounds I paid for my machine. Then I considered that I was free to go, and I went.

SIR HARRY: All this going on in my house while you were living in the lap of luxury! *(She nods.)* By God you were determined.

KATE *(briefly)*: By God, I was.

SIR HARRY *(staring)*: How you must have hated me.

KATE *(smiling at the childish word)*: Not a bit—after I saw that there was a way out. From that hour you amused me, Harry; I was even sorry for you, for I saw that you couldn't help yourself. Success is just a fatal gift.

SIR HARRY: Oh, thank you.

KATE *(thinking, dear friends in front, of you and me perhaps)*: Yes, and some of your most successful friends knew it. One or two of them used to look very sad at times, as if they thought they might have come to something if they hadn't got on.

SIR HARRY *(who has a horror of sacrilege)*: The battered crew you live among now—what are they but folk who have tried to succeed and failed?

KATE: That's it; they try, but they fail.

SIR HARRY: And always will fail.

KATE: Always. Poor souls—I say of them. Poor soul—they say of me. It keeps us human. That is why I never tire of them.

SIR HARRY *(comprehensively)*: Bah! Kate, I tell you I'll be worth half a million yet.

KATE: I'm sure you will. You're getting stout, Harry.

SIR HARRY: No, I'm not.

KATE: What was the name of that fat old fellow who used to fall asleep at our dinner parties?

SIR HARRY: If you mean Sir William Crackley—

KATE: That was the man. Sir William was to me a perfect picture of the grand success. He had got on so well that he was very, very stout, and when he sat on a chair it was thus *(Her hands meeting in front of her.)*—as if he were holding his success together. That is what you are working for, Harry. You will have that and the half million about the same time.

SIR HARRY *(who has surely been very patient)*: Will you please to leave my house.

KATE *(putting on her gloves, soiled things)*: But don't let us part in anger. How do you think I am looking, Harry, compared to the dull, inert thing that used to roll round in your padded carriages?

SIR HARRY *(in masterly fashion)*: I forget what you were like. I'm very sure you never could have held a candle to the present Lady Sims.

KATE: That is a picture of her, is it not?

SIR HARRY *(seizing his chance again)*: In her wedding-gown. Painted by an R.A.

KATE *(wickedly)*: A knight?

SIR HARRY *(deceived)*: Yes.

KATE *(who likes* LADY SIMS*: a piece of presumption on her part)*: It is a very pretty face.

SIR HARRY *(with the pride of possession)*: Acknowledged to be a beauty everywhere.

KATE: There is a merry look in the eyes, and character in the chin.

SIR HARRY *(like an auctioneer)*: Noted for her wit.

KATE: All her life before her when that was painted. It is a *spirituelle*[3] face too.

(Suddenly she turns on him with anger, for the first and only time in the play.)

Oh, Harry, you brute!

3. Refined and graceful.

SIR HARRY *(staggered)*: Eh? What?

KATE: That dear creature capable of becoming a noble wife and mother—she is the spiritless woman of no account that I saw here a few minutes ago. I forgive you for myself, for I escaped, but that poor lost soul, oh, Harry, Harry.

SIR HARRY *(waving her to the door)*: I'll thank you—If ever there was a woman proud of her husband and happy in her married life, that woman is Lady Sims.

KATE: I wonder.

SIR HARRY: Then you needn't wonder.

KATE *(slowly)*: If I was a husband—it is my advice to all of them—I would often watch my wife quietly to see whether the twelve-pound look was not coming into her eyes. Two boys, did you say, and both like you?

SIR HARRY: What is that to you?

KATE *(with glistening eyes)*: I was only thinking that somewhere there are two little girls who, when they grow up—the dear, pretty girls who are all meant for the men that don't get on! Well, good-bye, Sir Harry.

SIR HARRY *(showing a little human weakness, it is to be feared)*: Say first that you're sorry.

KATE: For what?

SIR HARRY: That you left me. Say you regret it bitterly. You know you do.

(She smiles and shakes her head. He is pettish. He makes a terrible announcement.)

You have spoilt the day for me.

KATE *(to hearten him)*: I'm sorry for that; but it is only a pin-prick, Harry. I suppose it is a little jarring in the moment of your triumph to find that there is—one old friend—who does not think you a success; but you will soon forget it. Who cares what a typist thinks?

SIR HARRY *(heartened)*: Nobody. A typist at eighteen shillings a week!

KATE *(proudly)*: Not a bit of it, Harry. I double that.

SIR HARRY *(neatly)*: Magnificent! *(There is a timid knock at the door.)*

LADY SIMS: May I come in?

SIR HARRY *(rather appealingly)*: It is Lady Sims.

KATE: I won't tell. She is afraid to come into her husband's room without knocking!

SIR HARRY: She is not. *(Uxoriously.)* Come in, dearest.

(Dearest enters carrying the sword. She might have had the sense not to bring it in while this annoying person is here.)

LADY SIMS *(thinking she has brought her welcome with her)*: Harry, the sword has come.

SIR HARRY *(who will dote on it presently)*: Oh, all right.

LADY SIMS: But I thought you were so eager to practice with it.

(The person smiles at this. He wishes he had not looked to see if she was smiling.)

SIR HARRY *(sharply)*: Put it down. *(*LADY SIMS *flushes a little as she lays the sword aside.)*

KATE *(with her confounded courtesy)*: It is a beautiful sword, if I may say so.

LADY SIMS *(helped)*: Yes. *(The person thinks she can put him in the wrong, does she? He'll show her.)*

SIR HARRY *(with one eye on* KATE*)*: Emmy, the one thing your neck needs is more jewels.

LADY SIMS *(faltering)*: More!

SIR HARRY: Some ropes of pearls. I'll see to it. It's a bagatelle[4] to me. *(*KATE *conceals her chagrin, so she had better be shown the door. He rings.)* I won't detain you any longer, miss.

KATE: Thank you.

LADY SIMS: Going already? You have been very quick.

SIR HARRY: The person doesn't suit, Emmy.

LADY SIMS: I'm sorry.

KATE: So am I, madam, but it can't be helped. Good-bye, your ladyship—good-bye, Sir Harry.

(There is a suspicion of an impertinent curtsey, and she is escorted off the premises by TOMBES. *The air of the room is purified by her going.* SIR HARRY *notices it at once.)*

LADY SIMS *(whose tendency is to say the wrong thing)*: She seemed such a capable woman.

SIR HARRY *(on his hearth)*: I don't like her style at all.

LADY SIMS *(meekly)*: Of course you know best. *(This is the right kind of woman.)*

SIR HARRY *(rather anxious for corroboration)*: Lord, how she winced when I said I was to give you those ropes of pearls.

LADY SIMS: Did she? I didn't notice. I suppose so.

SIR HARRY *(frowning)*: Suppose? Surely I know enough about women to know that.

LADY SIMS: Yes, oh yes.

SIR HARRY *(odd that so confident a man should ask this)*: Emmy, I know you well, don't I? I can read you like a book, eh?

LADY SIMS *(nervously)*: Yes, Harry.

SIR HARRY *(jovially, but with an inquiring eye)*: What a different existence yours is from that poor lonely wretch's.

LADY SIMS: Yes, but she has a very contented face.

4. A trifle.

SIR HARRY *(with a stamp of his foot)*: All put on. What?
LADY SIMS *(timidly)*: I didn't say anything.
SIR HARRY *(snapping)*: One would think you envied her.
LADY SIMS: Envied? Oh no—but I thought she looked so alive. It was while she was working the machine.
SIR HARRY: Alive! That's no life. It is you that are alive. *(Curtly.)* I'm busy, Emmy. *(He sits at his writing table.)*
LADY SIMS *(dutifully)*: I'm sorry; I'll go, Harry. *(Inconsequentially.)* Are they very expensive?
SIR HARRY: What?
LADY SIMS: Those machines?

(When she has gone the possible meaning of her question startles him. The curtain hides him from us, but we may be sure that he will soon be bland again. We have a comfortable feeling, you and I, that there is nothing of HARRY SIMS *in us.)*

Questions

1. Why do you think Barrie provided all the humorous stage directions that would be lost to an audience seeing the play in a theatre?
2. Describe Sir Harry. Why do you suppose he fails to see reality?
3. What comic devices does Barrie use in this play?
4. Discuss the role of predictability in *The Twelve-Pound Look.*
5. What can you infer are the various reasons that Kate left Sir Harry?
6. How do you feel about Kate's saying, "One's religion is whatever he is most interested in, and yours is Success."
7. Kate's biggest insult to Sir Harry is her accusation that he wasn't a man. Why do you suppose she said this? What did she mean?
8. Where does the turning point occur? Were you surprised by the ending? Why or why not?

DOROTHY PARKER

Here We Are

DOROTHY PARKER is probably best known as a writer of biting and sardonic short fiction. But she began her literary career as a drama critic for *Vanity Fair* and a book reviewer for the *New Yorker.*

Born in 1893 in New Jersey, Parker also wrote light verse and film scripts. Her plays include *The Coast of Illyria,* based on the life of the English essayist Charles Lamb, and *Ladies of the Corridor.* The first play was coauthored with Ross Evans, the second with Arnaud d'Usseau.

HERE WE ARE is similar to Chekhov's *A Marriage Proposal* in that it provides a humorous look at human foibles that come to light under the best of circumstances. Chekhov dealt with two young people shortly before they become committed to each other; Parker shows they are just as prone to quarrel and disagree afterward.

The play illustrates that, no matter what the circumstances, people cannot get along together for more than a short time. Underlying the humor is a look at the uncertainties of the two young people.

Here We Are Dorothy Parker

Characters:

HE
SHE

Setting:

A compartment in a Pullman car. HE *is storing the suitcases in the rack and hanging up coats.* SHE *is primping.* HE *finishes disposing of the luggage and sits.*

HE: Well!

SHE: Well!

HE: Well, here we are.

SHE: Here we are, aren't we?

HE: Eeyop. I should say we are. Here we are.

SHE: Well!

HE: Well! Well! How does it feel to be an old married lady?

SHE: Oh, it's too soon to ask me that. At least—I mean. Well, I mean, goodness, we've only been married about three hours, haven't we?

HE: We have been married exactly two hours and twenty-six minutes.

SHE: My, it seems like longer.

HE: No, it isn't hardly half-past six yet.

SHE: It seems like later. I guess it's because it starts getting dark so early.

HE: It does, at that. The nights are going to be pretty long from now on. I mean. I mean—well, it starts getting dark early.

SHE: I didn't have any idea what time it was. Everything was so mixed up, I sort of don't know where I am, or what it's all about. Getting back from the church, and then all those people, and then changing all my clothes, and then everybody throwing things, and all. Goodness, I don't see how people do it every day.

HE: Do what?

SHE: Get married. When you think of all the people, all over the world, getting married just as if it was nothing. Chinese people and everybody. Just as if it wasn't anything.

HE: Well, let's not worry about people all over the world. Let's don't think about a lot of Chinese. We've got something better to think about. I mean. I mean—well, what do we care about them?

SHE: I know, but I just sort of got to thinking of them, all of them, all over everywhere, doing it all the time. At least, I mean—getting married, you know. And it's—well, it's sort of such a big thing to do, it makes you feel queer. You think of them, all of them, all doing it just like it wasn't anything. And how does anybody know what's going to happen next?

HE: Let them worry, we don't have to. We know darn well what's going to happen next. I mean—well, we know it's going to be great. Well, we know we're going to be happy. Don't we?

SHE: Oh, of course. Only you think of all the people, and you have to sort of keep thinking. It makes you feel funny. An awful lot of people that get married, it doesn't turn out so well. And I guess they all must have thought it was going to be great.

HE: Aw, come on, now, this is no way to start a honeymoon, with all this thinking going on. Look at us—all married and everything done. I mean. The wedding all done and all.

SHE: Ah, it was nice, wasn't it? Did you really like my veil?

HE: You looked great, just great.

SHE: Oh, I'm terribly glad. Ellie and Louise looked lovely, didn't they? I'm terribly glad they did finally decide on pink. They looked perfectly lovely.

HE: Listen, I want to tell you something. When I was standing up there in that old church waiting for you to come up, and I saw those two bridesmaids, I thought to myself, I thought, "Well, I never knew Louise could look like that!" I thought she'd have knocked anybody's eye out.

SHE: Oh, really? Funny. Of course, everybody thought her dress and hat were lovely, but a lot of people seemed to think she looked sort of tired. People have been saying that a lot, lately. I tell them I think it's awfully mean of them to go around saying that about her. I tell them they've got to remember that Louise isn't so terribly young any more, and they've got to expect her to look like that. Louise can say she's twenty-three all she wants to, but she's a good deal nearer twenty-seven.

HE: Well, she was certainly a knockout at the wedding. Boy!

SHE: I'm terribly glad you thought so. I'm glad someone did. How did you think Ellie looked?

HE: Why, I honestly didn't get a look at her.

SHE: Oh, really? Well, I certainly think that's too bad. I don't suppose I ought to say it about my own sister, but I never saw anybody look as beautiful as Ellie looked today. And always so sweet and unselfish, too. And you didn't even notice her. But you never pay attention to Ellie, anyway. Don't think I haven't noticed it. It makes me feel just terrible. It makes me feel just awful that you don't like my own sister.

HE: I do so like her! I'm crazy for Ellie, I think she's a great kid.

SHE: Don't think it makes any difference to Ellie! Ellie's got enough people crazy about her. It isn't anything to her whether you like her or not. Don't flatter yourself she cares! Only, the only thing is, it makes it awfully hard for me you don't like her, that's the only thing. I keep thinking, when we come back and get in the apartment and everything, it's going to be awfully hard for me that you won't want all my family around. I know how you feel about my family. Don't think I haven't seen it. Only, if you don't ever want to see them, that's your loss. Not theirs. Don't flatter yourself!

HE: Oh, now, come on! What's all this talk about not wanting your family around? Why, you know how I feel about your family. I think your old lady—I think your mother's swell. And Ellie. And your father. What's all this talk?

SHE: Well, I've seen it. Don't think I haven't. Lots of people they get married, and they think it's going to be great and everything, and then it all goes to pieces because people don't like people's families, or something like that. Don't tell me! I've seen it happen.

HE: Honey, what is all this? What are you getting all angry about? Hey, look, this is our honeymoon. What are you trying to start a fight for? Ah, I guess you're just feeling sort of nervous.

SHE: Me? What have I got to be nervous about? I mean. I mean, goodness, I'm not nervous.

HE: You know, lots of times, they say that girls get kind of nervous and yippy on account of thinking about—I mean. I mean—well, it's like you said, things are all so sort of mixed up and everything, right now. But afterwards, it'll be all right. I mean. I mean—well, look, honey, you don't look any too comfortable. Don't you want to take your hat off? And let's don't ever fight, ever. Will we?

SHE: Ah, I'm sorry I was cross. I guess I did feel a little bit funny. All mixed up, and then thinking of all those people all over everywhere, and then being sort of 'way off here, all alone with you. It's so sort of different. It's sort of such a big thing. You can't blame a person for thinking, can you? Yes, don't let's ever, ever fight. We won't be like a whole lot of them. We won't fight or be nasty or anything. Will we?

HE: You bet your life we won't.

SHE: I guess I will take this darned old hat off. It kind of presses. Just put it up on the rack, will you, dear? Do you like it, sweetheart?

HE: Looks good on you.

SHE: No, but I mean, do you really like it?

HE: Well, I'll tell you, I know this is the new style and everything like that, and it's probably great. I don't know anything about things like that. Only I like the kind of a hat like that blue hat you had. Gee, I like that hat.

SHE: Oh, really? Well, that's nice. That's lovely. The first thing you say to me, as soon as you get me off on a train away from my family and everything, is that you don't like my hat. The first thing you say to your wife is you think she has terrible taste in hats. That's nice, isn't it?

HE: Now, honey, I never said anything like that. I only said—

SHE: What you don't seem to realize is this hat cost twenty-two dollars. Twenty-two dollars. And that horrible old blue thing you think you're so crazy about, that cost three ninety-five.

HE: I don't give a darn what they cost. I only said—I said I liked that blue hat. I don't know anything about hats. I'll be crazy about this one as soon as I get used to it. Only it's kind of not like your other hats. I don't know about the new style. What do I know about women's hats?

SHE: It's too bad you didn't marry somebody that would get the kind of hats you'd like. Hats that cost three ninety-five. Why didn't you marry Louise? You always think she looks so beautiful. You'd love her taste in hats. Why didn't you marry her?

HE: Ah, now, honey, for heaven's sakes!

SHE: Why didn't you marry her? All you've done, ever since we got on this train, is talk about her. Here I've sat and sat, and just listened to you saying how wonderful Louise is. I suppose that's nice, getting me off here all alone with you, and then raving about Louise right in front of my face. Why didn't you ask her to marry you? I'm sure she would have jumped at the chance. There aren't so many people asking her to marry them. It's too bad you didn't marry her. I'm sure you'd have been much happier.

HE: Listen, baby, while you're talking about things like that, why didn't you marry Joe Brooks? I suppose he could have given you all the twenty-two-dollar hats you wanted, I suppose!

SHE: Well, I'm not so sure I'm not sorry I didn't. There! Joe Brooks wouldn't have waited until he got me all off alone and then sneered at my taste in clothes. Joe Brooks wouldn't ever hurt my feelings. Joe Brooks has always been fond of me.

HE: Yeah, he's fond of you. He was so fond of you he didn't even send a wedding present. That's how fond of you he was.

SHE: I happen to know for a fact that he was away on business, and as soon as he comes back he's going to give me anything I want for the apartment.

HE: Listen, I don't want anything he gives you in our apartment. Anything he gives you, I'll throw right out the window. That's what I think of your friend Joe Brooks. And how do you know where he is and what he's going to do, anyway? Has he been writing to you?

SHE: I suppose my friends can correspond with me. I didn't hear there was any law against that.

HE: Well, I suppose they can't! And what do you think of that? I'm not going to have my wife getting a lot of letters from cheap traveling salesmen!

SHE: Joe Brooks is not a cheap traveling salesman! He is not! He gets a wonderful salary.

HE: Oh yeah? Where did you hear that?

SHE: He told me so himself.

HE: Oh, he told you so himself. I see. He told you so himself.

SHE: You've got a lot of right to talk about Joe Brooks. You and your friend Louise. All you ever talk about is Louise.

HE: Oh, for heaven's sakes! What do I care about Louise? I just thought she was a friend of yours, that's all. That's why I ever noticed her.

SHE: Well, you certainly took an awful lot of notice of her today. On our wedding day! You said yourself when you were standing there in the church you just kept thinking of her. Right up at the altar. Oh, right in the presence of God! And all you thought about was Louise.

HE: Listen, honey, I never should have said that. How does anybody know what kind of crazy things come into their heads when they're standing there waiting to get married? I was just telling you that because it was so kind of crazy. I thought it would make you laugh.

SHE: I know, I've been all sort of mixed up today, too. I told you that. Everything so strange and everything. And me all the time thinking about all those people all over the world, and now us here all alone, and everything. I know you get all mixed up. Only I did think, when you kept talking about how beautiful Louise looked, you did it with malice and forethought.

HE: I never did anything with malice and forethought! I just told you that about Louise because I thought it would make you laugh.

SHE: Well, it didn't.

HE: No, I know it didn't. It certainly did not. Ah, baby, and we ought to be laughing, too. Hell, honey lamb, this is our honeymoon. What's the matter?

SHE: I don't know. We used to squabble a lot when we were going together and then engaged and everything, but I thought everything would be so different as soon as you were married. And now I feel so sort of strange and everything. I feel so sort of alone.

HE: Well, you see, sweetheart, we're not really married yet. I mean. I mean—well, things will be different afterwards. Oh, hell. I mean, we haven't been married very long.

SHE: No.

HE: Well, we haven't got much longer to wait now. I mean—well, we'll be in New York in about twenty minutes. Then we can have dinner, and sort of see what we feel like doing. Or, I mean—is there anything special you want to do tonight?

SHE: What?

HE: What I mean to say, would you like to go to a show or something?

SHE: Why, whatever you like. I sort of didn't think people went to theaters and things on their—I mean, I've got a couple of letters I simply must write. Don't let me forget.

HE: Oh, you're going to write letters tonight?

SHE: Well, you see, I've been perfectly terrible. What with all the excitement and everything. I never did thank poor old Mrs. Sprague for her berry spoon, and I never did a thing about those book ends the McMasters sent. It's just too awful of me. I've got to write them this very night.

HE: And when you've finished writing your letters, maybe I could get you a magazine or a bag of peanuts.

SHE: What?

HE: I mean, I wouldn't want you to be bored.

SHE: As if I could be bored with you! Silly! Aren't we married? Bored!

HE: What I thought, I thought when we got in, we could go right up to the Biltmore and anyway leave our bags, and maybe have a little dinner in the room, kind of quiet, and then do whatever we wanted. I mean. I mean—well, let's go right up there from the station.

SHE: Oh, yes, let's. I'm so glad we're going to the Biltmore. I just love it. The twice I've stayed in New York we've always stayed there, Papa and Mamma and Ellie and I, and I was crazy about it. I always sleep so well there. I go right off to sleep the minute I put my head on the pillow.

HE: Oh, you do?

SHE: At least, I mean, 'way up high it's so quiet.

HE: We might go to some show or other tomorrow night instead of tonight. Don't you think that would be better?

SHE: Yes, I think it might.

HE: Do you really have to write those letters tonight?

SHE: Well, I don't suppose they'd get there any quicker than if I wrote them tomorrow.

HE: And we won't ever fight any more, will we?

SHE: Oh, no. Not ever! I don't know what made me do like that. It all got so sort of funny, sort of like a nightmare, the way I got thinking of all those people getting married all the time; and so many of them, everything spoils on account of fighting and everything. I got all mixed up thinking about them. Oh, I don't want to be like them. But we won't be, will we?

HE: Sure we won't.

SHE: We won't go all to pieces. We won't fight. It'll all be different, now we're married. It'll all be lovely. Reach me down my hat, will you, sweetheart? It's time I was putting it on. Thanks. Ah, I'm sorry you don't like it.

HE: I do so like it!

SHE: You said you didn't. You said you thought it was perfectly terrible.

HE: I never said any such thing. You're crazy.

SHE: All right, I may be crazy. Thank you very much. But that's what you said. Not that it matters—it's just a little thing. But it makes you feel pretty funny to think you've gone and married somebody that says you have perfectly terrible taste in hats. And then goes and says you're crazy, besides.

HE: Now, listen here, nobody said any such thing. Why, I love that hat. The more I look at it the better I like it. I think it's great.

SHE: That isn't what you said before.

HE: Honey, stop it, will you? What do you want to start all this for? I love the damned hat. I mean, I love your hat. I love anything you wear. What more do you want me to say?

SHE: Well, I don't want you to say it like that.

HE: I said I think it's great. That's all I said.

SHE: Do you really? Do you honestly? Ah, I'm so glad. I'd hate you not to like my hat. It would be—I don't know, it would be sort of such a bad start.

HE: Well, I'm crazy for it. Now we've got that settled, for heaven's sakes. Ah, baby. Baby lamb. We're not going to have any bad starts. Look at us—we're on our honeymoon. Pretty soon we'll be regular old married people. I mean. I mean, in a few minutes we'll be getting in to New York, and then we'll be going to the hotel, and then everything will be all right. I mean—well, look at us! Here we are married! Here we are!

SHE: Yes, here we are, aren't we?

Curtain

Questions

1. What part does jealousy play in *Here We Are?*
2. For a time the man tries to placate his new wife. At what point do her comments begin to upset him?
3. Why do you think the man told the woman He kept thinking of Louise? Was her reaction justified? Why do you think so?

4. Why do you suppose She thinks everything will be fine once She's married?
5. Discuss the use of sarcasm in the play.
6. What do you think the man and woman's relationship will be like in ten years? In twenty?
7. Where are the turning point and the climax? Explain.

LOUIS PHILLIPS

Carwash

LOUIS PHILLIPS often tends to view the world humorously, as seen in such plays as *Goin' West,* which pokes fun at the American dreams of fame, fortune, and happiness, and *Carwash.*

An extremely versatile writer, Phillips writes humor pieces for magazines and newspapers and is the author of some twenty-five books for children and adults, including *How Do You Get a Horse Out of a Bathtub?* and *Who Stole the Atlantic Ocean?*

Phillips is equally well known as a poet. His *The Time, the Hour, the Solitariness of the Place,* was cowinner of the 1984 Swallow's Tale Press Poetry Award, and he was one of several poets whose work was selected to appear in *New York: Beijing,* a poetry anthology that accompanied American art exhibited in Beijing, Shanghai, and Hong Kong in 1987 as part of a cultural exchange between China and the United States.

His plays have been widely produced in regional theatres across the country as well as in New York City. The recipient of numerous playwriting awards, including a National Endowment for the Arts Fellowship in 1983, Phillips was playwright-in-residence for four years at the Colonnades Theatre Lab in New York City where three of his plays were produced.

Phillips currently teaches creative writing at the School of Visual Arts in New York City.

CARWASH is intended mainly for enjoyment, even though it pokes fun at people who measure success solely by monetary gain and status symbols.

The play poses this situation: Suppose the laws governing the physical universe were suspended—at least in part, at least for a time. How would people react? Would they go crazy? Would they insist on finding rational explanations for the irrational? Such questions interest Louis Phillips, and he explores them imaginatively in this play.

Carwash Louis Phillips

Characters:

KEN PFEIFFER
SUE WHISTLER
DARLENE SILVERMAN
WOMAN

Setting:

In the dark we hear the sound of a carwash at full throttle. The water hums a powerful spray, the brushes create a concerto of scrub, the vacuum cleaners vacuum, pulling dust and dirt out of some kind of universe. The noise subsides. When the lights come on on the Charm School Carwash, we see a few buckets of soap, large sponges, two or three folding chairs, dirty towels.

On stage are two men. KEN PFEIFFER, *who is dressed in a dark suit and who is carrying a briefcase, and* JOE WHISTLER, *a worker at the carwash. Joe is in simple workpants, sneakers, and a white shirt with the name:* CHARM SCHOOL CARWASH.

PFEIFFER: Get me the manager!

JOE: I am the manager.

PFEIFFER: No, you're not the manager. You're a car thief.

JOE: Keep calm.

PFEIFFER: I am calm.

JOE: You're not calm.

PFEIFFER: You're not the manager!

JOE: I am one of the managers. Everyone on the lot is a manager. It's part of a new psychological theory of increasing profits. Make everybody feel the way the owner feels. We learned it from a book about the Japanese.

PFEIFFER: I don't want to hear about the Japanese right now.

JOE: Why? Are they ruining your business too?

PFEIFFER: I don't have a business. And, at the moment, I don't even have a car!

JOE: You have a car. You came in here with a car. You will leave with one.

PFEIFFER: I want to leave with the one I came in.

JOE: You will.

PFEIFFER: Where is it?

JOE: It has to be in there somewhere.

PFEIFFER: It's not in there. I keep telling you. It's not in there. Look!

(The owner of the carwash enters. She is DARLENE SILVERMAN. *In her mid-thirties, she is short, with frizzled hair. She wears a blue jumpsuit.)*

DARLENE: What seems to be the trouble here.

PFEIFFER: I want the manager.

DARLENE: I am the manager.

PFEIFFER: Of course. Everybody's a manager in this business. It's something you learned from the Japanese. . . .

DARLENE: What's that suppose to mean?

JOE: He's upset because he lost his car.

DARLENE: He lost his car?

JOE: He lost his car.

PFEIFFER: I lost my car.

DARLENE: You lost your car?

PFEIFFER: What are we talking about here?

JOE: I thought we were talking about losing your car.

PFEIFFER: That's right. That's exactly what I'm talking about. Losing my car.

DARLENE: If you lost your car, what are you doing at a carwash? It doesn't make any sense to come to a carwash without any car.

PFEIFFER: Are you crazy? What are you talking about? I came here with my car. And now I don't have a car. I put it in there *(Points to the carwash tunnel.)*.

DARLENE (*to* JOE): What's he talking about?

JOE: He lost his car.

DARLENE: He lost his car?

PFEIFFER: I lost my car. . . in there.

DARLENE: Is this some kind of a joke? You lost your car in there?

PFEIFFER: I didn't lose the car. You lost the car.

DARLENE (*to* JOE): What's he talking about? It's impossible to lose a car in there.

PFEIFFER: You did something to it.

JOE: I didn't touch the car.

PFEIFFER: Somebody touched the car!

JOE: I don't touch the cars until they come out of the tunnel. Your car didn't come out of the tunnel. Therefore, I didn't touch it.

DARLENE (*to* PFEIFFER): See?

PFEIFFER: See what?

DARLENE: He didn't touch your car. So what are you complaining about?

PFEIFFER: What am I complaining about?

DARLENE: What are you complaining about?

JOE: What's he complaining about?

PFEIFFER: Stop it! I don't want you trying any of your charm school stuff on me.

JOE: What charm school stuff?

PFEIFFER: I don't find any of it charming.

DARLENE: I still don't understand what you're complaining about.
PFEIFFER: I told you.
DARLENE: You didn't tell me.
PFEIFFER: I drove my car into this Charm School and Carwash. . . .
DARLENE: It's not charm school and carwash. It's Charm School Carwash. It's owned by a woman named Charm School.
PFEIFFER: There's actually a woman named Charm School?
DARLENE: Of course there is. You don't think that we would actually name a carwash Charm School unless the owner wanted her name upon it. But maybe you think it's funny to make fun of a person's name.
PFEIFFER: Are you the owner?
DARLENE: No, I'm the manager.
JOE: One of the managers.
DARLENE: My name's Darlene. This is Joe. What's your name?
PFEIFFER: Pfeiffer. . . Salten Pfeiffer.
DARLENE: Salten Pfeiffer and you make fun of someone named Charm School?
PFEIFFER: Don't do this to me!
DARLENE: Do what to you?
PFEIFFER: Put me on the defensive. It's you people who are at fault. Not me. I drove my car in here in good faith. Put it on the conveyor belt, got out, came over here, listened to the water, the brushes, and waited for my car to emerge fully cleansed, brand-new as it were. . . .
JOE: And for less than two dollars too. What kind of a bargain is that?
PFEIFFER: But my car didn't come out. What kind of a bargain is that? The $80,000 car wash.
DARLENE: $80,000? What kind of car are you driving?
PFEIFFER: It was designed for a movie star.
DARLENE: Oh.
PFEIFFER: Oh? What do you mean by "oh"?
DARLENE: I mean you can't expect a movie star's car to act like everybody else's car.
PFEIFFER: I expect it to come out of a carwash.
DARLENE: Maybe it's still in there?
JOE: We looked. It's not in there.
PFEIFFER: What is this? The Bermuda Triangle? I bring my car in here and it goes up in a puff of smoke.
DARLENE: Smoke? Did you actually see a puff of smoke?
PFEIFFER: I didn't see anything. I have been waiting for my car to come out and it didn't come out.
DARLENE: Then why did you say a puff of smoke?
PFEIFFER: It was a figure of speech. A way of talking.
DARLENE: Well, don't say it if you don't mean it.

PFEIFFER: I mean it. I just don't believe it. What do you people do? Is it some kind of illusion? Some magician taught you to pluck people's cars out of thin air?

DARLENE: How do we know it happened?

PFEIFFER: What do you mean?

DARLENE: How do we know you actually came in here with a car?

PFEIFFER: Of course I came in here with a car. What else would I bring to a carwash. My laundry? . . . That's what I did. I brought you my underwear and called it a Mercedes.

DARLENE: No need to talk dirty.

PFEIFFER: I drove in here. I put my Mercedes on the conveyor belt. I got out. . . The car went through and didn't emerge.

DARLENE: You can't prove it. I think you would actually have a difficult time proving you actually brought a car in here.

PFEIFFER: I don't have to prove it!

DARLENE: Of course you do. You don't think the owner is going to pay for a car that doesn't exist.

PFEIFFER: Of course it exists. I have it registered.

DARLENE: I mean exist here.

PFEIFFER: He saw me drive it in. *(To* JOE.) Tell her you saw me drive it in.

JOE: I don't know. It was very busy at the time. A lot of cars were coming through.

PFEIFFER: Not an $80,000 silver Mercedes! What kind of a racket are you two running here?

JOE: Be careful what you say.

DARLENE: We're not running any racket. It seems to be that you're the one trying to cheat us.

JOE: How long do you think we could get away with stealing people's cars?

PFEIFFER: You're not stealing my car and getting away with it.

DARLENE: No one is stealing your car.

PFEIFFER: Get me another manager.

JOE: We're the only two managers left.

PFEIFFER: Sorry. Somehow I had gotten the impression that everybody on this lot is a manager. It's a Japanese theory.

JOE: You're not a manager.

PFEIFFER: I'm not even the owner of my automobile anymore. I'm going to the police. This charm school is out of business.

DARLENE: Wait. . . Tell me something.

PFEIFFER: I've been telling you something for the past twenty minutes, but nobody seems to be listening.

DARLENE: Just because we're not strong in communications theory, it doesn't mean you have to yell at us.

PFEIFFER: I want my car back.

JOE: That we understand.

DARLENE: We want your car back too. Believe us. It doesn't help the reputation of a carwash to be losing cars.

PFEIFFER: When it comes to reputation, you people are dead. Of course, you can always change your name to Automobiles Anonymous.

DARLENE: It may not be our fault. It may be the manufacturer's fault.

PFEIFFER: How can it be the manufacturer's fault?

DARLENE: Have you ever had the car washed before?

PFEIFFER: What do you mean?

DARLENE: They're always recalling cars for something.

PFEIFFER: Not Mercedes! And not in the middle of a carwash. The manufacturer didn't come in and pluck it right out of the tunnel.

DARLENE: I mean there might have been a glitch in the paint job. Some kind of chemical so that if water is added to it, it just evaporates.

PFEIFFER: Mercedes don't evaporate. Buicks evaporate! Volkswagens! Maybe even a Greyhound bus or two. But not an $80,000 custom-made Mercedes.

JOE: She's talking about the paint.

PFEIFFER: What? You don't think the car has been in the rain?

JOE: You have an $80,000 Mercedes and you leave it out in the rain. You don't deserve a car like that.

PFEIFFER: Oh, I get it. You take it away from me because you think I don't deserve it? Of all the carwashes in the United States, I have to pick one that's Marxist. . . .

DARLENE: Wait a minute, mister. You're going too far.

PFEIFFER: I'm not going too far. I'm not going anywhere because I don't have my car!

DARLENE: We didn't take away your car because you didn't deserve it.

PFEIFFER: Oh, really! Then just what was your motive in stealing my car?

JOE: We had no motive.

PFEIFFER: A bit cold-blooded, isn't it? To steal a valuable automobile without a motive?

DARLENE: We didn't steal your car at all! What are you trying to do? Pull that old lawyer's stunt—"When did you stop beating your wife?"

PFEIFFER: You're lucky I'm not a lawyer.

DARLENE: You're lucky I'm not a lawyer.

PFEIFFER: Ah, but I know lawyers.

JOE: Don't look at me. I'm just the manager of a carwash.

DARLENE: Everybody knows a lawyer. It's nothing to be proud of.

PFEIFFER: But you're going to have the privilege of knowing my lawyers. We're going to sue you for everything you're worth.

DARLENE: We don't own the place.

JOE: And there are so many managers, we hardly manage it. Japanese theory only works if you have an emperor.

PFEIFFER: What a 20th Century phenomenon: to absolve one's self of responsibility.

JOE: He should be a lawyer because I don't understand anything he's said nor anything that's happened. It's like a modern play.

PFEIFFER: You'll have plenty of time in jail to think about it.

DARLENE: We're not absolving ourselves of anything. Joe and I have been working at carwashes for years, but we have never lost a car yet.

JOE *(sing-song)*:

The cars go in,
The cars go out,
And all of us
Run about. . .

PFEIFFER: I don't see much running about here. In fact, I see very little heartfelt concern for my plight.

DARLENE *(takes up a clipboard)*: I think that what has happened is so far out of the ordinary that we do not know how to cope with it.

PFEIFFER: Likely story. The extraordinary is easy to cope with; it's the ordinary that leaves everybody helpless.

DARLENE: Very well. We'll cope. What was the year of your car?

PFEIFFER: I don't understand.

DARLENE: Is it such a difficult question?

PFEIFFER: What? You have so many $80,000 Mercedes zipping through here, you think it got lost in the shuffle?

DARLENE: When we recover your automobile, we wish to be certain you get the right one.

PFEIFFER: You're stalling. You're playing for time.

DARLENE: Of course I am. Even as we talk, the molecules that we call automobile might be reassembling themselves. . . and then we'll just turn around and there it will be. . . . *(She turns back to the carwash. The Mercedes has not appeared.)*

PFEIFFER: It's still not there.

JOE: Can I go home?

PFEIFFER: No. No one's leaving this lot until I get my car back.

DARLENE: What year was it?

PFEIFFER: Was? In the past tense already. That doesn't seem optimistic. Very well, it was a 1990.

JOE: 1990?

DARLENE: Please don't joke. We have reputation to maintain.

PFEIFFER: I'm not joking. It's this year's model.

DARLENE: But this is 1989.

PFEIFFER: 1990.

DARLENE: 1989.

JOE: Do I get to vote?

PFEIFFER: A year is not a politician. It's not something you vote upon.

DARLENE: If we can't agree what year it is, how are we going to agree about getting your car back?

PFEIFFER: Please, Lord, don't let me be in a time warp!

JOE: What's a time warp?

PFEIFFER: What's a carwash?

DARLENE: Ontology[1] is not our strong suit. Now may we continue with the business at hand?

PFEIFFER: It started out to be such a simple day. When I drove in here to wash my car, I really thought I had a handle on my life. I thought I had a clue to things.

JOE: It's television.

PFEIFFER: What's television?

JOE: Everything. Television is the reason that everything in life is going wrong.

PFEIFFER: That's a bit of a generalization, isn't it?

JOE: I'm just trying to be of help.

DARLENE: We watch old movies and lose our sense of time.

PFEIFFER: I'm losing something, that's for certain. My car and my sense of time. Perhaps I have been living a year ahead of everybody else.

JOE: Oh good.

PFEIFFER: What's good about it?

JOE: You can tell me who's going to be in the World Series.

PFEIFFER: Who cares who's going to be in the World Series.

JOE: Well, who cares about losing a silly car?

PFEIFFER: Silly? A Mercedes silly? Religion is silly. War is silly. Selling insurance is silly. But an $80,000 Mercedes is serious business.

JOE: There. You said it yourself. Why are you so upset about losing your car when it's a material object completely covered by insurance?

PFEIFFER: I'm covered for theft, fire, and collision. I doubt if there is anything in the policy about losing it in a carwash!

DARLENE: What about an act of God?

PFEIFFER: Ask Him, not me!

JOE: Who? Me?

PFEIFFER: No, God! If losing something in a carwash is an act of God, then I'd hate to think how the Pope discusses earthquakes.

JOE: Maybe that's it.

PFEIFFER: What's it?

1. A particular theory about the nature of being.

JOE: Maybe while your Mercedes was being washed, there was an earthquake. The floor just opened up and swallowed the car.

PFEIFFER: In there?

JOE: In there.

PFEIFFER: No where else all around us? Just in there, those few cubic feet where my Mercedes happened to be standing? Boom! And we didn't hear it? We didn't feel a thing?

JOE: It's possible.

PFEIFFER: Maybe a million ants left over from an old Charlton Heston movie crawled out of the jungles and climbed over the car and ate it!

DARLENE: No need to vent your sarcasm on us.

PFEIFFER: I'm not sarcastic. I'm insane. There's a difference. I've lost my mind.

DARLENE: Maybe the car is right in front of us, but we just can't see it.

JOE: See? There's the advantage of having more than one manager on the lot. It gives you a different perspective to the same problem. Those Japanese theories really work. *(*DARLENE *gives* PFEIFFER *the clipboard.)*

DARLENE: Here. Hold this.

PFEIFFER: Why?

DARLENE: I'm going in there and get your car.

PFEIFFER: You're going in there and get my car?

DARLENE: I'm going in there and get your car.

JOE: I don't think I would go in there myself.

PFEIFFER: Don't stop her. If she thinks my car is in there, let her go get it. Of course if it's really in there, how she will get in there is more than I know, because it is a law of physics: No two separate pieces of matter can occupy the same place at the same time.

DARLENE *(pulls some wires out of the socket)*: I'll just make certain everything is unplugged.

JOE: No. Don't go in there.

PFEIFFER: It's only a carwash. Stop treating it like the Black Lagoon. *(All three peer into the carwash.)*

JOE: We can see from this side all the way through to the other side. That means there's nothing in there.

PFEIFFER: Oh no. She thinks she can find it.

DARLENE: I'll just walk in. If there's nothing there, then I'll emerge at the other side.

PFEIFFER: Sounds logical to me.

JOE: Let's all go together.

PFEIFFER: There is nothing to be frightened of. There's nothing in there.

DARLENE: I'll be right back.

PFEIFFER: One small natural law is broken and we go to pieces. *(*DARLENE *enters the carwash.* JOE *and* PFEIFFER *watch her every move.)*

JOE: If it can happen once, it can happen again. And then we won't be able to trust anything ever again.

PFEIFFER *(to* DARLENE*)*: Any clues?

JOE: We won't even be able to trust the law of gravity. Things will go flying off the earth.

PFEIFFER: No need to be melodramatic about it.

JOE: You're right. It's just a car. Why should the entire world depend upon the appearance or disappearance of a single object?

PFEIFFER: I've always hated miracles. . . even when I was a little boy.

JOE: Darlene, do you see anything?

PFEIFFER: How can she see anything? There's nothing there to see.

JOE: Perhaps your Mercedes is of a very sophisticated design. You can only see it when you're right on top of it.

PFEIFFER: Where is she?

JOE: Behind the big brushes?

PFEIFFER: No.

JOE *(calls):* Darlene!

PFEIFFER: She's gone!

JOE: She's not gone! Don't say that! . . . Darlene!

PFEIFFER: If she's not gone, then where is she?

JOE: We count on the world acting a certain way and when it doesn't act that way. . . Darlene!

PFEIFFER: I don't want to look.

JOE: I knew this was going to happen.

PFEIFFER: Are you crazy? Nobody could know it was going to happen!

JOE: I just knew it. I felt it.

PFEIFFER: Call the police.

JOE: You think the police understand physics better than us?

PFEIFFER: If you keep sending things through your carwash and they keep disappearing, you're going to lose your license.

JOE: Darlene isn't a thing. . . .

PFEIFFER: Why didn't I go to the carwash down the street, the one recommended to me by my friends. All of this could have been avoided.

JOE: Your friends recommended the other carwash?

PFEIFFER: I didn't mean to offend you!

JOE: The other carwash is not run on sound business principles as set forth by the Japanese.

PFEIFFER: At least all their cars and managers don't disappear into thin air. Things go in and then they come out. . . usually clean. . . it makes for a clear profit margin.

JOE: How do you know? Maybe cars have been disappearing from carwashes for years and everybody's been keeping silent about it. . . . Darlene!

PFEIFFER: She's not there. There's no sense to keep calling after her.

JOE: Where is she?

PFEIFFER: She's probably out somewhere riding around in my Mercedes.

JOE: She doesn't know how to drive.

PFEIFFER: She shouldn't be practising on my Mercedes somewhere in Never Never Land.

JOE: Maybe it's like a black hole.

PFEIFFER: Then that is what it should be called—everything in the universe should be correctly labeled.

JOE: Whatever is happening should not be happening. It's not right.

PFEIFFER: Black holes exist somewhere in outer space, not on the corner of 5th and Main.

JOE: I don't know.

PFEIFFER: Me neither.

JOE: Now what?

PFEIFFER *(throws up his arms in despair):* Got me.

JOE: I can't stand such an irrational universe.

PFEIFFER: I know.

JOE: I want things to make sense.

PFEIFFER: I know.

JOE: If one little thing can't be explained, everything flies out the window.

PFEIFFER: I know.

JOE: That's why books on corporative management, especially as written by the Japanese, make so much sense.

PFEIFFER: I never read one.

JOE: You should. You want me to lend you Darlene's? She's probably not coming back for it.

PFEIFFER: No, thanks.

JOE: Are you depressed?

PFEIFFER: Yes. Are you?

JOE: I don't know. It's weird. To watch a car disappear off the face of the earth should be the most wonderful thing that could happen, something beyond the ordinary, trivial events of the day. . . .

PFEIFFER: You can say that. . . it's not your car. . . .

DARLENE's VOICE *(calls from the carwash tunnel):* Joe! . . . Mr. Pfeiffer . . . Are you there?

JOE: I'm here . . . We're here . . . Are you?

DARLENE's VOICE: I think I've got a clue. . . .

JOE: What?

DARLENE's VOICE: I think I've got a clue. . . .

JOE: She says she thinks she has a clue.

PFEIFFER: I hear her, but I can't see her.

JOE: We're coming.

PFEIFFER: Wait a minute. You can't leave me here. I need you to substantiate my story. . . . (JOE *disappears into the carwash.)*

PFEIFFER: Hold on! Come back. . . No one's going to believe me! *(*PFEIFFER *waits. No response.)*

PFEIFFER *(peering into the carwash):* Now what?

(He disappears into the tunnel. The lot is completely deserted. Then we hear the sound of a car horn from the street. It blasts two or three times and then in comes a young WOMAN *in blouse, slacks, her hair tied under a bandana.)*

WOMAN: Hey, I would like to get my car washed. What happened to all the managers that used to be here? *(She peers into the carwash. She sees nothing.)*

WOMAN: All right. I get the message. If you don't want my business, I can go elsewhere. This is not the only carwash in town. *(She walks off to her own car.)*

WOMAN: It's no way to run a business. A person could come in here and steal you blind. *(She's gone. The sound of a car starting.)*

WOMAN's VOICE: You've just lost a customer! *(Car drives away. Lights out.)*

Questions

1. What is the play's central idea, the message it conveys to the audience? How do you know this? Do you agree with the central idea? Why or why not?
2. The play is not grounded in reality; that is, there can be no logical explanation for what happens. What about the three major characters? Are they realistic? What makes you think so? Is the dialogue realistic? Support your answer.
3. The employees of the carwash refer to themselves as managers. What is the significance of this?
4. What is the significance of the name, the Charm School Carwash? Why do you think Phillips used a name like this?

5. Did you like the play? Why or why not? If you were the playwright, is there anything about it that you would change? If so, what? Why would you change it?
6. Why didn't Phillips end his play with the disappearance of Pfeiffer? What is the point of having the young woman pull up at the carwash demanding service?
7. What do you think happened first to the car and then to the people who entered the carwash? Let your imagination run free in answering the question. Now write a brief second act to the play that reveals what you imagined.

Melodrama

Melodrama is a genre that combines some of the elements of comedy and tragedy. It's similar to comedy in that it most often has a happy ending. It's related to tragedy in that it concerns a serious subject and the audience identifies or empathizes with the characters. But unlike tragic characters, those in melodrama are one-dimensional.

Melodrama often relies on creating feelings of terror, and coincidence or fate plays a large part in the outcome. Good always triumphs. The form includes sentimentality. Melodrama is often episodic in that the most exciting events and situations are included in the script. There also is comic relief provided by the minor characters.

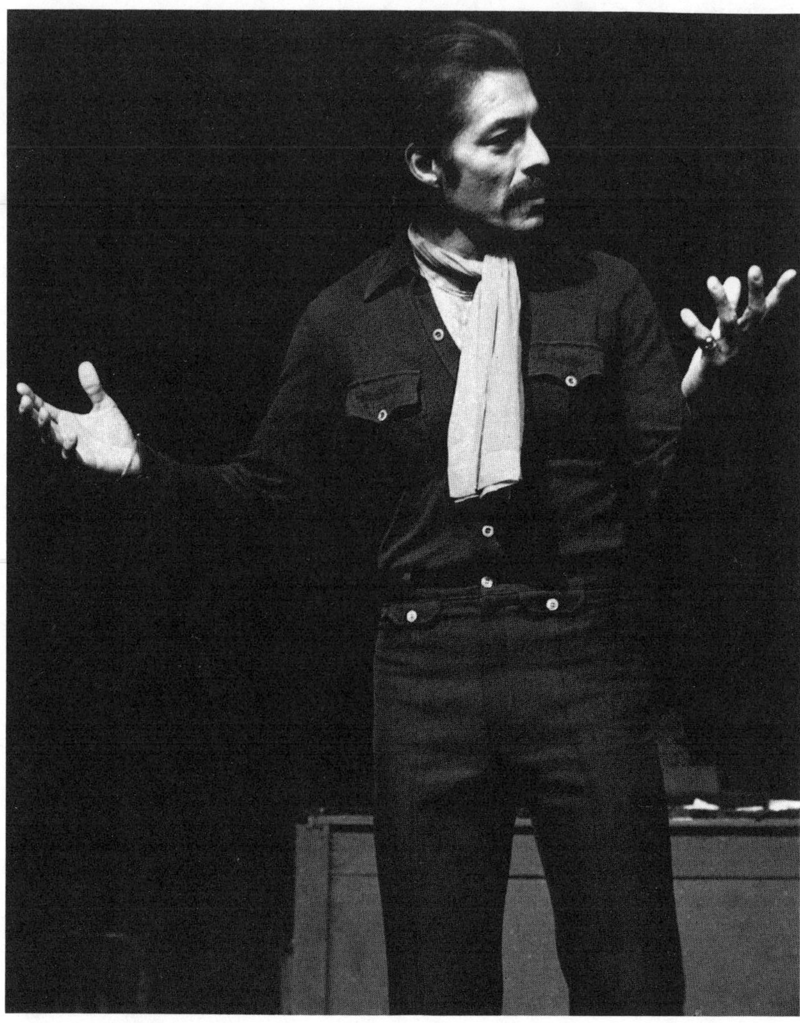

Mr. Scratch pleads his case in a scene from The Devil and Daniel Webster. *(Photography by Wanda Tritten-Robin, courtesy of Marquis Public Theatre, San Diego, California)*

STEPHEN VINCENT BENÉT

The Devil and Daniel Webster

STEPHEN VINCENT BENÉT was a native Pennsylvanian who lived from 1898 until 1943. His first book, six dramatic dialogues written in verse, was published when he was only seventeen. For the rest of his life, he held no other jobs besides writing.

As did many other twentieth-century playwrights, he wrote in several genres, including both fiction and poetry. *John Brown's Body,* a long narrative poem about events during the Civil War, won Benét a Pulitzer Prize.

THE DEVIL AND DANIEL WEBSTER is a melodrama because the characters are lacking in complexity and are presented in a one-sided manner. Generally, they are all good or all bad, with Jabez Stone being a good man who is simply a victim of temptation.

The legend of a person's selling his soul to the devil is an old one, going back at least as far as Christopher Marlowe's *The Tragical History of Doctor Faustus,* written near the end of the 1500s. Benét, however, gives the play a new twist in letting Webster face the jury to try to convince them to allow Stone's soul to be returned to him.

The Devil and Daniel Webster Stephen Vincent Benét

Characters:

JABEZ STONE
MARY STONE
DANIEL WEBSTER
MR. SCRATCH
THE FIDDLER
JUSTICE HATHORNE
JUSTICE HATHORNE'S CLERK
KING PHILIP
TEACH
WALTER BUTLER
SIMON GIRTY
DALE
MEN AND WOMEN OF CROSS CORNERS, NEW HAMPSHIRE

Setting:

Jabez Stone's Farmhouse. Time—1841. The scene is the main room of a New Hampshire farmhouse in 1841, a big comfortable room that hasn't yet developed the stuffiness of a front-parlor. A door, right, leads to the kitchen—a door, left, to the outside. There is a fireplace, right. Windows, in center, show a glimpse of summer landscape. Most of the furniture has been cleared away for the dance which follows the wedding of JABEZ *and* MARY STONE, *but there is a settle or bench by the fireplace, a table, left, with some wedding presents upon it, at least three chairs by the table, and a cider barrel on which the* FIDDLER *sits, in front of the table. Near the table, against the side-wall, there is a cupboard where there are glasses and a jug. There is a clock.*

A country wedding has been in progress—the wedding of JABEZ *and* MARY STONE. *He is a husky young farmer, around twenty-eight or thirty. The bride is in her early twenties. He is dressed in stiff, store clothes but not ridiculously—they are of good quality and he looks important. The bride is in a simple white or cream wedding-dress and may carry a small, stiff bouquet of country flowers.*

Now the wedding is over and the guests are dancing. The FIDDLER *is perched on the cider barrel. He plays and calls square-dance figures. The guests include the recognizable types of a small new England town, doctor, lawyer, storekeeper, old maid, schoolteacher, farmer, etc. There is an air of prosperity and hearty country mirth about the whole affair.*

At rise, JABEZ *and* MARY *are up left center, receiving the congratulations of a few last guests who talk to them and pass on to the dance. The others are dancing. There is a buzz of conversation that follows the tune of the dance music.*

FIRST WOMAN: Right nice wedding.

FIRST MAN: Handsome couple.

SECOND WOMAN *(passing through crowd with dish of oyster stew)*: Oysters for supper!

SECOND MAN *(passing cake)*: And layer-cake—layer-cake—

AN OLD MAN *(hobbling toward cider barrel)*: Makes me feel young again! Oh, by jingo!

AN OLD WOMAN *(pursuing him)*: Henry, Henry, you've been drinking cider!

FIDDLER: Set to your partners! Dosy-do!

WOMAN: Mary and Jabez.

MEN: Jabez and Mary.

A WOMAN: Where's the State Senator?

A MAN: Where's the lucky bride?

(With cries of "Mary—Jabez—strike it up, Fiddler—make room for the bride and groom," the CROWD *drags* MARY *and* JABEZ, *pleased but embarrassed, into the center of the room and* MARY *and* JABEZ *do a little solo-dance, while the* CROWD *claps, applauds and makes various remarks.)*

A MAN: Handsome steppers!

A WOMAN: She's pretty as a picture.

A SECOND MAN: Cut your pigeon-wing,[1] Jabez!

THE OLD MAN: Young again, young again, that's the way I feel! *(He tries to cut a pigeon-wing himself.)*

THE OLD WOMAN: Henry, Henry, careful of your rheumatiz!

A THIRD WOMAN: Makes me feel all teary—seeing them so happy. *(The solo-dance ends, the music stops for a moment.)*

THE OLD MAN *(gossiping to a neighbor)*: Wonder where he got it all—Stones was always poor.

HIS NEIGHBOR: Ain't poor now—makes you wonder just a mite.

A THIRD MAN: Don't begrudge it to him—but I wonder where he got it.

THE OLD MAN *(starting to whisper)*: Let me tell you something—

THE OLD WOMAN *(quickly)*: Henry, Henry, don't you start to gossip. *(She drags him away.)*

FIDDLER *(cutting in)*: Set to your partners! Scratch for corn! *(The dance resumes, but as it does so, the* CROWD *chants back and forth.)*

WOMEN: Gossip's got a sharp tooth.

MEN: Gossip's got a mean tooth.

WOMEN: She's a lucky woman. They're a lucky pair.

MEN: That's true as gospel. But I wonder where he got it.

WOMEN: Money, land and riches.

1. A fancy dance step.

MEN: Just came out of nowhere.

WOMEN and MEN *(together)*: Wonder where he got it all— But that's his business.

FIDDLER: Left and right—grand chain!

(The dance rises to a pitch of ecstasy with the final figure—the fiddle squeaks and stops. The dancers mop their brows.)

FIRST MAN: Whew! Ain't danced like that since I was knee-high to a grasshopper!

SECOND MAN: Play us "The Portland Fancy," fiddler!

THIRD MAN: No, wait a minute, neighbor. Let's hear from the happy pair! Hey, Jabez!

FOURTH MAN: Let's hear from the State Senator! *(They crowd around* JABEZ *and push him up on the settle.)*

OLD MAN: Might as well. It's the last time he'll have the last word!

OLD WOMAN: Now, Henry Banks, you ought to be ashamed of yourself!

OLD MAN: Told you so, Jabez!

THE CROWD: Speech!

JABEZ *(embarrassed)*: Neighbors—friends—I'm not much of a speaker—spite of your 'lecting me to State Senate—

THE CROWD: That's the ticket, Jabez. Smart man, Jabez. I voted for ye. Go ahead, Senator, you're doing fine.

JABEZ: But we're certainly glad to have you here—me and Mary. And we want to thank you for coming and—

A VOICE: Vote the Whig ticket!

ANOTHER VOICE: Hooray for Daniel Webster!

JABEZ: And I'm glad Hi Foster said that, for those are my sentiments, too. Mr. Webster has promised to honor us with his presence here tonight.

THE CROWD: Hurray for Dan'l! Hurray for the greatest man in the U. S.!

JABEZ: And when he comes, I know we'll give him a real New Hampshire welcome.

THE CROWD: Sure we will—Webster forever—and to hell with Henry Clay!

JABEZ: And meanwhile—well, there's Mary and me *(Takes her hand.)*—and, if you folks don't have a good time, well, we won't feel right about getting married at all. Because I know I've been lucky—and I hope she feels that way, too. And, well, we're going to be happy or bust a trace![2] *(He wipes his brow to terrific applause. He and* MARY *look at each other.)*

A WOMAN *(in kitchen doorway)*: Come and get the cider, folks!

(The CROWD *begins to drift away—a few to the kitchen—a few toward the door that*

2. A strap or connecting piece of a harness, such as one joining a horse and buggy.

leads to the outside. They furnish a shifting background to the next little scene, where MARY *and* JABEZ *are left alone by the fireplace.)*

JABEZ: Mary.

MARY: Mr. Stone.

JABEZ: Mary.

MARY: My husband.

JABEZ: That's a big word, husband.

MARY: It's a good word.

JABEZ: Are you happy, Mary?

MARY: Yes. So happy, I'm afraid.

JABEZ: Afraid?

MARY: I suppose it happens to every girl—just for a minute. It's like spring turning into summer. You want it to be summer. But the spring was sweet. *(Dismissing the mood.)* I'm sorry. Forgive me. It just came and went, like something cold. As if we'd been too lucky.

JABEZ: We can't be too lucky, Mary. Not you and me.

MARY *(rather mischievously)*: If you say so, Mr. Stone. But you don't even know what sort of housekeeper I am. And Aunt Hepsy says—

JABEZ: Bother your Aunt Hepsy! There's just you and me and that's all that matters in the world.

MARY: And you don't know something else—

JABEZ: What's that?

MARY: How proud I am of you. Ever since I was a little girl. Ever since you carried my books. Oh, I'm sorry for women who can't be proud of their men. It must be a lonely feeling.

JABEZ *(uncomfortably)*: A man can't always be proud of everything, Mary. There's some things a man does, or might do—when he has to make his way.

MARY *(laughing)*: I know—terrible things—like being the best farmer in the county and the best State Senator—

JABEZ *(quietly)*: And a few things, besides. But you remember one thing, Mary, whatever happens. It was all for you. And nothing's going to happen. Because he hasn't come yet—and he would have come if it was wrong.

MARY: But it's wonderful to have Mr. Webster come to us.

JABEZ: I wasn't thinking about Mr. Webster. *(He takes both her hands.)* Mary, I've got something to tell you. I should have told you before, but I couldn't seem to bear it. Only, now that it's all right, I can. Ten years ago—

A VOICE *(from off stage)*: Dan'l! Dan'l Webster!

*(*JABEZ *drops* MARY's *hands and looks around. The* CROWD *begins to mill and gather toward the door. Others rush in from the kitchen.)*

ANOTHER VOICE: Black Dan'l! He's come!
ANOTHER VOICE: Three cheers for the greatest man in the U. S.!
ANOTHER VOICE: Three cheers for Daniel Webster!

(And, to the cheering and applause of the crowd, DANIEL WEBSTER *enters and stands for a moment upstage, in the familiar pose, his head thrown back, his attitude leonine.*[3] *He stops the cheering of the crowd with a gesture.)*

WEBSTER: Neighbors—old friends—it does me good to hear you. But don't cheer me—I'm not running for President this summer. *(A laugh from the* CROWD.*)* I'm here on a better errand—to pay my humble respects to a most charming lady and her very fortunate spouse. *(There is the twang of a fiddlestring breaking.)*

FIDDLER: 'Tarnation! Busted a string!

A VOICE: He's always bustin' strings. *(*WEBSTER *blinks at the interruption but goes on.)*

WEBSTER: We're proud of State Senator Stone in these parts—we know what he's done. Ten years ago he started out with a patch of land that was mostly rocks and mortgages and now—well, you've only to look around you. I don't know that I've ever seen a likelier farm, not even at Marshfield—and I hope, before I die, I'll have the privilege of shaking his hand as Governor of this State. I don't know how he's done it—I couldn't have done it myself. But I know this—Jabez Stone wears no man's collar. *(At this statement there is a discordant squeak from the fiddle and* JABEZ *looks embarrassed.* WEBSTER *knits his brows.)* And what's more, if I know Jabez, he never will. But I didn't come here to talk politics—I came to kiss the bride. *(He does so among great applause. He shakes hands with* JABEZ.*)* Congratulations, Stone—you're a lucky man. And now, if our friend in the corner will give us a tune on his fiddle—

(The CROWD *presses forward to meet the great man. He shakes hands with several.)*

A MAN: Remember me, Mr. Webster? Saw ye up at the State House at Concord.

ANOTHER MAN: Glad to see ye, Mr. Webster. I voted for ye ten times.

*(*WEBSTER *receives their homage politely, but his mind is still on the music.)*

WEBSTER *(a trifle irritated)*: I said, if our friend in the corner would give us a tune on his fiddle—

FIDDLER *(passionately, flinging the fiddle down)*: Hell's delight—excuse me, Mr. Webster. But the very devil's got into that fiddle of mine. She

3. Like a lion.

was doing all right up to just a minute ago. But now I've tuned her and tuned her and she won't play a note I want.

(And, at this point, MR. SCRATCH *makes his appearance. He has entered, unobserved, and mixed with the crowd while all eyes were upon* DANIEL WEBSTER. *He is, of course, the devil—a New England devil, dressed like a rather shabby attorney but with something just a little wrong in clothes and appearance. For one thing, he wears black gloves on his hands. He carries a large black tin box, like a botanist's collecting-box, under one arm. Now he slips through the crowd and taps the* FIDDLER *on the shoulder.)*

SCRATCH *(insinuatingly)*: Maybe you need some rosin on your bow, fiddler?

FIDDLER: Maybe I do and maybe I don't. *(Turns and confronts the stranger.)* But who are you? I don't remember seeing you before.

SCRATCH: Oh, I'm just a friend—a humble friend of the bridegroom's. *(He walks toward* JABEZ. *Apologetically.)* I'm afraid I came in the wrong way, Mr. Stone. You've improved the place so much since I last saw it that I hardly knew the front door. But, I assure you, I came as fast as I could.

JABEZ *(obviously shocked)*: It—it doesn't matter. *(With a great effort.)* Mary—Mr. Webster—this is a—a friend of mine from Boston—a legal friend. I didn't expect him today but—

SCRATCH: Oh, my dear Mr. Stone—an occasion like this—I wouldn't miss it for the world. *(He bows.)* Charmed, Mrs. Stone. Delighted, Mr. Webster. But—don't let me break up the merriment of the meeting. *(He turns back toward the table and the* FIDDLER.*)*

FIDDLER *(with a grudge, to* SCRATCH*)*: Boston lawyer, eh?

SCRATCH: You might call me that.

FIDDLER *(tapping the tin box with his bow)*: And what have you got in that big tin box of yours? Lawpapers?

SCRATCH: Oh—curiosities for the most part. I'm a collector, too.

FIDDLER: Don't hold much with Boston curiosities, myself. And you know about fiddling too, do you? Know all about it?

SCRATCH: Oh— *(A deprecatory shrug.)*

FIDDLER: Don't shrug your shoulders at me—I ain't no Frenchman. Telling me I needed more rosin!

MARY: *(trying to stop the quarrel)*: Isaac—please—

FIDDLER: Sorry, Mary—Mrs. Stone. But I have been playing the fiddle at Cross Corners weddings for twenty-five years. And now here comes a stranger from Boston and tells me I need more rosin!

SCRATCH: But, my good friend—

FIDDLER: Rosin indeed! Here—play it yourself then and see what you can make of it!

(He thrusts the fiddle at SCRATCH. *The latter stiffens, slowly lays his black collecting-box on the table, and takes the fiddle.)*

SCRATCH *(with feigned embarrassment)*: But really, I— *(He bows toward* JABEZ*).* Shall I—Mr. Senator? *(*JABEZ *makes a helpless gesture of assent.)*

MARY *(to* JABEZ*)*: Mr. Stone—Mr. Stone—are you ill?

JABEZ: No—no—but I feel—it's hot—

WEBSTER *(chuckling)*: Don't you fret, Mrs. Stone. I've got the right medicine for him. *(He pulls a flask from his pocket.)* Ten-year-old Medford, Stone—I buy it by the keg down at Marshfield. Here— *(He tries to give some of the rum to* JABEZ.*)*

JABEZ: No—*(he turns)*—Mary—Mr. Webster— *(But he cannot explain. With a burst.)* Oh, let him play—let him play! Don't you see he's bound to? Don't you see there's nothing we can do?

(A rustle of discomfort among the guests. SCRATCH *draws the bow across the fiddle in a horrible discord.)*

FIDDLER *(triumphantly)*: I told you so, stranger. The devil's in that fiddle!

SCRATCH: I'm afraid it needs special tuning. *(Draws the bow in a second discord.)* There—that's better. *(Grinning.)* And now for this happy—this very happy occasion—in tribute to the bride and groom—I'll play something appropriate—a song of young love—

MARY: Oh, Jabez—Mr. Webster—stop him! Do you see his hands? He's playing with gloves on his hands.

*(*WEBSTER *starts forward, but, even as he does so,* SCRATCH *begins to play and all freeze as* SCRATCH *goes on with the extremely inappropriate song that follows. At first his manner is oily and mocking—it is not till he reaches the line "The devil took the words away" that he really becomes terrifying and the crowd starts to be afraid.)*

SCRATCH *(accompanying himself fantastically)*:

Young William was a thriving boy.
(Listen to my doleful tale.)

Young Mary Clark was all his joy.
(Listen to my doleful tale.)

He swore he'd love her all his life.
She swore she'd be his loving wife.

But William found a gambler's den
And drank with livery-stable men.

He played the cards, he played the dice.
He would not listen to advice.

And when in church he tried to pray,
The devil took the words away.

(SCRATCH, *still playing, starts to march across the stage.)*

The devil got him by the toe
And so, alas, he had to go.

"Young Mary Clark, young Mary Clark,
I now must go into the dark."

(These last two verses have been directed at JABEZ, SCRATCH *continues, now turning on* MARY.*)*

Young Mary lay upon her bed.
"Alas my Will-i-am is dead."

He came to her a bleeding ghost—

(He rushes at MARY *but* WEBSTER *stands between them.)*

WEBSTER: Stop! Stop! You miserable wretch—can't you see that you're frightening Mrs. Stone? *(He wrenches the fiddle out of* SCRATCH's *hands and tosses it aside.)* And now, sir—out of this house!

SCRATCH *(facing him)*: You're a bold man, Mr. Webster. Too bold for your own good, perhaps. And anyhow, it wasn't my fiddle. It belonged to— *(He wheels and sees the* FIDDLER *tampering with the collecting-box that has been left on the table.)* Idiot! What are you doing with my collecting-box? *(He rushes for the* FIDDLER *and chases him round the table, but the* FIDDLER *is just one jump ahead.)*

FIDDLER: Boston lawyer, eh? Well, I don't think so. I think you've got something in that box of yours you're afraid to show. And, by jingo—*(He throws open the lid of the box. The lights wink and there is a clap of thunder. All eyes stare upward. Something has flown out of the box. But what?* FIDDLER, *with relief.)* Why, 'tain't nothing but a moth.

MARY: A white moth—a flying thing.

WEBSTER: A common moth—*telea polyphemus*—

THE CROWD: A moth—just a moth—a moth—

FIDDLER *(terrified)*: But it ain't. It ain't no common moth! I seen it! And it's got a death's-head on it! *(He strikes at the invisible object with his bow to drive it away.)*

VOICE OF THE MOTH: Help me, neighbors! Help me!

WEBSTER: What's that? It wails like a lost soul.

MARY: A lost soul.

THE CROWD: A lost soul—lost—in darkness—in the darkness.

VOICE OF THE MOTH: Help me, neighbors!

FIDDLER: It sounds like Miser Stevens.

JABEZ: Miser Stevens!

THE CROWD: The Miser—Miser Stevens—a lost soul—lost.

FIDDLER *(frantically)*: It sounds like Miser Stevens—and you had him in your box. But it can't be. He ain't dead.

JABEZ: He ain't dead—I tell you he ain't dead! He was just as spry and mean as a woodchuck Tuesday.

THE CROWD: Miser Stevens—soul of Miser Stevens—but he ain't dead.

SCRATCH *(dominating them)*: Listen! *(A bell off stage begins to toll a knell, slowly, solemnly.)*

MARY: The bell—the church bell—the bell that rang at my wedding.

WEBSTER: The church bell—the passing bell.

JABEZ: The funeral bell.

THE CROWD: The bell—the passing bell—Miser Stevens—dead.

VOICE OF THE MOTH: Help me, neighbors, help me! I sold my soul to the devil. But I'm not the first or the last. Help me. Help Jabez Stone!

SCRATCH: Ah, would you!

(He catches the moth in his red bandanna, stuffs it back into his collecting-box, and shuts the lid with a snap.)

VOICE OF THE MOTH *(fading)*: Lost—lost forever, forever. Lost, like Jabez Stone. *(The* CROWD *turns on* JABEZ. *They read his secret in his face.)*

THE CROWD: Jabez Stone—Jabez Stone—answer us—answer us.

MARY: Tell them, dear—answer them—you are good—you are brave—you are innocent. *(But the* CROWD *is all pointing hands and horrified eyes.)*

THE CROWD: Jabez Stone—Jabez Stone. Who's your friend in black, Jabez Stone? *(They point to* SCRATCH.*)*

WEBSTER: Answer them, Mr. State Senator.

THE CROWD: Jabez Stone—Jabez Stone. Where did you get your money, Jabez Stone? *(*SCRATCH *grins and taps his collecting-box.* JABEZ *cannot speak.)*

JABEZ: I—I— *(He stops.)*

THE CROWD: Jabez Stone—Jabez Stone. What was the price you paid for it, Jabez Stone?

JABEZ *(looking around wildly)*: Help me, neighbors! Help me! *(This cracks the built-up tension and sends the* CROWD *over the edge into fanaticism.)*

A WOMAN'S VOICE *(high and hysterical)*: He's sold his soul to the devil! *(She points to* JABEZ.*)*

OTHER VOICES: To the devil!

THE CROWD: He's sold his soul to the devil! The devil himself! The devil's playing the fiddle! The devil's come for his own!

JABEZ *(appealing)*: But, neighbors—I didn't know—I didn't mean—oh, help me!

THE CROWD *(inexorably)*: He's sold his soul to the devil!

SCRATCH *(grinning)*: To the devil!

THE CROWD: He's sold his soul to the devil! There's no help left for him, neighbors! Run, hide, hurry, before we're caught! He's a lost soul—Jabez Stone—he's the devil's own! Run, hide, hasten!

(They stream across the stage like a flurry of bats, the cannier picking up the wedding-presents they have given to take along with them. MR. SCRATCH *drives them out into the night, fiddle in hand, and follows them.* JABEZ *and* MARY *are left with* WEBSTER. JABEZ *has sunk into a chair, beaten, with his head in his hands.* MARY *is trying to comfort him.* WEBSTER *looks at them for a moment and shakes his head, sadly. As he crosses to exit to the porch, his hand drops for a moment on* JABEZ's *shoulder, but* JABEZ *makes no sign.* WEBSTER *exits.* JABEZ *lifts his head.)*

MARY *(comforting him)*: My dear—my dear—

JABEZ: I—it's all true, Mary. All true. You must hurry.

MARY: Hurry?

JABEZ: Hurry after them—back to the village—back to your folks. Mr. Webster will take you—you'll be safe with Mr. Webster. You see, it's all true and he'll be back in a minute. *(With a shudder.)* The other one. *(He groans.)* I've got until twelve o'clock. That's the contract. But there isn't much time.

MARY: Are you telling me to run away from you, Mr. Stone?

JABEZ: You don't understand, Mary. It's true.

MARY: We made some promises to each other. Maybe you've forgotten them. But I haven't. I said, it's for better or worse. It's for better or worse. I said, in sickness or in health. Well, that covers the ground, Mr. Stone.

JABEZ: But, Mary, you must—I command you.

MARY: "For thy people shall be my people and thy God my God." *(Quietly.)* That was Ruth, in the Book. I always liked the name of Ruth—always liked the thought of her. I always thought—I'll call a child Ruth, some time. I guess that was just a girl's notion. *(She breaks.)* But, oh, Jabez—why?

JABEZ: It started years ago, Mary. I guess I was a youngster then—guess I must have been. A youngster with a lot of ambitions and no way in the world to get there. I wanted city clothes and a big white house—I wanted to be State Senator and have people look up to me. But all I got on the farm was a crop of stones. You could work all day and all night but that was all you got.

MARY *(softly)*: It was pretty—that hill-farm, Jabez. You could look all the way across the valley.

JABEZ: Pretty? It was fever and ague—it was stones and blight. If I had a horse, he got colic—if I planted garden-truck, the woodchucks ate it. I'd lie awake nights and try to figure out a way to get somewhere—but there wasn't any way. And all the time you were growing up, in the town. I couldn't ask you to marry me and take you to a place like that.

MARY: Do you think it's the place makes the difference to a woman? I'd—I'd have kept your house. I'd have stroked the cat and fed the chickens and seen you wiped your shoes on the mat. I wouldn't have asked for more. Oh, Jabez—why didn't you tell me?

JABEZ: It happened before I could. Just an average day—you know—just an average day. But there was a mean east wind and a mean small rain. Well, I was plowing, and the share broke clean off on a rock where there hadn't been any rock the day before. I didn't have money for a new one—I didn't have money to get it mended. So I said it and I said loud, "I'll sell my soul for about two cents," I said. *(He stops.* MARY *stares at him.)* Well, that's all there is to it, I guess. He came along that afternoon—that fellow from Boston—and the dog looked at him and ran away. Well, I had to make it more than two cents, but he was agreeable to that. So I pricked my thumb with a pin and signed the paper. It felt hot when you touched it, that paper. I keep remembering that. *(He pauses.)* And it's all come true and he's kept his part of the bargain. I got the riches and I've married you. And, oh, God Almighty, what shall I do?

MARY: Let us run away! Let us creep and hide!

JABEZ: You can't run away from the devil—I've seen his horses. Miser Stevens tried to run away.

MARY: Let us pray—let us pray to the God of Mercy that He redeem us.

JABEZ: I can't pray, Mary. The words just burn in my heart.

MARY: I won't let you go! I won't! There must be someone who could help us. I'll get the judge and the squire—

JABEZ: Who'll take a case against old Scratch? Who'll face the devil himself and do him brown? There isn't a lawyer in the world who'd dare do that. *(*WEBSTER *appears in the doorway.)*

WEBSTER: Good evening, neighbors. Did you say something about lawyers—

MARY: Mr. Webster!

JABEZ: Dan'l Webster! But I thought—

WEBSTER: You'll excuse me for leaving you for a moment. I was just taking a stroll on the porch, in the cool of the evening. Fine summer evening, too.

JABEZ: Well, it might be, I guess, but that kind of depends on the circumstances.

WEBSTER: H'm. Yes. I happened to overhear a little of your conversation. I gather you're in trouble, Neighbor Stone.

JABEZ: Sore trouble.

WEBSTER *(delicately)*: Sort of law case, I understand.

JABEZ: You might call it that, Mr. Webster. Kind of a mortgage case, in a way.

MARY: Oh, Jabez!

WEBSTER: Mortgage case. Well, I don't generally plead now, except before the Supreme Court, but this case of yours presents some very unusual features and I never deserted a neighbor in trouble yet. So, if I can be of any assistance—

MARY: Oh, Mr. Webster, will you help him?

JABEZ: It's a terrible lot to ask you. But—well, you see, there's Mary. And, if you could see your way to it—

WEBSTER: I will.

MARY *(weeping with relief)*: Oh, Mr. Webster!

WEBSTER: There, there, Mrs. Stone. After all, if two New Hampshire men aren't a match for the devil, we might as well give the country back to the Indians. When is he coming, Jabez?

JABEZ: Twelve o'clock. The time's getting late.

WEBSTER: Then I'd better refresh my memory. The—er—mortgage was for a definite term of years?

JABEZ: Ten years.

WEBSTER: And it falls due—?

JABEZ: Tonight. Oh, I can't see how I came to be such a fool!

WEBSTER: No use crying over spilt milk, Stone. We've got to get you out of it, now. But tell me one thing. Did you sign this precious document of your own free will?

JABEZ: Yes, it was my own free will. I can't deny that.

WEBSTER: H'm, that's a trifle unfortunate. But we'll see.

MARY: Oh, Mr. Webster, can you save him? Can you?

WEBSTER: I shall do my best, madam. That's all you can ever say till you see what the jury looks like.

MARY: But even you, Mr. Webster—oh, I know you're Secretary of State—I know you're a great man—I know you've done wonderful things. But it's different—fighting the devil!

WEBSTER *(towering)*: I've fought John C. Calhoun, madam. And I've fought Henry Clay. And, by the great shade of Andrew Jackson, I'd fight ten thousand devils to save a New Hampshire man!

JABEZ: You hear, Mary?

MARY: Yes. And I trust Mr. Webster. But—oh, there must be some way that I can help!

WEBSTER: There is one, madam, and a hard one. As Mr. Stone's counsel, I must formally request your withdrawal.

MARY: No.

WEBSTER: Madam, think for a moment. You cannot help Mr. Stone—since you are his wife, your testimony would be prejudiced. And frankly, madam, in a very few moments this is going to be no place for a lady.

MARY: But I can't—I can't leave him—I can't bear it!

JABEZ: You must go, Mary. You must.

WEBSTER: Pray, madam—you can help us with your prayers. Are the prayers of the innocent unavailing?

MARY: Oh, I'll pray—I'll pray. But a woman's more than a praying machine, whatever men think. And how do I know?

WEBSTER: Trust me, Mrs. Stone.

*(*MARY *turns to go, and, with one hand on* JABEZ'S *shoulder, as she moves to the door, says the following prayer:)*

MARY:

Now may there be a blessing and a light betwixt thee and me,
  forever.
For, as Ruth unto Naomi, so do I cleave unto thee.
Set me as a seal upon thy heart, as a seal upon thine arm, for love
  is strong as death.
Many waters cannot quench love, neither can the floods drown it.
As Ruth unto Naomi, so do I cleave unto thee.
The Lord watch between thee and me when we are absent, one
  from the other.
Amen. Amen. *(She goes out.)*

WEBSTER: Amen.

JABEZ: Thank you, Mr. Webster. She ought to go. But I couldn't have made her do it.

WEBSTER: Well, Stone—I know ladies—and I wouldn't be surprised if she's still got her ear to the keyhole. But she's best out of this night's business. How long have we got to wait?

JABEZ *(beginning to be terrified again)*: Not long—not long.

WEBSTER: Then I'll just get out the jug, with your permission, Stone. Somehow or other, waiting's wonderfully shorter with a jug. *(He crosses to the cupboard, gets out jug and glasses, pours himself a drink.)* Ten-year-old Medford. There's nothing like it. I saw an inchworm take a drop of it once and he stood right up on his hind legs and bit a bee. Come—try a nip.

JABEZ: There's no joy in it for me.

WEBSTER: Oh, come, man, come! Just because you've sold your soul to the devil, that needn't make you a teetotaller.

(He laughs and passes the jug to JABEZ *who tries to pour from it. But at that moment the clock whirs and begins to strike the three-quarters, and* JABEZ *spills the liquor.)*

JABEZ: Oh, God!

WEBSTER: Never mind—it's a nervous feeling, waiting for a trial to begin. I remember my first case—

JABEZ: 'Tain't that. *(He turns to* WEBSTER.*)* Mr. Webster—Mr. Webster—for God's sake harness your horses and get away from this place as fast as you can!

WEBSTER *(placidly)*: You've brought me a long way, neighbor, to tell me you don't like my company.

JABEZ: I've brought you the devil's own way. I can see it all, now. He's after both of us—him and his damn collecting-box! Well, he can have me, if he likes—I don't say I relish it but I made the bargain. But you're the whole United States! He can't get you, Mr. Webster—he mustn't get you!

WEBSTER: I'm obliged to you, Neighbor Stone. It's kindly thought of. But there's a jug on the table and a case in hand. And I never left a jug or a case half-finished in my life. *(There is a knock at the door.* JABEZ *gives a cry.)* Ah, I thought your clock was a trifle slow, Neighbor Stone. Come in! *(*SCRATCH *enters from the night.)*

SCRATCH: Mr. Webster! This *is* a pleasure!

WEBSTER: Attorney of record for Jabez Stone. Might I ask your name?

SCRATCH: I've gone by a good many. Perhaps Scratch will do for the evening. I'm often called that in these regions. May I? *(He sits at the table and pours a drink from the jug. The liquor steams as it pours into the glass while* JABEZ *watches, terrified.* SCRATCH *grins, toasting* WEBSTER *and* JABEZ *silently in the liquor. Then he becomes businesslike. To* WEBSTER.*)* And now I call upon you, as a law-abiding citizen, to assist me in taking possession of my property.

WEBSTER: Not so fast, Mr. Scratch. Produce your evidence, if you have it. *(*SCRATCH *takes out a black pocketbook and examines papers.)*

SCRATCH: Slattery—Stanley—Stone. *(Takes out a deed.)* There, Mr. Webster. All open and above board and in due and legal form. Our firm has its reputation to consider—we deal only in the one way.

WEBSTER *(taking deed and looking it over)*: H'm. This appears—I say, it appears—to be properly drawn. But, of course, we contest the signature. *(Tosses it back, contemptuously.)*

SCRATCH *(suddenly turning on* JABEZ *and shooting a finger at him)*: Is that your signature?

JABEZ *(wearily)*: You know damn well it is.

WEBSTER *(angrily)*: Keep quiet, Stone. *(To* SCRATCH.*)* But that is a minor matter. This precious document isn't worth the paper it's written on. The law permits no traffic in human flesh.

SCRATCH: Oh, my dear Mr. Webster! Courts in every State in the Union have held that human flesh is property and recoverable. Read your Fugitive Slave Act. Or, shall I cite Brander versus McRae?

WEBSTER: But, in the case of the State of Maryland versus Four Barrels of Bourbon—

SCRATCH: That was overruled, as you know, sir. North Carolina versus Jenkins and Co.

WEBSTER *(unwillingly)*: You seem to have an excellent acquaintance with the law, sir.

SCRATCH: Sir, that is no fault of mine. Where I come from, we have always gotten the pick of the Bar.

WEBSTER *(changing his note, heartily)*: Well, come now, sir. There's no need to make hay and oats of a trifling matter when we're both sensible men. Surely we can settle this little difficulty out of court. My client is quite prepared to offer a compromise. (SCRATCH *smiles.)* A very substantial compromise. (SCRATCH *smiles more broadly, slowly shaking his head.)* Hang it, man, we offer ten thousand dollars! (SCRATCH *signs "No.")* Twenty thousand—thirty—name your figure! I'll raise it if I have to mortgage Marshfield!

SCRATCH: Quite useless, Mr. Webster. There is only one thing I want from you—the execution of my contract.

WEBSTER: But this is absurd. Mr. Stone is now a State Senator. The property has greatly increased in value!

SCRATCH: The principle of *caveat emptor*[4] still holds, Mr. Webster. *(He yawns and looks at the clock.)* And now, if you have no further arguments to adduce[5]—I'm rather pressed for time—*(He rises briskly as if to take* JABEZ *into custody.)*

WEBSTER *(thundering)*: Pressed or not, you shall not have this man. Mr. Stone is an American citizen and no American citizen may be forced into the service of a foreign prince. We fought England for that, in '12, and we'll fight all hell for it again!

SCRATCH: Foreign? And who calls me a foreigner?

WEBSTER: Well, I never yet heard of the dev—of your claiming American citizenship?

SCRATCH: And who with better right? When the first wrong was done to the first Indian, I was there. When the first slaver put out for the Congo, I stood on her deck. Am I not in your books and stories and beliefs, from the first settlements on? Am I not spoken of, still, in every church in New England? 'Tis true, the North claims me for a Southerner and the South for a Northerner, but I am neither. I am

4. Lat., Let the buyer beware.

5. To bring forward as evidence.

merely an honest American like yourself—and of the best descent—for, to tell the truth, Mr. Webster, though I don't like to boast of it, my name is older in the country than yours.

WEBSTER: Aha! Then I stand on the Constitution! I demand a trial for my client!

SCRATCH: The case is hardly one for an ordinary jury—and indeed, the lateness of the hour—

WEBSTER: Let it be any court you choose, so it is an American judge and an American jury. Let it be the quick or the dead, I'll abide the issue.

SCRATCH: The quick or the dead! You have said it!

(He points his finger at the place where the jury is to appear. There is a clap of thunder and a flash of light. The stage blacks out completely. All that can be seen is the face of SCRATCH, *lit with a ghastly green light as he recites the invocation that summons the* JURY. *As, one by one, the important* JURYMEN *are mentioned, they appear.)*

I summon the jury Mr. Webster demands.
From churchyard mould and gallows grave,
Brimstone pit and burning gulf,
I summon them!
Dastard,[6] liar, scoundrel, knave,
I summon them! Appear!
There's Simon Girty, the renegade,
The haunter of the forest glade
Who joined with Indian and wolf
To hunt the pioneer.
The stains upon his hunting-shirt
Are not the blood of the deer.
There's Walter Butler, the loyalist,
Who carried a firebrand in his fist
Of massacre and shame.
King Philip's eye is wild and bright.
They slew him in the great Swamp Fight,
But still, with terror and affright,
The land recalls his name.
Blackbeard Teach, the pirate fell,
Smeet the strangler, hot from hell,
Dale, who broke men on the wheel,
Morton, of the tarnished steel,
I summon them, I summon them
From their tormented flame!
Quick or dead, quick or dead,

6. Mean, sneaky coward.

Broken heart and bitter head,
True Americans, each one,
Traitor and disloyal son,
Cankered[7] earth and twisted tree,
Outcasts of eternity,
Twelve great sinners, tried and true,
For the work they are to do!
I summon them, I summon them!
Appear, appear, appear!

(The JURY *has now taken its place in the box—*WALTER BUTLER *in the place of foreman. They are eerily lit and so made-up as to suggest the unearthly. They sit stiffly in their box. At first, when one moves, all move, in stylized gestures. It is not till the end of* WEBSTER's *speech that they begin to show any trace of humanity. They speak rhythmically, and, at first, in low, eerie voices.)*

JABEZ *(seeing them, horrified)*: A jury of the dead!
JURY: Of the dead!
JABEZ: A jury of the damned!
JURY: Of the damned!
SCRATCH: Are you content with the jury, Mr. Webster?
WEBSTER: Quite content. Though I miss General Arnold from the company.
SCRATCH: Benedict Arnold is engaged upon other business. Ah, you asked for a justice, I believe. *(He points his finger and* JUSTICE HATHORNE, *a tall, lean, terrifying Puritan, appears, followed by his* CLERK.*)* Justice Hathorne is a jurist of experience. He presided at the Salem witch-trials. There were others who repented of the business later. But not he, not he!
HATHORNE: Repent of such notable wonders and undertakings? Nay, hang them, hang them all!

(He takes his place on the bench. The CLERK, *an ominous little man with clawlike hands, takes his place. The room has now been transformed into a courtroom.)*

CLERK *(in a gabble of ritual)*: Oyes, oyes, oyes. All ye who have business with this honorable court of special session this night, step forward!
HATHORNE *(with gavel)*: Call the first case.
CLERK: The World, the Flesh and the Devil versus Jabez Stone.
HATHORNE: Who appears for the plaintiff?
SCRATCH: I, Your Honor.
HATHORNE: And for the defendant?
WEBSTER: I.

7. Ulcerated.

JURY: The case—the case—he'll have little luck with this case.
HATHORNE: The case will proceed.
WEBSTER: Your Honor, I move to dismiss this case on the grounds of improper jurisdiction.
HATHORNE: Motion denied.
WEBSTER: On the grounds of insufficient evidence.
HATHORNE: Motion denied.
JURY: Motion denied—denied. Motion denied.
WEBSTER: I will take an exception.
HATHORNE: There are no exceptions in this court.
JURY: No exceptions—no exceptions in this court. It's a bad case, Daniel Webster—a losing case.
WEBSTER: Your Honor—
HATHORNE: The prosecution will proceed—
SCRATCH: Your Honor—gentlemen of the jury. This is a plain, straightforward case. It need not detain us long.
JURY: Detain us long—it will not detain us long.
SCRATCH: It concerns one thing alone—the transference, barter and sale of a certain piece of property, to wit, his soul, by Jabez Stone, farmer, of Cross Corners, New Hampshire. That transference, barter or sale is attested by a deed. I offer that deed in evidence and mark it Exhibit A.
WEBSTER: I object.
HATHORNE: Objection denied. Mark it Exhibit A.

*(*SCRATCH *hands the deed—an ominous and impressive document—to the* CLERK *who hands it to* HATHORNE. HATHORNE *hands it back to the* CLERK *who stamps it. All very fast and with mechanical gestures.)*

JURY: Exhibit A—mark it Exhibit A. *(*SCRATCH *takes the deed from the* CLERK *and offers it to the* JURY, *who pass it rapidly among them, hardly looking at it, and hand it back to* SCRATCH.*)* We know the deed—the deed—it burns in our fingers—we do not have to see the deed. It's a losing case.
SCRATCH: It offers incontestable evidence of the truth of the prosecution's claim. I shall now call Jabez Stone to the witness-stand.
JURY *(hungrily)*: Jabez Stone to the witness-stand, Jabez Stone. He's a fine, fat fellow, Jabez Stone. He'll fry like a batter-cake, once we get him where we want him.
WEBSTER: Your Honor, I move that this jury be discharged for flagrant and open bias!
HATHORNE: Motion denied.
WEBSTER: Exception.
HATHORNE: Exception denied.

JURY: His motion's always denied. He thinks himself smart and clever—lawyer Webster. But his motion's always denied.
WEBSTER: Your Honor! *(He chokes with anger.)*
CLERK *(advancing)*: Jabez Stone to the witness-stand!
JURY: Jabez Stone—Jabez Stone.

*(*WEBSTER *gives* JABEZ *an encouraging pat on the back, and* JABEZ *takes his place in the witness-stand, very scared.)*

CLERK *(offering a black book)*: Do you solemnly swear—testify—so help you—and it's no good for we don't care what you testify?
JABEZ: I do.
SCRATCH: What's your name?
JABEZ: Jabez Stone.
SCRATCH: Occupation?
JABEZ: Farmer.
SCRATCH: Residence?
JABEZ: Cross Corners, New Hampshire.

(These three questions are very fast and mechanical on the part of SCRATCH. *He is absolutely sure of victory and just going through a form.)*

JURY: A farmer—he'll farm in hell—we'll see that he farms in hell.
SCRATCH: Now, Jabez Stone, answer me. You'd better, you know. You haven't got a chance and there'll be a cooler place by the fire for you.
WEBSTER: I protest! This is intimidation! This mocks all justice!
HATHORNE: The protest is irrelevant, incompetent and immaterial. We have our own justice. The protest is denied.
JURY: Irrelevant, incompetent and immaterial—we have our own justice—oh, ho, Daniel Webster! *(The* JURY's *eyes fix upon* WEBSTER *for an instant, hungrily.)*
SCRATCH: Did you or did you not sign this document?
JABEZ: Oh, I signed it! You know I signed it. And, if I have to go to hell for it, I'll go! *(A sigh sweeps over the* JURY.*)*
JURY: One of us—one of us now—we'll save a place by the fire for you, Jabez Stone.
SCRATCH: The prosecution rests.
HATHORNE: Remove the prisoner.
WEBSTER: But I wish to cross-examine—I wish to prove—
HATHORNE: There will be no cross-examination. We have our own justice. You may speak, if you like. But be brief.
JURY: Brief—be very brief—we're weary of earth—incompetent, irrelevant and immaterial—they say he's a smart man, Webster, but he's lost his case tonight—be very brief—we have our own justice here. *(*WEBSTER *stares around him like a baited bull. Can't find words.)*

MARY'S VOICE *(from off stage)*: Set me as a seal upon thy heart, as a seal upon thine arm, for love is strong as death—

JURY *(loudly)*: A seal!—ha, ha—a burning seal!

MARY'S VOICE: Love is strong—

JURY *(drowning her out)*: Death is stronger than love. Set the seal upon Daniel Webster—the burning seal of the lost. Make him one of us—one of the damned—one with Jabez Stone!

(The JURY's *eyes all fix upon* WEBSTER. *The* CLERK *advances as if to take him into custody. But* WEBSTER *silences them all with a great gesture.)*

WEBSTER: Be still!

I was going to thunder and roar. I shall not do that.

I was going to denounce and defy. I shall not do that.

You have judged this man already with your abominable justice. See that you defend it. For I shall not speak of this man.

You are demons now, but once you were men. I shall speak to every one of you.

Of common things I speak, of small things and common.

The freshness of morning to the young, the taste of food to the hungry, the day's toil, the rest by the fire, the quiet sleep.

These are good things.

But without freedom they sicken, without freedom they are nothing.

Freedom is the bread and the morning and the risen sun.

It was for freedom we came in the boats and the ships. It was for freedom we came.

It has been a long journey, a hard one, a bitter one.

But, out of the wrong and the right, the sufferings and the starvations, there is a new thing, a free thing.

The traitors in their treachery, the wise in their wisdom, the valiant in their courage—all, all have played a part.

It may not be denied in hell nor shall hell prevail against it.

Have you forgotten this? *(He turns to the* JURY.*)* Have you forgotten the forest?

GIRTY *(as in a dream)*: The forest, the rustle of the forest, the free forest.

WEBSTER *(to* KING PHILIP*)*: Have you forgotten your lost nation?

KING PHILIP: My lost nation—my fires in the wood—my warriors.

WEBSTER *(to* TEACH*)*: Have you forgotten the sea and the way of ships?

TEACH: The sea—and the swift ships sailing—the blue sea.

JURY: Forgotten—remembered—forgotten yet remembered.

WEBSTER: You were men once. Have you forgotten?

JURY: We were men once. We have not thought of it nor remembered. But we were men.

WEBSTER:

Now here is this man with good and evil in his heart.

Do you know him? He is your brother. Will you take the law of the oppressor and bind him down?

It is not for him that I speak. It is for all of you.

There is sadness in being a man but it is a proud thing, too.

There is failure and despair on the journey—the endless journey of mankind.

We are tricked and trapped—we stumble into the pit—but, out of the pit, we rise again.

No demon that was ever foaled can know the inwardness of that—only men—bewildered men.

They have broken freedom with their hands and cast her out from the nations—yet shall she live while man lives.

She shall live in the blood and the heart—she shall live in the earth of this country—she shall not be broken.

When the whips of the oppressors are broken and their names forgotten and destroyed,

I see you, mighty, shining, liberty, liberty! I see free men walking and talking under a free star.

God save the United States and the men who have made her free.

The defense rests.

JURY *(exultantly)*: We were men—we were free—we were men—we have not forgotten—our children—our children shall follow and be free.

HATHORNE *(rapping with gavel)*: The jury will retire to consider its verdict.

BUTLER *(rising)*: There is no need. The jury has heard Mr. Webster. We find for the defendant, Jabez Stone!

JURY: Not guilty!

SCRATCH *(in a screech, rushing forward)*: But, Your Honor—

(But, even as he does so, there is a flash and a thunderclap, the stage blacks out again, and when the lights come on, JUDGE *and* JURY *are gone. The yellow light of dawn lights the windows.)*

JABEZ: They're gone and it's morning—Mary, Mary!

MARY *(in doorway)*: My love—my dear.

(She rushes to him. Meanwhile SCRATCH *has been collecting his papers and trying to sneak out. But* WEBSTER *catches him.)*

WEBSTER: Just a minute, Mr. Scratch. I'll have that paper first, if you please. *(He takes the deed and tears it.)* And, now, sir, I'll have *you!*

SCRATCH: Come, come, Mr. Webster. This sort of thing is ridic—ouch—is ridiculous. If you're worried about the costs of the case, naturally, I'd be glad to pay.

WEBSTER: And so you shall! First of all, you'll promise and covenant never to bother Jabez Stone or any other New Hampshire man from now till doomsday. For any hell we want to raise in this State, we can raise ourselves, without any help from you.

SCRATCH: Ouch! Well, they never did run very big to the barrel but—ouch—I agree!

WEBSTER: See you keep to the bargain! And then—well, I've got a ram named Goliath. He can butt through an iron door. I'd like to turn you loose in his field and see what he could do to you. *(*SCRATCH *trembles.)* But that would be hard on the ram. So we'll just call in the neighbors and give you a shivaree.[8]

SCRATCH: Mr. Webster—please—oh—

WEBSTER: Neighbors! Neighbors! Come in and see what a long-barrelled, slab-sided, lantern-jawed, fortune-telling note-shaver I've got by the scruff of the neck! Bring on your kettles and your pans! *(A noise and murmur outside.)* Bring on your muskets and your flails!

JABEZ: We'll drive him out of New Hampshire!

MARY: We'll drive old Scratch away!

(The CROWD *rushes in, with muskets, flails, brooms, etc. They pursue* SCRATCH *around the stage, chanting.)*

THE CROWD:

We'll drive him out of New Hampshire!
We'll drive old Scratch away!
Forever and a day, boys,
Forever and a day!

(They finally catch SCRATCH *between two of them and fling him out of the door, bodily.)*

A MAN: Three cheers for Dan'l Webster!

ANOTHER MAN: Three cheers for Daniel Webster! He's licked the devil!

WEBSTER *(moving to center stage, and joining* JABEZ's *hands and* MARY's.*)*: And whom God hath joined let no man put asunder. *(He kisses* MARY *and turns, dusting his hands.)* Well, that job's done. I hope there's pie for breakfast, Neighbor Stone. *(And, as some of the women, dancing, bring in pies from the kitchen.)*

Curtain!

8. A mock serenade with noisemakers.

Questions

1. What is the play's central idea? How is it supported?
2. Do you think it's logical, considering the framework of the play, that Webster would agree to any judge and jury Scratch wants to provide? Why?
3. Was Webster's plea to the jury convincing to you? Was it believable?
4. Do you think the idea of a person's selling his soul to Scratch is a good basis for a play?
5. The members of the Crowd, except for the Fiddler, are interchangeable and indistinguishable. Why do you think Benét presented them this way?
6. The Crowd reacts generally as one character, and so does the Jury. It's as though there are no individuals. What parallels can you draw between the two groups? Why do you think Benét drew these parallels?
7. What is your opinion of the character of Jabez Stone? Of his wife, Mary? Do you find them believable?
8. Is the behavior of the characters logical throughout? Support your answer. Was Scratch's utter defeat logical?

EUGENE O'NEILL

Where the Cross Is Made

EUGENE O'NEILL was born in 1888, son of a well-known actor. Although his biographers disagree on when he started writing plays, his long career as a dramatist was greatly aided in 1914 when he enrolled in George Pierce Baker's playwriting workshop at Harvard University. Two years later, he became associated with the Provincetown Players, an important part of the little-theatre movement just beginning in the United States.

O'Neill, who wrote many one-act and full-length plays, experimented with different styles, often intermingled in his plays, and is largely responsible for the worldwide acceptance of American drama. He won three Pulitzer Prizes for his work and in 1936 was awarded a Nobel Prize in Literature. Most of his writing is highly personal and subjective.

WHERE THE CROSS IS MADE is one of eleven plays of O'Neill's that deal with the sea. Copyrighted in 1919, the play uses realistic dialogue and situations, but the events are seen through the eyes of the protagonist, Nat Bartlett, who, like his father, has been driven to madness by the thought of buried treasure. Thus the play is expressionistic in that it shows Nat Bartlett's perception of reality.

Melodramatic in content, the play's primary purpose is to entertain; the major theme of greed is of secondary importance.

Where the Cross Is Made Eugene O'Neill

Characters:

CAPTAIN ISAIAH BARTLETT
NAT BARTLETT, *his son*
SUE BARTLETT, *his daughter*
DOCTOR HIGGINS
SILAS HORNE, *mate* } *of the schooner* MARY ALLEN
CATES, *bo'sun* } *of the schooner* MARY ALLEN
JIMMY KANAKA, *harpooner* } *of the schooner* MARY ALLEN

Setting:

Captain Bartlett's "cabin"—a room erected as a lookout post at the top of his house situated on a high point of land on the California coast. The inside of the compartment is fitted up like the captain's cabin of a deep-sea sailing vessel. On the left, forward, a porthole. Farther back, the stairs of the companionway. Still farther, two more portholes. In the rear, left, a marble-topped sideboard with a ship's lantern on it. In the rear, center, a door opening on stairs which lead to the lower house. A cot with a blanket is placed against the wall to the right of the door. In the right wall, five portholes. Directly under them, a wooden bench. In front of the bench, a long table with two straight-backed chairs, one in front, the other to the left of it. A cheap, dark-colored rug is on the floor. In the ceiling, midway from front to rear, a skylight extending from opposite the door to above the left edge of the table. In the right extremity of the skylight is placed a floating ship's compass. The light from the binnacle sheds over this from above and seeps down into the room, casting a vague globular shadow of the compass on the floor.

The time is an early hour of a clear windy night in the fall of the year 1900. Moonlight, winnowed by the wind which moans in the stubborn angles of the old house, creeps wearily in through the portholes and rests like tired dust in circular patches upon the floor and table. An insistent monotone of thundering surf, muffled and far-off, is borne upward from the beach below.

After the curtain rises the door in the rear is opened slowly and the head and shoulders of NAT BARTLETT *appear over the sill. He casts a quick glance about the room, and seeing no one there, ascends the remaining steps and enters. He makes a sign to some one in the darkness beneath: "All right, Doctor."* DOCTOR HIGGINS *follows him into the room and, closing the door, stands looking with great curiosity around him. He is a slight, medium-sized professional-looking man of about thirty-five.* NAT BARTLETT *is very tall, gaunt, and loose-framed. His right arm has been amputated at the shoulder and the sleeve on that side of the heavy mackinaw he wears hangs flabbily or flaps against his body as he moves. He appears much older than his thirty years. His shoulders have a weary stoop as if worn down by the burden of his massive head with its heavy shock of tangled black hair. His face is long, bony, and sallow, with deep-set black eyes, a large aquiline nose, a wide thin-lipped mouth shadowed by an unkempt bristle of mustache. His voice is low and deep with a penetrating, hollow, metallic quality. In addition to the mackinaw, he wears corduroy trousers stuffed down into high laced boots.*

NAT: Can you see, Doctor?

HIGGINS *(in the too-casual tones which betray an inward uneasiness)*: Yes—perfectly—don't trouble. The moonlight is so bright—

NAT: Luckily. *(Walking slowly toward the table.)* He doesn't want any light—lately—only the one from the binnacle[1] there.

HIGGINS: He? Ah—you mean your father?

NAT *(impatiently)*: Who else?

HIGGINS *(a bit startled—gazing around him in embarrassment)*: I suppose this is all meant to be like a ship's cabin?

NAT: Yes—as I warned you.

HIGGINS *(in surprise)*: Warned me? Why, warned? I think it's very natural—and interesting—this whim of his.

NAT *(meaningly)*: Interesting, it may be.

HIGGINS: And he lives up here, you said—never comes down?

NAT: Never—for the past three years. My sister brings his food up to him. *(He sits down in the chair to the left of the table.)* There's a lantern on the sideboard there, Doctor. Bring it over and sit down. We'll make a light. I'll ask your pardon for bringing you to this room on the roof—but—no one'll hear us here; and by seeing for yourself the mad way he lives—. Understand that I want you to get all the facts—just that, facts!—and for that light is necessary. Without that—they become dreams up here—dreams, Doctor.

HIGGINS *(with a relieved smile carries over the lantern)*: It is a trifle spooky.

NAT *(not seeming to notice this remark)*: He won't take any note of this light. His eyes are too busy—out there. *(He flings his left arm in a wide gesture seaward.)* And if he does notice—well, let him come down. You're bound to see him sooner or later. *(He scratches a match and lights the lantern.)*

HIGGINS: Where is—he?

NAT *(pointing upward)*: Up on the poop.[2] Sit down, man! He'll not come—yet awhile.

HIGGINS *(sitting gingerly on the chair in front of table)*: Then he has the roof too rigged up like a ship?

1. A stand for housing and supporting a compass.
2. The poop is a superstructure at the stern of a ship. The poop deck is a weather deck on top of the poop.

NAT: I told you he had. Like a deck, yes. A wheel, compass, binnacle light, the companionway[3] there *(He points.)*, a bridge to pace up and down on—*and keep watch*. If the wind wasn't so high you'd hear him now—back and forth—all the live-long night. *(With a sudden harshness.)* Didn't I tell you he's mad?

HIGGINS *(with a professional air)*: That was nothing new. I've heard that about him from all sides since I first came to the asylum yonder. You say he only walks at night—up there?

NAT: Only at night, yes. *(Grimly.)* The things he wants to see can't be made out in daylight—dreams and such.

HIGGINS: But just what is he trying to see? Does any one know? Does he tell?

NAT *(impatiently)*: Why, every one knows what Father looks for, man! The ship, of course.

HIGGINS: What ship?

NAT: His ship—the Mary Allen—named for my dead mother.

HIGGINS: But—I don't understand— Is the ship long overdue—or what?

NAT: Lost in a hurricane off the Celebes[4] with all on board—three years ago!

HIGGINS *(wonderingly)*: Ah. *(After a pause.)* But your father still clings to a doubt—

NAT: There is no doubt for him or any one else to cling to. She was sighted bottom up, a complete wreck, by the whaler John Slocum. That was two weeks after the storm. They sent a boat out to read her name.

HIGGINS: And hasn't your father ever heard—

NAT: He was the first to hear, naturally. Oh, he *knows* right enough, if that's what you're driving at. *(He bends toward the doctor—intensely.)* He *knows,* Doctor, he *knows*—but he won't *believe.* He can't—and keep living.

HIGGINS *(impatiently)*: Come, Mr. Bartlett, let's get down to brass tacks. You didn't drag me up here to make things more obscure, did you? Let's have the facts you spoke of. I'll need them to give sympathetic treatment to his case when we get him to the asylum.

NAT *(anxiously—lowering his voice)*: And you'll come to take him away tonight—for sure?

HIGGINS: Twenty minutes after I leave here I'll be back in the car. That's positive.

NAT: And you know your way through the house?

HIGGINS: Certainly, I remember—but I don't see—

NAT: The outside door will be left open for you. You must come right up.

3. A stair or ladder within the hull of a ship.

4. Former name of Sulawesi.

My sister and I will be here—with him. And you understand— Neither of us knows anything about this. The authorities have been complained to—not by us, mind—but by some one. He must never know—

HIGGINS: Yes, yes—but still I don't— Is he liable to prove violent?

NAT: No—no. He's quiet always—too quiet; but he might do something—anything—if he knows—

HIGGINS: Rely on me not to tell him, then; but I'll bring along two attendants in case— *(He breaks off and continues in matter-of-fact tones.)* And now for the facts in this case, if you don't mind, Mr. Bartlett.

NAT *(shaking his head—moodily)*: There are cases where facts— Well, here goes—the brass tacks. My father was a whaling captain as his father before him. The last trip he made was seven years ago. He expected to be gone two years. It was four before we saw him again. His ship had been wrecked in the Indian Ocean. He and six others managed to reach a small island on the fringe of the Archipelago—an island barren as hell, Doctor—after seven days in an open boat. The rest of the whaling crew never were heard from again—gone to the sharks. Of the six who reached the island with my father only three were alive when a fleet of Malay canoes picked them up, mad from thirst and starvation, the four of them. These four men finally reached Frisco.[5] *(With great emphasis.)* They were my father; Silas Horne, the mate; Cates, the bo'sun, and Jimmy Kanaka, a Hawaiian harpooner. Those four! *(With a forced laugh.)* There are facts for you. It was all in the papers at the time—my father's story.

HIGGINS: But what of the other three who were on the island?

NAT *(harshly)*: Died of exposure, perhaps. Mad and jumped into the sea, perhaps. That was the told story. Another was whispered—killed and eaten, perhaps! But gone—vanished—that, undeniably. That was the fact. For the rest—who knows? And what does it matter?

HIGGINS *(with a shudder)*: I should think it would matter—a lot.

NAT *(fiercely)*: We're dealing with facts, Doctor! *(With a laugh.)* And here are some more for you. My father brought the three down to this house with him—Horne and Cates and Jimmy Kanaka. We hardly recognized my father. He had been through hell and looked it. His hair was white. But you'll see for yourself—soon. And the others—they were all a bit queer, too—mad, if you will. *(He laughs again.)* So much for the facts, Doctor. They leave off there and the dreams begin.

HIGGINS *(doubtfully)*: It would seem—the facts are enough.

NAT: Wait. *(He resumes deliberately.)* One day my father sent for me and in the presence of the others told me the dream. I was to be heir to the

5. San Francisco.

secret. Their second day on the island, he said, they discovered in a sheltered inlet the rotten, waterlogged hulk of a Malay prau[6]—a proper war prau such as the pirates used to use. She had been there rotting—God knows how long. The crew had vanished—God knows where, for there was no sign on the island that man had ever touched there. The Kanakas went over the prau—they're devils for staying underwater, you know—and they found—in two chests—*(he leans back in his chair and smiles ironically)*—Guess what, Doctor?

HIGGINS *(with an answering smile)*: Treasure, of course.

NAT *(leaning forward and pointing his finger accusingly at the other)*: You see! The root of belief is in you, too! *(Then he leans back with a hollow chuckle.)* Why, yes. Treasure, to be sure. What else? They landed it and—you can guess the rest, too—diamonds, emeralds, gold ornaments—innumerable, of course. Why limit the stuff of dreams? Ha-ha! *(He laughs sardonically as if mocking himself.)*

HIGGINS *(deeply interested)*: And then?

NAT: They began to go mad—hunger, thirst, and the rest—and they began to forget. Oh, they forgot a lot, and lucky for them they did, probably. But my father realizing, as he told me, what was happening to them, insisted that while they still knew what they were doing they should—guess again now, Doctor. Ha-ha!

HIGGINS: Bury the treasure?

NAT *(ironically)*: Simple, isn't it? Ha-ha. And then they made a map—the same old dream, you see—with a charred stick, and my father had care of it. They were picked up soon after, mad as hatters, as I have told you, by some Malays. *(He drops his mocking and adopts a calm, deliberate tone again.)* But the map isn't a dream, Doctor. We're coming back to facts again. *(He reaches into the pocket of his mackinaw and pulls out a crumpled paper.)* Here. *(He spreads it out on the table.)*

HIGGINS *(craning his neck eagerly)*: Dammit! This is interesting. The treasure, I suppose, is where—

NAT: Where the cross is made.

HIGGINS: And here are the signatures, I see. And that sign?

NAT: Jimmy Kanaka's. He couldn't write.

HIGGINS: And below? That's yours, isn't it?

NAT: As heir to the secret, yes. We all signed it here the morning the Mary Allen, the schooner my father had mortgaged this house to fit out, set sail to bring back the treasure. Ha-ha.

HIGGINS: The ship he's still looking for—that was lost three years ago?

NAT: The Mary Allen, yes. The other three men sailed away on her. Only father and the mate knew the approximate location of the island—and I—as heir. It's—*(He hesitates, frowning.)* No matter. I'll keep the

6. A prow; a ship.

mad secret. My father wanted to go with them—but my mother was dying. I dared not go either.

HIGGINS: Then you wanted to go? You believed in the treasure then?

NAT: Of course. Ha-ha. How could I help it? I believed until my mother's death. Then *he* became mad, entirely mad. He built this cabin—to wait in—and he suspected my growing doubt as time went on. So, as final proof, he gave me a thing he had kept hidden from them all—a sample of the richest of the treasure. Ha-ha. Behold!

(He takes from his pocket a heavy bracelet thickly studded with stones and throws it on the table near the lantern.)

HIGGINS *(picking it up with eager curiosity—as if in spite of himself)*: Real jewels?

NAT: Ha-ha! You want to believe, too. No—paste and brass—Malay ornaments.

HIGGINS: You had it looked over?

NAT: Like a fool, yes. *(He puts it back in his pocket and shakes his head as if throwing off a burden.)* Now you know why he's mad—waiting for that ship—and why in the end I had to ask you to take him away where he'll be safe. The mortgage—the price of that ship—is to be foreclosed. We have to move, my sister and I. We can't take him with us. She is to be married soon. Perhaps away from the sight of the sea he may—

HIGGINS *(perfunctorily)*: Let's hope for the best. And I fully appreciate your position. *(He gets up, smiling.)* And thank you for the interesting story. I'll know how to humor him when he raves about treasure.

NAT *(somberly)*: He is quiet always—too quiet. He only walks to and fro—watching—

HIGGINS: Well, I must go. You think it's best to take him tonight?

NAT *(persuasively)*: Yes, Doctor. The neighbors—they're far away but—for my sister's sake—you understand.

HIGGINS: I see. It must be hard on her—this sort of thing—Well.—*(He goes to the door, which* NAT *opens for him.)* I'll return presently. *(He starts to descend.)*

NAT *(urgently)*: Don't fail us, Doctor. And come right up. He'll be here. *(He closes the door and tiptoes carefully to the companionway. He ascends it a few steps and remains for a moment listening for some sound from above. Then he goes over to the table, turning the lantern very low, and sits down, resting his elbows, his chin on his hands, staring somberly before him. The door in the rear is slowly opened. It creaks slightly and* NAT *jumps to his feet—in a thick voice of terror.)* Who's there?

(The door swings wide open, revealing SUE BARTLETT. *She ascends into the room and shuts the door behind her. She is a tall, slender woman of twenty-five, with a pale, sad face framed in a mass of dark red hair. This hair furnishes the only touch*

of color about her. Her full lips are pale; the blue of her wistful wide eyes is fading into a twilight gray. Her voice is low and melancholy. She wears a dark wrapper and slippers.)

SUE *(stands and looks at her brother accusingly)*: It's only I. What are you afraid of?

NAT *(averts his eyes and sinks back on his chair again)*: Nothing. I didn't know—I thought you were in your room.

SUE *(comes to the table)*: I was reading. Then I heard some one come down the stairs and go out. Who was it? *(With sudden terror.)* It wasn't—Father?

NAT: No. He's up there—watching—as he always is.

SUE *(sitting down—insistently)*: Who was it?

NAT *(evasively)*: A man—I know.

SUE: What man? What is he? You're holding something back. Tell me.

NAT *(raising his eyes defiantly)*: A doctor.

SUE *(alarmed)*: Oh! *(With quick intuition.)* You brought him up here—so that I wouldn't know!

NAT *(doggedly)*: No. I took him up here to see how things were—to ask him about Father.

SUE *(as if afraid of the answer she will get)*: Is he one of them—from the asylum? Oh, Nat, you haven't—

NAT *(interrupting her—hoarsely)*: No, no! Be still.

SUE: That would be—the last horror.

NAT *(defiantly)*: Why? You always say that. What could be more horrible than things as they are? I believe—it would be better for him—away—where he couldn't see the sea. He'll forget his mad idea of waiting for a lost ship and a treasure that never was. *(As if trying to convince himself—vehemently.)* I believe this!

SUE *(reproachfully)*: You don't, Nat. You know he'd die if he hadn't the sea to live with.

NAT *(bitterly)*: And you know old Smith will foreclose the mortgage. Is that nothing? We cannot pay. He came yesterday and talked with me. He knows the place is his—to all purposes. He talked as if we were merely his tennants, curse him! And he swore he'd foreclose immediately unless—

SUE *(eagerly)*: What?

NAT *(in a hard voice)*: Unless we have—Father—taken away.

SUE *(in anguish)*: Oh! But why, why? What is Father to him?

NAT: The value of the property—our home which is his, Smith's. The neighbors are afraid. They pass by on the road at nights coming back to their farms from the town. They see *him* up there walking back and forth—waving his arms against the sky. They're afraid. They talk of a complaint. They say for his own good he must be taken away.

They even whisper the house is haunted. Old Smith is afraid of his property. He thinks that *he* may set fire to the house—do anything—

SUE *(despairingly)*: But you told him how foolish that was, didn't you? That Father is quiet, always quiet.

NAT: What's the use of telling—when they believe—when they're afraid? *(Sue hides her face in her hands—a pause—*NAT *whispers hoarsely)*: I've been afraid myself—at times.

SUE: Oh Nat! Of what?

NAT *(violently)*: Oh, him and the sea he calls to! Of the damned sea he forced me on as a boy—the sea that robbed me of my arm and made me the broken thing I am!

SUE *(pleadingly)*: You can't blame Father—for your misfortune.

NAT: He took me from school and forced me on his ship, didn't he? What would I have been now but an ignorant sailor like him if he had had his way? No. It's the sea I should not blame, that foiled him by taking my arm and then throwing me ashore—another one of *his* wrecks!

SUE *(with a sob)*: You're bitter, Nat—and hard. It was so long ago. Why can't you forget?

NAT *(bitterly)*: Forget! You can talk! When Tom comes home from this voyage you'll be married and out of this with life before you—a captain's wife as our mother was. I wish you joy.

SUE *(supplicatingly)*: And you'll come with us, Nat—and father, too—and then—

NAT: Would you saddle your young husband with a madman and a cripple? *(Fiercely.)* No, no, not I! *(Vindictively.)* And not him, either! *(With sudden meaning—deliberately.)* I've got to stay here. My book is three-fourths done—my book that will set me free! But I know, I feel, as sure as I stand here living before you, that I must finish it here. It could not live for me outside of this house where it was born. *(Staring at her fixedly.)* So I will stay—in spite of hell! *(*SUE *sobs hopelessly. After a pause he continues:)* Old Smith told me I could live here indefinitely without paying—as caretaker—if—

SUE *(fearfully—like a whispered echo)*: If?

NAT *(staring at her—in a hard voice)*: If I have *him* sent—where he'll no longer harm himself—nor others.

SUE *(with horrified dread)*: No—no, Nat! For our dead mother's sake.

NAT *(struggling)*: Did I say I had? Why do you look at me—like that?

SUE: Nat! Nat! For our mother's sake!

NAT *(in terror)*: Stop! Stop! She's dead—and at peace. Would you bring her tired soul back to him again to be bruised and wounded?

SUE: Nat!

NAT *(clutching at his throat as though to strangle something within him—hoarsely)*: Sue! Have mercy! *(His sister stares at him with dread foreboding.* NAT *calms himself with an effort and continues deliberately:)* Smith said he would give two thousand cash if I would sell the place to him—and he would let me stay, rent free, as caretaker.

SUE *(scornfully)*: Two thousand! Why, over and above the mortgage its worth—

NAT: It's not what it's worth. It's what one can get, cash—for my book—for freedom!

SUE: So that's why he wants Father sent away, the wretch! He must know the will Father made—

NAT: Gives the place to me. Yes, he knows. I told him.

SUE *(dully)*: Ah, how vile men are!

NAT *(persuasively)*: If it were to be done—if it were, I say—there'd be half for you for your wedding portion. That's fair.

SUE *(horrified)*: Blood money! Do you think I could touch it?

NAT *(persuasively)*: It would be only fair. I'd give it to you.

SUE: My God, Nat, are you trying to bribe me?

NAT: No. It's yours in all fairness. *(With a twisted smile.)* You forget I'm heir to the treasure, too, and can afford to be generous. Ha-ha.

SUE *(alarmed)*: Nat! You're so strange. You're sick, Nat. You couldn't talk this way if you were yourself. Oh, we must go away from here—you and father and I! Let Smith foreclose. There'll be something over the mortgage; and we'll move to some little house—by the sea so that father—

NAT *(fiercely)*: Can keep up his mad game with me—whispering dreams in my ear—pointing out to sea—mocking me with stuff like this! *(He takes the bracelet from his pocket. The sight of it infuriates him and he hurls it into a corner, exclaiming in a terrible voice:)* No! No! It's too late for dreams now. It's too late! I've put them behind me tonight—forever!

SUE *(looks at him and suddenly understands that what she dreads has come to pass—letting her head fall on her outstretched arms with a long moan)*: Then—you've done it! You've sold him! Oh, Nat, you're cursed!

NAT *(with a terrified glance at the roof above)*: Ssshh! What are you saying? He'll be better off—away from the sea.

SUE *(dully)*: You've sold him.

NAT *(wildly)*: No! No! *(He takes the map from his pocket.)* Listen, Sue! For God's sake, listen to me! See! The map of the island. *(He spreads it out on the table.)* And the treasure—where the cross is made. *(He gulps and his words pour out incoherently.)* I've carried it about for years. Is that nothing? You don't know what it means. It stands between me and my book. It's stood between me and life—driving me mad! *He* taught me to wait and hope with him—wait and hope—day after day. He made me doubt my brain and give the lie to my eyes—when hope was dead—when I knew it was all a dream—I couldn't kill it! *(His eyes starting from his head.)* God forgive me, I still believe! And that's mad—mad, do you hear?

SUE *(looking at him with horror)*: And that is why—you hate him!

NAT: No, I don't— *(Then in a sudden frenzy.)* Yes! I do hate him! He's stolen my brain! I've got to free myself, can't you see, from him—and his madness.

SUE *(terrified—appealingly)*: Nat! Don't! You talk as if—

NAT *(with a wild laugh)*: As if I were mad? You're right—but I'll be mad no more! See! *(He opens the lantern and sets fire to the map in his hand. When he shuts the lantern again it flickers and goes out. They watch the paper burn with fascinated eyes as he talks.)* See how I free myself and become sane. And now for facts, as the doctor said. I lied to you about him. He was a doctor from the asylum. See how it burns! It must all be destroyed—this poisonous madness. Yes, I lied to you—see—it's gone—the last speck—and the only other map is the one Silas Horne took to the bottom of the sea with him. *(He lets the ash fall to the floor and crushes it with his foot.)* Gone! I'm free of it—at last! *(His face is very pale, but he goes on calmly.)* Yes, I sold him, if you will—to save my soul. They're coming from the asylum to get him—

(There is a loud, muffled cry from above, which sounds like "Sail-ho," and a stamping of feet. The slide to the companionway above is slid back with a bang. A gust of air tears down into the room. NAT *and* SUE *have jumped to their feet and stand petrified.* CAPTAIN BARTLETT *tramps down the stairs.)*

NAT *(with a shudder)*: God! Did he hear?

SUE: Ssshh! *(*CAPTAIN BARTLETT *comes into the room. He bears a striking resemblance to his son, but his face is more stern and formidable, his form more robust, erect and muscular. His mass of hair is pure white, his bristly mustache the same, contrasting with the weather-beaten leather color of his furrowed face. Bushy gray brows overhang the obsessed glare of his fierce dark eyes. He wears a heavy, double-breasted blue coat, pants of the same material, and rubber boots turned down from the knee.)*

BARTLETT *(in a state of mad exultation strides toward his son and points an accusing finger at him.* NAT *shrinks backward a step)*: Bin thinkin' me mad, did ye? Thinkin' it for the past three years, ye bin—ever since them fools on the Slocum tattled their damn lie o' the Mary Allen bein' a wreck.

NAT *(swallowing hard—chokingly)*: No—Father—I—

BARTLETT: Don't lie, ye whelp! You that I'd made my heir—aimin' to git me out o' the way. Aimin' to put me behind the bars o' the jail for mad folk!

SUE: Father—no!

BARTLETT *(waving his hand for her to be silent)*: Not you, girl, not you. You're your mother.

NAT *(very pale)*: Father—do you think—I—

BARTLETT *(fiercely)*: A lie in your eyes! I bin a-readin' 'em. My curse on you!

SUE: Father! Don't!

BARTLETT: Leave me be, girl. He believed, didn't he? And ain't he turned traitor—mockin' at me and sayin' it's all a lie—mockin' at himself, too, for bein' a fool to believe in dreams, as he calls 'em.

NAT *(placatingly)*: You're wrong, Father. I do believe.

BARTLETT *(triumphantly)*: Aye, now ye do! Who wouldn't credit their own eyes?

NAT *(mystified)*: Eyes?

BARTLETT: Have ye not seen her, then? Did ye not hear me hail?

NAT *(confusedly)*: Hail? I heard a shout. But—hail what?—seen what?

BARTLETT *(grimly)*: Aye, now's your punishment, Judas. *(Explosively.)* The Mary Allen, ye blind fool, come back from the Southern Seas—come back as I swore she must!

SUE *(trying to soothe him)*: Father! Be quiet. It's nothing.

BARTLETT *(not heeding her—his eyes fixed hypnotically on his son's)*: Turned the pint a half-hour back—the Mary Allen—loaded with gold as I swore she would be—carryin' her lowers—not a reef in 'em—makin' port, boy, as I swore she must—too late for traitors, boy, too late!—droppin' her anchor just when I hailed her.

NAT *(a haunted, fascinated look in his eyes, which are fixed immovably on his father's)*: The Mary Allen! But how do you know?

BARTLETT: Not know my own ship! 'Tis you're mad!

NAT: But at night—some other schooner—

BARTLETT: No other, I say! The Mary Allen—clear in the moonlight. And heed this: D'you call to mind the signal I gave to Silas Horne if he made this port o' a night?

NAT *(slowly)*: A red and a green light at the mainmast-head.

BARTLETT *(triumphantly)*: Then look out if ye dare! *(He goes to the porthole, left forward.)* Ye can see it plain from here. *(Commandingly.)* Will ye believe your eyes? Look—and then call me mad!

(NAT *peers through the porthole and starts back, a dumbfounded expression on his face.)*

NAT *(slowly)*: A red and a green at the mainmast-head. Yes—clear as day.

SUE *(with a worried look at him)*: Let me see. *(She goes to the porthole.)*

BARTLETT *(to his son with fierce satisfaction)*: Aye, ye see now clear enough—too late for you. *(*NAT *stares at him spellbound.)* And from above I saw Horne and Cates and Jimmy Kanaka plain on the deck in the moonlight lookin' up at me. Come!

(He strides to the companionway, followed by NAT. *The two of them ascend.* SUE *turns from the porthole, an expression of frightened bewilderment on her face. She shakes her head sadly. A loud "Mary Allen, ahoy!" comes from above in* BARTLETT's *voice, followed like an echo by the same hail from* NAT. SUE *covers her face with her hands, shuddering.* NAT *comes down the companionway, his eyes wild and exulting.)*

SUE *(brokenly)*: He's bad tonight, Nat. You're right to humor him. It's the best thing.

NAT *(savagely)*: Humor him? What in hell do you mean?

SUE *(pointing to the porthole)*: There's nothing there, Nat. There's not a ship in harbor.

NAT: You're a fool—or blind! The Mary Allen's there in plain sight of any one, with the red and the green signal lights. Those fools lied about her being wrecked. And I've been a fool, too.

SUE: But, Nat, there's nothing. *(She goes over to the porthole again.)* Not a ship. See.

NAT: I saw, I tell you! From above it's all plain.

(He turns from her and goes back to his seat by the table. SUE *follows him, pleading frightenedly.)*

SUE: Nat! You mustn't let this— You're all excited and trembling, Nat. *(She puts a soothing hand on his forehead.)*

NAT *(pushing her away from him roughly)*: You blind fool!

*(*BARTLETT *comes down the steps of the companionway. His face is transfigured with the ecstasy of a dream come true.)*

BARTLETT: They've lowered a boat—the three—Horne and Cates and Jimmy Kanaka. They're a-rowin' ashore. I heard the oars in the locks. Listen! *(A pause.)*

NAT *(excitedly)*: I hear!

SUE *(who has taken the chair by her brother—in a warning whisper)*: It's the wind and sea you hear, Nat. Please!

BARTLETT *(suddenly)*: Hark! They've landed. They're back on earth again as I swore they'd come back. They'll be a-comin' up the path now.

(He stands in an attitude of rigid attention. NAT *strains forward in his chair. The sound of the wind and sea suddenly ceases and there is a heavy silence. A dense green glow floods slowly in rhythmic waves like a liquid into the room—as of great depths of the sea faintly penetrated by light.)*

NAT *(catching at his sister's hand—chokingly)*: See how the light changes! Green and gold! *(He shivers.)* Deep under the sea! I've been drowned for years! *(Hysterically.)* Save me! Save me!

SUE *(patting his hand comfortingly)*: Only the moonlight, Nat. It hasn't changed. Be quiet, dear, it's nothing. *(The green light grows deeper and deeper.)*

BARTLETT *(in a crooning, monotonous tone)*: They move slowly—slowly. They're heavy, I know, heavy—the two chests. Hark! They're below at the door. You hear?

NAT *(starting to his feet)*: I hear! I left the door open.

BARTLETT: For them?

NAT: For them.

SUE *(shuddering)*: Ssshh!

(The sound of a door being heavily slammed is heard from way down in the house.)

NAT *(to his sister—excitedly)*: There! You hear?

SUE: A shutter in the wind.

NAT: There is no wind.

BARTLETT: Up they come! Up, bullies! They're heavy—heavy! *(The padding of bare feet sounds from the floor below—then comes up the stairs.)*

NAT: You hear them now?

SUE: Only the rats running about. It's nothing, Nat.

BARTLETT *(rushing to the door and throwing it open)*: Come in, lads, come in!—and welcome home!

(The forms of SILAS HORNE, CATES, *and* JIMMY KANAKA *rise noiselessly into the room from the stairs. The last two carry heavy inlaid chests.* HORNE *is a parrot-nosed, angular old man dressed in gray cotton trousers and a singlet torn open across his hairy chest.* JIMMY *is a tall, sinewy, bronzed young Kanaka. He wears only a breech cloth.* CATES *is squat and stout and is dressed in dungaree pants and a shredded white sailor's blouse, stained with iron rust. All are in their bare feet. Water drips from their soaked and rotten clothes. Their hair is matted, intertwined with slimy strands of seaweed. Their eyes, as they glide silently into the room, stare frightfully wide at nothing. Their flesh in the green light has the suggestion of decomposition. Their bodies sway limply, nervelessly, rhythmically as if to the pulse of long swells of the deep sea.)*

NAT *(making a step toward them)*: See! *(Frenziedly.)* Welcome home, boys!

SUE *(grabbing his arm)*: Sit down, Nat. It's nothing. There's no one there. Father—sit down!

BARTLETT *(grinning at the three and putting his finger to his lips)*: Not here, boys, not here—not before him. *(He points to his son.)* He has no right, now. Come. The treasure is ours only. We'll go away with it together. Come. *(He goes to the companionway. The three follow. At the foot of it* HORNE *puts a swaying hand on his shoulder and with the other holds out a piece of paper to him.* BARTLETT *takes it and chuckles exultantly.)* That's right—for him—that's right! *(He ascends. The figures sway up after him.)*

NAT *(frenziedly)*: Wait! *(He struggles toward the companionway.)*

SUE *(trying to hold him back)*: Nat—don't! Father—come back!

NAT: Father!

(He flings her away from him and rushes up the companionway. He pounds against the slide, which seems to have been shut down on him.)

SUE *(hysterically—runs wildly to the door in rear)*: Help! Help! *(As she gets to the door* DOCTOR HIGGINS *appears, hurrying up the stairs.)*

HIGGINS *(excitedly)*: Just a moment, Miss. What's the matter?

SUE *(with a gasp)*: My father—up there!

HIGGINS: I can't see—where's my flash? Ah. *(He flashes it on her terror-stricken face, then quickly around the room. The green glow disappears. The wind and sea are heard again. Clear moonlight floods through the portholes.* HIGGINS *springs to the companionway.* NAT *is still pounding.)* Here, Bartlett. Let me try.

NAT *(coming down—looking dully at the doctor)*: They've locked it. I can't get up.

HIGGINS *(looks up—in an astonished voice)*: What's the matter, Bartlett? It's all open. *(He starts to ascend.)*

NAT *(in a voice of warning)*: Look out, man! Look out for them!

HIGGINS *(calls down from above)*: Them? Who? There's no one here. *(Suddenly—in alarm.)* Come up! Lend a hand here! He's fainted!

*(*NAT *goes up slowly.* SUE *goes over and lights the lantern, then hurries back to the foot of the companionway with it. There is a scuffling noise from above. They reappear, carrying* CAPTAIN BARTLETT's *body.)*

HIGGINS: Easy now! *(They lay him on the couch in rear.* SUE *sets the lantern down by the couch.* HIGGINS *bends and listens for a heartbeat. Then he rises, shaking his head.)* I'm sorry—

SUE *(dully)*: Dead?

HIGGINS *(nodding)*: Heart failure, I should judge. *(With an attempt at consolation.)* Perhaps it's better so, if—

NAT *(as if in a trance)*: There was something Horne handed him. Did you see?

SUE *(wringing her hands)*: Oh, Nat, be still! He's dead. *(To* HIGGINS *with pitiful appeal.)* Please go—go—

HIGGINS: There's nothing I can do?

SUE: Go—please—

*(*HIGGINS *bows stiffly and goes out.* NAT *moves slowly to his father's body, as if attracted by some irresistible fascination.)*

NAT: Didn't you see? Horne handed him something.

SUE *(sobbing)*: Nat! Nat! Come away! Don't touch him, Nat! Come away.

(But her brother does not heed her. His gaze is fixed on his father's right hand, which hangs downward over the side of the couch. He pounces on it and forcing the clenched fingers open with a great effort, secures a crumpled ball of paper.)

NAT *(flourishing it above his head with a shout of triumph)*: See! *(He bends down and spreads it out in the light of the lantern.)* The map of the island! Look! It isn't lost for me after all! There's still a chance—*my* chance! *(With mad, solemn decision.)* When the house is sold I'll go—and I'll find it! Look! It's written here in his handwriting: "The treasure is buried where the cross is made."

SUE *(covering her face with her hands—brokenly)*: Oh, God! Come away, Nat! Come away!

Curtain.

Questions

1. In what ways did O'Neill use exaggeration in this play?
2. The theme of the play is greed. How many instances of greed can you find? Explain your answer.
3. Are the situations portrayed in the play believable? Why or why not?
4. What is the significance of the book Nat is writing? What does he mean when he says it will set him free?
5. What clues can you find that Nat is insane? When do you begin to suspect that he is?
6. With which character do you most sympathize? Why? With whom do you sympathize the least? Why?

SUSAN GLASPELL

Trifles

SUSAN GLASPELL was an American novelist and playwright who was active in the formation of the Provincetown Players, the group with which Eugene O'Neill worked. The group produced Glaspell's one-act plays and in 1915 her first three-act play, *Bernice,* in which she herself played a servant.

Her best work usually is considered to be *Alison's House,* suggested by the life of Emily Dickinson. For the play, the dramatist received a Pulitzer Prize.

Susan Glaspell was born in 1882 in Iowa. *Trifles,* published in 1916, is one of her earliest one-act plays.

TRIFLES shows a mastery of dialogue and perception and deals with the battle of the sexes. As such, it could be considered an early example of feminist writing. The story concerns the idea that although men tend to patronize women, Mrs. Peters and Mrs. Hale are, in fact, far more perceptive and knowledgeable than the men.

Trifles Susan Glaspell

Characters:

COUNTY ATTORNEY
MRS. PETERS
SHERIFF
MRS. HALE
HALE

Setting:

The kitchen in the now-abandoned farmhouse of JOHN WRIGHT, *a gloomy kitchen, and left without having been put in order—the walls covered with a faded wall paper. Downstage right is a door leading to the parlor. On the right wall above this door is a built-in kitchen cupboard with shelves in the upper portion and drawers below. In the rear wall at right, up two steps is a door opening onto stairs leading to the second floor. In the rear wall at left is a door to the shed and from there to the outside. Between these two doors is an old-fashioned black iron stove. Running along the left wall from the shed door is an old iron sink and sink shelf, in which is set a hand pump. Downstage of the sink is an uncurtained window. Near the window is an old wooden rocker. Center stage is an unpainted wooden kitchen table with straight chairs on either side. There is a small chair downstage right. Unwashed pans under the sink, a loaf of bread outside the breadbox, a dish towel on the table—other signs of incompleted work. At the rear the shed door opens and the* SHERIFF *comes in followed by the* COUNTY ATTORNEY *and* HALE. *The* SHERIFF *and* HALE *are men in middle life, the* COUNTY ATTORNEY *is a young man; all are much bundled up and go at once to the stove. They are followed by the two women—the* SHERIFF'S *wife,* MRS. PETERS, *first; she is a slight wiry woman, a thin nervous face.* MRS. HALE *is larger and would ordinarily be called more comfortable looking, but she is disturbed now and looks fearfully about as she enters. The women have come in slowly, and stand close together near the door.*

COUNTY ATTORNEY *(at stove rubbing his hands)*: This feels good. Come up to the fire, ladies.

MRS. PETERS *(after taking a step forward)*: I'm not—cold.

SHERIFF *(unbuttoning his overcoat and stepping away from the stove to right of table as if to mark the beginning of official business)*: Now, Mr. Hale, before we move things about, you explain to Mr. Henderson just what you saw when you came here yesterday morning.

COUNTY ATTORNEY *(crossing down to left of the table)*: By the way, has anything been moved? Are things just as you left them yesterday?

SHERIFF *(looking about)*: It's just the same. When it dropped below zero last night I thought I'd better send Frank out this morning to make a fire for us—*(Sits right of center table.)* no use getting pneumonia with a big case on, but I told him not to touch anything except the stove—and you know Frank.

COUNTY ATTORNEY: Somebody should have been left here yesterday.

SHERIFF: Oh—yesterday. When I had to send Frank to Morris Center for that man who went crazy—I want you to know I had my hands full yesterday. I knew you could get back from Omaha by today and as long as I went over everything here myself—

COUNTY ATTORNEY: Well, Mr. Hale, tell just what happened when you came here yesterday morning.

HALE *(crossing down to above table)*: Harry and I had started to town with a load of potatoes. We came along the road from my place and as I got here I said, "I'm going to see if I can't get John Wright to go in with me on a party telephone." I spoke to Wright about it once before and he put me off, saying folks talked too much anyway, and all he asked was peace and quiet—I guess you know about how much he talked himself; but I thought maybe if I went to the house and talked about it before his wife, though I said to Harry that I didn't know as what his wife wanted made much difference to John—

COUNTY ATTORNEY: Let's talk about that later, Mr. Hale. I do want to talk about that, but tell now just what happened when you got to the house.

HALE: I didn't hear or see anything; I knocked at the door, and still it was all quiet inside. I knew they must be up, it was past eight o'clock. So I knocked again, and I thought I heard somebody say, "Come in." I wasn't sure, I'm not sure yet, but I opened the door—this door *(Indicating the door by which the two women are still standing.)* and there in that rocker—*(Pointing to it.)* sat Mrs. Wright. *(They all look at the rocker downstage left.)*

COUNTY ATTORNEY: What—was she doing?

HALE: She was rockin' back and forth. She had her apron in her hand and was kind of—pleating it.

COUNTY ATTORNEY: And how did she—look?

HALE: Well, she looked queer.

COUNTY ATTORNEY: How do you mean—queer?

HALE: Well, as if she didn't know what she was going to do next. And kind of done up.

COUNTY ATTORNEY *(takes out notebook and pencil and sits left of center table)*: How did she seem to feel about your coming?

HALE: Why, I don't think she minded—one way or other. She didn't pay much attention. I said, "How do, Mrs. Wright, it's cold, ain't it?" And she said, "Is it?"—and went on kind of pleating at her apron. Well, I was surprised; she didn't ask me to come up to the stove, or to set down, but just sat there, not even looking at me, so I said, "I want to see John." And then she—laughed. I guess you would call it a laugh. I thought of Harry and the team outside, so I said a little sharp: "Can't I see John?" "No," she says, kind o' dull like. "Ain't he home?" says I. "Yes," says she, "he's home." "Then why can't I see him?" I asked her, out of patience. " 'Cause he's dead," says she. *"Dead?"* says I. She just nodded her head, not getting a big excited, but rockin' back and forth. "Why—where is he?" says I, not knowing what to say. She just pointed upstairs—like that. *(Himself pointing to the room above.)* I started for the stairs, with the idea of going up there. I walked from there to here—then I says, "Why, what did he die of?" "He died of a rope round his neck," says she, and just went on pleatin' at her apron. Well, I went out and called Harry. I thought I might—need help. We went upstairs and there he was lyin'—

COUNTY ATTORNEY: I think I'd rather have you go into that upstairs, where you can point it all out. Just go on now with the rest of the story.

HALE: Well, my first thought was to get that rope off. It looked . . . *(Stops, his face twitches.)* . . . but Harry, he went up to him, and he said, "No, he's dead all right, and we'd better not touch anything." So we went back downstairs. She was still sitting that same way. "Has anybody been notified?" I asked. "No," says she, unconcerned. "Who did this, Mrs. Wright?" said Harry. He said it business-like—and she stopped pleatin' of her apron. "I don't know," she says. "You don't *know*?" says Harry. "No," says she. "Weren't you sleepin' in the bed with him?" says Harry. "Yes," says she, "but I was on the inside." "Somebody slipped a rope round his neck and strangled him and you didn't wake up?" says Harry. "I didn't wake up," she said after him. We must 'a' looked as if we didn't see how that could be, for after a minute she said, "I sleep sound." Harry was going to ask her more questions but I said maybe we ought to let her tell her story first to the coroner, or the sheriff, so Harry went fast as he could to Rivers' place, where there's a telephone.

COUNTY ATTORNEY: And what did Mrs. Wright do when she knew that you had gone for the coroner?

HALE: She moved from the rocker to that chair over there *(Pointing to a small chair in the downstage right corner.)* and just sat there with her hands held together and looking down. I got a feeling that I ought to make some conversation, so I said I had come in to see if John wanted to put in a telephone, and at that she started to laugh, and then she stopped and looked at me—scared. *(The* COUNTY ATTORNEY, *who has had his notebook out, makes a note.)* I dunno, maybe it wasn't scared. I wouldn't like to say it was. Soon Harry got back, and then Dr. Lloyd came, and you, Mr. Peters, and so I guess that's all I know that you don't.

COUNTY ATTORNEY *(rising and looking around)*: I guess we'll go upstairs first—and then out to the barn and around there. *(To the* SHERIFF.*)* You're convinced that there was nothing important here—nothing that would point to any motive?

SHERIFF: Nothing here but kitchen things.

(The COUNTY ATTORNEY, *after again looking around the kitchen, opens the door of a cupboard closet in right wall. He brings a small chair from right—gets up on it and looks on a shelf. Pulls his hand away, sticky.)*

COUNTY ATTORNEY: Here's a nice mess. *(The women draw nearer upstage center.)*

MRS. PETERS *(to the other woman)*: Oh, her fruit; it did freeze. *(To the* LAWYER.*)* She worried about that when it turned so cold. She said the fire'd go out and her jars would break.

SHERIFF *(rises)*: Well, can you beat the woman! Held for murder and worryin' about her preserves.

COUNTY ATTORNEY *(getting down from chair)*: I guess before we're through she may have something more serious than preserves to worry about. *(Crosses down right center.)*

HALE: Well, women are used to worrying over trifles. *(The two women move a little closer together.)*

COUNTY ATTORNEY *(with the gallantry of a young politician)*: And yet, for all their worries, what would we do without the ladies?

(The women do not unbend. He goes below the center table to the sink, takes a dipperful of water from the pail and pouring it into a basin, washes his hands. While he is doing this the SHERIFF *and* HALE *cross to cupboard, which they inspect. The* COUNTY ATTORNEY *starts to wipe his hands on the roller towel, turns it for a cleaner place.)*

Dirty towels! *(Kicks his foot against the pans under the sink.)* Not much of a housekeeper, would you say, ladies?

MRS. HALE *(stiffly)*: There's a great deal of work to be done on a farm.

COUNTY ATTORNEY: To be sure. And yet *(With a little bow to her.)* I know there are some Dickson County farmhouses which do not have such roller towels. *(He gives it a pull to expose its full length again.)*

MRS. HALE: Those towels get dirty awful quick. Men's hands aren't always as clean as they might be.

COUNTY ATTORNEY: Ah, loyal to your sex, I see. But you and Mrs. Wright were neighbors. I suppose you were friends, too.

MRS. HALE *(shaking her head)*: I've not seen much of her of late years. I've not been in this house—it's more than a year.

COUNTY ATTORNEY *(crossing to women upstage center)*: And why was that? You didn't like her?

MRS. HALE: I liked her all well enough. Farmers' wives have their hands full, Mr. Henderson. And then—

COUNTY ATTORNEY: Yes—?

MRS. HALE *(looking about)*: It never seemed a very cheerful place.

COUNTY ATTORNEY: No—it's not cheerful. I shouldn't say she had the homemaking instinct.

MRS. HALE: Well, I don't know as Wright had, either.

COUNTY ATTORNEY: You mean that they didn't get on very well?

MRS. HALE: No, I don't mean anything. But I don't think a place'd be any cheerfuller for John Wright's being in it.

COUNTY ATTORNEY: I'd like to talk more of that a little later. I want to get the lay of things upstairs now. *(He goes past the women to upstage right where steps lead to a stair door.)*

SHERIFF: I suppose anything Mrs. Peters does'll be all right. She was to take in some clothes for her, you know, and a few little things. We left in such a hurry yesterday.

COUNTY ATTORNEY: Yes, but I would like to see what you take, Mrs. Peters, and keep an eye out for anything that might be of use to us.

MRS. PETERS: Yes, Mr. Henderson.

(The men leave by upstage right door to stairs. The women listen to the men's steps on the stairs, then look about the kitchen.)

MRS. HALE *(crossing left to sink)*: I'd hate to have men coming into my kitchen, snooping around and criticizing.

(She arranges the pans under sink which the LAWYER *had shoved out of place.)*

MRS. PETERS: Of course, it's no more than their duty. *(Crosses to cupboard upstage right.)*

MRS. HALE: Duty's all right, but I guess that deputy sheriff that came out to make the fire might have got a little of this on. *(Gives the roller towel a pull.)* Wish I'd thought of that sooner. Seems mean to talk about her for not having things slicked up when she had to come away in such a hurry. *(Crosses right to* MRS. PETERS *at cupboard.)*

MRS. PETERS *(who has been looking through cupboard, lifts one end of a towel that covers a pan)*: She had bread set. *(Stands still.)*

MRS. HALE *(eyes fixed on a loaf of bread beside the breadbox, which is on a low shelf of the cupboard)*: She was going to put this in there. *(Picks up loaf, then abruptly drops it. In a manner of returning to familiar things.)* It's a shame about her fruit. I wonder if it's all gone. *(Gets up on the chair and looks.)* I think there's some here that's all right, Mrs. Peters. Yes—here; *(Holding it toward the window.)* this is cherries, too. *(Looking again.)* I declare I believe that's the only one. *(Gets down, jar in her hand. Goes to the sink and wipes it off on the outside.)* She'll feel awful bad after all her hard work in the hot weather. I remember the afternoon I put up my cherries last summer.

(She puts the jar on the big kitchen table, center of the room. With a sigh, is about to sit down in the rocking chair. Before she is seated realizes what chair it is; with a slow look at it, steps back. The chair which she has touched rocks back and forth. MRS. PETERS *moves to center table and they both watch the chair rock for a moment or two.)*

MRS. PETERS *(shaking off the mood which the empty rocking chair has evoked. Now in a businesslike manner she speaks)*: Well, I must get those things from the front room closet. *(She goes to the door at the right, but, after looking into the other room, steps back.)* You coming with me, Mrs. Hale? You could help me carry them. *(They go in the other room; reappear,* MRS. PETERS *carrying a dress, petticoat and skirt,* MRS. HALE *following with a pair of shoes.)* My, it's cold in there. *(She puts the clothes on the big table, and hurries to the stove.)*

MRS. HALE *(right of center table examining the skirt)*: Wright was close. I think maybe that's why she kept so much to herself. She didn't even belong to the Ladies' Aid. I suppose she felt she couldn't do her part, and then you don't enjoy things when you feel shabby. I heard she used to wear pretty clothes and be lively, when she was Minnie Foster, one of the town girls singing in the choir. But that—oh, that was thirty years ago. This all you was to take in?

MRS. PETERS: She said she wanted an apron. Funny thing to want, for there isn't much to get you dirty in jail, goodness knows. But I suppose just to make her feel more natural. *(Crosses to cupboard.)* She said they was in the top drawer in this cupboard. Yes, here. And then her little shawl that always hung behind the door. *(Opens stair door and looks.)* Yes, here it is. *(Quickly shuts door leading upstairs.)*

MRS. HALE *(abruptly moving toward her)*: Mrs. Peters?

MRS. PETERS: Yes, Mrs. Hale? *(At upstage right door.)*

MRS. HALE: Do you think she did it?

MRS. PETERS *(in a frightened voice)*: Oh, I don't know.

MRS. HALE: Well, I don't think she did. Asking for an apron and her little shawl. Worrying about her fruit.

MRS. PETERS *(starts to speak, glances up, where footsteps are heard in the room above. In a low voice)*: Mr. Peters says it looks bad for her. Mr. Henderson is awful sarcastic in a speech and he'll make fun of her sayin' she didn't wake up.

MRS. HALE: Well, I guess John Wright didn't wake when they was slipping that rope under his neck.

MRS. PETERS *(crossing slowly to table and placing shawl and apron on table with other clothing)*: No, it's strange. It must have been done awful crafty and still. They say it was such a—funny way to kill a man, rigging it all up like that.

MRS. HALE *(crossing to left of* MRS. PETERS *at table)*: That's just what Mr. Hale said. There was a gun in the house. He says that's what he can't understand.

MRS. PETERS: Mr. Henderson said coming out that what was needed for the case was a motive; something to show anger, or—sudden feeling.

MRS. HALE *(who is standing by the table)*: Well, I don't see any signs of anger around here. *(She puts her hand on the dish towel which lies on the table, stands looking down at table, one-half of which is clean, the other half messy.)* It's wiped to here. *(Makes a move as if to finish work, then turns and looks at loaf of bread outside the breadbox. Drops towel. In that voice of coming back to familiar things.)* Wonder how they are finding things upstairs. *(Crossing below table to downstage right.)* I hope she had it a little more red-up up there. You know, it seems kind of *sneaking*. Locking her up in town and then coming out here and trying to get her own house to turn against her!

MRS. PETERS: But, Mrs. Hale, the law is the law.

MRS. HALE: I s'pose 'tis. *(Unbuttoning her coat.)* Better loosen up your things, Mrs. Peters. You won't feel them when you go out.

*(*MRS. PETERS *takes off her fur tippet, goes to hang it on chair back left of table, stands looking at the work basket on floor near downstage left window.)*

MRS. PETERS: She was piecing a quilt.

(She brings the large sewing basket to the center table and they look at the bright pieces, MRS. HALE *above the table and* MRS. PETERS *left of it.)*

MRS. HALE: It's a log cabin pattern. Pretty, isn't it? I wonder if she was goin' to quilt it or just knot it?

(Footsteps have been heard coming down the stairs. The SHERIFF *enters followed by* HALE *and the* COUNTY ATTORNEY.*)*

SHERIFF: They wonder if she was going to quilt it or just knot it! *(The men laugh, the women look abashed.)*

COUNTY ATTORNEY *(rubbing his hands over the stove)*: Frank's fire didn't do much up there, did it? Well, let's go out to the barn and get that cleared up. *(The men go outside by upstage left door.)*

MRS. HALE *(resentfully)*: I don't know as there's anything so strange, our takin' up our time with little things while we're waiting for them to get the evidence. *(She sits in chair right of table smoothing out a block with decision.)* I don't see as it's anything to laugh about.

MRS. PETERS *(apologetically)*: Of course they've got awful important things on their minds. *(Pulls up a chair and joins* MRS. HALE *at the left of the table.)*

MRS. HALE *(examining another block)*: Mrs. Peters, look at this one. Here, this is the one she was working on, and look at the sewing! All the rest of it has been so nice and even. And look at this! It's all over the place! Why, it looks as if she didn't know what she was about!

(After she has said this they look at each other, then start to glance back at the door. After an instant MRS. HALE *has pulled at a knot and ripped the sewing.)*

MRS. PETERS: Oh, what are you doing, Mrs. Hale?

MRS. HALE *(mildly)*: Just putting out a stitch or two that's not sewed very good. *(Threading a needle.)* Bad sewing always made me fidgety.

MRS. PETERS *(with a glance at door, nervously)*: I don't think we ought to touch things.

MRS. HALE: I'll just finish up this end. *(Suddenly stopping and leaning forward.)* Mrs. Peters?

MRS. PETERS: Yes, Mrs. Hale?

MRS. HALE: What do you suppose she was so nervous about?

MRS. PETERS: Oh—I don't know. I don't know as she was nervous. I sometimes sew awful queer when I'm just tired. *(*MRS. HALE *starts to say something, looks at* MRS. PETERS, *then goes on sewing.)* Well, I must get these things wrapped up. They may be through sooner than we think. *(Putting apron and other things together.)* I wonder where I can find a piece of paper, and string. *(Rises.)*

MRS. HALE: In that cupboard, maybe.

MRS. PETERS *(crosses right looking in cupboard)*: Why, here's a bird-cage. *(Holds it up.)* Did she have a bird, Mrs. Hale?

MRS. HALE: Why, I don't know whether she did or not—I've not been here for so long. There was a man around last year selling canaries cheap, but I don't know as she took one; maybe she did. She used to sing real pretty herself.

MRS. PETERS *(glancing around)*: Seems funny to think of a bird here. But she must have had one, or why would she have a cage? I wonder what happened to it?

MRS. HALE: I s'pose maybe the cat got it.

MRS. PETERS: No, she didn't have a cat. She's got that feeling some people have about cats—being afraid of them. My cat got in her room and she was real upset and asked me to take it out.

MRS. HALE: My sister Bessie was like that. Queer, ain't it?

MRS. PETERS *(examining the cage)*: Why, look at this door. It's broke. One hinge is pulled apart. *(Takes a step down to* MRS. HALE's *right.)*

MRS. HALE *(looking too)*: Looks as if someone must have been rough with it.

MRS. PETERS: Why, yes. *(She brings the cage forward and puts it on the table.)*

MRS. HALE *(glancing toward upstage left door)*: I wish if they're going to find any evidence they'd be about it. I don't like this place.

MRS. PETERS: But I'm awful glad you came with me, Mrs. Hale. It would be lonesome for me sitting here alone.

MRS. HALE: It would, wouldn't it? *(Dropping her sewing.)* But I tell you what I do wish, Mrs. Peters. I wish I had come over sometimes when *she* was here. I—*(Looking around the room.)*—wish I had.

MRS. PETERS: But of course you were awful busy, Mrs. Hale—your house and your children.

MRS. HALE *(rises and crosses left)*: I could've come. I stayed away because it weren't cheerful—and that's why I ought to have come. I—*(Looking out left window.)*—I've never liked this place. Maybe because it's down in a hollow and you don't see the road. I dunno what it is, but it's a lonesome place and always was. I wish I had come over to see Minnie Foster sometimes. I can see now—*(Shakes her head.)*

MRS. PETERS *(left of table and above it)*: Well, you mustn't reproach yourself, Mrs. Hale. Somehow we just don't see how it is with other folks until—something turns up.

MRS. HALE: Not having children makes less work—but it makes a quiet house, and Wright out to work all day, and no company when he did come in. *(Turning from window.)* Did you know John Wright, Mrs. Peters?

MRS. PETERS: Not to know him; I've seen him in town. They say he was a good man.

MRS. HALE: Yes—good; he didn't drink, and kept his word as well as most, I guess, and paid his debts. But he was a hard man, Mrs. Peters. Just to pass the time of day with him— *(Shivers.)* Like a raw wind that gets to the bone. *(Pauses, her eye falling on the cage.)* I should think she would 'a' wanted a bird. But what do you suppose went with it?

MRS. PETERS: I don't know, unless it got sick and died.

(She reaches over and swings the broken door, swings it again, both women watch it.)

MRS. HALE: You weren't raised round here, were you? *(*MRS. PETERS *shakes her head.)* You didn't know—her?

MRS. PETERS: Not till they brought her yesterday.

MRS. HALE: She—come to think of it, she was kind of like a bird herself—real sweet and pretty, but kind of timid and—fluttery. How—she—did—change. *(Silence; then as if struck by a happy thought and relieved to get back to everyday things. Crosses right above* MRS. PETERS *to cupboard, replaces small chair used to stand on to its original place downstage right.)* Tell you what, Mrs. Peters, why don't you take the quilt in with you? It might take up her mind.

MRS. PETERS: Why, I think that's a real nice idea, Mrs. Hale. There couldn't possibly be any objection to it, could there? Now, just what would I take? I wonder if her patches are in here—and her things. *(They look in the sewing basket.)*

MRS. HALE *(crosses to right of table)*: Here's some red. I expect this has got sewing things in it. *(Brings out a fancy box.)* What a pretty box. Looks like something somebody would give you. Maybe her scissors are in here. *(Opens box. Suddenly puts her hand to her nose)*. Why— *(*MRS. PETERS *bends nearer, then turns her face away.)* There's something wrapped up in this piece of silk.

MRS. PETERS: Why, this isn't her scissors.

MRS. HALE *(lifting the silk)*: Oh, Mrs. Peters—it's— *(*MRS. PETERS *bends closer.)*

MRS. PETERS: It's the bird.

MRS. HALE: But, Mrs. Peters—look at it! Its neck! Look at its neck! It's all—other side *to.*

MRS. PETERS: Somebody—wrung—its—neck.

(Their eyes meet. A look of growing comprehension, of horror. Steps are heard outside. MRS. HALE *slips box under quilt pieces, and sinks into her chair. Enter* SHERIFF *and* COUNTY ATTORNEY. MRS. PETERS *steps downstage left and stands looking out of window.)*

COUNTY ATTORNEY *(as one turning from serious things to little pleasantries)*: Well, ladies, have you decided whether she was going to quilt it or knot it? *(Crosses to center above table.)*

MRS. PETERS: We think she was going to—knot it.

*(*SHERIFF *crosses to right of stove, lifts stove lid and glances at fire, then stands warming hands at stove.)*

COUNTY ATTORNEY: Well, that's interesting, I'm sure. *(Seeing the bird-cage.)* Has the bird flown?

MRS. HALE *(putting more quilt pieces over the box)*: We think the—cat got it.

COUNTY ATTORNEY *(preoccupied)*: Is there a cat? *(*MRS. HALE *glances in a quick covert way at* MRS. PETERS.*)*

MRS. PETERS *(turning from window takes a step in)*: Well, not *now.* They're superstitious, you know. They leave.

COUNTY ATTORNEY *(to* SHERIFF PETERS, *continuing an interrupted conversation)*: No sign at all of anyone having come from the outside. Their own rope. Now let's go up again and go over it piece by piece. *(They start upstairs.)* It would have to have been someone who knew just the—

*(*MRS. PETERS *sits down left of the table. The two women sit there not looking at one another, but as if peering into something and at the same time holding back. When they talk now it is in the manner of feeling their way over strange ground, as if afraid of what they are saying, but as if they cannot help saying it.)*

MRS. HALE *(hesitatively and in hushed voice)*: She liked the bird. She was going to bury it in that pretty box.

MRS. PETERS *(in a whisper):* When I was a girl—my kitten—there was a boy took a hatchet, and before my eyes—and before I could get there—*(Covers her face an instant.)* If they hadn't held me back I would have—*(Catches herself, looks upstairs where steps are heard, falters weakly.)*—hurt him.

MRS. HALE *(with a slow look around her)*: I wonder how it would seem never to have had any children around. *(Pause.)* No, Wright wouldn't like the bird—a thing that sang. She used to sing. He killed that, too.

MRS. PETERS *(moving uneasily)*: We don't know who killed the bird.

MRS. HALE: I knew John Wright.

MRS. PETERS: It was an awful thing was done in this house that night, Mrs. Hale. Killing a man while he slept, slipping a rope around his neck that choked the life out of him.

MRS. HALE: His neck. Choked the life out of him. *(Her hand goes out and rests on the birdcage.)*

MRS. PETERS *(with rising voice)*: We don't know who killed him. We don't *know.*

MRS. HALE *(her own feeling not interrupted)*: If there'd been years and years of nothing, then a bird to sing to you, it would be awful—still, after the bird was still.

MRS. PETERS *(something within her speaking)*: I know what stillness is. When we homesteaded in Dakota, and my first baby died—after he was two years old, and me with no other then—

MRS. HALE *(moving)*: How soon do you suppose they'll be through looking for the evidence?

MRS. PETERS: I know what stillness is. *(Pulling herself back.)* The law has got to punish crime, Mrs. Hale.

MRS. HALE *(not as if answering that)*: I wish you'd seen Minnie Foster when she wore a white dress with blue ribbons and stood up there in the choir and sang. *(A look around the room.)* Oh, I *wish* I'd come over here once in a while! That was a crime! That was a crime! Who's going to punish that?

MRS. PETERS *(looking upstairs)*: We mustn't—take on.

MRS. HALE: I might have known she needed help! I know how things can be—for women. I tell you, it's queer, Mrs. Peters. We live close together and we live far apart. We all go through the same things—it's all just a different kind of the same thing. *(Brushes her eyes, noticing the jar of fruit, reaches out for it.)* If I was you I wouldn't tell her her fruit was gone. Tell her it *ain't*. Tell her it's all right. Take this in to prove it to her. She—she may never know whether it was broke or not.

MRS. PETERS *(takes the jar, looks about for something to wrap it in; takes petticoat from the clothes brought from the other room, very nervously begins winding this around the jar. In a false voice)*: My, it's a good thing the men couldn't hear us. Wouldn't they just laugh! Getting all stirred up over a little thing like a—dead canary. As if that could have anything to do with—with—wouldn't they *laugh! (The men are heard coming downstairs.)*

MRS. HALE *(under her breath)*: Maybe they would—maybe they wouldn't.

COUNTY ATTORNEY: No, Peters, it's all perfectly clear except a reason for doing it. But you know juries when it comes to women. If there was some definite thing. *(Crosses slowly to above table.* SHERIFF *crosses downstage right* MRS. HALE *and* MRS. PETERS *remain seated at either side of table.)* Something to show—something to make a story about—a thing that would connect up with this strange way of doing it— *(The women's eyes meet for an instant. Enter* HALE *from outer door.)*

HALE *(remaining upstage left by door)*: Well, I've got the team around. Pretty cold out there.

COUNTY ATTORNEY: I'm going to stay awhile by myself. *(To the* SHERIFF.*)* You can send Frank out for me, can't you? I want to go over everything. I'm not satisfied we can't do better.

SHERIFF: Do you want to see what Mrs. Peters is going to take in? *(The* LAWYER *picks up the apron, laughs.)*

COUNTY ATTORNEY: Oh, I guess they're not very dangerous things the ladies have picked out. *(Moves a few things about, disturbing the quilt pieces which cover the box. Steps back.)* No, Mrs. Peters doesn't need supervising. For that matter a sheriff's wife is married to the law. Ever think of it that way, Mrs. Peters?

MRS. PETERS: Not—just that way.

SHERIFF *(chuckling)*: Married to the law. *(Moves to downstage right door to the other room.)* I just want you to come in here a minute, George. We ought to take a look at these windows.

COUNTY ATTORNEY *(scoffingly)*: Oh, windows!

SHERIFF: We'll be right out, Mr. Hale.

*(*HALE *goes outside. The* SHERIFF *follows the* COUNTY ATTORNEY *into the other room. Then* MRS. HALE *rises, hands tight together, looking intensely at* MRS. PETERS, *whose eyes make a slow turn, finally meeting* MRS. HALE's. *A moment* MRS. HALE *holds her, then her own eyes point the way to where the box is concealed. Suddenly* MRS. PETERS *throws back quilt pieces and tries to put the box in the bag she is carrying. It is too big. She opens box, starts to take bird out, cannot touch it, goes to pieces, stands there helpless. Sound of a knob turning in the other room.* MRS. HALE *snatches the box and puts it in the pocket of her big coat. Enter* COUNTY ATTORNEY *and* SHERIFF, *who remains downstage right.)*

COUNTY ATTORNEY *(crosses to upstage left door facetiously)*: Well, Henry, at least we found out that she was not going to quilt it. She was going to—what is it you call it, ladies.

MRS. HALE *(standing center below table facing front, her hand against her pocket)*: We call it—knot it, Mr. Henderson.

Curtain.

Questions

1. What is the significance of the title? Support your answer through specific instances in the play.
2. Why do you think the women were more perceptive in discovering motive than the men, who supposedly were trained to look for such things?
3. Find examples of the men's patronizing of the women. Why do you think they do this? Do you think this attitude was more common at the time the play was written than it is today?
4. Do you think the women should have concealed the motive for the murder? Do you feel sympathetic toward Mrs. Wright? Why or why not?

5. The play has many examples of sexual chauvinism, both male and female. Try to find as many as you can and discuss probable reasons.
6. Do you think *Trifles* is a well-written play? Do you like it? Why or why not?
7. From evidence provided in the play, can you speculate on Susan Glaspell's manner of looking at life? How do you think she viewed the world?
8. What makes this play a melodrama? How is it typical of this form of drama? How is it atypical?

LUCILLE FLETCHER

Sorry, Wrong Number

LUCILLE FLETCHER was born in Brooklyn, New York, in 1913, and attended Vassar College. She wrote a number of novels, two in collaboration with Allan Ullman—*Sorry, Wrong Number* and *Night Man*. She wrote several other novels and a number of radio and television plays.

SORRY, WRONG NUMBER has been presented as a radio play, a film, a stage play, and a television show. Even though it presents characters who are one-dimensional, audience members identify with Mrs. Stephenson and worry about what will happen to her.

The play is a typical melodrama in its use of shallow characters, its reliance on coincidence, its exaggeration of circumstances, and its foreboding atmosphere.

Sorry, Wrong Number Lucille Fletcher

Characters:

MRS. STEVENSON
1ST OPERATOR
1ST MAN
2ND MAN
CHIEF OPERATOR
2ND OPERATOR
3RD OPERATOR
4TH OPERATOR
5TH OPERATOR
INFORMATION
HOSPITAL RECEPTIONIST
WESTERN UNION
SERGEANT DUFFY
A LUNCH ROOM COUNTER ATTENDANT

Setting:

As curtain rises, we see a divided stage, only the center part of which is lighted and furnished as MRS. STEVENSON's *bedroom. Expensive, rather fussy furnishings. A large bed, on which* MRS. STEVENSON, *clad in bed-jacket, is lying. A night-table close by, with phone, lighted lamp, and pill bottles. A mantel, with clock, right. A closed door, right. A window, with curtains closed, rear. The set is lit by one lamp on night-table. It is enclosed by three flats. Beyond this central set, the stage, on either side, is in darkness.*

MRS. STEVENSON *is dialing a number on phone, as curtain rises. She listens to phone, slams down receiver in irritation. As she does so, we hear sound of a train roaring by in the distance. She reaches for her pill bottle, pours herself a glass of water, shakes out pill, swallows it, then reaches for phone again, dials number nervously.* SOUND: *Number being dialed on phone: Busy signal.*

MRS. STEVENSON *(a querulous, self-centered neurotic):* Oh—*dear! (Slams down receiver. Dials* OPERATOR.*)*

*(*SCENE: *A spotlight, left of side flat, picks up out of peripheral darkness, figure of* 1ST OPERATOR, *sitting with headphones at small table. If spotlight not available, use flashlight, clicked on by* 1ST OPERATOR, *illumining her face.)*

OPERATOR: Your call, please?

MRS. STEVENSON: Operator? I have been dialing Murray Hill 4-0098 now for the last three-quarters of an hour, and the line is always busy. But I don't see how it *could* be busy that long. Will you try it for me, please?

OPERATOR: Murray Hill 4-0098? One moment, please. *(SCENE: She makes gesture of plugging in call through a switchboard.)*

MRS. STEVENSON: I don't see how it could be busy all this time. It's my husband's office. He's working late tonight, and I'm all alone here in the house. My health is very poor—and I've been feeling so nervous all day. . . .

OPERATOR: Ringing Murray Hill 4-0098. . . .

(SOUND: Phone buzz. It rings three times. Receiver is picked up at other end. (SCENE: Spotlight picks up figure of a heavy-set man, seated at desk with phone on right side of dark periphery of stage. He is wearing a hat. Picks up phone, which rings three times.)

MAN: Hello.

MRS. STEVENSON: Hello . . . ? *(A little puzzled.)* Hello. Is Mr. Stevenson there?

MAN *(into phone, as though he had not heard)*: Hello . . . . *(Louder.)* Hello.

(SCENE: Spotlight on left now moves from OPERATOR *to another man,* GEORGE. *A killer type, also wearing hat, but standing as in a phone booth. A three-sided screen may be used to suggest this.)*

2ND MAN *(slow heavy quality, faintly foreign accent)*: Hello.

1ST MAN: Hello. George?

GEORGE: Yes, sir.

MRS. STEVENSON *(louder and more imperious, to phone)*: Hello. Who's this? What number am I calling, please?

1ST MAN: We have heard from our client. He says the coast is clear for tonight.

GEORGE: Yes, sir.

1ST MAN: Where are you now?

GEORGE: In a phone booth.

1ST MAN: Okay. You know the address. At eleven o'clock the private patrolman goes around to the bar on Second Avenue for a beer. Be sure that all the lights downstairs are out. There should be only one light visible from the street. At eleven-fifteen a subway train crosses the bridge. It makes a noise in case her window is open, and she should scream.

MRS. STEVENSON *(shocked)*: Oh—HELLO! What number is this, please?

GEORGE: Okay. I understand.

1ST MAN: Make it quick. As little blood as possible. Our client does not wish to make her suffer long.

GEORGE: A knife okay, sir?

1ST MAN: Yes. A knife will be okay. And remember—remove the rings and bracelets, and the jewelry in the bureau drawer. Our client wishes it to look like simple robbery.

GEORGE: Okay—I get—

*(*SCENE: *Spotlight suddenly goes out on* GEORGE.*)* *(*SOUND: *A bland buzzing signal.)* *(*SCENE: *Spotlight goes off on* 1ST MAN.*)*

MRS. STEVENSON *(clicking phone):* Oh . . . ! *(Bland buzzing signal continues. She hangs up):* How awful! How unspeakably . . .

*(*SCENE: *She lies back on her pillows, overcome for a few seconds, then suddenly pulls herself together, reaches for phone.)* *(*SOUND: *Dialing. Phone buzz.)* *(*SCENE: *Spotlight goes on at* 1ST OPERATOR's *switchboard,* 1ST *and* 2ND MAN *exit as unobtrusively as possible, in darkness.)*

OPERATOR: Your call, please?

MRS. STEVENSON *(unnerved and breathless, into phone):* Operator. I—I've just been cut off.

OPERATOR: I'm sorry, madam. What number were you calling?

MRS. STEVENSON: Why—it was supposed to be Murray Hill 4-0098, but it wasn't. Some wires must have crossed—I was cut into a wrong number—and—I've just heard the most dreadful thing—a—a murder—and—*(Imperiously.)* Operator, you'll simply have to retrace that call at once.

OPERATOR: I beg your pardon, madam—I don't quite—

MRS. STEVENSON: Oh—I know it was a wrong number, and I had no business listening—but these two men—they were cold-blooded fiends—and they were going to murder somebody—some poor innocent woman—who was all alone—in a house near a bridge. And we've got to stop them—we've got to—

OPERATOR *(patiently)*: What number were you calling, madam?

MRS. STEVENSON: That doesn't matter. This was a *wrong* number. And *you* dialed it. And we've got to find out what it was—immediately!

OPERATOR: But—madam—

MRS. STEVENSON: Oh—why are you so stupid? Look—it was obviously a case of some little slip of the finger. I told you to try Murray Hill 4-0098 for me—you dialed it but your finger must have slipped—and I was connected with some other number—and I could hear them, but they couldn't hear me. Now, I simply fail to see why you couldn't make that same mistake again—on purpose—why you couldn't *try* to dial Murray Hill 4-0098 in the same careless sort of way. . . .

OPERATOR *(quickly)*: Murray Hill 4-0098? I will try to get it for you, madam.

MRS. STEVENSON *(sarcastically)*: *Thank* you.

(SCENE: *She bridles, adjusts herself on her pillows, reaches for handkerchief, wipes forehead, glancing uneasily for a moment toward window, while still holding phone.) (Sound of ringing: Busy signal.)*

OPERATOR: I am sorry. Murray Hill 4-0098 is busy.

MRS. STEVENSON *(frantically clicking receiver)*: Operator. Operator.

OPERATOR: Yes, Madam.

MRS. STEVENSON *(angrily)*: You *didn't* try to get that wrong number at all. I asked explicitly. And all you did was dial correctly.

OPERATOR: I am sorry. What number were you calling?

MRS. STEVENSON: Can't you, for once, forget what number I was calling, and do something specific? Now I want to trace that call. It's my civic duty—it's *your* civic duty—to trace that call. . . and to apprehend those dangerous killers—and if *you* won't. . .

OPERATOR *(glancing around wearily)*: I will connect you with the Chief Operator.

MRS. STEVENSON: *Please! (Sound of ringing.)*

(SCENE: OPERATOR *puts hand over mouthpiece of phone, gestures into darkness. A half whisper:)*

OPERATOR: Miss Curtis. Will you pick up on 17, please?

(MISS CURTIS, *Chief Operator, enters. Middle-aged, efficient type, pleasant. Wearing headphones.)*

MISS CURTIS: Yes, dear. What's the trouble?

OPERATOR: Somebody wanting a call traced. I can't make head nor tail of it. . . .

MISS CURTIS *(sitting down at desk, as* OPERATOR *gets up):* Sure, dear. 17? *(She makes gesture of plugging in her headphone, coolly and professionally.)* This is the Chief Operator.

MRS. STEVENSON: Chief Operator? I want you to trace a call. A telephone call. Immediately. I don't know where it came from, or who was making it, but it's absolutely necessary that it be tracked down. Because it was about a murder. Yes, a terrible, cold-blooded murder of a poor innocent woman—tonight—at eleven-fifteen.

CHIEF OPERATOR: I see.

MRS. STEVENSON *(high-strung, demanding)*: Can you trace it for me? Can you track down those men?

CHIEF OPERATOR: It depends, madam.

MRS. STEVENSON: Depends on what?

CHIEF OPERATOR: It depends on whether the call is still going on. If it's a live call, we can trace it on the equipment. If it's been disconnected, we can't.

MRS. STEVENSON: Disconnected?

CHIEF OPERATOR: If the parties have stopped talking to each other.

MRS. STEVENSON: Oh—but—but of course they must have stopped talking to each other by *now.* That was at least five minutes ago—and they didn't sound like the type who would make a long call.

CHIEF OPERATOR: Well, I can try tracing it. *(*SCENE: *She takes pencil out of her hair-do.)* Now—what is your name, madam?

MRS. STEVENSON: Mrs. Stevenson. Mrs. Elbert Stevenson. But—listen—

CHIEF OPERATOR *(writing it down)*: And your telephone number?

MRS. STEVENSON *(more irritated)*: Plaza 4-2295. But if you go on wasting all this time— *(*SCENE: *She glances at clock on mantel.)*

CHIEF OPERATOR: And what is your reason for wanting this call traced?

MRS. STEVENSON: My reason? Well—for Heaven's sake—isn't it obvious? I overhear two men—they're killers—they're planning to murder this woman—it's a matter for the police.

CHIEF OPERATOR: Have you told the police?

MRS. STEVENSON: No. How could I?

CHIEF OPERATOR: You're making this check into a private call purely as a private individual?

MRS. STEVENSON: Yes. But meanwhile—

CHIEF OPERATOR: Well, Mrs. Stevenson—I seriously doubt whether we could make this check for you at this time just on your say-so as a private individual. We'd have to have something more official.

MRS. STEVENSON: Oh—for Heaven's sake! You mean to tell me I can't report a murder without getting tied up in all this redtape? Why—it's perfectly idiotic. All right, then. I *will* call the police. *(She slams down receiver.) (*SCENE: *Spotlight goes off on two* OPERATORS.*)* Ridiculous!

*(Sound of dialing.) (*SCENE: MRS. STEVENSON *dials numbers on phone, as two* OPERATORS *exit unobtrusively in darkness.) (On right of stage, spotlight picks up a* 2ND OPERATOR, *seated like first, with headphones at table [same one vacated by* 1ST MAN*].)*

2ND OPERATOR: Your call, please?

MRS. STEVENSON *(very annoyed)*: The Police Department—*please.*

2ND OPERATOR: Ringing the Police Department.

*(Ring twice. Phone is picked up.) (*SCENE: *left stage, at table vacated by* 1ST *and* CHIEF OPERATOR, *spotlight now picks up* SERGEANT DUFFY, *seated in a relaxed position. Just entering beside him is a young man in cap and apron, carrying a large brown paper parcel, delivery boy for a local lunch counter. Phone is ringing.)*

YOUNG MAN: Here's your lunch, Sarge. They didn't have no jelly doughnuts, so I give you French crullers.[1] Okay, Sarge?

1. A sweet roll in a twisted shape.

S. DUFFY: French crullers. I got ulcers. Whyn't you make it apple pie? *(Picks up phone, which has rung twice.)* Police department. Precinct 43. Duffy speaking.

(SCENE: LUNCHROOM ATTENDANT, *anxiously.* We don't have no apple pie, either, Sarge—)

MRS. STEVENSON: Police Department? Oh. This is Mrs. Stevenson—Mrs. Elbert Smythe Stevenson of 53 North Sutton Place. I'm calling up to report a murder.

(SCENE: DUFFY *has been examining lunch, but double-takes suddenly on above.)*

DUFFY: Eh?

MRS. STEVENSON: I mean—the murder hasn't been committed yet. I just overheard plans for it over the telephone . . . over a wrong number that the operator gave me. (SCENE: DUFFY *relaxes, sighs, starts taking lunch from bag.)* I've been trying to trace down the call myself, but everybody is so stupid—and I guess in the end you're the only people who could *do* anything.

DUFFY *(not too impressed)*: (SCENE: ATTENDANT, *who exits.)* Yes, ma'am.

MRS. STEVENSON *(trying to impress him)*: It was a perfectly *definite* murder. I heard their plans distinctly. (SCENE: DUFFY *begins to eat sandwich, phone at his ear.)* Two men were talking, and they were going to murder some woman at eleven-fifteen tonight—she lived in a house near a bridge.

DUFFY: Yes, ma'am.

MRS. STEVENSON: And there was a private patrolman on the street. He was going to go around for a beer on Second Avenue. And there was some third man—a client, who was paying to have this poor woman murdered—they were going to take her rings and bracelets—and use a knife . . . well, it's unnerved me dreadfully—and I'm not well. . . .

DUFFY: I see. (SCENE: *Having finished sandwich, he wipes mouth with paper napkin.)* When was all this, ma'am?

MRS. STEVENSON: About eight minutes ago. Oh . . . *(Relieved.)* Then you *can* do something? You *do* understand—

DUFFY: And what is your name, ma'am? (SCENE: *He reaches for pad.)*

MRS. STEVENSON *(impatiently)*: Mrs. Stevenson. Mrs. Elbert Stevenson.

DUFFY: And your address?

MRS. STEVENSON: 53 North Sutton Place. *That's* near a bridge. The Queensboro Bridge, you know—and *we* have a private patrolman on *our* street—and Second Avenue—

DUFFY: And what was that number you were calling?

MRS. STEVENSON: Murray Hill 4-0098. (SCENE: DUFFY *writes it down.)* But—that wasn't the number I overheard. I mean Murray Hill 4-0098 is my husband's office. (SCENE: DUFFY, *in exasperation, holds pencil poised.)* He's working late tonight, and I was trying to reach him to ask him to come home. I'm an invalid, you know—and it's the maid's night off—and I *hate* to be alone—even though he says I'm perfectly safe as long as I have the telephone right beside my bed.

DUFFY *(stolidly)*: (SCENE: *He has put pencil down, pushes pad away.)* Well—we'll look into it, Mrs. Stevenson—and see if we can check it with the telephone company.

MRS. STEVENSON *(getting impatient)*: But the telephone company said they couldn't check the call if the parties had stopped talking. I've already taken care of *that.*

DUFFY: Oh—yes? (SCENE: *He yawns slightly.)*

MRS. STEVENSON *(high-handed)*: Personally I feel you ought to do something far more immediate and drastic than just check the call. What good does checking the call do, if they've stopped talking? By the time you track it down, they'll already have committed the murder.

DUFFY (SCENE: *He reaches for paper cup of coffee.)* Well—we'll take care of it, lady. Don't worry. (SCENE: *He begins to take off paper top of coffee container.)*

MRS. STEVENSON: I'd say the whole thing calls for a search—a complete and thorough search of the whole city. (SCENE: DUFFY *puts down phone for a moment, to work on cup, as her voice continues.)* I'm very near a bridge, and I'm not far from Second Avenue. And I know *I'd* feel a whole lot better if you sent around a radio car to *this* neighborhood at once.

DUFFY (SCENE: *Picks up phone again, drinks coffee)*: And what makes you think the murder's going to be committed in your neighborhood, ma'am?

MRS. STEVENSON: Oh—I don't know. The coincidence is so horrible. Second Avenue—the patrolman—the bridge . . .

DUFFY (SCENE: *He sips coffee)*: Second Avenue is a very long street, ma'am. And do you happen to know how many bridges there are in the city of New York alone? Not to mention Brooklyn, Staten Island, Queens, and the Bronx? And how do you know there isn't some little house out on Staten Island—on some little Second Avenue you never heard about? (SCENE: *A long gulp of coffee.)* How do you know they were even talking about New York at all?

MRS. STEVENSON: But I heard the call on the New York dialing system.

DUFFY: How do you know it wasn't a long distance call you overheard? Telephones are funny things. (SCENE: *He sets down coffee.)* Look, lady, why don't you look at it this way? Supposing you hadn't broken in on that telephone call? Supposing you'd got your husband the way you always do? Would this murder have made any difference to you then?

MRS. STEVENSON: I suppose not. But it's so inhuman—so cold-blooded . . .

DUFFY: A lot of murders are committed in this city every day, ma'am. If we could do something to stop 'em, we would. But a clue of this kind that's so vague isn't much more use to us than no clue at all.

MRS. STEVENSON: But, surely—

DUFFY: Unless, of course, you have some reason for thinking this call is phoney—and that someone may be planning to murder *you?*

MRS. STEVENSON: *Me?* Oh—no—I hardly think so. I—I mean—why should anybody? I'm alone all day and night—I see nobody except my maid Eloise—she's a big two-hundred-pounder—she's too lazy to bring up my breakfast tray—and the only other person is my husband Elbert—he's crazy about me—adores me—waits on me hand and foot—he's scarcely left my side since I took sick twelve years ago—

DUFFY: Well—then—there's nothing for you to worry about, is there? *(*SCENE: LUNCHROOM ATTENDANT *has entered. He is carrying a piece of apple pie on a plate. Points it out to* DUFFY *triumphantly.)* And now—if you'll just leave the rest of this to us—

MRS. STEVENSON: But what will you *do?* It's so late—it's nearly eleven o'clock.

DUFFY *(firmly)*: (SCENE: *He nods to* ATTENDANT, *pleased.)* We'll take care of it, lady.

MRS. STEVENSON: Will you broadcast it all over the city? And send out squads? And warn your radio cars to watch out—especially in suspicious neighborhoods like mine?

*(*SCENE: ATTENDANT, *in triumph, has put pie down in front of* DUFFY. *Takes fork out of his pocket, stands at attention, waiting.)*

DUFFY *(more firmly)*: Lady, I *said* we'd take care of it. *(*SCENE: *Glances at pie.)* Just now I've got a couple of other matters here on my desk that require my immediate—

MRS. STEVENSON: Oh! *(She slams down receiver hard.)* Idiot. *(*SCENE: DUFFY, *listening at phone, hangs up. Shrugs. Winks at* ATTENDANT *as though to say, "What a crazy character!" Attacks his pie as spotlight fades out). (*MRS. STEVENSON, *in bed, looking at phone nervously.)* Now—why did I do that? Now—he'll think I *am* a fool. *(*SCENE: *She sits there tensely, then throws herself back against pillows, lies there a moment, whimpering with self-pity.)* Oh—why doesn't Elbert come home? *Why* doesn't he?

*(*SCENE: *We hear sound of train roaring by in the distance. She sits up reaching for phone.) (Sound of dialing operator). (*SCENE: *Spotlight picks up* 2ND OPERATOR, *seated right.)*

OPERATOR: Your call, please?

MRS. STEVENSON: Operator—for Heaven's sake—will you ring that Murray

Hill 4-0098 number again? I can't think what's keeping him so long.

OPERATOR: Ringing Murray Hill 4-0098. *(Rings. Busy signal.)* The line is busy. Shall I—

MRS. STEVENSON *(nastily)*: I can hear it. You don't have to tell me. I know it's busy. *(Slams down receiver.)* (SCENE: *Spotlight fades off on* 2ND OPERATOR.) (SCENE: MRS. STEVENSON *sinks back against pillows again, whimpering to herself fretfully. She glances at clock, then turning, punches her pillows up, trying to make herself comfortable. But she isn't. Whimpers to herself as she squirms restlessly in bed.)* If I could only get out of this bed for a little while. If I could get a breath of fresh air—or just lean out the window—and see the street. . . . (SCENE: *She sighs, reaches for pill bottle, shakes out a pill. As she does so:) (The phone rings. She darts for it instantly.)* Hello. Elbert? Hello. Hello. Hello. Oh—what's the *matter* with this phone? HELLO? HELLO? *(Slams down the receiver.)* (SCENE: *She stares at it tensely.) (The phone rings again. Once. She picks it up.)* Hello? Hello. . . . Oh—for Heaven's sake—who *is* this? Hello. Hello. HELLO. *(Slams down receiver. Dials operator.)* (SCENE: *Spotlight comes on left, showing* 3RD OPERATOR, *at spot vacated by* DUFFY.)

3RD OPERATOR: Your call, please?

MRS. STEVENSON *(very annoyed and imperious)*: Hello. Operator. I don't know what's the matter with this telephone tonight, but it's positively driving me crazy. I've never seen such inefficient, miserable service. Now, look. I'm an invalid, and I'm very nervous, and I'm *not* supposed to be annoyed. But if this keeps on much longer. . .

3RD OPERATOR *(a young sweet type)*: What seems to be the trouble, madam?

MRS. STEVENSON: Well—everything's wrong. The whole world could be murdered, for all you people care. And now—my phone keeps ringing. . . .

OPERATOR: Yes, madam?

MRS. STEVENSON: Ringing and ringing and ringing every five seconds or so, and when I pick it up, there's no one there.

OPERATOR: I am sorry, madam. If you will hang up, I will test it for you.

MRS. STEVENSON: I don't want you to test it for me. I want you to put through that call—whatever it is—at once.

OPERATOR *(gently)*: I am afraid that is not possible, madam.

MRS. STEVENSON *(storming)*: Not possible? And why—may I ask?

OPERATOR: The system is automatic, madam. If someone is trying to dial your number, there is no way to check whether the call is coming through the system or not—unless the person who is trying to reach you complains to his particular operator—

MRS. STEVENSON: Well, of all the stupid, complicated. . .! And meanwhile *I've* got to sit here in my bed, *suffering* every time that phone rings—imagining everything. . . .

OPERATOR: I will try to check it for you, madam.

MRS. STEVENSON: Check it! Check it! That's all anybody can do. Of all the stupid, idiotic...! *(She hangs up.)* Oh—what's the use... (SCENE: 3RD OPERATOR *fades out of spotlight, as) (Instantly* MRS. STEVENSON'S *phone rings again. She picks up receiver. Wildly.)* Hello. HELLO. Stop ringing, do you hear me? Answer me? What do you want? Do you realize you're driving me crazy? (SCENE: *Spotlight goes on right. We see a* MAN *in eye-shade and shirt-sleeves, at desk with phone and telegrams.)* Stark, staring...

MAN *(dull flat voice):* Hello. Is this Plaza 4-2295?

MRS. STEVENSON *(catching her breath)*: Yes. Yes. This is Plaza 4-2295.

WESTERN UNION: This is Western Union. I have a telegram here for Mrs. Elbert Stevenson. Is there anyone there to receive the message?

MRS. STEVENSON *(trying to calm herself)*: I am Mrs. Stevenson.

WESTERN UNION *(reading flatly)*: The telegram is as follows: "Mrs. Elbert Stevenson. 53 North Sutton Place, New York, New York. Darling. Terribly sorry. Tried to get you for last hour, but line busy. Leaving for Boston eleven p. m. tonight on urgent business. Back tomorrow afternoon. Keep happy. Love. Signed. Elbert."

MRS. STEVENSON *(breathlessly, aghast, to herself)*: Oh...no...

WESTERN UNION: (That is all, madam. Do you wish us to deliver a copy of the message?

MRS. STEVENSON: No—no, thank you.

WESTERN UNION: Thank you, madam. Good night. *(He hangs up phone.)* (SCENE: *Spotlight on* WESTERN UNION *immediately out.)*

MRS. STEVENSON *(mechanically, to phone)*: Good night. *(She hangs up slowly. Suddenly bursting into.)* No—no—it isn't true! He couldn't do it! Not when he knows I'll be all alone. It's some trick—some fiendish...

(SCENE: *We hear sound of train roaring by outside. She half rises in bed, in panic, glaring toward curtains. Her movements are frenzied. She beats with her knuckles on bed, then suddenly stops, and reaches for phone. She dials operator.)* (SCENE: *Spotlight picks up* 4TH OPERATOR, *seated left.)*

OPERATOR *(coolly)*: Your call, please?

MRS. STEVENSON: Operator—try that Murray Hill 4-0098 number for me just once more, please.

OPERATOR: Ringing Murray Hill 4-0098. *(Call goes through. We hear ringing at other end. Ring after ring.)*

(SCENE: *If telephone noises are not used audibly, have* OPERATOR *say after a brief pause: "They do not answer.")*

MRS. STEVENSON: He's gone. Oh—Elbert, how could you? How could you...? *(She hangs up phone, sobbing pityingly to herself, turning rest-*

lessly.) (SCENE: *Spotlight goes out on* 4TH OPERATOR.) But I can't be alone tonight. I can't. If I'm alone one more second . . . (SCENE: *She runs hands wildly through hair.)* I don't care what he says—or what the expense is—I'm a sick woman—I'm entitled . . .

(SCENE: *With trembling fingers she picks up receiver again.) (She dials* INFORMATION. SCENE: *The spotlight picks up* INFORMATION OPERATOR, *seated right.)*

INFORMATION: This is information.

MRS. STEVENSON: I want the telephone number of Henchley Hospital.

INFORMATION: Henchley Hospital? Do you have the address, madam?

MRS. STEVENSON: No. It's somewhere in the 70's, though. It's a very small, private and exclusive hospital where I had my appendix out two years ago. Henchley. H-E-N-C—

INFORMATION: One moment, please.

MRS. STEVENSON: Please—hurry. And please—what *is* the time?

INFORMATION: I do not know, madam. You may find out the time by dialing Meridan 7-1212.

MRS. STEVENSON *(irritated)*: Oh—for Heaven's sake! Couldn't you—?

INFORMATION: The number of Henchley Hospital is Butterfield 7-0105, madam.

MRS. STEVENSON: Butterfield 7-0105.

(She hangs up before she finishes speaking, and immediately dials number as she repeats it. SCENE: *Spotlight goes out on* INFORMATION. *Phone rings.* SCENE: *Spotlight picks up* WOMAN *in nurse's uniform, seated at desk, left.)*

WOMAN *(middle-aged, solid, firm, practical)*: Henchley Hospital, good evening.

MRS. STEVENSON: Nurses' Registry.

WOMAN: Who was it you wished to speak to, please?

MRS. STEVENSON *(high-handed)*: I want the Nurses' Registry at once. I want a trained nurse. I want to hire her immediately. For the night.

WOMAN: I see. And what is the nature of the case, madam?

MRS. STEVENSON: Nerves. I'm very nervous. I need soothing—and companionship. My husband is away—and I'm—

WOMAN: Have you been recommended to us by any doctor in particular, madam?

MRS. STEVENSON: No. But I really don't see why all this catechizing is necessary. I want a trained nurse. I was a patient in your hospital two years ago. And after all, I *do* expect to *pay* this person—

WOMAN: We quite understand that, madam. But registered nurses are very scarce just now—and our superintendent has asked us to send people out only on cases where the physician in charge feels it is absolutely necessary.

MRS. STEVENSON *(growing hysterical)*: Well—it *is* absolutely necessary. I'm a sick woman. I—I'm very upset. Very. I'm alone in this house—and I'm an invalid—and tonight I overheard a telephone conversation that upset me dreadfully. About a murder—a poor woman who was going to be murdered at eleven-fifteen tonight—in fact, if someone doesn't come at once—I'm afraid I'll go out of my mind. . . . *(Almost off handle by now.)*

WOMAN *(calmly)*: I see. Well—I'll speak to Miss Phillips as soon as she comes in. And what is your name, madam?

MRS. STEVENSON: Miss Phillips. And when do you expect her in?

WOMAN: I really don't know, madam. She went out to supper at eleven o'clock.

MRS. STEVENSON: Eleven o'clock. But it's not eleven yet. *(She cries out.)* Oh, my clock *has* stopped. I thought it was running down. What time is it? *(*SCENE: WOMAN *glances at wristwatch.)*

WOMAN: Just fourteen minutes past eleven. . . .

(Sound of phone receiver being lifted on same line as MRS. STEVENSON's. *A click.)*

MRS. STEVENSON *(crying out)*: What's *that?*

WOMAN: What was what, madam?

MRS. STEVENSON: That—that click just now—in my own telephone? As though someone had lifted the receiver off the hook of the extension phone downstairs. . . .

WOMAN: I didn't hear it, madam. Now—about this. . .

MRS. STEVENSON *(scared)*: But I *did*. There's someone in this house. Someone downstairs in the kitchen. And they're listening to me now. They're. . . *(*SCENE: *She puts hand over her mouth. Hangs up phone.* SCENE: *She sits there, in terror, frozen, listening. In a suffocated voice.)* I won't pick it up, I won't let them hear me. I'll be quiet—and they'll think. . . *(With growing terror.)* But if I don't call someone now—while they're still down there—there'll be no time. . . .

(She picks up receiver. Bland buzzing signal. She dials operator. Ring twice. SCENE: *On second ring, spotlight goes on right. We see* 5TH OPERATOR.*)*

OPERATOR *(fat and lethargic)*: Your call, please?

MRS. STEVENSON *(a desperate whisper)*: Operator—I—I'm in desperate trouble. . . I—

OPERATOR: I cannot hear you, madam. Please speak louder.

MRS. STEVENSON *(still whispering)*: I don't dare. I—there's someone listening. Can you hear me now?

OPERATOR: Your call, please? What number are you calling, madam?

MRS. STEVENSON *(desperately)*: You've got to hear me. Oh—please. You've got to help me. There's someone in this house. Someone who's going to murder me. And you've got to get in touch with the. . . *(Click of receiver being put down on* MRS. STEVENSON's *line. Bursting out wildly.)* Oh—there it is. . . he's put it down. . . he's coming. . . *(She screams.)* He's coming up the stairs. . . (SCENE: *She thrashes in bed, phone cord catching in lamp wire, lamp topples, goes out. Darkness. Hoarsely.)* Give me the Police Department. . . . (SCENE: *We see on the dark center stage, the shadow of door opening. Screaming.)* The police!. . .

(SCENE: *On stage, swift rush of a shadow, advancing to bed—sound of her voice is choked out, as)*

OPERATOR: Ringing the Police Department.

(Phone is rung. We hear sound of a train beginning to fade in. On second ring, MRS. STEVENSON *screams again, but roaring of train drowns out her voice. For a few seconds we hear nothing but roaring of train, then dying away, phone at police headquarters ringing.* SCENE: *Spotlight goes on* DUFFY, *left stage.)*

DUFFY: Police Department. Precinct 43. Duffy speaking. *(Pause.* SCENE: *Nothing visible but darkness on center stage.)* Police Department. Duffy speaking.

(SCENE: *A flashlight goes on, illuminating open phone to one side of* MRS. STEVENSON's *bed. Nearby, hanging down, is her lifeless hand. We see the second man,* GEORGE, *in black gloves, reach down and pick up phone. He is breathing hard.)*

GEORGE: Sorry. Wrong number.

(Hangs up. SCENE: *He replaces receiver on hook quietly, exits, as* DUFFY *hangs up with a shrug, and* CURTAIN FALLS.*)*

Questions

1. What creates the feeling of suspense? How is this feeling intensified?
2. When do you first begin to suspect that Mrs. Stevenson is the intended murder victim?
3. Why do you suppose the Operator says she has difficulty understanding Mrs. Stevenson? Is this believable?

4. Why is Duffy, the policeman, so inattentive and bored when Mrs. Stevenson calls him?
5. Do you like Mrs. Stevenson? Why or why not? Use three or four adjectives that describe her character.
6. Why do you suppose the playwright had Mrs. Stevenson complain about her maid?

Tragicomedy

Another genre that mingles elements of the comic and serious is tragicomedy. The term is paradoxical in that a protagonist who is truly noble cannot appear comic, nor can a comic protagonist possess the scope of a tragic hero. Nevertheless, some playwrights do mingle comic and tragic elements, but it takes a skillful writer to do this without confusing the audience. Often a situation appears comic, but later the audience realizes it is serious. Tragicomedy generally tries to show how life intermingles the comic and the tragic.

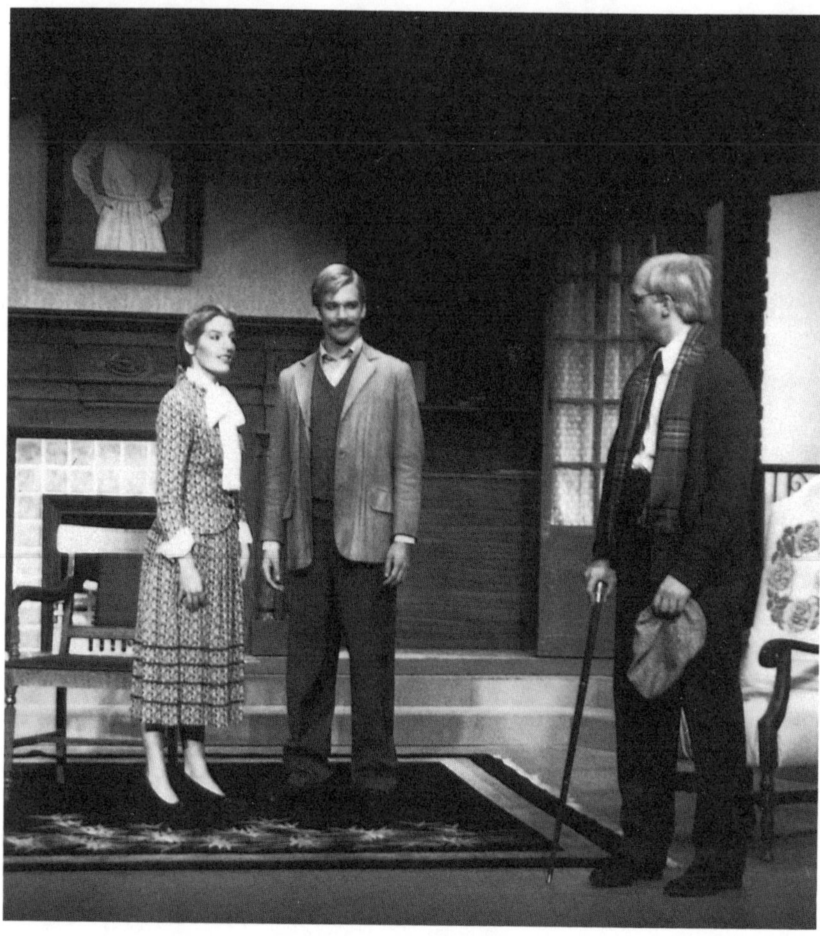

Andrew interrupts his wife, Millie, and his colleague, Frank, in a scene from The Browning Version. *(Photography by David Weeks, courtesy of Grossmont College Theatre Arts Department, El Cajon, California)*

TERENCE RATTIGAN

The Browning Version

TERENCE RATTIGAN first received wide attention with *French Without Tears* in 1936. It ran for more than a thousand performances in London's West End. Although he gained prominence as a writer of light comedy, Rattigan later showed a more serious side with such plays as *The Winslow Boy,* which in 1946 won the Ellen Terry Award for best play produced in London and the New York Drama Critics Circle Award as the season's best foreign play. One of his best-known plays is *Separate Tables.* Rattigan also wrote many film and television plays.

THE BROWNING VERSION was first produced in 1948 and won the Ellen Terry Award. It is the story of a man who appears to be weak but has a hidden reserve of strength. Caught up in a life for which he is unsuited, he has decided to make the best of things, only later realizing that he doesn't have to accept what others try to thrust upon him.

The central idea is that we don't have to accept what life has given us but can fight against it, if only we are given the slightest encouragement to break away from established patterns.

The Browning Version Terence Rattigan

Characters:

JOHN TAPLOW
FRANK HUNTER
MILLIE CROCKER-HARRIS
ANDREW CROCKER-HARRIS
DR. FROBISHER
PETER GILBERT
MRS. GILBERT

Setting:

The sitting-room in the Crocker-Harris's flat in a public school[1] *in the south of England. About 6:30* P.M. *of a day in July.*

The building in which the flat is situated is large and Victorian, and at some fairly recent time has been converted into flats of varying size for masters, married and unmarried. The Crocker-Harris's have the ground floor and their sitting-room is probably the biggest—and gloomiest—room in the house. It boasts, however, access (through a stained glass door left) to a small garden, and is furnished with chintzy and genteel cheerfulness. Another door, up right, leads into the hall and a third, up center, to the rest of the flat. The hall door is partially concealed by a screen. There is a large bay-window in the left wall below the garden door. Near the window is a flat-topped desk with a swivel chair behind it and an upright chair on the other side. The fireplace is down right. Below it is an easy chair and a small table with a telephone. A settee stands in front of the fireplace at right center. There is an oval dining-table with two chairs up center. Right of the door up center is a sideboard; and against the wall left of the door up right is a hall-stand, in which some walking-sticks are kept. A small cupboard stands against the wall down right.

When the CURTAIN *rises the room is empty. There are copies of "The Times" and the "Tatler" on the settee. We hear the front door opening and closing and immediately after there is a timorous knock on the door up right. After a pause the knock is repeated. The door opens and* JOHN TAPLOW *makes his appearance. He is a plain, moon-faced boy of about sixteen, with glasses. He carries a book and an exercise-book. He is dressed in grey flannels, a dark blue coat and white scarf. He stands in doubt at the door for a moment, then goes back into the hall.*

TAPLOW *(off; calling)*: Sir! Sir! *(After a pause he comes back into the room, crosses to the garden door up left and opens it. He calls.)* Sir!

1. Private boarding school.

(There is no reply. TAPLOW, *standing in the bright sunshine at the door, emits a plaintive sigh, then closes it firmly and comes down right of the desk on which he places the book, the notebook and a pen. He sits in the chair right of the desk. He looks round the room. On the table center is a small box of chocolates, probably the Crocker-Harris's ration for the month.* TAPLOW *rises, moves above the table and opens the box. He counts the number inside, and removes two. One of these he eats and the other, after a second's struggle, either with his conscience or his judgment of what he might be able to get away with, virtuously replaces in the box. He puts back the box on the table, and moves up right to the hall-stand. He selects a walking-stick with a crooked handle, comes down center, and makes a couple of golf-swings, with an air of great concentration.* FRANK HUNTER *enters up right and appears from behind the screen covering the door. He is a rugged young man—not perhaps quite as rugged as his deliberately cultivated manner of ruthless honesty makes him appear, but wrapped in all the self-confidence of the popular master. He watches* TAPLOW, *whose back is to the door, making his swing.)*

FRANK *(coming down behind* TAPLOW*)*: Roll the wrists away from the ball. Don't break them like that. *(He puts his large hands over the abashed* TAPLOW's.*)* Now swing. *(*TAPLOW, *guided by* FRANK's *evidently expert hands, succeeds in hitting the carpet with more effect than before. He breaks away right of* TAPLOW.*)* Too quick. Slow back and stiff left arm. It's no good just whacking the ball as if you were the headmaster and the ball was you. It'll never go more than fifty yards if you do. Get a rhythm. A good golf swing is a matter of aesthetics, not of brute strength. *(*TAPLOW, *only half listening, is gazing at the carpet.)*

FRANK: What's the matter?

TAPLOW: I think we've made a tear in the carpet, sir. *(*FRANK *examines the spot perfunctorily.)*

FRANK *(taking the stick from* TAPLOW*)*: Nonsense. That was there already. *(He crosses up right and puts the stick in the hall-stand.)* Do I know you? *(He comes down left of the settee to right of* TAPLOW.*)*

TAPLOW: No, sir.

FRANK: What's your name?

TAPLOW: Taplow.

FRANK: Taplow? No, I don't. You're not a scientist, I gather.

TAPLOW: No, sir. I'm still in the lower fifth. I can't specialize until next term—that's to say if I've got my remove[2] all right.

FRANK: Don't you know yet if you've got your remove?

TAPLOW: No, sir. Mr. Crocker-Harris doesn't tell us the results like the other masters.

FRANK: Why not?

TAPLOW: Well, you know what he's like, sir.

2. A passing grade.

FRANK *(moving away to the fireplace)*: I believe there *is* a rule that form[3] results should only be announced by the headmaster on the last day of term.

TAPLOW: Yes; but who else pays any attention to it—except Mr. Crocker-Harris?

FRANK: I don't, I admit—but that's no criterion. So you've got to wait until tomorrow to know your fate, have you?

TAPLOW: Yes, sir.

FRANK: Supposing the answer is favorable—what then?

TAPLOW: Oh—science sir, of course.

FRANK *(sadly)*: Yes. We get all the slackers.

TAPLOW *(protestingly)*: I'm extremely interested in science, sir.

FRANK: Are you? I'm not. Not at least in the science I have to teach.

TAPLOW *(moving above the desk)*: Well, anyway, sir, it's a good deal more exciting than this muck. *(He indicates the book he put on the desk.)*

FRANK: What is this muck?

TAPLOW: Aeschylus, sir. *The Agamemnon.*

FRANK *(moving to the left end of the couch)*: And your considered view is that *The Agamemnon* of Aeschylus is muck, is it?

TAPLOW: Well, no, sir. I don't think the play is muck—exactly. I suppose, in a way, it's rather a good plot, really; a wife murdering her husband and having a lover and all that. I only meant the way it's taught to us—just a lot of Greek words strung together and fifty lines if you get them wrong.

FRANK: You sound a little bitter, Taplow.

TAPLOW: I am rather, sir.

FRANK: Kept in, eh?

TAPLOW: No, sir. Extra work.

FRANK: Extra work—on the last day of school?

TAPLOW: Yes, sir—and I might be playing golf. *(He moves into the window, upstage end.)* You'd think *he'd* have enough to do anyway himself, considering he's leaving tomorrow for good—but oh no. I missed a day last week when I had 'flu—so here I am—and look at the weather, sir.

FRANK: Bad luck. Still there's one consolation. You're pretty well bound to get your remove tomorrow for being a good boy in taking extra work.

TAPLOW *(crossing to center)*: Well, I'm not so sure, sir. That would be true of the ordinary masters all right. They just wouldn't dare not give a chap a remove after his taking extra work—it would be such a bad advertisement for them. But those sort of rules don't apply to the Crock—Mr. Crocker-Harris. I asked him yesterday outright if he'd given me a remove and do you know what he said, sir?

3. Class/grade.

FRANK: No. What?

TAPLOW *(mimicking a very gentle, rather throaty voice)*: "My dear Taplow, I have given you exactly what you deserve. No less; and certainly no more." Do you know, sir, I think he may have marked me down, rather than up, for taking extra work. I mean, the man's barely human. *(He breaks off quickly.)* Sorry, sir. Have I gone too far?

FRANK *(sitting on the settee, left end, and picking up "The Times"):* Yes. Much too far.

TAPLOW: Sorry, sir. I got sort of carried away.

FRANK: Evidently. *(He opens "The Times" and reads.* TAPLOW *moves to the chair right of the desk and sits.)* Er—Taplow.

TAPLOW: Yes, sir?

FRANK: What was that Mr. Crocker-Harris said to you? Just—er—repeat it, would you?

TAPLOW *(mimicking)*: "My dear Taplow, I have given you exactly what you deserve. No less; and certainly no more." *(*FRANK *snorts, then looks stern.)*

FRANK: Not in the least like him. Read your nice Aeschylus and be quiet.

TAPLOW *(with weary disgust)*: Aeschylus.

FRANK: Look, what time did Mr. Crocker-Harris tell you to be here?

TAPLOW: Six-thirty, sir.

FRANK: Well, he's ten minutes late. Why don't you cut? You could still get nine holes in before lock-up.

TAPLOW *(genuinely shocked)*: Oh, no, I couldn't cut. Cut the Crock—Mr. Crocker-Harris? I shouldn't think it's ever been done in the whole time he's been here. God knows what would happen if I did. He'd probably follow me home, or something.

FRANK: I must admit I envy him the effect he seems to have on you boys in his form. You all seem scared to death of him. What does he do—beat you all, or something?

TAPLOW *(rising and moving to the left end of the settee)*: Good Lord, no. He's not a sadist, like one or two of the others.

FRANK: I beg your pardon?

TAPLOW: A sadist, sir, is someone who gets pleasure out of giving pain.

FRANK: Indeed? But I think you went on to say that some other masters . . .

TAPLOW: Well, of course they are, sir. I won't mention names, but you know them as well as I do. Of course I know most masters think we boys don't understand a thing—but dash it, sir, you're different. You're young—well comparatively anyway—and you're science and you canvassed for Labour in the last election. You must know what sadism is. *(*FRANK *stares for a moment at* TAPLOW, *then turns away.)*

FRANK: Good Lord! What are public schools coming to?

TAPLOW *(crossing to right of the desk, below the chair, and leaning against it)*: Anyway, the Crock isn't a sadist. That's what I'm saying. He wouldn't be so frightening if he were—because at least it would show he had some feelings. But he hasn't. He's all shrivelled up inside like a nut and he seems to hate people to like him. It's funny, that. I don't know any other master who doesn't like being liked.

FRANK: And I don't know any boy who doesn't trade on that very foible.

TAPLOW: Well, it's natural, sir. But not with the Crock.

FRANK *(making a feeble attempt at re-establishing the correct relationship)*: Mr. Crocker-Harris.

TAPLOW: Mr. Crocker-Harris. The funny thing is that in spite of everything, I do rather like him. I can't help it. And sometimes I think he sees it and that seems to shrivel him up even more.

FRANK: I'm sure you're exaggerating.

TAPLOW: No, sir. I'm not. In form the other day he made one of his little classical jokes. Of course nobody laughed because nobody understood it, myself included. Still, I knew he'd meant it as funny, so I laughed. Not out of sucking-up, sir, I swear, but ordinary common politeness, and feeling a bit sorry for him having made a dud joke. *(He moves round below the desk to left of it)*. Now I can't remember what the joke was—but let's say it was—*(mimicking)* Benedictus, benedicatur, benedictine. . . Now, you laugh, sir. *(*FRANK *laughs formally.* TAPLOW *looks at him over an imaginary pair of spectacles, and then, very gently crooks his forefinger to him in indication to approach the table.* FRANK *rises. He is genuinely interested in the incident. In a gentle, throaty voice.)* Taplow—you laughed at my little pun, I noticed. I must confess I am flattered at the evident advance your Latinity has made that you should so readily have understood what the rest of the form did not. Perhaps, now, you would be good enough to explain it to them, so that they too can share your pleasure. *(The door up right is pushed open and* MILLIE CROCKER-HARRIS *enters. She is a thin woman in the late thirties, rather more smartly dressed than the general run of schoolmasters' wives. She is wearing a cape and carries a shopping basket. She closes the door and then stands by the screen watching* TAPLOW *and* FRANK. *It is a few seconds before they notice her.)* Come along, Taplow. *(*FRANK *moves slowly above the desk.)* Do not be so selfish as to keep a good joke to yourself. Tell the others. . . *(He breaks off suddenly, noticing* MILLIE.*)* Oh Lord! *(*FRANK *turns quickly, and seems infinitely relieved at seeing* MILLIE.*)*

FRANK: Oh, hullo.

MILLIE *(without expression)*: Hullo. *(She comes down to the sideboard and puts her basket on it.)*

TAPLOW *(moving up to left of* FRANK; *whispering frantically)*: Do you think she heard? *(*FRANK *shakes his head comfortingly.* MILLIE *takes off her cape and hangs it on the hall-stand.)* I think she did. She was standing there quite a time. If she did and she tells him, there goes my remove.

FRANK: Nonsense.

(He crosses to the fireplace. MILLIE *takes the basket from the sideboard, moves above the table center and puts the basket on it.)*

MILLIE *(to* TAPLOW*)*: Waiting for my husband?

TAPLOW *(moving down left of the table center)*: Er—yes.

MILLIE: He's at the Bursar's and might be there quite a time. If I were you I'd go.

TAPLOW *(doubtfully)*: He said most particularly I was to come.

MILLIE: Well, why don't you run away for a quarter of an hour and come back? *(She unpacks some things from the basket.)*

TAPLOW: Supposing he gets here before me?

MILLIE *(smiling)*: I'll take the blame. *(She takes a prescription out of the basket.)* I tell you what—you can do a job for him. Take this prescription to the chemist and get it made up.

TAPLOW: All right, Mrs. Crocker-Harris. *(He crosses towards the door up right.)*

MILLIE: And while you're there you might as well slip into Stewart's and have an ice. Here. Catch. *(She takes a shilling from her bag and throws it to him.)*

TAPLOW *(turning and catching it)*: Thanks awfully. *(He signals to* FRANK *not to tell, and moves to the door up right.)*

MILLIE: Oh, Taplow. *(She crosses to him.)*

TAPLOW *(turning on the step)*: Yes, Mrs. Crocker-Harris.

MILLIE: I had a letter from my father today in which he says he once had the pleasure of meeting your mother.

TAPLOW *(uninterested but polite)*: Oh, really?

MILLIE: Yes. It was at some fête[4] or other in Bradford. My uncle—that's Sir William Bartop, you know—made a speech and so did your mother. My father met her afterwards at tea.

TAPLOW: Oh really?

MILLIE: He said he found her quite charming.

TAPLOW: Yes, she's jolly good at those sort of functions. *(Becoming aware of his lack of tact.)* I mean—I'm sure she found him charming, too. So long. *(He goes out up right.)*

MILLIE *(coming down to the left end of the settee)*: Thank you for coming round.

FRANK: That's all right.

MILLIE: You're staying for dinner?

FRANK: If I may.

MILLIE: If you may! *(She crosses below the settee to him.)* Give me a cigarette. *(*FRANK *takes out his case and extends it to her.* MILLIE *takes a cigarette. Indicating the case.)* You haven't given it away yet, I see.

4. A large, elaborate party.

FRANK: Do you think I would?

MILLIE: Frankly, yes. Luckily it's a man's case. I don't suppose any of your girlfriends would want it.

FRANK: Don't be silly.

MILLIE: Where have you been all this week?

FRANK *(sitting in the easy chair)*: Correcting exam papers—making reports. You know what end of term is like.

MILLIE *(crossing below the settee and moving above the table center)*: I do know what end of term is like. But even Andrew has managed this last week to take a few hours off to say good-bye to people. *(She takes some packages out of the shopping basket.)*

FRANK: I really have been appallingly busy. Besides, I'm coming to stay with you in Bradford.

MILLIE: Not for over a month. Andrew doesn't start his new job until September first. That's one of the things I had to tell you.

FRANK: Oh. I had meant to be in Devonshire in September.

MILLIE *(quickly)*: Who with?

FRANK: My family.

MILLIE: Surely you can go earlier, can't you? Go in August.

FRANK: It'll be difficult.

MILLIE: Then you'd better come to me in August.

FRANK: But Andrew will still be there. *(There is a pause.* MILLIE *crosses to left of the desk, opens a drawer and takes out some scissors.)* I think I can manage September.

MILLIE *(shutting the drawer)*: That'd be better—from every point of view. *(She moves below the table center and puts down the scissors.)* Except that it means I shan't see you for six weeks.

FRANK *(lightly)*: You'll survive that, all right.

MILLIE: Yes, I'll survive it—*(She moves to the left end of the settee)* but not as easily as you will. *(*FRANK *says nothing.)* I haven't much pride, have I? *(She crosses to* FRANK *and stands above the easy chair.)* Frank, darling—*(She sits on the arm of the chair and kisses him.)* I love you so much. *(*FRANK *kisses her on the mouth, but a trifle perfunctorily, and then rises and breaks quickly away, as if afraid someone had come into the room. He moves below the settee. She laughs)*. You're very nervous.

FRANK: I'm afraid of that screen arrangement. You can't see people coming in.

MILLIE: Oh yes. *(She rises and stands by the fireplace.)* That reminds me. What were you and Taplow up to when I came in just now? Making fun of my husband?

FRANK: Afraid so. Yes.

MILLIE: It sounded rather a good imitation. I must get him to do it for me sometime. It was very naughty of you to encourage him.

FRANK: I know. It was.

MILLIE *(ironically)*: Bad for discipline.

FRANK *(sitting on the settee)*: Exactly. Currying favor with the boys, too. My God, how easy it is to be popular. I've only been a master three years, but I've already slipped into an act and a vernacular that I just can't get out of. Why can't anyone ever be natural with the little blighters?

MILLIE: They probably wouldn't like it if you were.

(She crosses below the settee and moves above the table center. She picks up the scissors and a packet of luggage labels and cuts the latter one by one from the packet.)

FRANK: I don't see why not. No one seems to have tried it yet, anyway. I suppose the trouble is—we're all too scared of them. Either one gets forced into an attitude of false and hearty and jocular bonhomie like myself, or into the sort of petty, soulless tyranny which your husband uses to protect himself against the lower fifth.

MILLIE *(rather bored with this)*: He'd never be popular—whatever he did.

FRANK: Possibly not. He ought never to have become a schoolmaster really. Why did he?

MILLIE: It was his vocation, he said. He was sure he'd make a big success of it, especially when he got his job here first go off. *(Bitterly.)* Fine success he's made, hasn't he?

FRANK: You should have stopped him.

MILLIE: How was I to know? He talked about getting a house, then a headmastership.

FRANK *(rising)*: The Crock a headmaster! That's a pretty thought.

MILLIE: Yes, it's funny to think of now, all right. Still, he wasn't always the Crock, you know. He had a bit more gumption once. At least I thought he had. Don't let's talk any more about him—*(She comes right round the table to center.)* it's too depressing. *(She starts to move left.)*

FRANK: I'm sorry for him.

MILLIE *(stopping and turning; indifferently)*: He's not sorry for himself, so why should you be? It's me you should be sorry for.

FRANK: I am.

MILLIE *(moving in a few steps towards* FRANK; *smiling)*: Then show me.

(She stretches out her arms to him. FRANK *moves to her and kisses her again quickly and lightly. She holds him hungrily. He has to free himself almost roughly.)*

FRANK *(crossing to the fireplace)*: What have you been doing all day?

MILLIE: Calling on the other masters' wives—saying fond farewells. I've worked off twelve. I've another seven to do tomorrow.

FRANK: You poor thing! I don't envy you.

MILLIE *(moving above the desk to left of it with some labels)*: It's the housemasters' wives that are the worst. *(She picks up a pen and writes on the la-*

bels.) They're all so damn patronizing. You should have heard Betty Carstairs. "My dear—it's such terrible bad luck on you both—that your husband should get this heart trouble just when, if only he'd stayed on, he'd have been bound to get a house. I mean, he's considerably senior to my Arthur as it is, and they simply couldn't have gone on passing him over, could they?"

FRANK: There's a word for Betty Carstairs, my dear, that I would hesitate to employ before a lady.

MILLIE: She's got her eye on you, anyway.

FRANK: Betty Carstairs? What utter rot!

MILLIE: Oh yes, she has. I saw you at that concert. Don't think I didn't notice.

FRANK: Millie, darling! Really! I detest the woman.

MILLIE: Then what were you doing in her box at Lord's?

FRANK: Carstairs invited me. I went there because it was a good place to see the match from.

MILLIE: Yes, I'm sure it was. Much better than the grandstand, anyway.

FRANK *(remembering something suddenly)*: Oh, my God!

MILLIE *(coming below the desk)*: It's all right, my dear. Don't bother to apologize. We gave the seat away, as it happens.

FRANK: I'm most terribly sorry.

MILLIE: It's all right. *(She moves to right of the desk.)* We couldn't afford a box, you see.

FRANK *(moving a few steps towards right center)*: It wasn't that. You know it wasn't that. It's just that I—well, I clean forgot.

MILLIE: Funny you didn't forget the Carstairs invitation.

FRANK: Millie—don't be a fool

MILLIE: It's you who are the fool. *(Appealingly)* Frank—have you never been in love? I know you're not in love with me—but haven't you ever been in love with anyone? Don't you realize what torture you inflict on someone who loves you when you do a thing like that?

FRANK: I've told you I'm sorry—I don't know what more I can say.

MILLIE: Why not the truth?

FRANK: The truth is—I clean forgot.

MILLIE: The truth is—you had something better to do—and why not say it?

FRANK: All right. Believe that if you like. It happens to be a lie, but believe it all the same. Only for God's sake stop this. *(He turns and moves down right.)*

MILLIE: Then for God's sake show me some pity. Do you think it's any pleasanter for me to believe that you cut me because you forgot? Do you think that doesn't hurt either? *(FRANK turns away. She moves above the up right corner of the desk and faces the door up left.)* Oh damn! I was so determined to be brave and not mention Lord's. Why did I?

Frank, just tell me one thing. Just tell me you're not running away from me—that's all I want to hear.

FRANK: I'm coming to Bradford.

MILLIE *(turning to* FRANK*)*: I think, if you don't, I'll kill myself.

FRANK *(turning and taking a few steps in towards* MILLIE*)*: I'm coming to Bradford.

(The door up right opens. FRANK *stops at the sound.* MILLIE *recovers herself and crosses above the table center to the sideboard.* ANDREW CROCKER-HARRIS *enters and appears from behind the screen. Despite the summer sun he wears a serge suit and a stiff collar. He carries a mackintosh and a rolled-up timetable and looks, as ever, neat, complacent and unruffled. He speaks in a very gentle voice which he rarely raises.)*

ANDREW *(hanging his mackintosh on the hall-stand)*: Is Taplow here? *(*FRANK *eases towards the fireplace.)*

MILLIE: I sent him to the chemist to get your prescription made up.

ANDREW: What prescription?

MILLIE: Your heart medicine. Don't you remember? You told me this morning it had run out.

ANDREW: Of course I remember, my dear, but there was no need to send Taplow for it. If you had telephoned the chemist he would have sent it round in plenty of time. He knows the prescription. *(He comes down to the left end of the settee.)* Now Taplow will be late and I am so pressed for time I hardly know how to fit him in. *(He sees* FRANK.*)* Ah, Hunter! How are you? *(He moves right to* FRANK.*)*

FRANK: Very well, thanks. *(They shake hands.)*

ANDREW: Most kind of you to drop in, but, as Millie should have warned you, I am expecting a pupil for extra work and. . .

MILLIE: He's staying to dinner, Andrew.

ANDREW: Good. Then I shall see something of you. However, when Taplow returns I'm sure you won't mind. . .

FRANK *(making a move)*: No, of course not. I'll make myself scarce now, if you'd rather—I mean, if you're busy. . . *(He turns away and moves center.)*

ANDREW: Oh no. There is no need for that. Sit down, do. Will you smoke? I don't, as you know, but Millie does. *(He crosses below the desk and moves up left of it.)* Millie, give our guest a cigarette.

MILLIE *(moving down to the table center)*: I haven't any, I'm afraid. I've had to cadge from him.

(She takes a copy of the "Tatler" from the basket. ANDREW *opens the drawer that should contain the scissors.* FRANK *takes out his cigarette case, crosses to right of the table center, and offers it to* MILLIE. *She exchanges a glance with him as she takes a cigarette.)*

ANDREW *(looking for the scissors)*: We expected you at Lord's, Hunter.

FRANK: What? Oh yes. I'm most terribly sorry. I. . .

MILLIE *(crossing behind the settee)*: He clean forgot, Andrew. Imagine.

ANDREW: Forgot?

MILLIE: Not everyone is blessed with your superhuman memory, you see.

FRANK: I really can't apologize enough.

ANDREW: Please don't bother to mention it. On the second day we managed to sell the seat to a certain Dr. Lambert, who wore, I regret to say, the colors of the opposing faction, but who otherwise seemed a passably agreeable person. *(He moves above the table center.)* You liked him, didn't you, Millie?

MILLIE *(looking at* FRANK*)*: Very much indeed. I thought him quite charming.

ANDREW: A charming old gentleman. *(To* FRANK.*)* You have had tea? *(He picks up the scissors.)*

FRANK: Yes—thank you.

ANDREW: Is there any other refreshment I can offer you?

FRANK: No, thank you.

ANDREW *(cutting the string round the timetable)*: Would it interest you to see the new timetable I have drafted for next term?

FRANK: Yes, very much. *(He moves up right of* ANDREW. ANDREW *opens out a long roll of paper, made by pasting pieces of foolscap together, and which is entirely covered by his meticulous writing.)* I never knew you drafted our timetables.

ANDREW: Didn't you? I have done so for the last fifteen years. *(*MILLIE *wanders down right of the settee.)* Of course, they are always issued in mimeograph under the headmaster's signature. Now what form do you take? Upper fifth Science—there you are—that's the general picture; but on the back you will see each form specified under separate headings—there—that's a new idea of mine—Millie, this might interest you.

MILLIE *(sitting in the easy chair; suddenly harsh)*: You know it bores me to death.

*(*FRANK *looks up, surprised and uncomfortable.* ANDREW *does not remove his eyes from the timetable.)*

ANDREW: Millie has no head for this sort of work. There you see. Now here you can follow the upper fifth Science throughout every day of the week.

FRANK *(indicating the timetable)*: I must say, I think this is a really wonderful job.

ANDREW: Thank you. It has the merit of clarity, I think. *(He starts to roll up the timetable.)*

FRANK: I don't know what they'll do without you.

ANDREW *(without expression)*: They'll find somebody else, I expect. *(There is a pause.)*

FRANK: What sort of job is this you're going to?

ANDREW *(looking at* MILLIE *for the first time)*: Hasn't Millie told you?

FRANK: She said it was a cr— a private school.

ANDREW: A crammer's[5]—for backward boys. It is run by an old Oxford contemporary of mine who lives in Dorset. *(He moves round left of the table center and finishes rolling up the timetable.)* The work will not be so arduous as here and my doctor seems to think I will be able to undertake it without—er, danger.

FRANK *(with genuine sympathy)*: It's the most rotten bad luck for you. I'm awfully sorry.

ANDREW *(raising his voice a little)*: My dear Hunter, there is nothing whatever to be sorry for. I am looking forward to the change. *(There is a knock at the door up right.)* Come in. *(He crosses below the table to center.* TAPLOW *enters up right, a trifle breathless and guilty-looking. He carries a medicine bottle wrapped and sealed.)* Ah, Taplow. Good. You have been running, I see.

TAPLOW: Yes, sir. *(He crosses to the left end of the settee.)*

ANDREW: There was a queue at the chemist's, I suppose?

TAPLOW: Yes, sir.

ANDREW: And doubtless an even longer one at Stewart's?

TAPLOW: Yes, sir—I mean—no, sir—I mean—*(He looks at* MILLIE.*)* yes, sir. *(He crosses below the settee to* MILLIE *and hands her the medicine.)*

MILLIE: You were late yourself, Andrew.

ANDREW: Exactly. And for that I apologize, Taplow.

TAPLOW: That's all right, sir.

ANDREW *(crossing below the desk and moving left of it)*: Luckily we have still a good hour before lock-up, so nothing has been lost. *(He puts the timetable on the desk.)*

FRANK *(moving to the door up left; to* MILLIE*)*: May I use the short cut? I'm going back to my digs. *(*ANDREW *sits at his desk and opens a book.)*

MILLIE *(rising and moving up right of the settee)*: Yes. Go ahead. Come back soon. If Andrew hasn't finished we can sit in the garden. *(She crosses above the table center and picks up the shopping basket. She puts the medicine on the sideboard.)* I'd better go and see about dinner. *(She goes out up center.)*

ANDREW *(to* FRANK*)*: Taplow is desirous of obtaining a remove from my form, Hunter, so that he can spend the rest of his career here playing happily with the crucibles, retorts, and bunsen burners of your science fifth.

5. School for intensive work on one subject; a tutoring program.

FRANK *(turning at the door)*: Oh. Has he?

ANDREW: Has he what?

FRANK: Obtained his remove?

ANDREW *(after a pause)*: He has obtained exactly what he deserves. No less; and certainly no more. *(*TAPLOW *mutters an explosion of mirth.* FRANK *nods, thoughtfully, and goes out.* ANDREW *has caught sight of* TAPLOW's *contorted face, but passes no remark on it. He beckons* TAPLOW *across and signs to him to sit in the chair right of the desk.* TAPLOW *sits.* ANDREW *picks up a copy of "The Agamemnon" and* TAPLOW *does the same.)* Line thirteen hundred and ninety-nine. Begin. *(He leans back.)*

TAPLOW *(reading slowly)*: Chorus. We—are surprised at . . .

ANDREW *(automatically)*: We marvel at.

TAPLOW: We marvel at—thy tongue—how bold thou art—that you . . .

ANDREW: Thou. *(His interruptions are automatic. His thoughts are evidently far distant.)*

TAPLOW: Thou—can . . .

ANDREW: Canst.

TAPLOW: Canst—boastfully speak . . .

ANDREW: Utter such a boastful speech.

TAPLOW: Utter such a boastful speech—over—*(in a sudden rush of inspiration)* the bloody corpse of the husband you have slain.

*(*ANDREW *puts on his glasses and looks down at his text for the first time.* TAPLOW *looks apprehensive.)*

ANDREW *(after a pause)*: Taplow—I presume you are using a different text from mine.

TAPLOW: No, sir.

ANDREW: That is strange, for the line as I have it reads: "heetis toiond ep andri compadzise logon." However diligently I search I can discover no "bloody"—no "corpse"—no "you have slain." Simply "husband".

TAPLOW: Yes, sir. That's right.

ANDREW: Then why do you invent words that simply are not there?

TAPLOW: I thought they sounded better, sir. More exciting. After all, she did kill her husband, sir. *(With relish.)* She's just been revealed with his dead body and Cassandra's weltering in gore.

ANDREW: I am delighted at this evidence, Taplow, of your interest in the rather more lurid aspects of dramaturgy, but I feel I must remind you that you are supposed to be construing Greek, not collaborating with Aeschylus. *(He leans back.)*

TAPLOW *(greatly daring)*: Yes, but still, sir, translator's licence, sir—I didn't get anything wrong—and after all it *is* a play and not just a bit of Greek construe.

ANDREW *(momentarily at a loss):* I seem to detect a note of end of term in your remarks. I am not denying that *The Agamemnon* is a play. It is perhaps the greatest play ever written. *(He leans forward.)*

TAPLOW *(quickly):* I wonder how many people in the form think that? *(He pauses; instantly frightened of what he has said.)* Sorry, sir. Shall I go on? *(*ANDREW *does not answer. He sits motionless, staring at his book.)* Shall I go on, sir? *(There is another pause.* ANDREW *raises his head slowly from his book.)*

ANDREW *(murmuring gently, not looking at* TAPLOW*)*: When I was a very young man, only two years older than you are now, Taplow, I wrote, for my own pleasure, a translation of *The Agamemnon*—a very free translation—I remember—in rhyming couplets.

TAPLOW: The whole *Agamemnon*—in verse? That must have been hard work, sir.

ANDREW: It was hard work; but I derived great joy from it. The play had so excited and moved me that I wished to communicate, however imperfectly, some of that emotion to others. When I had finished it, I remember, I thought it very beautiful—almost more beautiful than the original. *(He leans back.)*

TAPLOW: Was it ever published, sir?

ANDREW: No. Yesterday I looked for the manuscript while I was packing my papers. I was unable to find it. I fear it is lost—like so many other things. Lost for good.

TAPLOW: Hard luck, sir. *(*ANDREW *is silent again.* TAPLOW *steals a timid glance at him)*. Shall I go on, sir? *(*ANDREW, *with a slight effort, lowers his eyes again to his text.)*

ANDREW *(leaning forward; raising his voice slightly)*: No. Go back and get that last line right.

*(*TAPLOW, *out of* ANDREW's *vision, as he thinks, makes a disgusted grimace in his direction.)*

TAPLOW: That—thou canst utter such a boastful speech over thy husband.

ANDREW: Yes. And now, if you would be so kind, you will do the line again, without the facial contortion which you just found necessary to accompany it.

*(*TAPLOW *is about to begin the line again.* MILLIE *enters up center, hurriedly. She is wearing an apron.* TAPLOW *rises.)*

MILLIE: The headmaster's just coming up the drive. Don't tell him I'm in. The fish pie isn't in the oven yet. *(She exits up center.)*

TAPLOW *(turning hopefully to* ANDREW*)*: I'd better go, hadn't I, sir? I mean—I don't want to be in the way.

ANDREW: We do not yet know that it is I the headmaster wishes to see.

Other people live in this building. *(There is a knock at the door up right.)* Come in.

*(*DR. FROBISHER *enters up right. He looks more like a distinguished diplomat than a doctor of literature and a classical scholar. He is in the middle fifties and goes to a very good tailor.* ANDREW *rises.)*

FROBISHER: Ah, Crocker-Harris, I've caught you in. I'm so glad. *(He crosses behind the settee and comes down left of it.)* I hope I'm not disturbing you?

ANDREW: I have been taking a pupil in extra work. *(*TAPLOW *eases below the table center.)*

FROBISHER: On the penultimate day of term? That argues either great conscientiousness on your part or considerable backwardness on his.

ANDREW: Perhaps a combination of both.

FROBISHER: Quite so, but as this is my only chance of speaking to you before tomorrow, I think that perhaps your pupil will be good enough to excuse us. *(He turns politely to* TAPLOW.*)*

TAPLOW: Oh yes, sir. That's really quite all right. *(He grabs his books off* ANDREW's *desk.)*

ANDREW *(crossing to* TAPLOW*)*: I'm extremely sorry, Taplow. You will please explain to your father exactly what occurred over this lost hour and tell him that I shall in due course be writing to him to return the money involved. *(*FROBISHER *moves below the settee to the fireplace.)*

TAPLOW *(hurriedly)*: Yes, sir. But please don't bother, sir. *(He dashes to the door up right.)* I know it's all right, sir. Thank you, sir. *(He darts out.)*

FROBISHER *(idly picking up an ornament on the mantelpiece)*: Have the Gilberts called on you yet? *(He turns to* ANDREW.*)*

ANDREW *(moving center)*: The Gilberts, sir? Who are they?

FROBISHER: Gilbert is your successor with the lower fifth. He is down here today with his wife, and as they will be taking over this flat I thought perhaps you wouldn't mind if they came in to look it over.

ANDREW: Of course not.

FROBISHER: I've told you about him, I think. He is a very brilliant young man and won exceptionally high honours at Oxford.

ANDREW: So I understand, sir.

FROBISHER: Not, of course, as high as the honours you yourself won there. He didn't, for instance, win the Chancellor's prize for Latin verse or the Gainsford.

ANDREW: He won the Hertford Latin, then?

FROBISHER *(replacing the ornament)*: No. *(Mildly surprised.)* Did you win that, too? *(*ANDREW *nods.)* It's sometimes rather hard to remember that you are perhaps the most brilliant classical scholar we have ever had at the school.

ANDREW: You are very kind.

FROBISHER *(urbanely correcting his gaffe)*: Hard to remember, I mean—because of your other activities—your brilliant work on the school timetable, for instance, and also for your heroic battle for so long and against such odds with the soul-destroying lower fifth.

ANDREW: I have not found that my soul has been destroyed by the lower fifth, Headmaster.

FROBISHER: I was joking, of course.

ANDREW: Oh. I see.

FROBISHER: Is your wife in?

ANDREW: Er—no. Not at the moment.

FROBISHER: I shall have a chance of saying good-bye to her tomorrow. *(He moves in a few steps below the settee.)* I am rather glad I have got you to myself. I have a delicate matter—two rather delicate matters—to broach.

ANDREW *(moving in slightly; indicating the settee)*: Please sit down. *(He stands at the left end of the settee.)*

FROBISHER: Thank you. *(He sits.)* Now you have been with us, in all, eighteen years, haven't you? (ANDREW *nods.)* It is extremely unlucky that you should have had to retire at so comparatively early an age and so short a time before you would have been eligible for a pension.

(He is regarding his nails, as he speaks, studiously avoiding meeting ANDREW's *gaze.* ANDREW *crosses below the settee to the fireplace and stands facing it.)*

ANDREW *(after a pause)*: You have decided, then, not to award me a pension?

FROBISHER: Not I, my dear fellow. It has nothing at all to do with me. It's the governors who, I'm afraid, have been forced to turn down your application. I put your case to them as well as I could— (ANDREW *turns and faces* FROBISHER.*)*—but they decided with great regret, that they couldn't make an exception to the rule.

ANDREW: But I thought—my wife thought, that an exception was made some five years ago . . .

FROBISHER: Ah! In the case of Buller, you mean? True. But the circumstances with Buller were quite remarkable. It was, after all, in playing rugger against the school that he received that injury.

ANDREW: Yes. I remember.

FROBISHER: And then the governors received a petition from boys, old boys and parents, with over five hundred signatures.

ANDREW: I would have signed that petition myself, but through some oversight I was not asked.

FROBISHER: He was a splendid fellow, Buller. Splendid. Doing very well, too, now, I gather.

ANDREW: I'm delighted to hear it.

FROBISHER: Your own case, of course, is equally deserving. If not more so—for Buller was a younger man. Unfortunately—rules are rules—and are not made to be broken every few years; at any rate that is the governors' view.

ANDREW: I quite understand.

FROBISHER: I knew you would. Now might I ask you a rather impertinent question?

ANDREW: Certainly.

FROBISHER: You have, I take it, private means?

ANDREW: My wife has some.

FROBISHER: Ah, yes. Your wife has often told me of her family connexions. I understand her father has a business in—Bradford—isn't it?

ANDREW: Yes. He runs a men's clothing shop in the Arcade.

FROBISHER: Indeed? Your wife's remarks have led me to imagine something a little more—extensive.

ANDREW: My father-in-law made a settlement on my wife at the time of our marriage. She has about three hundred a year of her own. I have nothing. Is that the answer to your question, Headmaster?

FROBISHER: Yes. Thank you for your frankness. Now, this private school you are going to . . .

ANDREW: My salary at the crammer's is to be two hundred pounds a year.

FROBISHER: Quite so. With board and lodging, of course?

ANDREW: For eight months of the year.

FROBISHER: Yes, I see. *(He ponders a second.)* Of course, you know, there is the School Benevolent Fund that deals with cases of actual hardship.

ANDREW: There will be no actual hardship, Headmaster.

FROBISHER: No. I am glad you take that view. I must admit, though, I had hoped that your own means had proved a little more ample. Your wife had certainly led me to suppose . . .

ANDREW: I am not denying that a pension would have been very welcome, Headmaster, but I see no reason to quarrel with the governors' decision. What is the other delicate matter you have to discuss?

FROBISHER: Well, it concerns the arrangements at prize-giving tomorrow. You are, of course, prepared to say a few words?

ANDREW: I had assumed you would call on me to do so.

FROBISHER: Of course. It is always done, and I know the boys appreciate the custom.

ANDREW *(crossing to the upstage end of the desk)*: I have already made a few notes of what I am going to say. Perhaps you would care . . .

FROBISHER: No, no. That isn't necessary at all. I know I can trust your discretion—not to say your wit. It will be, I know, a very moving moment for you—indeed for us all—but, as I'm sure you realize, it is far better to keep these occasions from becoming too heavy and distressing. You know how little the boys appreciate sentiment.

ANDREW: I do.

FROBISHER: That is why I've planned my own reference to you at the end of my speech to be rather more light and jocular than I would otherwise have made it.

ANDREW: I quite understand. *(He moves to left of the desk, puts on his glasses and picks up his speech.)* I too have prepared a few little jokes and puns for my speech. One—a play of words on *vale,* farewell, and Wally, the Christian name of a backward boy in my class, is, I think, rather happy.

FROBISHER: Yes. *(He laughs belatedly.)* Very neat. That should go down extremely well.

ANDREW: I'm glad you like it.

FROBISHER *(rising and crossing to right of the desk)*: Well, now—there is a particular favour I have to ask of you in connexion with the ceremony, and I know I shall not have to ask in vain. Fletcher, as you know, is leaving too.

ANDREW: Yes. He is going into the city, they tell me.

FROBISHER: Yes. Now he is, of course, considerably junior to you. He has only been here—let me see—five years. But, as you know, he has done great things for our cricket—positive wonders, when you remember what doldrums we were in before he came.

ANDREW: Our win at Lord's this year was certainly most inspiriting.

FROBISHER: Exactly. *(He moves above the desk.)* Now I'm sure that tomorrow the boys will make the occasion of his farewell speech a tremendous demonstration of gratitude. The applause might go on for minutes—you know what the boys feel about Lord's—and I seriously doubt my ability to cut it short or even, I admit, the propriety of trying to do so. Now, you see the quandary in which I am placed?

ANDREW: Perfectly. You wish to refer to me and for me to make my speech before you come to Fletcher?

FROBISHER: It's extremely awkward, and I feel wretched about asking it of you—but it's more for your own sake than for mine or Fletcher's that I do. After all, a climax is what one must try to work up to on these occasions.

ANDREW: Naturally, Headmaster, I wouldn't wish to provide an anticlimax.

FROBISHER: You really mustn't take it amiss, my dear fellow. The boys, in applauding Fletcher for several minutes and yourself say—for—well, for not quite so long—won't be making any personal demonstration between you. It will be quite impersonal—I assure you—quite impersonal.

ANDREW: I understand.

FROBISHER *(patting* ANDREW's *shoulder; warmly)*: I knew you would *(He looks at his watch.)* and I can hardly tell you how wisely I think you have chosen. Well now—as that is all my business, I think perhaps I had better be getting along. *(He crosses to right of the table center.)* This has been a terribly busy day for me—for you too, I imagine.

ANDREW: Yes.

*(*MILLIE *enters up center. She has taken off her apron, and tidied herself up. She comes to left of* FROBISHER.*)*

MILLIE *(in her social manner)*: Ah, Headmaster. How good of you to drop in.

FROBISHER *(more at home with her than with* ANDREW*)*: Mrs. Crocker-Harris. How are you? *(They shake hands.)* You're looking extremely well, I must say. *(To* ANDREW.*)* Has anyone ever told you, Crocker-Harris, that you have a very attractive wife?

ANDREW: Many people, sir. But then I hardly need to be told.

MILLIE: Can I persuade you to stay a few moments and have a drink, Headmaster? It's so rarely we have the pleasure of seeing you.

FROBISHER: Unfortunately, dear lady, I was just on the point of leaving. I have two frantic parents waiting for me at home. You are dining with us tomorrow—both of you, aren't you?

MILLIE: Yes, indeed—and so looking forward to it. *(*FROBISHER *and* MILLIE *move to the door up right.)*

FROBISHER: I'm so glad. We can say our sad farewells then. *(To* ANDREW.*)* Au revoir, Crocker-Harris, and thank you very much.

(He opens the door. ANDREW *gives a slight bow.* MILLIE *holds the door open.* FROBISHER *goes out.)*

MILLIE *(To* ANDREW*)*: Don't forget to take your medicine, dear, will you? *(She goes out.)*

ANDREW: No.

FROBISHER *(off)*: Lucky invalid! To have such a very charming nurse.

MILLIE *(off)*: I really don't know what to say to all these compliments, Headmaster. I don't believe you mean a word of them. *(*ANDREW *turns and looks out of the window.)*

FROBISHER *(off)*: Every word. Till tomorrow, then? Good-bye.

(The outer door is heard to slam. ANDREW *is staring out of the window.* MILLIE *enters up right.)*

MILLIE: Well? Do we get it? *(She stands on the step.)*

ANDREW *(turning and moving below the chair left of his desk; absently)*: Get what?

MILLIE: The pension, of course. Do we get it?

ANDREW: No.

MILLIE *(crossing above the settee to center):* My God! Why not?

ANDREW *(sitting at his desk)*: It's against the rules.

MILLIE: Buller got it, didn't he? Buller got it? What's the idea of giving it to him and not to us?

ANDREW: The governors are afraid of establishing a precedent.

MILLIE: The mean old brutes! My God, what I wouldn't like to say to them! *(She moves above the desk and rounds on* ANDREW.*)* And what did you say? Just sat there and made a joke in Latin, I suppose?

ANDREW: There wasn't very much I could say, in Latin or any other language.

MILLIE: Oh, wasn't there? I'd have said it all right. I wouldn't just have sat there twiddling my thumbs and taking it from that old phoney of a headmaster. But, then, of course, I'm not a man. *(*ANDREW *is turning the pages of "The Agamemnon," not looking at her.)* What do they expect you to do? Live on my money, I suppose.

ANDREW: There has never been any question of that. I shall be perfectly able to support myself.

MILLIE: Yourself? Doesn't the marriage service say something about the husband supporting his wife? *(She leans on the desk.)* Doesn't it? You ought to know.

ANDREW: Yes, it does.

MILLIE: And how do you think you're going to do that on two hundred a year?

ANDREW: I shall do my utmost to save some of it. You're welcome to it, if I can.

MILLIE: Thank you for precisely nothing. *(*ANDREW *underlines a word in the text he is reading.)* What else did the old fool have to say? *(She moves to right of the chair, right of the desk.)*

ANDREW: The headmaster? He wants me to make my speech tomorrow before instead of after Fletcher.

MILLIE *(sitting right of the desk)*: Yes. I knew he was going to ask that.

ANDREW *(without surprise)*: You knew?

MILLIE: Yes. He asked my advice about it a week ago. I told him to go ahead. I knew you wouldn't mind, and as there isn't a Mrs. Fletcher to make *me* look a fool, I didn't give two hoots. *(There is a knock on the door up right.)* Come in.

*(*MR. *and* MRS. GILBERT *enter up right. He is about twenty-two, and his wife a year or so younger.* MILLIE *rises and stands at the downstage corner of the desk.)*

GILBERT: Mr. Crocker-Harris?

ANDREW: Yes. *(He rises.)* Is it Mr. and Mrs. Gilbert? The headmaster told me you might look in.

MRS. GILBERT *(crossing above the settee to center)*: I do hope we're not disturbing you. *(*GILBERT *follows* MRS. GILBERT *and stands downstage of, and slightly behind, her.)*

ANDREW: Not at all. This is my wife.

MRS. GILBERT: How do you do?

ANDREW: Mr. and Mrs. Gilbert are our successors to this flat, my dear.

MILLIE: Oh yes. *(She moves to left of* MRS. GILBERT.*)* How nice to meet you both.

GILBERT: How do you do? We really won't keep you more than a second—my wife thought as we were here you wouldn't mind us taking a squint at our future home.

MRS. GILBERT *(unnecessarily)*: This is the drawing-room, I suppose?

*(*GILBERT *crosses to the fireplace. He looks for a moment at the picture above the mantelpiece, then turns and watches the others.)*

MILLIE: Well, it's really a living-room. Andrew uses it as a study.

MRS. GILBERT: How charmingly you've done it!

MILLIE: Oh, do you think so? I'm afraid it isn't nearly as nice as I'd like to make it—but a schoolmaster's wife has to think of so many other things besides curtains and covers. Boys with dirty books and a husband with leaky fountain pens, for instance.

MRS. GILBERT: Yes, I suppose so. Of course, I haven't been a schoolmaster's wife for very long, you know.

GILBERT: Don't swank, darling. You haven't been a schoolmaster's wife at all yet.

MRS. GILBERT: Oh yes, I have—for two months. You were a schoolmaster when I married you.

GILBERT: Prep school doesn't count.

MILLIE: Have you only been married two months?

MRS. GILBERT: Two months and sixteen days.

GILBERT: Seventeen.

MILLIE *(sentimentally)*: Andrew, did you hear? They've only been married two months.

ANDREW: Indeed? Is that all?

MRS. GILBERT *(crossing above* MILLIE *to the window)*: Oh, look, darling. They've got a garden. It is yours, isn't it?

MILLIE: Oh, yes. It's only a pocket hankerchief, I'm afraid, but it's very useful to Andrew. He often works out there, don't you, dear?

ANDREW: Yes, indeed. I find it very agreeable.

MILLIE *(moving to the door up center)*: Shall I show you the rest of the flat? It's a bit untidy, I'm afraid, but you must forgive that. *(She opens the door.)*

MRS. GILBERT *(moving up to left of* MILLIE*)*: Oh, of course.

MILLIE: And the kitchen is in a terrible mess. I'm in the middle of cooking dinner.

MRS. GILBERT *(breathlessly)*: Oh, do you cook?

MILLIE: Oh, yes. I have to. We haven't had a maid for five years.

MRS. GILBERT: Oh! I do think that's wonderful of you. I'm scared stiff of having to do it for Peter—I know the first dinner I have to cook for him will wreck our married life.

GILBERT: Highly probable. (MRS. GILBERT *exits up center.)*

MILLIE *(following* MRS. GILBERT*)*: Well, these days we've all got to try and do things we weren't really brought up to do. *(She goes out, closing the door.)*

ANDREW *(to* GILBERT*)*: Don't you want to see the rest of the flat?

GILBERT *(crossing to center)*: No. I leave all that sort of thing to my wife. She's the boss. I thought perhaps you could tell me something about the lower fifth.

ANDREW: What would you like to know?

GILBERT: Well, sir, quite frankly, I'm petrified.

ANDREW: I don't think you need to be. May I give you some sherry? *(He comes down left to the cupboard.)*

GILBERT: Thank you.

ANDREW: They are mostly boys of about fifteen or sixteen. They are not very difficult to handle. *(He takes out a bottle and a glass.)*

GILBERT: The headmaster said you ruled them with a rod of iron. He called you "the Himmler[6] of the lower fifth."

ANDREW *(turning, bottle and glass in hand)*: Did he? "The Himmler of the lower fifth." I think he exaggerated. I hope he exaggerated. "The Himmler of the lower fifth." *(He puts the bottle on the desk, then fills the glass.)*

GILBERT *(puzzled)*: He only meant that you kept the most wonderful discipline. I must say I do admire you for that. I couldn't even manage that with eleven-year-olds, so what I'll be like with fifteens and sixteens I shudder to think. *(He moves below the chair right of the desk.)*

ANDREW: It is not so difficult. *(He hands* GILBERT *the glass.)* They aren't bad boys. Sometimes a little wild and unfeeling, perhaps—but not bad. "The Himmler of the lower fifth." Dear me! *(He turns to the cabinet with the bottle.)*

GILBERT: Perhaps I shouldn't have said that. I've been tactless, I'm afraid.

ANDREW: Oh no. *(He puts the bottle in the cupboard.)* Please sit down. *(He stands by the downstage end of the desk.)*

GILBERT: Thank you, sir. *(He sits right of the desk.)*

ANDREW: From the very beginning I realized that I didn't possess the

6. Reference to Heinrich Himmler, a Nazi leader in World War II Germany, head of the gestapo.

knack of making myself liked—a knack that you will find you do possess.

GILBERT: Do you think so?

ANDREW: Oh yes. I am quite sure of it. *(He moves up left of the desk.)* It is not a quality of great importance to a schoolmaster though, for too much of it, as you may also find, is as great a danger as the total lack of it. Forgive me lecturing, won't you?

GILBERT: I want to learn.

ANDREW: I can only teach you from my own experience. For two or three years I tried very hard to communicate to the boys some of my own joy in the great literature of the past. Of course I failed, as you will fail, nine hundred and ninety-nine times out of a thousand. But a single success can atone, and more than atone, for all the failure in the world. And sometimes—very rarely, it is true—but sometimes I had that success. That was in the early years.

GILBERT *(eagerly listening)*: Please go on, sir.

ANDREW: In early years too, I discovered an easy substitute for popularity. *(He picks up his speech.)* I had of course acquired—we all do—many little mannerisms and tricks of speech, and I found that the boys were beginning to laugh at me. I was very happy at that, and encouraged the boys' laughter by playing up to it. It made our relationship so very much easier. They didn't like me as a man, but they found me funny as a character, and you can teach more things by laughter than by earnestness—for I never did have much sense of humour. So, for a time, you see, I was quite a success as a schoolmaster . . . *(He stops.)* I fear this is all very personal and embarrassing to you. Forgive me. You need have no fears about the lower fifth.

(He puts the speech into his pocket and turns to the window. GILBERT *rises and moves above the desk.)*

GILBERT *(after a pause)*: I'm afraid I said something that hurt you very much. It's myself you must forgive, sir. Believe me, I'm desperately sorry.

ANDREW *(turning down stage and leaning slightly on the back of the swivel chair)*: There's no need. You were merely telling me what I should have known for myself. Perhaps I did in my heart, and hadn't the courage to acknowledge it. I knew, of course, that I was not only not liked, but now positively disliked. I had realized too that the boys—for many long years now—had ceased to laugh at me. I don't know why they no longer found me a joke. Perhaps it was my illness. No, I don't think it was that. Something deeper than that. Not a sickness of the body, but a sickness of the soul. At all events it didn't take much discernment on my part to realize I had become an utter failure as a schoolmaster. Still, stupidly enough, I hadn't realized that I was also feared. "The Himmler of the lower fifth." I suppose that will become my epitaph. *(*GILBERT *is now deeply embarrassed and rather upset, but he remains silent. He sits on the upstage end of the window seat. With a mild laugh.)* I cannot for the life of me imagine why I should choose to unburden myself to you—a total stranger—when I have been silent to others for so long. Perhaps it is because my very unworthy mantle is about to fall on your shoulders. If that is so I shall take a prophet's privilege and foretell that you will have a very great success with the lower fifth.

GILBERT: Thank you, sir. I shall do my best.

ANDREW: I can't offer you a cigarette, I'm afraid. I don't smoke.

GILBERT: That's all right, sir. Nor do I.

MRS. GILBERT *(off)*: Thank you so much for showing me round.

*(*MILLIE *and* MRS. GILBERT *enter up center.* ANDREW *rises.* MILLIE *comes down right of the table center, picks up the papers on the settee and puts them on the fender down right.* MRS. GILBERT *comes down left of the table center to right of* GILBERT.*)*

ANDREW: I trust your wife has found no major snags in your new flat.

MR. GILBERT: No. None at all.

MRS. GILBERT: Just imagine, Peter. Mr. and Mrs. Crocker-Harris first met each other on a holiday in the Lake District. Isn't that a coincidence?

GILBERT *(a little distrait)*: Yes. Yes, it certainly is. On a walking tour, too? *(*ANDREW *turns and looks out of the window.)*

MILLIE: Andrew was on a walking tour. No walking for me. I can't abide it. I was staying with my uncle—that's Sir William Bartop, you know—you may have heard of him. *(*GILBERT *and* MRS. GILBERT *try to look as though they had heard of him constantly. She moves below the settee.)* He'd taken a house near Windermere—quite a mansion it was really—rather silly for an old gentleman living alone—and Andrew knocked on our front door one day and asked the footman for a glass of water. So my uncle invited him in to tea.

MRS. GILBERT *(moving center)*: Our meeting wasn't quite as romantic as that.

GILBERT: I knocked her flat on her face. *(He moves behind* MRS. GILBERT *and puts his hands on her shoulders.)*

MRS. GILBERT: Not with love at first sight. With the swing doors of our hotel bar. So of course then he apologized and . . . *(*ANDREW *turns and faces into the room.)*

GILBERT *(brusquely)*: Darling. The Crocker-Harrises, I'm sure, have far more important things to do than to listen to your detailed but inaccurate account of our very sordid little encounter. Why not just say I married you for your money and leave it at that? Come on, we must go.

MRS. GILBERT *(moving above the settee; to* MILLIE*)*: Isn't he awful to me?

MILLIE *(moving round the right end of the settee to the door up right)*: Men have no souls, my dear. My husband is just as bad.

MRS. GILBERT: Good-bye, Mr. Crocker-Harris.

ANDREW *(with a slight bow)*: Good-bye.

MRS. GILBERT *(moving to the door up right; to* MILLIE*)*: I think your idea about the dining-room is awfully good—if only I can get the permit. . . (MILLIE *and* MRS. GILBERT *go out.* GILBERT *has dallied to say good-bye alone to* ANDREW.*)*

GILBERT: Good-bye, sir.

ANDREW *(crossing center to left of* GILBERT*)*: Er—you will, I know, respect the confidences I have just made to you.

GILBERT: I should hate you to think I wouldn't.

ANDREW: I am sorry to have embarrassed you. I don't know what came over me. I have not been very well, you know. Good-bye, my dear fellow, and my best wishes.

GILBERT: Thank you. The very best of good luck to you too, sir, in your future career.

ANDREW: My future career? Yes. Thank you.

GILBERT: Well, good-bye, sir.

(He crosses up right and goes out. ANDREW *moves to the chair right of the desk and sits. He picks up a book and looks idly at it.* MILLIE *enters up right. She crosses above the table center, picks up the box of chocolates and eats one as she speaks.)*

MILLIE: Good-looking couple.

ANDREW: Very.

MILLIE: He looks as if he'd got what it takes. I should think he'll be a success all right.

ANDREW: That's what I thought.

MILLIE: I don't think it's much of a career, though—a schoolmaster—for a likely young chap like that.

ANDREW: I know you don't.

MILLIE *(crossing down to the desk and picking up the luggage labels)*: Still, I bet when he leaves this place it won't be without a pension. It'll be roses, roses all the way, and tears and cheers and good-bye, Mr. Chips.

ANDREW: I expect so.

MILLIE: What's the matter with you?

ANDREW: Nothing.

MILLIE: You're not going to have another of your attacks, are you? You look dreadful.

ANDREW: I'm perfectly all right.

MILLIE *(indifferently)*: You know best. Your medicine's there, anyway, if you want it.

(She goes out up center. ANDREW, *left alone, continues for a time staring at the text he has been pretending to read. Then he puts one hand over his eyes. There is a knock on the door up right.)*

ANDREW: Come in. *(*TAPLOW *enters up right and appears timidly from behind the screen. He is carrying a small book behind his back. Sharply.)* Yes, Taplow? What is it?

TAPLOW: Nothing, sir.

ANDREW: What do you mean, nothing?

TAPLOW *(timidly)*: I just came back to say good-bye, sir.

ANDREW: Oh. *(He puts down the book and rises.)*

TAPLOW *(moving center)*: I didn't have a chance with the head here. I rather dashed out, I'm afraid. I thought I'd just come back and—wish you luck, sir.

ANDREW: Thank you, Taplow. That's good of you.

TAPLOW: I—er—thought this might interest you, sir. *(He quickly thrusts the small book towards* ANDREW.*)*

ANDREW *(taking out his glasses and putting them on)*: What is it?

TAPLOW: Verse translation of *The Agamemnon,* sir. The Browning version. It's not much good. I've been reading it in the Chapel gardens.

ANDREW *(taking the book)*: Very interesting, Taplow. *(He seems to have a little difficulty in speaking. He clears his throat and then goes on in his level, gentle voice.)* I know the translation, of course. It has its faults, I agree, but I think you will enjoy it more when you get used to the meter he employs. *(He hands the book back to* TAPLOW.*)*

TAPLOW *(brusquely thrusting the book back to* ANDREW*)*: It's for you, sir.

ANDREW: For me?

TAPLOW: Yes, sir. I've written in it. *(*ANDREW *opens the figleaf and reads whatever is written there.)*

ANDREW: Did you buy this?

TAPLOW: Yes, sir. It was only second-hand.

ANDREW: You shouldn't have spent your pocket-money this way.

TAPLOW: That's all right, sir. It wasn't very much. *(Suddenly appalled.)* The price isn't still inside, is it? *(*ANDREW *carefully wipes his glasses and puts them on again.)*

ANDREW *(at length)*: No. Just what you've written. Nothing else.

TAPLOW: Good. I'm sorry you've got it already. I thought you probably would have.

ANDREW: I haven't got it already. I may have had it once. I can't remember. But I haven't got it now.

TAPLOW: That's all right, then. *(*ANDREW *continues to stare at* TAPLOW's *inscription on the flyleaf. Suspiciously.)* What's the matter, sir? Have I got the accent wrong on "eumenose"?

ANDREW: No. The perispomenon is perfectly correct. *(His hands are shaking. He lowers the book and turns away above the chair right of the desk.)* Taplow, would you be good enough to take that bottle of medicine, which you so kindly brought in, and pour me out one dose in a glass which you will find in the bathroom?

TAPLOW *(seeing something is wrong)*: Yes, sir. *(He moves up to the sideboard and picks up the bottle.)*

ANDREW: The doses are clearly marked on the bottle. I usually put a little water with it.

TAPLOW: Yes, sir.

(He darts out up center. ANDREW, *the moment he is gone, breaks down and begins to sob uncontrollably. He sits in the chair left of the desk and makes a desperate attempt, after a moment, to control himself, but when* TAPLOW *comes back his emotion is still very apparent.* TAPLOW *re-enters with the bottle and a glass, comes to the upstage end of the desk and holds out the glass.)*

ANDREW *(taking the glass)*: Thank you. *(He drinks, turning his back on* TAPLOW *as he does so.)* You must forgive this exhibition of weakness, Taplow. The truth is I have been going through rather a strain lately.

TAPLOW *(putting the bottle on the desk)*: Of course, sir. I quite understand. *(He eases towards center. There is a knock on the door upper left.)*

ANDREW: Come in. *(*FRANK *enters up left.)*

FRANK: Oh, sorry. I thought you'd be finished by now. *(He moves to left of* TAPLOW.*)*

ANDREW: Come in, Hunter, do. It's perfectly all right. Our lesson was over some time ago, but Taplow most kindly came back to say goodbye.

*(*FRANK, *taking in* TAPLOW's *rather startled face and* ANDREW's *obvious emotion, looks a little puzzled.)*

FRANK: Are you sure I'm not intruding?

ANDREW: No, no. I want you to see this book that Taplow has given me, Hunter. Look. A translation of *The Agamemnon,* by Robert Browning. *(He rises.)* Do you see the inscription he has put into it? *(He hands the book open to* FRANK *across the desk.)*

FRANK *(glancing at the book)*: Yes, but it's no use to me, I'm afraid. I never learnt Greek.

ANDREW: Then we'll have to translate it for him, won't we, Taplow? *(He recites by heart.)* "ton kratownta malthecose theos prosothen eumenose prosdirkati."That means—in a rough translation: "God from afar looks graciously upon a gentle master." It comes from a speech of Agamemnon's to Clytaemnestra.

FRANK: I see. Very pleasant and very apt. *(He hands the book back to* ANDREW.*)*

ANDREW: Very pleasant. But perhaps not, after all, so very apt.

(He turns quickly away from both of them as emotion once more seems about to overcome him. FRANK *brusquely jerks his head to the bewildered* TAPLOW *to get out.* TAPLOW *nods.)*

TAPLOW: Good-bye, sir, and the best of luck.

ANDREW: Good-bye, Taplow, and thank you very much.

*(*TAPLOW *flees quickly up right and goes out.* FRANK *watches* ANDREW's *back with a mixture of embarrassment and sympathy.)*

ANDREW *(turning at length, slightly recovered)*: Dear me, what a fool I made of myself in front of that boy. And in front of you, Hunter. *(He moves in to the desk.)* I can't imagine what you must think of me.

FRANK: Nonsense.

ANDREW: I am not a very emotional person, as you know, but there was something so very touching and kindly about his action, and coming as it did just after . . . *(He stops, then glances at the book in his hand.)* This is a very delightful thing to have, don't you think?

FRANK: Delightful.

ANDREW: The quotation, of course, he didn't find entirely by himself. I happened to make some little joke about the line in form the other day. But he must have remembered it all the same to have found it so readily—and perhaps he means it.

FRANK: I'm sure he does, or he wouldn't have written it.

*(*MILLIE *enters up center with a tray of supper things. She puts the tray on the sideboard. She puts table napkins, mats and bread on the table.* ANDREW *turns and looks out of the window.)*

MILLIE: Hullo, Frank. I'm glad you're in time. Lend me a cigarette. I've been gasping for one for an hour.

*(*FRANK *moves up left of the table center and once more extends his case.* MILLIE *takes a cigarette.)*

FRANK: Your husband has just had a very nice present.

MILLIE: Oh? Who from?

FRANK: Taplow. *(He comes down left of the table.)*

MILLIE *(coming down right of the table; smiling)*: Oh, Taplow. *(*FRANK *lights* MILLIE's *cigarette.)*

ANDREW *(moving above the desk to the chair right of it)*: He bought it with his own pocket-money, Millie, and wrote a very charming inscription inside.

FRANK: "God looks kindly upon a gracious master."

ANDREW: No—not gracious—gentle, I think. "ton kratownta malthecose"—yes, I think gentle is the better translation. I would rather have had this present, I think, than almost anything I can think of. *(There is a pause.* MILLIE *laughs suddenly.)*

MILLIE *(holding out her hand)*: Let's see it. The artful little beast. *(*ANDREW *hands the book across to* MILLIE. MILLIE *opens it.)*

FRANK *(urgently)*: Millie. (MILLIE *looks at* ANDREW.*)*

ANDREW: Artful? *(*MILLIE *looks at* FRANK.*)* Why artful? *(*FRANK *stares meaningly at* MILLIE. MILLIE *looks at* ANDREW.*)* Why artful, Millie? *(*MILLIE *laughs again, quite lightly.)*

MILLIE: My dear, because I came into this room this afternoon to find him giving an imitation of you to Frank here. Obviously he was scared stiff I was going to tell you, and you'd ditch his remove or something. I don't blame him for trying a few bobs' worth of appeasement.

(She gives the book to ANDREW, *then moves up right of the table to the sideboard, where she stubs out her cigarette, picks up some cutlery and starts to lay the table.* ANDREW *stands quite still, looking down at the book.)*

ANDREW *(after a pause; nodding)*: I see.

(He puts down the book gently on the desk, picks up the bottle of medicine and moves up left of the table to the door up center.)

MILLIE: Where are you going, dear? Dinner's nearly ready.

ANDREW *(opening the door)*: Only to my room for a moment. I won't be long.

MILLIE: You've just had a dose of that, dear. I shouldn't have another, if I were you.

ANDREW: I am allowed two at a time.

MILLIE: Well, see it is two and no more, won't you?

*(*ANDREW *meets her eye for a moment, then goes out quietly.* MILLIE *moves to left of the table and lays the last knife and fork. She looks at* FRANK *with an expression half defiant and half ashamed.)*

FRANK *(with a note of real repulsion in his voice)*: Millie! My God! How could you?

MILLIE: Well, why not? *(She crosses above the table and comes down left of the settee.)* Why should he be allowed his comforting little illusions? I'm not.

FRANK *(advancing on her)*: Listen. You're to go to his room now and tell him that was a lie.

MILLIE: Certainly not. It wasn't a lie.

FRANK: If you don't, I will.

MILLIE: I shouldn't, if I were you. It'll only make things worse. He won't believe you.

FRANK *(moving up right of the table center)*: We'll see about that.

MILLIE: Go ahead. See what happens. He knows I don't lie to him. He knows what I told him was the truth, and he won't like your sympathy. He'll think you're making fun of him, like Taplow.

*(*FRANK *hesitates, then comes slowly down center again.* MILLIE *watches him, a little frightened.)*

FRANK *(after a pause)*: We're finished, Millie—you and I.

MILLIE *(laughing)*: Frank, really! Don't be hysterical.

FRANK: I'm not. I mean it.

MILLIE *(lightly)*: Oh yes, you mean it. Of course you mean it. Now just sit down, dear, and relax and forget all about artful little boys and their five bob presents, and talk to me. *(She pulls at his coat.)*

FRANK *(pulling away)*: Forget? If I live to be a hundred I shall never forget that little glimpse you've just given me of yourself.

MILLIE: Frank—you're making a frightening mountain out of an absurd little molehill.

FRANK: Of course, but the mountain I'm making in my imagination is so frightening that I'd rather try to forget both it and the repulsive little molehill that gave it birth. But as I know I never can, I tell you, Millie—from this moment you and I are finished.

MILLIE *(quietly)*: You can't scare me, Frank. *(She turns away towards the fireplace.)* I know that's what you're trying to do, but you can't do it.

FRANK *(quietly)*: I'm not trying to scare you, Millie. I'm telling you the simple truth. I'm not coming to Bradford. *(There is a pause.)*

MILLIE *(turning to face* FRANK*; with an attempt at bravado)*: All right, my dear, if that's the way you feel about it. Don't come to Bradford.

FRANK: Right. Now I think you ought to go to your room and look after Andrew. *(He crosses towards the door up left.)* I'm leaving.

MILLIE *(following* FRANK*)*: What is this? Frank, I don't understand, really I don't. What have I done?

FRANK: I think you know what you've done, Millie. Go and look after Andrew.

MILLIE *(moving to the left end of the settee)*: Andrew? Why this sudden concern for Andrew?

FRANK: Because I think he's just been about as badly hurt as a human being can be; and as he's a sick man and in a rather hysterical state it might be a good plan to go and see how he is.

MILLIE *(scornfully)*: Hurt? Andrew hurt? You can't hurt Andrew. He's dead.

FRANK *(moving to right of* MILLIE*)*: Why do you hate him so much, Millie?

MILLIE: Because he keeps me from you.

FRANK: That isn't true.

MILLIE: Because he's not a man at all.

FRANK: He's a human being.

MILLIE: You've got a fine right to be so noble about him, after deceiving him for six months.

FRANK: Twice in six months—at your urgent invitation. (MILLIE *slaps his face, in a violent paroxysm of rage.)* Thank you for that. I deserved it. *(He crosses to the chair right of the desk.)* I deserve a lot worse than that, too.

MILLIE *(running to him)*: Frank, forgive me—I didn't mean it.

FRANK *(quietly)*: You'd better have the truth, Millie, it had to come some time. *(He turns to face* MILLIE.*)* I've never loved you. I've never told you I loved you.

MILLIE: I know, Frank, I know. *(She backs away slightly.)* I've always accepted that.

FRANK: You asked me just now if I was running away from you. Well, I was.

MILLIE: I knew that, too.

FRANK: But I was coming to Bradford. It was going to be the very last time I was ever going to see you and at Bradford I would have told you that.

MILLIE: You wouldn't. You wouldn't. You've tried to tell me that so often before—*(She crosses to the fireplace.)* and I've always stopped you somehow—somehow. I would have stopped you again.

FRANK *(quietly)*: I don't think so, Millie. Not this time.

MILLIE *(crossing to right of the table center)*: Frank, I don't care what humiliations you heap on me. I know you don't give two hoots for me as a person. I've always known that. I've never minded so long as you cared for me as a woman. And you do, Frank. You do. You do, don't you? *(*FRANK *is silent. He crosses slowly to the fireplace.)* It'll be all right at Bradford, you see. It'll be all right, there.

FRANK: I'm not coming to Bradford, Millie.

(The door up center opens slowly and ANDREW *enters. He is carrying the bottle of medicine. He hands it to* MILLIE *and passes on crossing down left below the desk.* MILLIE *holds the bottle up to the light.)*

ANDREW *(gently)*: You should know me well enough by now, my dear, to realize how unlikely it is that I should ever take an overdose.

*(*MILLIE, *without a word, puts the bottle on the sideboard and goes out up center.* ANDREW *goes to the cupboard down left and takes out the sherry and one glass.)*

FRANK: I'm not staying to dinner, I'm afraid.

ANDREW: Indeed? I'm sorry to hear that. You'll have a glass of sherry?

FRANK: No, thank you.

ANDREW: You will forgive me if I do.

FRANK: Of course. Perhaps I'll change my mind. *(He crosses to center.* ANDREW *takes out a second glass and fills both of them.)* About Taplow . . .

ANDREW: Oh yes?

FRANK: It *is* perfectly true that he was imitating you. I, of course, was mostly to blame in that, and I'm very sorry.

ANDREW: That is perfectly all right. Was it a good imitation?

FRANK: No.

ANDREW: I expect it was. Boys are often very clever mimics.

FRANK: We talked about you, of course, before that. *(He moves in to right of the desk.)* He said—you probably won't believe this, but I thought I ought to tell you—he said he liked you very much. *(*ANDREW *smiles slightly.)*

ANDREW: Indeed? *(He drinks.)*

FRANK: I can remember very clearly his exact words. He said: "He doesn't seem to like people to like him—but in spite of that, I do—very much." *(Lightly.)* So you see it looks after all as if the book might not have been a mere question of—appeasement.

ANDREW: The book? *(He picks it up.)* Dear me! What a lot of fuss about a little book—and a not very good little book at that. *(He drops it on the desk.)*

FRANK: I would like you to believe me.

ANDREW: Possibly you would, my dear Hunter; but I can assure you I am not particularly concerned about Taplow's views of my character: or about yours either, if it comes to that.

FRANK *(hopelessly)*: I think you should keep that book all the same. You may find it'll mean something to you after all.

ANDREW *(turning to the cupboard and pouring himself another sherry)*: Exactly. It will mean a perpetual reminder to myself of the story with which Taplow is at this very moment regaling his friends in the House. "I gave the Crock a book, to buy him off, and he blubbed. The Crock blubbed. I tell you I was there. I saw it. The Crock blubbed." My mimicry is not as good as his, I fear. Forgive me. *(He moves up left of the desk.)* And now let us leave this idiotic subject and talk of more pleasant things. Do you like this sherry? I got it on my last visit to London.

FRANK: If Taplow ever breathes a word of that story to anyone at all, I'll murder him. But he won't. And if you think I will you greatly underestimate my character as well as his.

(He drains his glass and puts it on the desk. He moves to the door up left. ANDREW *comes down left, puts his glass on the cupboard, and stands facing downstage.)*

Good-bye.

ANDREW: Are you leaving so soon? Good-bye, my dear fellow.

*(*FRANK *stops. He takes out his cigarette case and places it on the left end of the table center.)*

FRANK: As this is the last time I shall probably ever see you, I'm going to offer you a word of advice.

ANDREW *(politely)*: I shall be glad to listen to it.

FRANK: Leave your wife. *(There is a pause.* ANDREW *looks out of the window.)*

ANDREW: So that you may the more easily carry on your intrigue with her?

FRANK *(moving in to the upstage end of the desk)*: How long have you known that?

ANDREW: Since it first began.

FRANK: How did you find out?

ANDREW: By information.

FRANK: By whose information?

ANDREW: By someone's whose word I could hardly discredit. *(There is a pause.)*

FRANK *(slowly, with repulsion)*: No! That's too horrible to think of.

ANDREW *(turning to* FRANK*)*: Nothing is ever too horrible to think of, Hunter. It is simply a question of facing facts.

FRANK: She might have told you a lie. Have you faced that fact?

ANDREW: She never tells me a lie. In twenty years she has never told me a lie. Only the truth.

FRANK: This was a lie.

ANDREW *(moving up left of* FRANK*)*: No, my dear Hunter. Do you wish me to quote you dates?

FRANK *(still unable to believe it)*: And she told you six months ago?

ANDREW *(moving down left)*: Isn't it seven?

FRANK *(savagely)*: Then why have you allowed me inside your home? Why haven't you done something—reported me to the governors—anything—made a scene, knocked me down?

ANDREW: Knocked you down?

FRANK: You didn't have to invite me to dinner.

ANDREW: My dear Hunter, if, over the last twenty years, I had allowed such petty considerations to influence my choice of dinner guests I would have found it increasingly hard to remember which master to invite and which to refuse. You see, Hunter, you mustn't flatter yourself you are the first. My information is a good deal better than yours, you understand. It's authentic. *(There is a pause.)*

FRANK: She's evil.

ANDREW: That's hardly a kindly epithet to apply to a lady whom, I gather, you have asked to marry.

FRANK: Did she tell you that?

ANDREW: She's a dutiful wife. She tells me everything.

FRANK: That, at least, was a lie.

ANDREW: She never lies.

FRANK *(leaning on the desk)*: That was a lie. Do you want the truth? Can you bear the truth?

ANDREW: I can bear anything. *(He crosses to the fireplace.)*

FRANK *(turning to face* ANDREW*)*: What I did I did coldbloodedly out of weakness and ignorance and crass stupidity. I'm bitterly, bitterly ashamed of myself, but, in a sense, I'm glad you know *(He moves center.)* though I'd rather a thousand times that you'd heard it from me than from your wife. I won't ask you to forgive me. I can only tell you, with complete truth, that the only emotion she has ever succeeded in arousing in me she aroused in me for the first time ten minutes ago—an intense and passionate disgust.

ANDREW: What a delightfully chivalrous statement.

FRANK *(moving below the settee)*: Forget chivalry, Crock, for God's sake. Forget all your fine mosaic scruples. You must leave her—it's your only chance.

ANDREW: She's my wife, Hunter. You seem to forget that. As long as she wishes to remain my wife, she may.

FRANK: She's out to kill you.

ANDREW: My dear Hunter, if that was indeed her purpose, you should know by now that she fulfilled it long ago.

FRANK: Why won't you leave her?

ANDREW: Because I wouldn't wish to add another grave wrong to one I have already done her.

FRANK: What wrong have you done her?

ANDREW: To marry her. *(There is a pause.* FRANK *stares at him in silence.)* You see, my dear Hunter, she is really quite as much to be pitied as I. We are both of us interesting subjects for your microscope. *(He sits on the fender.)* Both of us needing from the other something that would make life supportable for us, and neither of us able to give it. Two kinds of love. Hers and mine. Worlds apart as I know now, though when I married her I didn't think they were incompatible. In those days I hadn't thought that her kind of love—the love she requires and which I was unable to give her—was so important that its absence would drive out the other kind of love—the kind of love that I require and which I thought, in my folly, was by far the greater part of love. *(He rises.)* I may have been, you see, Hunter, a brilliant classical scholar, but I was woefully ignorant of the facts of life. I know better now, of course. I know that in both of us, the love that we should have borne each other has turned to bitter hatred. That's all the problem is. Not a very unusual one, I venture to think—nor nearly as tragic as you seem to imagine. Merely the problem of an unsatisfied wife and a henpecked husband. You'll find it all over the world. It is usually, I believe, a subject for farce. *(He turns to the mantelpiece and adjusts the hands of the clock.)* And now, if you have to leave us, my dear fellow, please don't let me detain you any longer. *(*FRANK *makes no move to go.)*

FRANK: Don't go to Bradford. Stay here, until you take up your new job.

ANDREW: I think I've already told you I'm not interested in your advice.

FRANK: Leave her. It's the only way.

ANDREW *(violently)*: Will you please go!

FRANK: All right. I'd just like you to say good-bye to me, properly, though. Will you? I shan't see you again. I know you don't want my pity, but, I would like to be of some help. *(*ANDREW *turns and faces* FRANK.*)*

ANDREW: If you think, by this expression of kindness, Hunter, that you can get me to repeat the shameful exhibition of emotion I made to Taplow a moment ago, I must tell you that you have no chance. My hysteria over that book just now was no more than a sort of reflex action of the spirit. The muscular twitchings of a corpse. It can never happen again.

FRANK: A corpse can be revived.

ANDREW: I don't believe in miracles.

FRANK: Don't you? Funnily enough, as a scientist, I do.

ANDREW *(turning to the fireplace)*: Your faith would be touching, if I were capable of being touched by it.

FRANK: You are, I think. *(He moves behind* ANDREW. *After a pause.)* I'd like to come and visit you at this crammer's.

ANDREW: That is an absurd suggestion.

FRANK: I suppose it is rather, but all the same I'd like to do it. May I?

ANDREW: Of course not.

FRANK *(sitting on the settee)*: Your term begins on the first of September, doesn't it? *(He takes out a pocket diary.)*

ANDREW: I tell you the idea is quite childish.

FRANK: I could come about the second week.

ANDREW: You would be bored to death. So, probably, would I.

FRANK *(glancing at his diary)*: Let's say Monday the twelfth, then.

ANDREW *(turning to face* FRANK, *his hands beginning to tremble)*: Say anything you like, only please go. Please go, Hunter.

FRANK *(writing in his book and not looking at* ANDREW*)*: That's fixed, then. Monday, September the twelfth. Will you remember that?

ANDREW *(after a pause; with difficulty)*: I suppose I'm at least as likely to remember it as you are.

FRANK: That's fixed, then. *(He rises, slips the book into his pocket and puts out his hand.)* Good-bye, until then. *(He moves in to* ANDREW. ANDREW *hesitates, then shakes his hand.)*

ANDREW: Good-bye.

FRANK: May I go out through your garden? *(He crosses to center.)*

ANDREW *(nodding)*: Of course.

FRANK: I'm off to have a quick word with Taplow. By the way, may I take him a message from you?

ANDREW: What message?

FRANK: Has he or has he not got his remove?

ANDREW: He has.

FRANK: May I tell him?

ANDREW: It is highly irregular. Yes, you may.

FRANK: Good. *(He turns to go, then turns back.)* Oh, by the way, I'd better have the address of that crammer's.

(He moves below the settee, takes out his diary, and points his pencil, ready to write. MILLIE *enters up center. She carries a casserole on three plates.)*

MILLIE *(coming above the table center)*: Dinner's ready. You're staying, Frank, aren't you? *(she puts the casserole and plates on the table.)*

FRANK *(politely)*: No. I'm afraid not. *(To* ANDREW.*)* What's that address?

ANDREW *(after great hesitation)*: The Old Deanery, Malcombe, Dorset.

FRANK: I'll write to you and you can let me know about trains. Good-bye. *(To* MILLIE.*)* Good-bye.

(He crosses to the door up left and goes out. MILLIE *is silent for a moment. Then she laughs.)*

MILLIE: That's a laugh, I must say.

ANDREW: What's a laugh, my dear?

MILLIE: You inviting him to stay with you.

ANDREW: I didn't. He suggested it.

MILLIE *(moving to the left end of the settee)*: He's coming to Bradford.

ANDREW: Yes. I remember your telling me so.

MILLIE: He's coming to Bradford. He's not going to you.

ANDREW: The likeliest contingency is, that he's not going to either of us.

MILLIE: He's coming to Bradford.

ANDREW: I expect so. Oh, by the way, I'm not. I shall be staying here until I go to Dorset.

MILLIE *(indifferently)*: Suit yourself. What makes you think I'll join you there?

ANDREW: I don't.

MILLIE: You needn't expect me.

ANDREW: I don't think either of us has the right to expect anything further from the other. *(The telephone rings.)* Excuse me. *(He moves to the table down right and lifts the receiver.)* Hullo . . . *(While he is speaking* MILLIE *crosses to left of the table center. About to sit, she sees the cigarette case. She picks it up, fingers it for a moment, and finally drops it into her pocket.)* Yes, Headmaster . . . The timetable? . . . It's perfectly simple. The middle fourth B division will take a ten-minute break on Tuesdays and a fifteen-minute break on alternate Wednesdays; while exactly the reverse procedure will apply to the lower Shell, C division. I thought I had sufficiently explained that on my chart . . . Oh, I see . . . Thank you, that is very good of you . . . Yes. I think you will find it will work out quite satisfactorily . . . Oh by the way, Headmaster. I have changed my mind about the prize-giving ceremony. I intend to speak after, instead of before, Fletcher, as is my privilege . . . Yes, I quite understand, but I am now seeing the matter in a different light . . . I know, but I am of opinion that occasionally an anti-climax can be surprisingly effective. Good-bye. *(He replaces the receiver, crosses to right of the table center, and sits.)* Come along, my dear. We mustn't let our dinner get cold. *(He unrolls his table napkin.* MILLIE *sits left of the table and unrolls her table napkin.* ANDREW *offers her the bread. She ignores it. He takes a piece. She removes the lid of the casserole as—*

Curtain

Questions

1. Why do you think Andrew is so willing to accept the way people treat him?
2. Why do you think the remark about Andrew's being "the Himmler of the lower fifth" hurts him so much?
3. Why does the gift of the book affect Andrew so deeply?

4. Why do you think Millie is so cruel and vicious in telling Andrew that Taplow was using the book as a form of bribery?
5. Is Andrew a believable character? Why or why not? Is Millie? Taplow? Frank?
6. Determine the turning point and climax.
7. Do you think this is a good play? Why or why not?

JOHN MILLINGTON SYNGE

In the Shadow of the Glen

JOHN MILLINGTON SYNGE is considered by many the greatest modern Irish dramatist. Born in 1871, he died in his late thirties, leaving only six plays. Yet in these plays he showed great control of dramatic structure, whether comic or tragic. In all six plays Synge dealt with the Irish character and thought.

IN THE SHADOW OF THE GLEN drew the open hostility of the Dublin audience when it was first produced. The text is highly condensed with nearly every line essential to its understanding.

This play defies classification in that it is half-serious and half-comic with elements of farce. It is serious in its portrayal of the poverty that existed in Ireland at the time but farcical in situation.

In pure farce, however, there are stock characters who have no depth, and the plot, which relies on physical actions and devious twists, is contrived. Also, there is never an important theme, and the progression of the action shows only how the major characters manage to release themselves from entanglements.

Often farce deals with illicit sexual relationships and infidelity but is amoral in outlook. The aim is only to provide laughter for the audience, and much of the fun is in the visual gags and absurdities of speech. The plot relies on misunderstandings, and many comic devices are used, including repetition, incongruity, and derision. There is often physical violence, misunderstandings, mistaken identity, and deception. The characters are victims of their vices and appear ridiculous when caught.

In the Shadow of the Glen John M. Synge

Characters:

DAN BURKE, *farmer and herd*
NORA BURKE, *his wife*
MICHEAL DARA, *a young herd*
A TRAMP

Setting:

The last cottage at the head of a long glen in County Wicklow.

(Cottage kitchen; turf fire on the right; a bed near it against the wall with a body lying on it covered with a sheet. A door is at the other end of the room, with a low table near it, and stools, or wooden chairs. There are a couple of glasses on the table, and a bottle of whisky, as if for a wake, with two cups, a teapot, and a homemade cake. There is another small door near the bed. NORA BURKE *is moving about the room, settling a few things, and lighting candles on the table, looking now and then at the bed with an uneasy look. Someone knocks softly at the door. She takes up a stocking with money from the table and puts it in her pocket. Then she opens the door.)*

TRAMP *(outside)*: Good evening to you, lady of the house.

NORA: Good evening, kindly stranger, it's a wild night, God help you, to be out in the rain falling.

TRAMP: It is, surely, and I walking to Brittas from the Aughrim fair.

NORA: Is it walking on your feet, stranger?

TRAMP: On my two feet, lady of the house, and when I saw the light below I thought maybe if you'd a sup of new milk and a quiet decent corner where a man could sleep. *(He looks in past her and sees the dead man.)* The Lord have mercy on us all!

NORA: It doesn't matter anyway, stranger, come in out of the rain.

TRAMP *(coming in slowly and going towards the bed)*: Is it departed he is?

NORA: It is, stranger. He's after dying on me, God forgive him, and there I am now with a hundred sheep beyond on the hills, and no turf drawn for the winter.

TRAMP *(looking closely at the dead man)*: It's a queer look is on him for a man that's dead.

NORA *(half-humorously)*: He was always queer, stranger, and I suppose them that's queer and they living men will be queer bodies after.

TRAMP: Isn't it a great wonder you're letting him lie there, and he is not tidied, or laid out itself?

NORA *(coming to the bed)*: I was afeard, stranger, for he put a black curse on me this morning if I'ld touch his body the time he'ld die sudden, or let any one touch it except his sister only, and it's ten miles away she lives in the big glen over the hill.

TRAMP *(looking at her and nodding slowly)*: It's a queer story he wouldn't let his own wife touch him, and he dying quiet in his bed.

NORA: He was an old man, and an odd man, stranger, and it's always up on the hills he was thinking thoughts in the dark mist. *(She pulls back a bit of the sheet.)* Lay your hand on him now, and tell me if it's cold he is surely.

TRAMP: Is it getting the curse on me you'ld be, woman of the house? I wouldn't lay my hand on him for the Lough[1] Nahanagan and it filled with gold.

NORA *(looking uneasily at the body)*: Maybe cold would be no sign of death with the like of him, for he was always cold, every day since I knew him,—and every night, stranger,—*(She covers up his face and comes away from the bed);* but I'm thinking it's dead he is surely, for he's complaining a while back of a pain in his heart, and this morning, the time he was going off to Brittas for three days or four, he was taken with a sharp turn. Then he went into his bed and he was saying it was destroyed he was, the time the shadow was going up through the glen, and when the sun set on the bog beyond he made a great lep, and let a great cry out of him, and stiffened himself out the like of a dead sheep.

TRAMP *(crosses himself)*: God rest his soul.

NORA *(pouring him out a glass of whisky)*: Maybe that would do you better than the milk of the sweetest cow in County Wicklow.

TRAMP: The Almighty God reward you, and may it be to your good health. *(He drinks.)*

NORA *(giving him a pipe and tobacco)*: I've no pipes saving his own, stranger, but they're sweet pipes to smoke.

TRAMP: Thank you kindly, lady of the house.

NORA: Sit down now, stranger, and be taking your rest.

TRAMP *(filling a pipe and looking about the room)*: I've walked a great way through the world, lady of the house, and seen great wonders, but I never seen a wake till this day with fine spirits, and good tobacco, and the best of pipes, and no one to taste them but a woman only.

NORA: Didn't you hear me say it was only after dying on me he was when the sun went down, and how would I go out into the glen and tell the neighbours, and I a lone woman with no house near me?

TRAMP *(drinking)*: There's no offence, lady of the house?

NORA: No offence in life, stranger. How would the like of you, passing in the dark night, know the lonesome way I was with no house near me at all?

TRAMP *(sitting down)*: I knew rightly. *(He lights his pipe so that there is a sharp*

1. Lake.

light beneath his haggard face.) And I was thinking, and I coming in through the door, that it's many a lone woman would be afeard of the like of me in the dark night, in a place wouldn't be as lonesome as this place, where there aren't two living souls would see the little light you have shining from the glass.

NORA *(slowly)*: I'm thinking many would be afeard, but I never knew what way I'd be afeard of beggar or bishop or any man of you at all. *(She looks towards the window and lowers her voice.)* It's other things than the like of you, stranger, would make a person afeard.

TRAMP *(looking round with a half-shudder)*: It is surely, God help us all!

NORA *(looking at him for a moment with curiosity)*: You're saying that, stranger, as if you were easy afeard.

TRAMP *(speaking mournfully)*: Is it myself, lady of the house, that does be walking round in the long nights, and crossing the hills when the fog is on them, the time a little stick would seem as big as your arm, and a rabbit as big as a bay horse, and a stack of turf as big as a towering church in the city of Dublin? If myself was easily afeard, I'm telling you, it's long ago I'ld have been locked into the Richmond Asylum, or maybe have run up into the back hills with nothing on me but an old shirt, and been eaten with crows the like of Patch Darcy—the Lord have mercy on him—in the year that's gone.

NORA *(with interest)*: You knew Darcy?

TRAMP: Wasn't I the last one heard his living voice in the whole world?

NORA: There were great stories of what was heard at that time, but would any one believe the things they do be saying in the glen?

TRAMP: It was no lie, lady of the house. . . . I was passing below on a dark night the like of this night, and the sheep were lying under the ditch and every one of them coughing, and choking, like an old man, with the great rain and the fog. Then I heard a thing talking—queer talk, you wouldn't believe at all, and you out of your dreams,—and "Merciful God," says I, "if I begin hearing the like of that voice out of the thick mist, I'm destroyed surely." Then I run, and I run, and I run, till I was below in Rathvanna. I got drunk that night, I got drunk in the morning, and drunk the day after,—I was coming from the races beyond—and the third day they found Darcy. . . . Then I knew it was himself I was after hearing, and I wasn't afeard any more.

NORA *(speaking sorrowfully and slowly)*: God spare Darcy, he'ld always look in here and he passing up or passing down, and it's very lonesome I was after him a long while *(she looks over at the bed and lowers her voice, speaking very clearly)*, and then I got happy again—if it's ever happy we are, stranger,—for I got used to being lonesome. *(A short pause; then she stands up.)*

NORA: Was there any one on the last bit of the road, stranger, and you coming from Aughrim?

TRAMP: There was a young man with a drift of mountain ewes, and he running after them this way and that.

NORA *(with a half-smile)*: Far down, stranger?

TRAMP: A piece only. *(She fills the kettle and puts it on the fire.)*

NORA: Maybe, if you're not easy afeard, you'ld stay here a short while alone with himself.

TRAMP: I would surely. A man that's dead can do no hurt.

NORA *(speaking with a sort of constraint)*: I'm going a little back to the west, stranger, for himself would go there one night and another and whistle at that place, and then the young man you're after seeing—a kind of a farmer has come up from the sea to live in a cottage beyond—would walk round to see if there was a thing we'ld have to be done, and I'm wanting him this night, the way he can go down into the glen when the sun goes up and tell the people that himself is dead.

TRAMP *(looking at the body in the sheet)*: It's myself will go for him, lady of the house, and let you not be destroying yourself with the great rain.

NORA: You wouldn't find your way, stranger, for there's a small path only, and it running up between two sluigs[2] where an ass and cart would be drowned. *(She puts a shawl over her head.)* Let you be making yourself easy, and saying a prayer for his soul, and it's not long I'll be coming again.

TRAMP *(moving uneasily)*: Maybe if you'd a piece of a grey thread and a sharp needle—there's great safety in a needle, lady of the house—I'ld be putting a little stitch here and there in my old coat, the time I'll be praying for his soul, and it going up naked to the saints of God.

NORA *(takes a needle and thread from the front of her dress and gives it to him)*: There's the needle, stranger, and I'm thinking you won't be lonesome, and you used to the back hills, for isn't a dead man itself more company than to be sitting alone, and hearing the winds crying, and you not knowing on what thing your mind would stay?

TRAMP *(slowly)*: It's true, surely, and the Lord have mercy on us all!

*(*NORA *goes out. The* TRAMP *begins stitching one of the tags in his coat, saying the "De Profundis" under his breath. In an instant the sheet is drawn slowly down, and* DAN BURKE *looks out. The* TRAMP *moves uneasily, then looks up, and springs to his feet with a movement of terror.)*

DAN *(with a hoarse voice)*: Don't be afeard, stranger; a man that's dead can do no hurt.

TRAMP *(trembling)*: I meant no harm, your honour; and won't you leave me easy to be saying a little prayer for your soul? *(A long whistle is heard outside.)*

DAN *(sitting up in his bed and speaking fiercely)*: Ah, the devil mend her. . . .

2. Swamplike area.

Do you hear that, stranger? Did ever you hear another woman could whistle the like of that with two fingers in her mouth? *(He looks at the table hurriedly.)* I'm destroyed with the drouth,[3] and let you bring me a drop quickly before herself will come back.

TRAMP *(doubtfully)*: Is it not dead you are?

DAN: How would I be dead, and I as dry as a baked bone, stranger?

TRAMP *(pouring out the whisky)*: What will herself say if she smells the stuff on you, for I'm thinking it's not for nothing you're letting on to be dead?

DAN: It is not, stranger, but she won't be coming near me at all, and it's not long now I'll be letting on, for I've a cramp in my back, and my hip's asleep on me, and there's been the devil's own fly itching my nose. It's near dead I was wanting to sneeze, and you blathering[4] about the rain, and Darcy *(bitterly)*—the devil choke him—and the towering church. *(Crying out impatiently.)* Give me that whisky. Would you have herself come back before I taste a drop at all? *(*TRAMP *gives him the glass.)*

DAN *(after drinking)*: Go over now to that cupboard, and bring me a black stick you'll see in the west corner by the wall.

TRAMP *(taking a stick from the cupboard)*: Is it that?

DAN: It is, stranger; it's a long time I'm keeping that stick for I've a bad wife in the house.

TRAMP *(with a queer look)*: Is it herself, master of the house, and she a grand woman to talk?

DAN: It's herself, surely, it's a bad wife she is—a bad wife for an old man, and I'm getting old, God help me, though I've an arm to me still. *(He takes the stick in his hand.)* Let you wait now a short while, and it's a great sight you'll see in this room in two hours or three. *(He stops to listen.)* Is that somebody above?

TRAMP *(listening)*: There's a voice speaking on the path.

DAN: Put that stick here in the bed and smooth the sheet the way it was lying. *(He covers himself up hastily.)* Be falling to sleep now and don't let on you know anything, or I'll be having your life. I wouldn't have told you at all but it's destroyed with the drouth I was.

TRAMP *(covering his head)*: Have no fear, master of the house. What is it I know of the like of you that I'ld be saying a word or putting out my hand to stay you at all?

(He goes back to the fire, sits down on a stool with his back to the bed and goes on stitching his coat.)

DAN *(under the sheet, querulously)*: Stranger.

3. Thirst.

4. Talking foolishly.

TRAMP *(quickly)*: Whisht, whisht. Be quiet I'm telling you, they're coming now at the door. *(*NORA *comes in with* MICHEAL DARA, *a tall, innocent young man behind her.)*

NORA: I wasn't long at all, stranger, for I met himself on the path.

TRAMP: You were middling long, lady of the house.

NORA: There was no sign from himself?

TRAMP: No sign at all, lady of the house.

NORA *(to* MICHEAL*)*: Go over now and pull down the sheet, and look on himself, Micheal Dara, and you'll see it's the truth I'm telling you.

MICHEAL: I will not, Nora, I do be afeard of the dead.

(He sits down on a stool next the table facing the TRAMP. NORA *puts the kettle on a lower hook of the pot-hooks, and piles turf under it.)*

NORA *(turning to* TRAMP*)*: Will you drink a sup of tea with myself and the young man, stranger, or *(speaking more persuasively)* will you go into the little room and stretch yourself a short while on the bed, I'm thinking it's destroyed you are walking the length of that way in the great rain.

TRAMP: Is it to go away and leave you, and you having a wake, lady of the house? I will not surely. *(He takes a drink from his glass which he has beside him.)* And it's none of your tea I'm asking either. *(He goes on stitching.* NORA *makes the tea.)*

MICHEAL *(after looking at the* TRAMP *rather scornfully for a moment)*: That's a poor coat you have, God help you, and I'm thinking it's a poor tailor you are with it.

TRAMP: If it's a poor tailor I am, I'm thinking it's a poor herd does be running back and forward after a little handful of ewes the way I seen yourself running this day, young fellow, and you coming from the fair. *(*NORA *comes back to the table.)*

NORA *(to* MICHEAL *in a low voice)*: Let you not mind him at all, Micheal Dara, he has a drop taken and it's soon he'll be falling asleep.

MICHEAL: It's no lie he's telling, I was destroyed surely. They were that wilful they were running off into one man's bit of oats, and another man's bit of hay, and tumbling into the red bogs till it's more like a pack of old goats than sheep they were. Mountain ewes is a queer breed, Nora Burke, and I'm not used to them at all.

NORA *(settling the tea things)*: There's no one can drive a mountain ewe but the men do be reared in the Glen Malure, I've heard them say, and above by Rathvanna, and the Glen Imaal, men the like of Patch Darcy, God spare his soul, who would walk through five hundred sheep and miss one of them, and he not reckoning them at all.

MICHEAL *(uneasily)*: Is it the man went queer in his head the year that's gone?

NORA: It is surely.

TRAMP *(plaintively)*: That was a great man, young fellow, a great man I'm telling you. There was never a lamb from his own ewes he wouldn't know before it was marked, and he'ld run from this to the city of Dublin and never catch for his breath.

NORA *(turning round quickly)*: He was a great man surely, stranger, and isn't it a grand thing when you hear a living man saying a good word of a dead man, and he mad dying?

TRAMP: It's the truth I'm saying, God spare his soul.

(He puts the needle under the collar of his coat, and settles himself to sleep in the chimney-corner. NORA *sits down at the table; their backs are turned to the bed.)*

MICHEAL *(looking at her with a queer look)*: I heard tell this day, Nora Burke, that it was on the path below Patch Darcy would be passing up and passing down, and I heard them say he'ld never pass it night or morning without speaking with yourself.

NORA *(in a low voice)*: It was no lie you heard, Micheal Dara.

MICHEAL: I'm thinking it's a power of men you're after knowing if it's in a lonesome place you live itself.

NORA *(giving him his tea)*: It's in a lonesome place you do have to be talking with some one, and looking for some one, in the evening of the day, and if it's a power of men I'm after knowing they were fine men, for I was a hard child to please, and a hard girl to please *(she looks at him a little sternly),* and it's a hard woman I am to please this day, Micheal Dara, and it's no lie I'm telling you.

MICHEAL *((looking over to see that the* TRAMP *is asleep, and then pointing to the dead man)*: Was it a hard woman to please you were when you took himself for your man?

NORA: What way would I live and I an old woman if I didn't marry a man with a bit of a farm, and cows on it, and sheep on the back hills?

MICHEAL *(considering)*: That's true, Nora, and maybe it's no fool you were, for there's good grazing on it, if it is a lonesome place, and I'm thinking it's a good sum he's left behind.

NORA *(taking the stocking with money from her pocket and putting it on the table)*: I do be thinking in the long nights it was a big fool I was that time, Micheal Dara, for what good is a bit of a farm with cows on it, and sheep on the back hills, when you do be sitting looking out from a door the like of that door, and seeing nothing but the mists rolling down the bog, and the mists again, and they rolling up the bog, and hearing nothing but the wind crying out in the bits of broken trees were left from the great storm, and the streams roaring with the rain.

MICHEAL *(looking at her uneasily)*: What is it ails you, this night, Nora Burke? I've heard tell it's the like of that talk you do hear from men, and they after being a great while on the back hills.

NORA *(putting out the money on the table)*: It's a bad night, and a wild night, Micheal Dara, and isn't it a great while I am at the foot of the back hills, sitting up here boiling food for himself, and food for the brood sow, and baking a cake when the night falls? *(She puts up the money, listlessly, in little piles on the table.)* Isn't it a long while I am sitting here in the winter and the summer, and the fine spring, with the young growing behind me and the old passing, saying to myself one time, to look on Mary Brien who wasn't that height *(holding out her hand),* and I a fine girl growing up, and there she is now with two children, and another coming on her in three months or four. *(She pauses.)*

MICHEAL *(moving over three of the piles)*: That's three pounds we have now, Nora Burke.

NORA *(continuing in the same voice)*: And saying to myself another time, to look on Peggy Cavanagh, who had the lightest hand at milking a cow that wouldn't be easy, or turning a cake, and there she is now walking round on the roads, or sitting in a dirty old house, with no teeth in her mouth, and no sense and no more hair than you'ld see on a bit of a hill and they after burning the furze from it.

MICHEAL: That's five pounds and ten notes, a good sum, surely! . . . It's not that way you'll be talking when you marry a young man, Nora Burke, and they were saying in the fair my lambs were the best lambs, and I got a grand price, for I'm no fool now at making a bargain when my lambs are good.

NORA: What was it you got?

MICHEAL: Twenty pound for the lot, Nora Burke. . . . We'ld do right to wait now till himself will be quiet awhile in the Seven Churches, and then you'll marry me in the chapel of Rathvanna, and I'll bring the sheep up on the bit of a hill you have on the back mountain, and we won't have anything we'ld be afeard to let our minds on when the mist is down.

NORA *(pouring him out some whisky)*: Why would I marry you, Mike Dara? You'll be getting old and I'll be getting old, and in a little while I'm telling you, you'll be sitting up in your bed—the way himself was sitting—with a shake in your face, and your teeth falling, and the white hair sticking out round you like an old bush where sheep do be leaping a gap.

*(*DAN BURKE *sits up noiselessly from under the sheet, with his hand to his face. His white hair is sticking out round his head.)*

NORA *(goes on slowly without hearing him)*: It's a pitiful thing to be getting old, but it's a queer thing surely. It's a queer thing to see an old man sitting up there in his bed with no teeth in him, and a rough word in his mouth, and his chin the way it would take the bark from the edge of an oak board you'ld have building a door. . . . God forgive me, Michael Dara, we'll all be getting old, but it's a queer thing surely.

MICHEAL: It's too lonesome you are from living a long time with an old man, Nora, and you're talking again like a herd that would be coming down the thick mist *(He puts his arm round her.)*, but it's a fine life you'll have now with a young man, a fine life surely. . . .

*(*DAN *sneezes violently.* MICHEAL *tries to get to the door, but before he can do so,* DAN *jumps out of the bed in queer white clothes, with his stick in his hand, and goes over and puts his back against it.)*

MICHEAL: Son of God deliver us. *(Crosses himself, and goes backward across the room.)*

DAN *(holding up his hand at him)*: Now you'll not marry her the time I'm rotting below in the Seven Churches, and you'll see the thing I'll give you will follow you on the back mountains when the wind is high.

MICHEAL *(to* NORA*)*: Get me out of it, Nora, for the love of God. He always did what you bid him, and I'm thinking he would do it now.

DAN *(turning towards her)*: It's little you care if it's dead or living I am, but there'll be an end now of your fine times, and all the talk you have of young men and old men, and of the mist coming up or going down. *(He opens the door.)* You'll walk out now from that door, Nora Burke, and it's not to-morrow, or the next day, or any day of your life, that you'll put in your foot through it again.

TRAMP *(standing up)*: It's a hard thing you're saying for an old man, master of the house, and what would the like of her do if you put her out on the roads?

DAN: Let her walk round the like of Peggy Cavanagh below, and be begging money at the cross-road, or selling songs to the men. *(To* NORA.*)* Walk out now, Nora Burke, and it's soon you'll be getting old with that life, I'm telling you; it's soon your teeth'll be falling and your head'll be the like of a bush where sheep do be leaping a gap. *(He pauses: she looks round at* MICHEAL.*)*

MICHEAL *(timidly)*: There's a fine Union below in Rathdrum.

DAN: The like of her would never go there. . . . It's lonesome roads she'll be going and hiding herself away till the end will come, and they find her stretched like a dead sheep with the frost on her, or the big spiders, maybe, and they putting their webs on her, in the butt of a ditch.

NORA *(angrily)*: What way will yourself be that day, Daniel Burke? What way will you be that day and you lying down a long while in your grave? For it's bad you are living, and it's bad you'll be when you're dead. *(She looks at him a moment fiercely, then half turns away and speaks plaintively again.)* Yet, if it is itself, Daniel Burke, who can help it at all, and let you be getting up into your bed, and not be taking your death with the wind blowing on you, and the rain with it, and you half in your skin.

DAN: It's proud and happy you'ld be if I was getting my death the day I was shut of yourself. *(Pointing to the door.)* Let you walk out through that door, I'm telling you, and let you not be passing this way if it's hungry you are, or wanting a bed.

TRAMP *(pointing to* MICHEAL*)*: Maybe himself would take her.

NORA: What would he do with me now?

TRAMP: Give you the half of a dry bed, and good food in your mouth.

DAN: Is it a fool you think him, stranger, or is it a fool you were born yourself? Let her walk out of that door, and let you go along with her, stranger—if it's raining itself—for it's too much talk you have surely.

TRAMP *(going over to* NORA*)*: We'll be going now, lady of the house—the rain is falling, but the air is kind and maybe it'll be a grand morning by the grace of God.

NORA: What good is a grand morning when I'm destroyed surely, and I going out to get my death walking the roads?

TRAMP: You'll not be getting your death with myself, lady of the house, and I knowing all the ways a man can put food in his mouth . . . .We'll be going now, I'm telling you, and the time you'll be feeling the cold, and the frost, and the great rain, and the sun again, and the south wind blowing in the glens, you'll not be sitting up on a wet ditch, the way you're after sitting in the place, making yourself old with looking on each day, and it passing you by. You'll be saying one time, "It's a grand evening, by the grace of God," and another time, "It's a wild night, God help us, but it'll pass surely." You'll be saying—

DAN *(goes over to them crying out impatiently)*: Go out of that door, I'm telling you, and do your blathering below in the glen. *(*NORA *gathers a few things into her shawl.)*

TRAMP *(at the door)*: Come along with me now, lady of the house, and it's not my blather you'll be hearing only, but you'll be hearing the herons crying out over the black lakes, and you'll be hearing the grouse and the owls with them, and the larks and the big thrushes when the days are warm, and it's not from the like of them you'll be hearing a talk of getting old like Peggy Cavanagh, and losing the hair off you, and the light of your eyes, but it's fine songs you'll be hearing when the sun goes up, and there'll be no old fellow wheezing, and the like of a sick sheep, close to your ear.

NORA: I'm thinking it's myself will be wheezing that time with lying down under the Heavens when the night is cold; but you've a fine bit of talk, stranger, and it's with yourself I'll go. *(She goes toward the door, then turns to* DAN.*)* You think it's a grand thing you're after doing with your letting on to be dead, but what is it at all? What way would a woman live in a lonesome place the like of this place, and she not making a talk with the men passing? And what way will yourself live from this day, with none to care for you? What is it you'll have now but a black life, Daniel Burke, and it's not long I'm telling you, till you'll be lying again under that sheet, and you dead surely.

(She goes out with the TRAMP. MICHEAL *is slinking after them, but* DAN *stops him.)*

DAN: Sit down now and take a little taste of the stuff, Micheal Dara. There's a great drouth on me, and the night is young.

MICHEAL *(coming back to the table)*: And it's very dry I am, surely, with the fear of death you put on me, and I after driving mountain ewes since the turn of the day.

DAN *(throwing away his stick)*: I was thinking to strike you, Micheal Dara, but you're a quiet man, God help you, and I don't mind you at all. *(He pours out two glasses of whisky, and gives one to* MICHEAL.*)*

DAN: Your good health, Micheal Dara.

MICHEAL: God reward you, Daniel Burke, and may you have a long life, and a quiet life, and good health with it. *(They drink.)*

Curtain

Questions

1. This play has both tragic and comic elements. What provides the tragic effect? The comic? What elements of farce does the play contain?
2. Why do you think Dan pretended to be dead? What is your opinion of what he did?

3. Which of the characters do you find the most likeable? The least likeable? Why?
4. What is the central idea of the play?
5. What is the purpose of the character of the Tramp?
6. Speculate on why you think the May-December romance between Dan and Nora occurred.
7. Did you like the use of the poetic dialogue? Why or why not?
8. Trace the play's story line.

Experimental Drama

Any new movement in theatre could, of course, be called experimental. Generally, however, experimental drama is considered to be something that is largely outside previously accepted or acknowledged forms.

Often, new directions in theatre and drama come from a desire for social reform. For instance, the popularity in the sixties and early seventies of street theatre, or guerilla theatre, was an attempt to bring plays to the people, rather than have audiences attend presentations in formal settings. Often these plays dealt directly with concerns and problems of the audience members and usually involved improvisation.

Another recent form of experimentation favored a return to the beginnings of theatre when drama was presented as ritual, such as at ancient Greek festivals. One of the pioneers in this movement was Antonin Artaud who wanted theatre to have a direct impact on social change. Others who favored theatre as ritual felt it could thus evoke stranger feelings in the viewers.

Theatre of the Absurd, popular in the fifties and sixties, was another type of experimentation. Absurdist drama often uses nonsensical dialogue that tells no logical story. Although the plays are usually comic, the source of the humor is different from that in most plays. Usually comedy deals with characters behaving abnormally in a normal society. Theatre of the Absurd, on the other hand, shows normal people in an insane world.

Although the first play that follows, *The Still Alarm,* was experimental in form, the playwright, George S. Kaufman, generally wrote easily understood story plays, whereas Saroyan generally deviated from the usual form and genre, at least to a degree. The other two playwrights, Anouilh and Ionesco, wrote largely in experimental veins. Ionesco, in fact, is largely responsible for beginning the Absurdist movement.

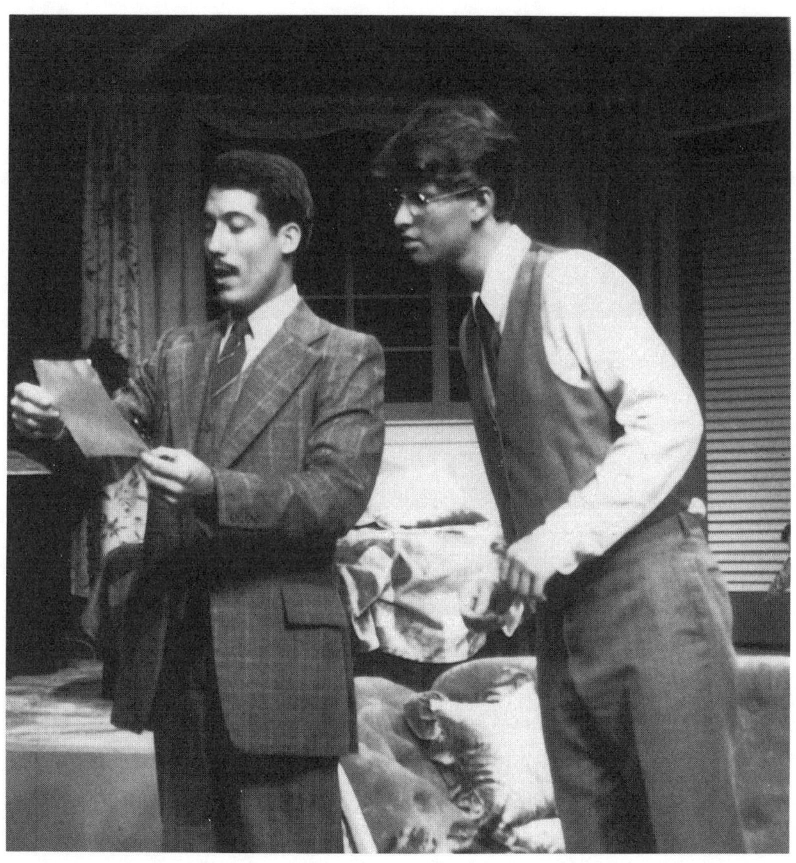

In a scene from The Still Alarm *by George S. Kaufman, Bob receives an important message. (Photograph courtesy of Grossmont College Theatre Arts Department, El Cajon, California)*

GEORGE S. KAUFMAN

The Still Alarm

GEORGE S. KAUFMAN nearly always collaborated with others on the writing of his plays. His partners included such well-known writers as Marc Connelly, Edna Ferber, Alexander Woollcott, and Moss Hart. Among his most-produced plays are *You Can't Take It with You,* which won a Pulitzer Prize, and *The Man Who Came to Dinner.* He received a second Pulitzer Prize for *Of Thee I Sing,* written with Morris Ryskind.

A journalist, a director, and a screenwriter, Kaufman often wrote light-hearted comedies. He directed *Guys and Dolls* in New York, and among his film scripts were several written for the Marx Brothers.

Kaufman was born in 1889 and died in 1961.

THE STILL ALARM exists purely for entertainment and the more seriously it is acted, the funnier it becomes. Very short, it can more appropriately be described as a sketch rather than a play in that it has little purpose other than to point up the absurdity of the situation.

The Still Alarm George S. Kaufman

Characters:

ED
BOB
THE BELLBOY
A FIREMAN
ANOTHER FIREMAN

Setting:

A hotel bedroom. VITAL NOTE: *It is important that the entire play should be acted calmly and politely, in the manner of an English drawing-room comedy. No actor ever raises his voice; every line must be read as though it were an invitation to a cup of tea. If this direction is disregarded, the play has no point at all. The Scene is a hotel bedroom. Two windows rear; door to the hall of the right, chair right center. Bed between windows. 'Phone stand right, downstage end of bed. Dresser left upstage corner. Another door at left. Small table and chairs downstage left center.*

ED *and* BOB *are on the stage.* ED *is getting into his overcoat as the curtain rises. Both are at right door.*

ED: Well, Bob, it's certainly been nice to see you again.

BOB: It was nice to see you.

ED: You come to town so seldom, I hardly ever get the chance to—

BOB: Well, you know how it is. A business trip is always more or less of a bore.

ED: Next time you've got to come out to the house.

BOB: I want to come out. I just had to stick around the hotel this trip.

ED: Oh, I understand. Well, give my best to Edith.

BOB *(remembering something)*: Oh, I say, Ed. Wait a minute.

ED: What's the matter?

BOB: I knew I wanted to show you something. *(Crosses left to table. Gets roll of blueprints from drawer.)* Did you know I'm going to build?

ED *(follows to right of table)*: A house?

BOB: You bet it's a house! *(Knock on right door.)* Come in! *(Spreads plans.)* I just got these yesterday.

ED *(sits)*: Well, that's fine! *(The knock is repeated—louder. Both men now give full attention to the door.)*

BOB: Come! Come in!

BELLBOY *(enters right)*: Mr. Barclay?

BOB: Well?

BELLBOY: I've a message from the clerk, sir. For Mr. Barclay personally.

BOB *(crosses to boy)*: I'm Mr. Barclay. What is the message?

BELLBOY: The hotel is on fire, sir.

BOB: What's that?

BELLBOY: The hotel is on fire.

ED: This hotel?

BELLBOY: Yes, sir.

BOB: Well—is it bad?

BELLBOY: It looks pretty bad, sir.

ED: You mean it's going to burn down?

BELLBOY: We think so—yes, sir.

BOB *(a low whistle of surprise)*: Well! We'd better leave.

BELLBOY: Yes, sir.

BOB: Going to burn down, huh?

BELLBOY: Yes, sir. If you'll step to the window you'll see. *(*BOB *goes to right window.)*

BOB: Yes, that is pretty bad. H'm. *(To* ED.*)* I say, you really ought to see this—

ED *(crosses up to right window—peering out)*: It's reached the floor right underneath.

BELLBOY: Yes, sir. The lower part of the hotel is about gone, sir.

BOB *(still looking out—looks up)*: Still all right up above, though. *(Turns to boy.)* Have they notified the Fire Department?

BELLBOY: I wouldn't know, sir. I'm only the bellboy.

BOB: Well, that's the thing to do, obviously—*(Nods head to each one as if the previous line was a bright idea.)*—notify the Fire Department. Just call them up, give them the name of the hotel—

ED: Wait a minute. I can do better than that for you. *(To the boy.)* Ring through to the Chief, and tell him that Ed Jamison told you to telephone him. *(To* BOB.*)* We went to school together, you know.

BOB: That's fine. *(To the boy.)* Now, get that right. Tell the Chief that Mr. Jamison said to ring him.

ED: *Ed* Jamison

BOB: Yes, *Ed* Jamison

BELLBOY: Yes, sir. *(Turns to go.)*

BOB: Oh! Boy! *(Pulls out handful of change; picks out a coin.)* Here you are.

BELLBOY: Thank you, sir.

(Exit BELLBOY. ED *sits right of table, lights cigarette and throws match downstage, then steps on it. There is a moment's pause.)*

BOB: Well! *(Crosses and looks out left window.)* Say, we'll have to get out of here pretty soon.

ED *(going to window)*: How is it—no better?

BOB: Worse, if anything. It'll be up here in a few moments.

ED: What floor *is* this?

BOB: Eleventh.

ED: Eleven. We couldn't jump, then.

BOB: Oh, no. You never could jump. *(Comes away from window to dresser.)* Well, I've got to get my things together. *(Pulls out suitcase.)*

ED *(smoothing out the plans)*: Who made these for you?

BOB: A fellow here—Rawlins. *(Turns a shirt in his hand.)* I ought to call one of the other hotels for a room.

ED: Oh, you can get in.

BOB: They're pretty crowded. *(Feels something on the sole of his foot; inspects it.)* Say, the floor's getting hot.

ED: I know it. It's getting stuffy in the room, too. Phew! *(He looks around, then goes to the phone.)* Hello.—Ice water in eleven-eighteen. *(Crosses to right of table.)*

BOB *(at bed)*: That's the stuff. *(Packs.)* You know, if I move to another hotel I'll never get my mail. Everybody thinks I'm stopping here.

ED *(studying the plans)*: Say, this isn't bad.

BOB *(eagerly)*: Do you like it? *(Remembers his plight.)* Suppose I go to another hotel and there's a fire there, too!

ED: You've got to take *some* chance.

BOB: I know, but here I'm sure. *('Phone rings.)* Oh, answer that, will you, Ed? *(To dresser and back.)*

ED *(crosses to 'phone)*: Sure. *(At 'phone.)* Hello— Oh, that's good. Fine. What?—Oh! Well, wait a minute. *(To* BOB.*)* The firemen are downstairs and some of them want to come up to this room.

BOB: Tell them, of course.

ED *(at 'phone)*: All right. Come right up. *(Hangs up, crosses and sits right of table.)* Now we'll get some action.

BOB *(looks out of window left)*: Say, there's an awful crowd of people on the street.

ED *(absently, as he pores over the plans)*: Maybe there's been some kind of accident.

BOB *(peering out, suitcase in hand)*: No. More likely they heard about the fire. *(A knock at the door right.)* Come in.

BELLBOY *(enters)*: I beg pardon, Mr. Barclay, the firemen have arrived.

BOB: Show them in.

(Crosses to right. The door opens. In the doorway appear two FIREMEN *in full regalia. The* FIRST FIREMAN *carries a hose and rubber coat; the* SECOND *has a violin case, right center.)*

FIRST FIREMAN *(enters right. Very apologetically)*: Mr. Barclay.

BOB: I'm Mr. Barclay.

FIRST FIREMAN: We're the firemen, Mr. Barclay. *(They remove their hats.)*

BOB: How de do?

ED: How de do?

BOB: A great pleasure, I assure you. Really must apologize for the condition of this room, but—

FIRST FIREMAN: Oh, that's all right. I know how it is at home.

BOB: May I present a friend of mine, Mr. Ed Jamison—

FIRST FIREMAN: How are you?

ED: How are you, boys? *(*SECOND FIREMAN *nods.)* I know your Chief.

FIRST FIREMAN: Oh, is that so? He knows the Chief—dear old Chiefie. *(*SECOND FIREMAN *giggles.)*

BOB *(embarrassed)*: Well, I guess you boys want to get to work, don't you?

FIRST FIREMAN: Well, if you don't mind. We would like to spray around a little bit.

BOB: May I help you?

FIRST FIREMAN: Yes, if you please.

*(*BOB *helps him into his rubber coat. At the same time the* SECOND FIREMAN, *without a word, lays the violin case on the bed, opens it, takes out the violin, and begins tuning it.)*

BOB *(watching him)*: I don't think I understand.

FIRST FIREMAN: Well, you see, Sid doesn't get much chance to practice at home. Sometimes, at a fire, while we're waiting for a wall to fall or something, why, a fireman doesn't really have anything to do, and personally I like to see him improve himself symphonically. I hope you don't resent it. You're not anti-symphonic?

BOB: Of course not—(BOB *and* ED *nod understandingly; the* SECOND FIREMAN *is now waxing the bow.)*

FIRST FIREMAN: Well, if you'll excuse me—

(To window right. Turns with decision toward the window. You feel that he is about to get down to business.)

BOB *(crosses to left)*: Charming personalities.

ED *(follows over to the window right)*: How *is* the fire?

FIRST FIREMAN *(feels the wall)*: It's pretty bad right now. This wall will go pretty soon now, but it'll fall out that way, so it's all right. *(Peers out.)* That next room is the place to fight it from. *(Crosses to door left.* BOB *shows ties as* ED *crosses.)*

ED *(sees ties)*: Oh! Aren't those gorgeous!

FIRST FIREMAN *(to* BOB*)*: Have you the key for this room?

BOB: Why, no. I've nothing to do with that room. I've just got this one. *(Folding a shirt as he talks.)*

ED: Oh, it's very comfortable.

FIRST FIREMAN: That's too bad, I had something up my sleeve. If I could have gotten in there. Oh, well, may I use your 'phone?

BOB: Please do. *(To* ED.*)* Do you think you might hold this? *(Indicates the hose.)*

ED: How?

FIRST FIREMAN: Just crawl under it. *(As he does that.)* Thanks. *(At phone.)* Hello. Let me have the clerk, please. *(To* SECOND FIREMAN.*)* Give us that little thing you played the night the Equitable Building burned down. *(Back to 'phone.)* Are you there? This is one of the firemen. Oh, you know. I'm in a room—ah—*(Looks at* BOB.*)*

BOB: Eleven-eighteen.

FIRST FIREMAN: Eleven-eighteen, and I want to get into the next room— Oh, goody. Will you send someone up with the key? There's no one in there? Oh, super-goody! Right away. *(Hangs up.)*

BOB: That's fine. *(To* FIREMAN.*)* Won't you sit down?

FIRST FIREMAN: Thanks.

ED: Have a cigar?

FIRST FIREMAN *(takes it)*: Much obliged.

BOB: A light?

FIRST FIREMAN: If you please.

ED *(failing to find a match)*: Bob, have you a match?

BOB *(crosses to left center)*: I thought there were some here. *(Hands in pockets.)*

FIRST FIREMAN: Oh, never mind.

(He goes to right window, leans out, and emerges with cigar lighted. BOB *crosses to left to dresser; slams drawer. The* SECOND FIREMAN *taps violin with bow.)*

FIRST FIREMAN: Mr. Barclay, I think he's ready now.

BOB *(takes chair from right table and sits center)*: Pardon me.

(They all sit. The SECOND FIREMAN *takes center of stage, with all the manner of a concert violinist. He goes into "Keep the Home Fires Burning."* BOB, ED, *and* FIRST FIREMAN *wipe brow as curtain falls slowly.)*

Copies of this play, in individual paper covered acting editions, are available from Samuel French, Inc., 25 W. 45th St., New York, N.Y. 10036 or 7623 Sunset Blvd., Hollywood Calif. 90046 or in Canada Samuel French, (Canada) Ltd., 80 Richmond Street East, Toronto M5C 1P1, Canada.

Questions

1. Did you enjoy the play? Why or why not?
2. List and give examples of the comic devices Kaufman used.

3. Can you offer any explanation for the characters' behavior?
4. Find as many instances as you can of illogical or impossible situations.
5. In what ways could *The Still Alarm* be considered experimental? In what ways does it follow established patterns?

JEAN ANOUILH

Episode in the Life of an Author

JEAN ANOUILH was born in Bordeaux, France, in 1910; his first play was produced in 1932. Although he wrote historic dramas, such as *The Lark* about Joan of Arc, most of his plays revolve around a domestic crisis, with the family the center of the action. Usually, the conflict stems from one character's failing to conform to the values of the others.

The characters often realize they are playing roles and then move in and out of their parts, both for comedy and ironic comments.

EPISODE IN THE LIFE OF AN AUTHOR is a mixture of the realistic and the nonrealistic. Although the characters use everyday dialogue, the setting is nonrealistic and the situations are highly exaggerated.

This play exists largely for entertainment, apparent through several comic devices, such as incongruity in the Author's attempt to act normally while everything is falling apart in his home and exaggeration, which presents situations that are beyond belief.

In effect, Anouilh is asking how much a person can endure and still continue to function.

Episode in the Life of an Author Jean Anouilh

Characters:

AUTHOR
ARDÈLE
MADAME BESSARABO
MAID
PHOTOGRAPHER
TWO PLUMBERS
WOMAN
FRIEND
MOTHER
LA SURETTE
INSPECTOR
GONTRAN

Setting:

The décor is as nonrealistic as possible, but the AUTHOR's *study should be distinguishable center, with three doors, a lobby stage left, the bottom of the staircase, and the front door. It is morning. The* AUTHOR *and* ARDÈLE *are discovered on stage in the study, both in dressing gowns. Standing face to face and both extremely agitated, they are shouting and banging on the desk. All the characters in this sketch are realistic, the women charming, but—and this production detail is indispensable—everyone is wearing a false nose.*

AUTHOR *(banging on the desk)*: Exactly!
ARDÈLE *(also banging on the desk)*: Exactly!
AUTHOR *(as above)*: Exactly!
ARDÈLE *(as above)*: Exactly!
AUTHOR *(suddenly icy)*: Good. The play's over. We've no more to say to each other.
ARDÈLE *(no less loftily)*: I hope not.
AUTHOR: Just one thing. That letter was not from your sister.
ARDÈLE: So you're rummaging in my drawers now. It's humiliating.
AUTHOR: Your sister's fond of you, of course, but hardly to the point of calling you "my own love."
ARDÈLE: So I'm not enough. You have to smear my sister.
AUTHOR: I'm not smearing your sister. I'm simply making an observation. Your sister isn't overloaded with culture, but after all she can spell. She wouldn't have systematically left out *all* the feminine endings on her past participles.
ARDÈLE: The things you pick on!
AUTHOR: That letter was from a man.
ARDÈLE: You're despicable. Might I be allowed to put one question?

AUTHOR: Put away.
ARDÈLE: Supposing it was all your fault?
AUTHOR *(laughing nastily)*: Ah-ha ha!
ARDÈLE: What are you doing?
AUTHOR: I'm laughing nastily.
ARDÈLE: How horrible! I deceive you and you laugh. You're not even capable of suffering. I've given you my youth and you rummage in my drawers.
AUTHOR: The letter was on the floor. In the closet.
ARDÈLE: Rummaging in closets. In two hours I shall have gone. I'm going back to my mother.
AUTHOR: She died in 1922.
ARDÈLE: Try—go on, *try* to make me more miserable by reminding me that my poor mother is dead and that I've nothing left in the world. All the same, she did leave a house. One twenty-two rue des Retaillons in Saint-Malo. My illiterate sister's living there. I'm going to her.
AUTHOR: Splendid.
ARDÈLE: You're delighted, of course. At last you'll be able to be unfaithful to me. For twelve years you've been waiting for this moment, and you've arranged it so that I'm the one that looks guilty.
AUTHOR *(yelling suddenly)*: For God's sake! Who sent you that letter?
ARDÈLE *(with marblelike contempt)*: What *can* be the matter? I suppose my sister can't write.

(At that moment someone rings. They listen. In the lobby, the MAID, *young and pleasant, but dissolved in tears, opens the door.)*

MADAME BESSARABO: I've come to see the Master. I have an appointment. Madame Bessarabo. This gentleman is the photographer.
AUTHOR: She's a Rumanian journalist. I sent her packing a week ago. We'll continue with this conversation later. And I'm not even shaved!
ARDÈLE *(sneering as she goes out)*: That makes twelve years you haven't been shaved.
AUTHOR *(passing his hand over his face)*: You exaggerate. It would have shown. Am I at least clean?
ARDÈLE *(slamming the door so hard that a picture falls down and the* AUTHOR *picks it up)*: No!

(The MAID, *still in tears, introduces* MADAME BESSARABO *and the* PHOTOGRAPHER, *who is weighed down with equipment.)*

MADAME B.: Master! I am overwhelmed by the tremendous favor. This gentleman is the photographer.
AUTHOR: Do sit down, madame. Excuse my receiving you in these clothes. I was working.

MADAME B.: Oh, Master! How very disturbing. I have interrupted a scene perhaps?

AUTHOR: Precisely. *(Recovering himself.)* I mean, er—no. It's of no importance. It wasn't my scene.

MADAME B. *(embarrassed)*: Oh! Please forgive me, I have been indiscreet. I shall go, Master; I shall go immediately. *(She installs herself.)* Do you mind if I smoke? I smoke like a—how do you say it?—like a chimney sweep.

AUTHOR: Like a chimney. Sweeps don't smoke—at least not on duty. In fact it's their job to stop the chimney smoking.

MADAME B.: What a fascinating detail! Everything French is quite extraordinary. Now, in Rumania we are all slaves. Master, I've come to talk to you about your last play. You know, of course, that *La Marguerite* had an enormous success in Bucharest. Three performances—for us that is much.

AUTHOR: Really?

MADAME B.: We have such a small theatre public. But very enthusiastic, too! We are traditionally devoted to anything French. The play made a great impression. The press was unanimous—we almost reached the fourth performance. The general opinion was that it was a little *dur* as you say—a little hard. We Rumanians are such great idealists. We believe enormously in sentiment. In fact, this explains why I am here. We want to know in my country what you really think about love. Our two cultures are so closely linked you cannot refuse us this. *(Someone rings.)* Well, Master, what do you say? I swear to you I shall be absolutely faithful.

AUTHOR *(suspicious)*: Why do you say that?

MADAME B.: Because there are journalists who betray. I shall never betray.

AUTHOR: Er . . . well, madame, truth to tell I feel somewhat embarrassed . . . What shall I say about love and *La Marguerite?* I think you have caught the subtle hint in the title. "Marguerite"—I love you, I love you not, I love you, I love you not. *(The* MAID, *still weeping, has been to open the door. She lets in* TWO PLUMBERS.*)*

PLUMBER: How do, gorgeous! We're here for the leak. *(The* MAID *knocks on the door of the study.)*

AUTHOR: Excuse me. Come in . . . what is it?

MAID: It's the plumbers, sir, for the leak.

AUTHOR: Well, let them look for it. You can see I'm busy.

PLUMBER *(shouting from the doorway)*: Where is it?

MAID: They're asking where it is.

AUTHOR: Why should we have sent for them if we knew where it was? Let them start in the attic and check the whole house.

PLUMBER: Okay, mister. We'll start with the attic. Which way, gorgeous?

MAID *(sobbing)*: This way.

PLUMBER *(going upstairs with her and his mate)*: What's up, gorgeous? Love's wonderful really, you know.

AUTHOR *(who has shut the door again)*: Please excuse me. Curious phenomenon. Water trickling about all over the place and nobody knows where from.

MADAME B.: How strange. You know, almost the same thing happened in the house of my great-uncle, the Archimandrite, in Rumania. I wake up one morning and there is water all over the drawing room.

AUTHOR: Same here!

MADAME B.: In the drawing room where there are no pipes.

AUTHOR: Same here!

MADAME B.: And the ceiling absolutely intact. As it was the house of a holy man, we thought for a moment it must be a miracle.

AUTHOR: Same here! Or rather, no, I wouldn't go that far. Now, "Marguerite"—I love you, I love you not, I love you, I love you not.

(The forestage left lights up and a WOMAN *dials a number on the telephone. Almost immediately, the telephone rings in the study.)*

AUTHOR: Please excuse me. Hello!

WOMAN: Is that you, Léon?

AUTHOR: I'm sorry, madame, whom did you wish to speak to?

WOMAN: Oh, Léon, it's you. Why are you disguising your voice?

AUTHOR: No, madame, it's not me. Which number did you want?

WOMAN: Jasmin one two, one two.

AUTHOR: I am Jasmin one two, one two, madame, but I regret to say that I am not Léon.

WOMAN: But listen, monsieur, Jasmin one two, one two is the number of my first husband!

AUTHOR: I'm sorry, madame. There's been a mistake. *(He hangs up and the light goes out forestage left.)* Some woman had the wrong number. It's very strange—they must make a habit of giving people my number.

MADAME B.: Do you know, exactly the same thing has happened to me in Rumania. You are aware, of course, that unlike yours in France, our numbers are very long. . . mine was seven, eighty-three, one, one two six two one four.

MAID *(bounding in)*: Monsieur, monsieur!

AUTHOR: What is it? I'm busy!

MAID *(tragically)*: They're asking if they can cut off the water.

AUTHOR: Certainly. But if they cut off the water, how will they find the leak? *(Noticing that she is weeping.)* What is the matter with you?

MAID: Oh! Monsieur, it's terrible what's going on.

AUTHOR: You mean, the leak?

MAID: Oh no. Not the leak.

AUTHOR: Madame, perhaps?

MAID: Oh, no. Not madame. *(She goes out, crying even more bitterly.)*

AUTHOR *(turning hesitantly back to* MADAME BESSARABO*)*: Strange.

MADAME B.: She's charming. Quite like one of Molière's.

AUTHOR *(smirking)*: You exaggerate, really! That's too high a compliment.

MADAME B.: I say what I think, Master, I have such an admiration for all your work—and for Molière's too, of course.

AUTHOR: Thank you. But we were saying—about the water in your drawing room . . .

MADAME B.: No—about my telephone number. But let us talk about *La Marguerite* instead. *(The* WOMAN *has redialed the number forestage.)*

AUTHOR: Well, I was saying that the title contains a subtle allusion. "Marguerite"—I love you, I love you not . . . *(The telephone rings.)*

WOMAN: Hello! Léon?

AUTHOR: Madame, you have the wrong number again. Are you dialing Jasmin one two, one two?

WOMAN: Of course, monsieur. I told you it is my first husband's number. Can you explain to me what you are doing on the line?

AUTHOR: What do you mean, what am I doing on the line? I'm waiting for someone to ring me on the line, madame; it happens to be mine! *(He hangs up.)* This is insane. I love you, I love you not, I love you, I love you not.

(There is a knock. It is ARDÈLE, *with nothing on but a bathrobe.)*

ARDÈLE: So that's how it is. You're starting that?

AUTHOR: Starting what? Do excuse me, madame.

ARDÈLE: Your oafish practical jokes. Cutting off the water just as I'm taking my shower. You know I'm leaving you, and as if that isn't enough, you want to put the blame on me. After what you've done!

AUTHOR: What *have* I done?

ARDÈLE: Don't play innocent—you know as well as I do! *(She goes out, banging the door. A picture falls down. The* AUTHOR *picks it up.)*

AUTHOR: I'm so sorry. Now, we were talking about love and *La Marguerite.*

MADAME B.: Quite. The rest is incidental. My great-uncle's leak, the telephone—I can tell you all about these things later when you come to Rumania. But, Master, you were so *dur,* so hard in *La Marguerite.* Tell me you were lying; confess that you believe in love just the same.

AUTHOR *(embarking)*: Well now, madame, to tell the truth, love, like the marguerite, has leaves, or rather petals . . .

(A man has dialed a number forestage right. The AUTHOR *picks up the receiver and yells into it.)*

AUTHOR: No, madame, I am not Léon!

FRIEND: What on earth's come over you, old thing? I know you're not Léon. This is Gustave. How are things, dear boy?

AUTHOR: Oh. It's you. Fine, thanks, fine. *(To* MADAME B.*)* One moment, please, I'm so sorry. How are things with you?

FRIEND: That's just it, they're not at all good, dear boy. You remember I had a simply fabulous idea for a scenario. I told you about it, I think?

AUTHOR: Yes, yes. I remember. *(To* MADAME B.*)* Please excuse me—a colleague of mine.

FRIEND: "The Woman with the Boas," I was calling it. You know, it's the story of a madly beautiful woman who meets a man in a train and falls in love with him.

AUTHOR: Yes, yes, I remember. Very original. . .

FRIEND: Paul Zed bought it from me. He was going to film it in the spring for Bourbanski. They'd got Liliane Trésor lined up. She'd accepted, and now she's refused.

AUTHOR *(politely)*: Oh, Lord, what a bore. Why was that? *(To* MADAME B.*)* I'm so sorry.

FRIEND: She doesn't want to die at the end.

AUTHOR: That's reasonable. Listen, old man, I'm so sorry, but I have someone with me.

FRIEND: How do you mean, it's reasonable? Look at it from my point of view. If I want to kill her off, who's going to stop me? After all, *I'm* the author. Anyway, it doesn't make sense. First of all, who's ever heard of an actress refusing to die? They usually fall over themselves for a good death agony. What's more, dear boy, if you remember the story, you'll see that she can't not die. Damn it, here's a woman who's deceived her husband with two men; she then falls in love on a train with a third man who turns out to be an ex-convict who was a counterspy in the war and takes drugs. That was the whole point. Producers can say what they like about happy endings—life is like that, dear boy, life is like that. I ask you, is life supposed to be a picnic?

AUTHOR: No, it isn't a picnic, but listen, old man, I've got someone here in my study—a journalist come specially from Rumania to see me about a leak in the water pipe.

FRIEND: About what?

AUTHOR: Oh—no—I mean about love, but there was a leak as well. I'll explain later. Call me again, do you mind?

FRIEND: Oh, all right, I'll call you in ten minutes.

(He hangs up. The forestage goes dark. Someone rings. The MAID *opens the door. This time it is an elderly woman, floweriły dressed.)*

MOTHER: Is my son at home?

MAID: Yes, madame.

AUTHOR: Do forgive me, what was I saying?

MADAME B.: That love had petals.

AUTHOR *(who has lost the drift)*: Petals.

MADAME B.: Yes, Master, you remember—the subtle allusion.

AUTHOR: Oh yes! The marguerite. So love, like the marguerite, has petals . . .

MADAME B. *(takes notes feverishly)*: How moving. I have the feeling no one has ever said that before.

MAID *(knocking at the study door)*: It's your mother, monsieur.

AUTHOR: Tell her I'm busy and ask her if she'd kindly call again.

MOTHER *(calling)*: It's very urgent, darling. I must have a word with you at once.

AUTHOR: Would you excuse me? All right, I'm coming. *(He goes out into the hall.)* What is it?

MOTHER: Aren't you going to kiss me? When you were little, you always used to kiss me.

AUTHOR: Yes, yes, I'm going to kiss you. What is it, now? I'm busy.

MOTHER: The pet. You know, for me, you'll always be a little boy. Now, it's about the apartment. I've been told about one that's up for exchange. I have to let them have my answer this morning.

AUTHOR: Just wait for me a second. I've someone with me from Rumania. She's going back any minute now.

MOTHER: Is Ardèle at home?

AUTHOR: Yes, but do please leave her where she is. Things aren't going so well this morning. No scenes between you, please.

MOTHER: How dare you say such a thing to your mother! Was I ever one to start anything? Don't you think it's painful enough already to see one's only son married to someone who hates one?

AUTHOR: Yes, I know it's rather painful. So don't stand about. Do sit down. Read the paper. I'll be back.

MOTHER *(holding him back)*: But you really must give me an answer about this flat. You know I've lost my lawsuit. That means I don't know how much in lawyers' fees and I may be thrown out on the street at any minute. If only you had a different wife—then I could come and live with you.

AUTHOR *(making her sit down and calmly but firmly placing a paper in her hands)*: Read the paper! *(He goes back into the study.)* So. Love has petals. Excuse me, I must be brief, I've so much to do. You've asked me a straight question, and I'll give you a straight answer. I believe in love.

MADAME B. *(with a cry of relief)*: Ah! At last! I shall send a cable at once, Master. It will be a great relief to the whole of Rumania!

(At this moment the door opens behind the AUTHOR *and the* TWO PLUMBERS *come in. They feel along the walls in silence, with an air of great mystery, weaving around everyone and putting the* PHOTOGRAPHER *in terror for his equipment. They then go out by another door without a word.)*

AUTHOR *(curtly)*: Man is alone, madame—left to himself, with his ridiculous freedom, and no one to call out to him in the desert! *(At this moment the* FRIEND *has dialed the number and the telephone rings.)*

AUTHOR: Excuse me, please. Hello!

FRIEND: Hello! Can I talk to you now, dear boy? Do you know what's happened to me? A phone call from Liliane Trésor. She agrees to die, provided it's consumption. The idea came to her when she had a bit of a cold. But now it's Paul Zed who won't play because he says it would be depressing. He says for Canada and the Channel Islands it would be better if she turned religious and went into a convent. He says that would make it sell better.

AUTHOR: Listen. I haven't finished with my visitor. Could you call me back later?

FRIEND: Right. Fine. I'll call you back. *(He hangs up.)*

(While they are speaking, someone rings. It is LA SURETTE, *a tramp, still quite young.)*

LA SURETTE: Is he in?

MAID *(who has opened the door to him, still sniffling)*: You again? But he gave you something only a week ago.

LA SURETTE: They're going to cut off the gas.

MAID *(at the door of the study)*: It's Monsieur La Surette, monsieur. He says they're going to cut off his gas.

AUTHOR *(getting up, furious, and coming into the hall)*: No! Do you hear me, man—no! I know we served together in the army. I know you saved me from being court-martialed the time I mislaid my bayonet, but damn it all! I gave you seven thousand last week!

LA SURETTE: That was for the potatoes.

AUTHOR: And you've eaten seven thousand francs' worth of potatoes in a week?

LA SURETTE: They're cutting off the gas. I can't cook them.

AUTHOR *(weakening)*: How much behind are you with the gas?

LA SURETTE: Nine months. They say if I pay half they won't cut me off. Better take the opportunity, hadn't I?

AUTHOR: How much?

LA SURETTE *(waving a hand)*: Oh! I don't know—here, here's the bill. You see I wasn't lying. Plus expenses, of course. They always add that. And then, I wanted to tell you—I think I've found a place. Only I can't go there with these boots. Maybe you've got an old pair.

AUTHOR: God in heaven! Wait there! I'll see in a minute.

(He turns to go back into the study when the MOTHER *comes out from behind the paper and seizes him.)*

MOTHER: Darling, do you know what I've just come across in the paper? Another flat. Eight rooms. At the Trocadéro. Furniture for sale, too. Only they don't say the price. What does it mean when they don't say the price?

AUTHOR *(going out)*: It means a million francs. Let's talk about it later.

MOTHER: A million francs for furniture? When I married, do you know how much an Empire commode was worth?

AUTHOR: I don't want to know. It's too late. *(He goes back into the study.)* I'm all yours, madame. Now, the marguerite . . . *(At this moment the* WOMAN *has dialed the number. He takes off the receiver.)*

WOMAN: Hello, Léon?

AUTHOR *(howling)*: No!

(He hangs up. There is a ring at the bell. LA SURETTE *opens the door. It is a serious-looking man in black. He greets the* MOTHER *and* LA SURETTE *and sits down to wait, having noticed that he is not the first. Meanwhile, the* AUTHOR *is addressing* MADAME B.*)*

AUTHOR: What was I saying?

MADAME B.: Man is alone, Master, man is desperately alone.

(The door at the back opens and ARDÈLE *comes in, dressed this time and wearing an outrageous hat.)*

ARDÈLE *(standing on the threshold, tragic)*: And what about the cats?

AUTHOR: You can see I'm busy.

ARDÈLE: Who's going to look after the cats now that I'm leaving?

AUTHOR: There's Léonie.

ARDÈLE: The maid! You'd leave the cats to the maid. You really mean that? Am I to believe my ears?

AUTHOR: Yes.

ARDÈLE: You monster! Clothaire's ill!

AUTHOR: What's the matter with him?

ARDÈLE: He's miaowing.

AUTHOR: All cats miaow. It's normal.

ARDÈLE: Insensitive brute. He's miaowing hoarsely. He suspects something.

AUTHOR: Talk to him then. Make him see reason. You see I'm busy. Open a tin of sardines.

ARDÈLE: Brute. Insensitive brute. That animal has more heart than you have. He'll refuse your old sardines. He's sad because I'm going. *(The man in black, tired of waiting, has come to knock on the study door.)*

MAN IN BLACK: Excuse me, monsieur. I see there are several people waiting to see you and I have to have a word with you urgently.

AUTHOR: What about, monsieur?

INSPECTOR: I am the housing inspector. A complaint has been lodged against you for insufficient occupation of the premises and you are under threat of a requisition order for your surplus accommodation.

AUTHOR: Requisition order? But I occupy the entire house, monsieur. Who do you want to put in?

INSPECTOR: A police officer, monsieur. Father of eight. Brigadier Lapomme. Top priority.

AUTHOR: I object, monsieur. The premises are legally occupied.

INSPECTOR: That's what I've come to find out. *(He glances at* MADAME BESSARABO.*)* Is madame one of the family?

AUTHOR: Madame is a Rumanian journalist.

INSPECTOR *(taking notes)*: Premises occupied by foreign émigrés. Have you a regular permit, madame?

MADAME: Monsieur, I am the Princess Bessarabo and I am staying at the Hotel Ritz.

INSPECTOR *(still taking notes)*: I see. Illegal occupation of further premises in Paris.

AUTHOR: Please don't confuse matters, monsieur! Madame has absolutely nothing to do with this house. Would you be so good as to wait next door for a moment, madame? *(To the* PHOTOGRAPHER.*)* You, too, please. And take your scrap iron with you.

INSPECTOR: Also one of the family?

AUTHOR: No, you can see perfectly well he's a photographer.

INSPECTOR: Doesn't stop him being one of the family. I've got an uncle who's a painter.

(While the AUTHOR *is easing the other two into the adjoining room,* ARDÈLE *has come up to the* INSPECTOR *gleefully.)*

ARDÈLE: You can send that policeman right along with his eight children. Let him make another one in the next nine months too if he wants to. He'll have plenty of room here because *I* am going, let me tell you, monsieur.

INSPECTOR *(taking more notes)*: You're vacating part of the property? I'll make a note of that.

ARDÈLE: Please do.

AUTHOR *(separating them)*: Ardèle! Inspector! Please. Let's keep calm. *(The* MOTHER *comes in, brandishing the paper.)*

MOTHER: A flat! Another flat! Darling, this time you'll be able to give your old mother a real treat. Twelve rooms in the Avenue Lamartine, just next door to dear Mademoiselle Pinocle. And for a song—only two million. And shall I tell you something? If I win my lawsuit, I shall keep my little flat at Asnières.

INSPECTOR *(noting)*: Twelve rooms, Avenue Lamartine, and you say you also have a small flat at Asnières? How many rooms?

MOTHER *(mutinous)*: Four, but I've been crafty and only declared two!

AUTHOR *(bawling)*: Mother, I order you to be quiet! And you—stop scribbling down everything people say to you. It's not normal. Damn it all, we're talking about *this* house, aren't we? You'll see that everything's in order here. I have my study on the ground floor, with my secretary's office, a drawing room and dining room, and this is the lobby.

LA SURETTE *(still in the lobby)*: Listen, the gas can wait, but about the boots—I've got to go there this afternoon.

AUTHOR: In a minute.

INSPECTOR *(taking a look at the staircase)*: What about the second floor? What have you got there?

AUTHOR: Three rooms. All occupied.

INSPECTOR: Is there a third floor?

AUTHOR: Only a trompe-l'oeil façade. There's no third floor really. It's just a sort of optical illusion. *(At this moment the* PLUMBERS *gallop down the stairs triumphantly.)*

PLUMBER: We've got it, mister. We've got it!

AUTHOR: What?

PLUMBER: The leak! It starts at the two big empty rooms on the third floor, runs right across the table tennis room, the winter garden, and the two libraries, and finishes up in that big room where you've got your collection of toy soldiers!

INSPECTOR *(rubbing his hands and mounting the staircase brandishing his notebook)*: Splendid! I'm going to have a look at all this.

AUTHOR *(somewhat discouraged)*: We've had it, now.

LA SURETTE: Look, do make an effort. When I lent you my bayonet so as to save you that court-martial, I didn't keep you waiting this long.

AUTHOR *(beside himself, suddenly rips off his shoes and throws them at* LA SURETTE*)*: Here you are, then! Take mine! But get out!

LA SURETTE *(putting them on immediately)*: Very well. But giving isn't everything. It's the way you do it. One may be poor, but one has one's dignity. *(He hands him the old boots.)* Do you want these! At least you can afford to have them mended. What have you decided about the gas?

AUTHOR *(who no longer knows what he is saying)*: Go and get mine, it's in the kitchen.

MOTHER *(plucking at him)*: Well, darling, what do you think about the flat? The twelve rooms at Avenue Lamartine or the eight at the Trocadéro? In a pinch I could make do with that, you know. I'm old now and I don't entertain much anymore.

ARDÈLE *(hooking him from the other side)*: So it's agreed, you're going to let me go, but it isn't going to be as easy as you're hoping. I demand, you hear me, I demand now to know the name of this woman.

AUTHOR: What woman?

ARDÈLE: Your mistress.

AUTHOR: What *do* you mean, my mistress?

ARDÈLE: Exactly what I said. Do you think I can be fooled by that letter? Let me tell you I can't. I knew all the time that letter was concealing something.

AUTHOR: Ah, you knew all the time? How clever of you. So what was it concealing, may I ask?

ARDÈLE: You may not! I'm asking you. You've discovered that I'm deceiving you. Why should you choose today to discover I'm deceiving you unless you're deceiving me?

AUTHOR *(taking her by the arm)*: Listen to me, Ardèle, I'm quite calm. I'm absolutely calm, and no matter what happens I shall stay calm.

ARDÈLE: You're molesting me! Deceiving me and molesting me! Look at him, your darling boy, look at the dear, sweet cherub.

MOTHER: Before he knew you, my son was sweetness itself. He has never failed his mother.

LA SURETTE *(putting his head through the door)*: What have you decided about the gas? You're not going to leave me with two hundred and fifty kilos of raw potatoes on my hands, are you?

AUTHOR *(disengaging himself from the two women and storming)*: Keep calm, everybody. We must keep exceedingly calm. *(At this moment the* WOMAN *dials his number.)*

WOMAN: Hello! Is that you, Léon?

AUTHOR *(smoothly)*: Yes, this is Léon speaking. I'd like to be Léon. Why shouldn't I be Léon?

WOMAN: Well then, why are you disguising your voice?

AUTHOR *(gloomily)*: Just to make you laugh.

WOMAN: Don't be cruel, Léon. I know you love another woman. But I'm ringing you because something terrible has happened to me. I can't stay here. I must find a flat.

AUTHOR *(very calmly)*: Oh, good. In that case I'll put you on to someone.

One moment. Mother. There's a woman here telephoning about a flat.

MOTHER *(rushing to the phone)*: A flat? A flat? Isn't he a darling? You see what a good son he is. Hello! Hello! Madame? Hello! Hello! You say you're ringing about a flat?

AUTHOR: That's one. Now—two: you. *(To* LA SURETTE.*)* To the kitchen. Eat everything you can find in the icebox. Empty all the bottles in sight.

LA SURETTE: What about the maid?

AUTHOR: Comfort her. Now, number three: you. *(To* ARDÈLE.*)* Listen to me carefully. Look me straight in the eye.

ARDÈLE: Oh, no! Don't start that. It's not fair. You know whenever you look me in the face I tell everything.

MOTHER *(at the telephone)*: So you really want to talk about a flat?

WOMAN: Yes, madame, I do, indeed.

MOTHER: How many rooms?

WOMAN: Oh, three or four, madame...

MOTHER: But that would be perfect, madame...

WOMAN: Really, would it really be suitable, do you think, madame? I cannot tell you how glad I am...

MOTHER: But it is I who am glad, madame...I don't wish to be indiscreet, of course, but about the furniture and fittings...

WOMAN: It's a little embarrassing, but...to tell the truth...I'd been hoping we needn't discuss furniture and fittings...

MOTHER: Ah! So had I, madame!

WOMAN: So, shall we say without furniture and fittings, then, madame? Do you agree?

MOTHER: Certainly, madame, without furniture and fittings...It is so much easier to come to an agreement with people of one's own kind? When may I come along to see you madame?

WOMAN: At once, madame, if that is possible. You can imagine I simply can't wait...

MOTHER: But it is I who cannot wait, madame. Please, what is your address?

WOMAN: One eighteen Boulevard Ravachol. Madame Fripon-Minet.

MOTHER: I shall wing my way, madame! I'll be with you immediately. *(She hangs up.)* Darling! Thank you! It's marvelous. Let me kiss you. Four rooms on the Boulevard Ravachol! A lovely quarter. And no furniture and fittings. Really one has only to deal with the right people. They are much less grasping than one thinks. Good-by now, good-by. Don't come with me, my turtledoves.

(She flies to the door, younger by fifty years. As she opens it, there is GONTRAN *on the threshold. He is a giant of a man.)*

GONTRAN: Is Jacques at home?

MOTHER: Yes, Gontran, yes. Come in, my little one. I adore you! *(She disappears.)*

AUTHOR *(left in the study with* ARDÈLE*)*: Now, listen to me carefully. I realize one may suffer a momentary lapse.

ARDÈLE: So you admit it?

AUTHOR: God almighty! Admit what?

ARDÈLE: Let me go, then. Your dishonesty sickens me. My mind's made up. I'm going.

GONTRAN *(coming in)*: So there you are, both of you!

AUTHOR *(somewhat ill-tempered)*: Yes, here we are. As you can see. What is it?

GONTRAN: I must say I didn't expect that sort of welcome from you on a day like this.

ARDÈLE: What's the matter, Gontran? You're so pale, little one.

GONTRAN *(sitting down suddenly)*: It's all over. Have you got a gun?

AUTHOR: Hell, no! I could do with one, though. Why a gun?

GONTRAN: Oh, never mind. I'd have preferred one, that's all. I'll get by.

ARDÈLE: But what on earth is the matter?

GONTRAN: You know I've left Lucienne?

AUTHOR *(embarrassed, as though it were himself)*: Oh, yes, I never told you; he's left Lucienne.

ARDÈLE: You mean he's left Lucienne? And you never told me? I suppose you thought it would put ideas into my head. Go on, admit that you were thinking of leaving me, too!

AUTHOR: Let's keep calm. He left Lucienne more than three months ago.

GONTRAN: I'm in love with Léa.

ARDÈLE: That stick!

GONTRAN: Please make your wife be quiet!

ARDÈLE: That shriveled prune? She hasn't even got any hair!

GONTRAN: I order you to make your wife be quiet, do you hear me?

AUTHOR: He's right. Be quiet. You have absolutely no right . . .

ARDÈLE: To say that she's a prune?

GONTRAN: Léa, a prune? She's blonde—well, anyway, now.

AUTHOR: Now you shut up, too! Let's all shut up. Don't let's ever say another word. Sign language only.

GONTRAN *(in tears)*: In any case, who said anything about Léa? I'm not talking about Léa.

ARDÈLE: That's better. At least I'm glad I don't know this . . . this . . . tart.

GONTRAN: I'm talking about Lucienne! That's what's so awful.

ARDÈLE: What has she done? Killed herself? I bet she's killed herself. Ring her up at once.

AUTHOR: Do be calm. What's the good if she's killed herself.

GONTRAN: She doesn't answer the phone. She doesn't answer my letters. *(He falls weeping into the* AUTHOR's *arms.)* She's deceiving me, old man; she's been deceiving me ever since I left her!

(He begins to sob like a child in the arms of the AUTHOR, *who supports his gigantic body as best he can.* ARDÈLE *meanwhile paces up and down the room laughing hysterically and breaking all the vases she can lay hands on.)*

GONTRAN: To do that to me! To do that to me! To do that to me!

AUTHOR *(yelling like a mad thing)*: Do let's be calm. Let's be absolutely calm. Let's try to be more and more calm.

(While all this is going on, the FRIEND *dials, forestage. The telephone rings. The* AUTHOR *drags himself to the telephone, loaded down by the dead weight of* GONTRAN, *who has fainted away.)*

AUTHOR: Hello!

FRIEND *(he, at least, is calm)*: Is that you, dear boy? Your line was busy. I've had a marvelous idea for the end of my film story.

AUTHOR *(not knowing what he is saying)*: Later, darling, later. The main thing is to keep calm. Please keep quite calm.

FRIEND: What do you mean, later darling? What on earth's come over you? Hello! Hello! Hello! Swine. *(He hangs up.)*

ARDÈLE *(bearing down on the* AUTHOR*)*: Caught in the act! Who were you talking to? I demand to know who you were talking to, you great coward. To your girl friend—weren't you? Deny it. You've just given yourself away. Take that! And that! *(She slaps his face. He lets go of* GONTRAN's *inert body and it crumples on the floor.)*

AUTHOR *(bending over him)*: He's fainted. We must call a doctor. Maybe he's taken poison. I'll go and look for some tincture of iodine.

(He goes off to the kitchen. ARDÈLE *calmly steps over the body and makes for the telephone.)*

ARDÈLE: Hello! Mademoiselle! This is Jasmin one two, one two. I've just had a call and I must find out immediately the number of my caller. Oh, you say it's difficult. Call the supervisor then, please. It's for security reasons. Your job and the whole future of the country depends upon it. You say I'll be in for it if I'm not speaking the truth? Do as I say, please, and check the facts afterward. Hello! Hello! Hello! Thank you, mademoiselle, you're a good Frenchwoman. I'll mention you to the Minister. You'll certainly be promoted. *(She dials a number. The* WOMAN *takes off the receiver, forestage.)*

WOMAN: Hello!

ARDÈLE: Hello. This is Jasmin one two, one two.

WOMAN: So you're Léon's new wife?

ARDÈLE: Oh, so he calls himself Léon these days? Coward!

WOMAN: I must confess I would like a word with you, madame! Was it you that sent this lunatic who wanted to snatch my flat from me?

ARDÈLE: Your flat? What in heaven's name do I care about your flat? You're trying to snatch my husband.

WOMAN: Let me remind you, madame, that it was you who snatched him from me! Léon adores me.

ARDÈLE: You! With that face? I can see it from here!

WOMAN: And yours, do you think I can't see that, too? I assure you I shall come and get him if you don't give him back to me.

ARDÈLE: Who, me?

WOMAN: Yes, you.

ARDÈLE: Yes, me.

(They continue with this incomprehensible exchange of "What, me?" "Yes, you," etc., while the AUTHOR *comes back from the kitchen, dragging* LA SURETTE *roughly by the collar.)*

AUTHOR: Parasite! Scrounger! Ill-bred boor! I'll teach you to monkey with the maid.

LA SURETTE: I lent you my rifle, didn't I, in time for that parade? Just because you've become a success in life, it doesn't mean you can grab everything for yourself. Anyway, you told me to comfort her.

AUTHOR: Not that way!

LA SURETTE: After all, she's only your maid!

AUTHOR: Scum! Leave her alone! *(Turning to the* MAID.*)* And you—stop crying like that. You've been irritating me all the morning!

MAID: But monsieur doesn't know. It's terrible.

AUTHOR: What is it that's so terrible still? Tell me. Like Oedipus, I want to know everything.

MAID: I'm pregnant.

AUTHOR *(sitting down, quietly)*: Whatever the case, we must keep calm.

MADAME B. *(bursting in)*: Master, Master, I can't wait any longer. The Rumanian intelligentsia is burning to know what you think of love . . .

AUTHOR *(getting up and going to her)*: Get out of here, you! Get the hell back to Rumania instantly!

MADAME B.: He's gone mad. It's terrific! *(She calls out to the* PHOTOGRAPHER.*)* We'll have to photograph him like that. It'll make sensational headlines.

AUTHOR: Madame, I don't know how these things are done in Rumania, but I warn you that if you have me photographed in these clothes I shall kill the photographer.

MADAME B.: That doesn't matter, we'll find another! Come along now, come along!

INSPECTOR *(looming)*: Ah, there you are, monsieur. I've made my inspection. A fine thing! A very fine thing! Twelve rooms to spare. You'll get your policeman all right. In fact, you'll probably get two!

ARDÈLE *(who has hung up a moment ago and has been listening, advances quietly)*: What do I hear? What were you saying while I was on the telephone? Well, *I've* got a revolver.

(She goes out, slamming the door. The picture falls down. The AUTHOR *picks it up.)*

AUTHOR: Let's keep calm. Let's keep calm to the end. Very well, monsieur. Gentlemen don't lose their heads.

INSPECTOR: Ah, so you want to be funny, my fine fellow? Sarcasm into the bargain. Right, you can have three policemen. A brigadier and two recruits. All of them fathers. And when their children are grown up, they'll make some more and they'll all live here until their children's children marry and make you some more!

AUTHOR: I'm quite calm. Yoga. Remember Yoga.

INSPECTOR: Remember what you like! You're certainly not going to forget me. I'll send you along some old-age pensioners—none under a hundred.

AUTHOR *(having attained a certain degree of concentration, chants)*: I am quite calm. Quite calm. I am becoming more and more calm.

MADAME B.: Admirable! Admirable! He really looks like a madman! What genius. What enormous genius. Another picture please, my friend. *(At this moment the* PLUMBERS *come in, shouting.)*

PLUMBERS: Look out, everyone! Look out! Look out!

AUTHOR: What's this?

PLUMBERS: The leak. The real one. We were wrong about the other one. We've only just found the real trouble, but something's gone wrong. There is water trickling all over the place. We can't control it anymore. It's everyone for himself now!

(At this very moment cascades of water begin to fall from the ceiling while MADAME BESSARABO, *the* MAID, *and the* MOTHER, *who has just returned, rush around in a panic, bellowing with fright.)*

MOTHER: A flat, indeed. A fine flat, I must say. No one in this family will ever get a flat again!

(The FRIEND *takes up his receiver. The* AUTHOR, *who has knocked the telephone over in passing, picks it up and says mechanically:)*

AUTHOR: Hello!

FRIEND: Hello, dear boy, am I disturbing you?

AUTHOR: *(trying to bring* GONTRAN *to by slapping his face)*: Not at all.

FRIEND: Ah! So you finally condescend to listen to me! I must say I've hit on a splendid idea for the end, old thing—a fire. Just like that. Everything ends in a fire.

(The AUTHOR *is standing calmly beneath the waterfall while the others are running in all directions trying to catch the pictures as they fall. Only the* INSPECTOR *has opened his umbrella and begins quietly making his report under the deluge.)*

AUTHOR: That's an excellent idea!

FRIEND: At the same time, you can hear gunfire. Do you follow me? Gunfire and fire—can you imagine the effect?

AUTHOR *(somewhat agitated, since he has just seen* ARDÈLE *come in with a pistol in her hand)*: Indeed!

*(*ARDÈLE *begins to shoot. He dodges the bullets and the water, at the same time trying to protect* GONTRAN'S *body.)*

AUTHOR: Indeed! I can well imagine it! *(Dodging a bullet.)* That'll be hilarious!

FRIEND *(pained)*: I don't think you can be paying attention, dear boy. One mustn't be selfish in this life, you know. There you are sitting quietly in your study, without a thought for the agony I've been going through trying to find an ending.

(During this time the WOMAN *has been nervously dialing the number, forestage. As the last shot is fired,* ARDÈLE *screams:)*

ARDÈLE: Darling! Tell me you're not hurt at least!

AUTHOR: No, my love. Everything's all right.

ARDÈLE: Oh, I was so frightened. *(She throws herself into his arms and falls limply in a faint.)*

AUTHOR *(shouting hysterically into the telephone)*: Everything's all right, do you hear me, everything's all right!

FRIEND *(furious)*: Do you want me to tell you something? You're impossible. You're just saying anything to keep me quiet. You're not even listening. Be honest, for once; tell me straight you don't think this ending's a good one.

AUTHOR *(holding up* ARDÈLE *and endeavoring to hoist up* GONTRAN*)*: Listen, dear boy, I'll be frank with you. I agree with Paul Zed. I know I wrote *La Marguerite,* but all the same I prefer a story to end happily.

FRIEND *(suddenly venomous)*: You're nothing but a cabaret turn! Just a piddling little unambitious cabaret turn! A lot of water'll flow under the bridge before I call you again!

(He hangs up furiously at this, while the waterfall brings down the ceiling. The WOMAN, *who has dialed the number for the tenth time, gives a cry of triumph.)*

WOMAN: Hello! Léon?

(She will go on shouting this until the curtain falls, while the AUTHOR *comes forward dragging with him* ARDÈLE *and* GONTRAN. *There is general panic in the background, and the décor falls to pieces as the* AUTHOR *addresses the public.)*

AUTHOR: Ladies and gentlemen—one does what one can . . . And there are so many serious writers in the theatre today, I am sure you will forgive the author's failings if he has only made you laugh.

Curtain

Questions

1. Are the characters realistic? Support your answer by pointing to specific lines in the play.
2. Character traits are often exaggerated. Determine how this is true for each character.
3. What purpose does each of the characters serve in advancing the story line?
4. Did you enjoy this play? Why or why not?
5. Even though the other characters are interrupting his work, the Author tries to be polite with them—at least up to a point. Why do you think Anouilh had him react this way?
6. What is the significance of the ending? Do you think it's logical? Why or why not?

WILLIAM SAROYAN

The New Play

WILLIAM SAROYAN was born in Fresno, California, of Armenian parents. Largely self-educated, he attained success as a short-story writer, novelist, playwright, and essayist.

His first published short story, *The Daring Young Man on the Flying Trapeze,* attracted wide attention and was later issued as a book. Among Saroyan's novels were *The Human Comedy, My Name is Aram,* and *Boys and Girls Together,* all highly successful.

Saroyan's first play, *My Heart's in the Highlands,* was also highly successful. This was followed by *The Time of Your Life,* the first play to win both a Pulitzer Prize and the New York Drama Critics Circle Award. This play had a great influence on later avant garde playwrights.

THE NEW PLAY mingles reality and imagination and certainly departs from the usual straight-line plotting of traditional plays. It seems to illustrate the idea that theatre and life are similar, and it is difficult to separate them because one blends so well into the other.

In reading *The New Play,* you can see why Saroyan had such an influence on the development of experimental styles of playwriting.

The New Play William Saroyan

Characters:

THE WRITER
THE SECRETARY
THE COCKTAIL PARTY MAN FOLGER
THE COCKTAIL PARTY WOMAN DINAH
THE MAN WHO LOOKS LIKE ABE LINCOLN IN THE MOVIES
THE PROFESSOR OF EVERYTHING

Setting:

A stage.

Scene One: A plain SECRETARY *brings the* WRITER *a cup of coffee. He takes a sip. She lights his cigarette. He takes a puff, inhales deeply, holds the smoke in a long time, then lets it out.*

SECRETARY: We were at work on The New Play.

WRITER: We were?

SECRETARY: Yes. We had come to where you were bored, and would not go on.

WRITER: When was *that?*

SECRETARY: Yesterday afternoon at half past two. You went to sleep. Shall we proceed?

WRITER: Well, first, let's think about it a minute.

SECRETARY: Yes, sir.

WRITER: Suppose I *do* write The New Play? Act One—flawless. Act Two—more flawless than Act One. Act Three—so flawless that half the people in the theatre *die.* They don't applaud. They just die. *(He reflects.)*

SECRETARY: Yes, sir.

WRITER: Is *that* what I want to do? Kill the people? Coffee and cigarettes in the morning for me, ideas all day long, money and fame? So much fame that it *bores* me. Fame *past* people—fame among little birds, animals, weeds, because I *am* a writer. *(Pause.)* Is that what I want to do? Kill the people?

SECRETARY: Oh, no, sir! Not *you!*

WRITER *(quickly)*: Just a minute. They can't live *forever.* Why *shouldn't* I kill them—with laughter? The other writers are killing them with lies, aren't they? Take the books one by one and look at them. All lies!

SECRETARY: Surely not—Shakespeare.

WRITER: Worst of all. Everybody rants and raves. And then somebody runs and somebody stabs somebody.

SECRETARY: Mr. Panafran, I came to work yesterday morning, and I'm sure it's going to take a day or two to get acquainted, but I'm afraid I can't stay on if you're the kind of writer who considers everybody else in the world dishonest. My father, Mr. Panafran . . .

WRITER: My name is *not* Panafran.

SECRETARY: Franapan . . .

WRITER: It's not Franapan, either.

SECRETARY: My father—was a gentleman.

WRITER: No doubt, and I'm a writer. Now, what the devil do you think you're doing to the *morning?* Here I am, ready to decide how to kill the people, and you've gone to work and half-stopped me from being wonderful, haven't you?

SECRETARY *(professionally)*: No, sir. I *am* writing everything down.

WRITER: Thank you. Let's just let *me* be the lunatic around here. Let's just let *you* be a good secretary. Got that?

SECRETARY: Yes, sir.

WRITER *(smiles, steps forward)*: As a matter of fact, I don't *work* with a secretary. *(He notices the* SECRETARY *writing quickly.)* Oh, no, that wasn't for *you*.

SECRETARY: I'm sorry, sir, I've written it all down. After all, I *am* a secretary and a very good one.

WRITER: Well, I'm glad, but I don't *have* a secretary.

SECRETARY: I'm writing it all down, Mr. Panafran.

WRITER: Go ahead, write it. I never had a secretary in my life.

SECRETARY: A secretary keeps *all* of a writer's ideas. She doesn't let him throw them away.

WRITER: I don't *have* any ideas.

SECRETARY: Oh, *yes,* you do.

WRITER: None at all.

SECRETARY: What's all this in the book, then?

WRITER: Morning. Coffee and cigarettes. If only I could be pompous. Existentialism. Do you know what that is?

SECRETARY: Yes, sir.

WRITER: The devil you do.

SECRETARY: It's a philosophy.

WRITER: Just like that! What was it *before* somebody said existentialism?

SECRETARY: Well, I'm sure you can't say anything against—food inspection!

WRITER: I can't say anything against *morning,* that's all.

SECRETARY: What can you say against afternoon?

WRITER: It's not the *same* as morning.

SECRETARY: Evening?

WRITER: By evening you're confused.

SECRETARY: Night?

WRITER: At night it's *all* lost. You've got to wait until morning again.

SECRETARY: Shall we go back to The New Play?

WRITER: I *wrote* it. I produced it. I directed it. It was *all* very exciting. It bored me. I throw away in ten minutes greater plays than the ones that win the prizes. I've thrown this one away, too.

SECRETARY: Shall we begin again, then?

WRITER: Well, it's still morning, if that's what you mean.

SECRETARY: Mr. Panafran, for six years I worked for Jerry, and Jerry always said a movie is only as good as its villain.

WRITER: What else did he say?

SECRETARY: He said a money-making movie must have a girl who, no matter how much clothes she wears, looks naked.

WRITER: Did he say anything about how a *naked* girl should look?

SECRETARY: No, he didn't, but my six years with Jerry were the happiest of my life because I knew I was contributing something.

WRITER: Why aren't you working for him now, then?

SECRETARY *(softly)*: Jerry died.

WRITER: The only decent thing he ever did, most likely.

SECRETARY *(outraged)*: Mr. Panafran, if you're going to make fun of everybody I hold dear, I don't have to keep this job. I can't imagine what kind of a writer you are, anyway. In your opinion everybody's an idiot. The fact that my father was a gentleman makes no difference. You haven't the slightest respect for story construction, plot atmosphere, or character development. I was told at the employment agency that the job was with a writer, and having had six years with Jerry, I felt I was qualified, but I don't think you want a secretary, Mr. Panafran, I think you want a—jezebel.

WRITER: I never had a secretary in my life. *(Pause.)* What *killed* Jerry?

SECRETARY: Heart attack. He was only thirty-three, poor boy.

WRITER: And he always said a movie is only as good as its villain?

SECRETARY: Yes.

WRITER: What a pompous bore!

SECRETARY: He's *dead,* Mr. Panafran. You can't speak that way of the dead.

WRITER: Why? Did he change when he died? He wasn't dead when he kept saying a movie is only as good as its villain, was he? He was alive *then,* if that's what you want to call it, wasn't he?

SECRETARY: Don't you dare imply that Jerry wasn't alive when he was alive. He *was*. He was the most alive young man that ever lived. You don't want a secretary, you want a . . .

WRITER: No, I don't. *(Smiles.)* That's all for today.

SECRETARY: But you haven't even gotten *started!*

WRITER: It's all right.

SECRETARY: You haven't even got a villain. You've *got* to have a villain.

WRITER: Not me.

SECRETARY: Well, I'll type out these crazy remarks, then. *(He goes in one direction. She goes in the other.)*

(Scene Two: The WRITER *is stretched out on a plain black sofa in the middle of the stage. The* SECRETARY *is seated on a plain chair at the head of the sofa, notebook and pencil ready.)*

SECRETARY *(to herself)*: I should have married Jerry. Instead, *he's* dead, and I work for a writer who sleeps. If I had been his wife, Jerry wouldn't have died.

WRITER: What would he have done?

SECRETARY: I thought you were asleep.

WRITER: I was. If you had married him, what would he have done?

SECRETARY: He would have lived.

WRITER: Where?

SECRETARY: Office and home. *(Pause.)* I'm ready if you are. *(She waits a moment, then looks at his face closely.)* Fast asleep again. Jerry *never* slept. Jerry created. He created and created. Stories, plots, characters, heroes, villains, themes, suspense, excitement. . .

WRITER *(jumps off the sofa)*: Write this down. I've waited forty-eight years for this. I knew I'd get it if I waited long enough.

SECRETARY *(following him around)*: Yes, sir.

WRITER *(softly)*: And.

SECRETARY *(writes)*: And.

WRITER: At last! *(He lies down on the sofa again.)*

SECRETARY: And *what? (Pause.)* Fast asleep again. He waited forty-eight years for *And*. I don't believe he's a writer at all. Perhaps he's a bank robber. *(Pause.)* No. They're all so sleepless. At least they were in Jerry's movies. And courteous, too, many of them. *(She looks at the* WRITER.*)* Perhaps he's the brains of an underworld gang that deals in counterfeit money. *(Pause.)* I should have married Jerry.

WRITER: And.

SECRETARY: I should have had a son.

WRITER: And.

SECRETARY: A daughter.

WRITER: And.

SECRETARY: A personal maid.

WRITER: And.

SECRETARY: A gardener.

WRITER: And.

SECRETARY: Everything! *(Pause.)* I never know when he's awake or asleep. I can't tell the difference, almost. When he jumps up I always think he's awake, but he isn't, he's still asleep, with his eyes wide open.

(Louder, directly to the WRITER.*)* And *everything! (Pause.)* God knows where he is now. Jerry was always awake, and I always knew what he was thinking. Success. *More* success. If he hadn't died he would now be thirty-six years old. If I had married him the year before he died, our son would now be three years old. Oh, what a handsome boy. Lost forever. There will never be another Jerry.

WRITER: How fortunate for us.

SECRETARY: Don't you dare speak that way of the dead! *(No answer.)*

SECRETARY: Oh, wake up, please.

WRITER: What for?

SECRETARY: It's half past two in the afternoon—time to work.

WRITER: This *is* my work.

SECRETARY: Your work is to write.

WRITER: I *am* writing.

SECRETARY *(comically shrill)*: It's got no plot!

WRITER: You refer, I presume, to Jerry's life.

SECRETARY: I refer to your play. *(No answer. She looks at his face intently again.)*

SECRETARY: Gone again. You never know when he's likely to arrive, or liable to go. I must ask the employment agency to send me to a mystery writer. *They're* dependable. Somebody kills somebody. It could be any one of six or seven people. Now it seems it's this one, now it seems it's that. I'm comfortable near a mystery. Not like here, where I never know whether I'm going or coming. *(She looks at him intently and with impatience.)* Oh, wake up, please. *(Pause.)* Well, then, if you won't wake up, I think the least you can do is tell me about your childhood. I'm sure you were desperately unhappy.

WRITER: Happy.

SECRETARY: *You?*

WRITER: All the time.

SECRETARY *(mocking)*: I'll *bet* you were.

WRITER: I *was*.

SECRETARY: *Prove* it.

WRITER: I'm happy *now*. What *better* proof is there?

SECRETARY: Well, I'm *not* happy now. As I child I was *bitterly* unhappy. My father was a gentleman, but my mother wasn't a lady. She humiliated my father. She humiliated *me*. I was terribly ashamed of her. *(Pause.)* May I stretch out on the sofa, too?

WRITER: Of course not.

SECRETARY: I can speak more freely if I'm stretched out.

WRITER: It's not necessary to speak more freely.

SECRETARY: It might do me good. I've always wanted to tell somebody about my mother, but I haven't had anybody to speak to freely.

WRITER: Keep it that way. I'm rather fond of your mother, and I'd rather she weren't belittled.

SECRETARY: Oh, please wake up, and let's get to work. At this rate, you'll never get the play written. *(No answer. She looks at his face intently again.)*

SECRETARY: One word. All afternoon. *And.* Great writer!

WRITER: Slob.

SECRETARY: Well, I'll say one thing, awake or asleep, you don't leave yourself out of your unkind thoughts for the human race.

WRITER: I *am* the human race.

SECRETARY *(quickly and comically)*: You are *not!*

WRITER: Am.

SECRETARY: Aren't.

WRITER: Who is, then?

SECRETARY: The multitudes.

WRITER: Where'd you get that from?

SECRETARY: Everybody knows the millions and millions of people all over the world, far away, are the human race. *(Again no answer.)* Asleep again. This is the lonesomest job I've ever had.

WRITER: There's no profession like it.

SECRETARY: He's fast asleep, of course.

WRITER: You bet your sweet life he is.

SECRETARY: Well, I've got *And* written down, but what good is it?

WRITER *(gets up, yawns, steps forward, smiles)*: The government is dirty.

SECRETARY: I refuse to write that down.

WRITER: I am speaking of the government of ancient Greece.

SECRETARY: You are *not* speaking of the government of ancient Greece.

WRITER: Rome?

SECRETARY: Not Rome, either.

WRITER: Sicily?

SECRETARY: No.

WRITER: Venice?

SECRETARY: No.

WRITER: Carthage? Corsica? Macedonia?

SECRETARY: No, *none* of them.

WRITER: Oh. In that case, the government *isn't* dirty.

SECRETARY: What government?

WRITER: The government of ancient Greece of course.

SECRETARY: But a moment ago you said the government of ancient Greece *was* dirty.

WRITER: That was a moment ago. The past is past, isn't it?

SECRETARY: Is the government going to be the villain, then?

WRITER: What villain?

SECRETARY: In the play?
WRITER: There is no play. That's the end of today's work.
SECRETARY: The *end* of it? It didn't *start*. You were asleep.
WRITER: Even so. *(He goes. She goes.)*

(Scene Three: The WRITER *has gotten out of his old clothes into rather neat ones. He is standing at a mobile bar-table, pouring gin into a large jar with ice cubes in it.*

A MAN *named* FOLGER *arrives; the* WRITER *hands him a drink.)*

FOLGER: I was thinking on my way here of the variety. *(He sips his drink.)* Thank you. Very good.

(A smiling, handsomely dressed WOMAN *of middle years named* DINAH *comes to the table, receives a drink.)*

FOLGER: Dinah, you're smiling about something. What is it?
DINAH: I haven't the faintest idea. Surely nothing new. *(She sips, as the* WRITER *watches. She sips again and again.)*
DINAH: Perfect, and, if I may, I believe I would like to cry. *(She smiles bigger than ever.)* Comfort me, dear Mr. Folger.
FOLGER: If you persist in smiling, I shall only continue to distrust you.
DINAH: Comfort me. *(She smiles.)*
FOLGER: What's your sorrow?
DINAH: It's untellable. *(She smiles.)*
WRITER: *(steps forward)*: You've listened to us before. We can speak of anything. Listen. *(He turns to* DINAH *and* FOLGER *who are speaking, unheard. He calls out in a strong voice.)* Apricots.
FOLGER: The tree is slender, with slender branches.
DINAH: A green soft leaf that stays cool even on the hottest day.
FOLGER: I especially like the freckles on the apricot itself.
DINAH: Yes. They're like freckles on a faceless cheek. New, smooth, tender, and the color of the sun.
FOLGER: Not at all, the color of the sun is orange.
DINAH: How absurd.
WRITER *(calls out again)*: Pennies.
DINAH: I saw a most astonishing play night before last. There they were, intoxicated with a theory of meaning when suddenly . . .
FOLGER: You needn't tell me. I was there, too. *(The* WRITER *listens closely, watching.)*
DINAH: I have always found the theory of meaning attractive only to children, but of course I mean only the very littlest of them.
FOLGER: My two small sons were quite good at knowing what they meant.
DINAH: What *did* they mean?

FOLGER: Why, nothing, of course, but while they were little they seemed to *believe* they meant a great deal, perhaps everything.

WRITER: No, no—*pennies.*

DINAH: The point of the play for me, whatever it may have been for you, dear Fred, was the unexpected behavior of the statesman from—oh, where *was* he from?

FOLGER: Gibraltar.

DINAH: Yes. When he was asked the metric weight of Gibraltar by the statesman from—now, where was *he* from?

FOLGER: Mesopotamia.

DINAH: Yes. And the man from Gibraltar misunderstood the question, believed he was being heckled, and began to bellow like a bull.

FOLGER: I was *there,* dear lady.

DINAH: I haven't said you weren't.

FOLGER: By which I mean the play bored me.

DINAH: You didn't go to be *amused,* I trust.

FOLGER: I went, to sleep. And wasn't permitted to.

DINAH: Whereupon the man from Iceland . . .

FOLGER: Gibraltar.

DINAH: I speak *now* of the man from Iceland.

FOLGER: I had no idea there *was* a man from Iceland.

DINAH: There *was.* Whereupon this man—performed I may say by a friend of my youngest daughter, and quite badly, too—I've asked her not to see him again . . .

WRITER: *Pennies.*

DINAH: . . . brought a handful of small coins out of his pocket, opened his hand, and held it out to the man bellowing like a bull. But this gentle Icelandic gesture of sympathy was *also* misunderstood by the bull—you know who I mean.

FOLGER: I haven't the faintest idea. I didn't like the play.

DINAH: Why must you imagine you *might* have? Who, then, in a rage, removed one of the small coins out of the hand of the man from Iceland, held it up for all to see, put it in his mouth and *swallowed* it. The bull did, I mean.

FOLGER: I don't remember that, and in any case I see nothing especially useful in your having brought it up.

DINAH: I am speaking of a number of people in a play, but apparently *you* are thinking of another kind of people, perhaps people like ourselves, who do *not* do, or say, fanciful things.

FOLGER: I am drinking. I am thinking of no one, certainly not ourselves.

WRITER *(to the audience)*: The coin the man swallowed may have been a penny, but the fact remains that we can speak of anything. *(He turns back to* DINAH *and* FOLGER.*)*

DINAH: The man from Gibraltar was a scoundrel of course, but I *like* them. I simply can't stand the righteous in plays. They're certainly difficult enough *out* of them.

WRITER *(returns to* DINAH *and* FOLGER, *fills their glasses)*: Have you wept? Has he comforted you?

DINAH *(sips)*: I've cried my eyes out, and he most certainly *hasn't* comforted me. I know of no one more heartless, and I love him for it.

FOLGER: You are much too attractive for *me* to understand. I have considerable difficulty with *plain* women. Pray, *when* did you weep?

DINAH: Oh, poor silly, I arrived in tears and I've been blubbering ever since. Every time we meet I become increasingly aware of the depth and enormity of your wisdom from the steadfast manner in which you hold out for arithmetic or nothing.

FOLGER: I am drinking, and the working of numbers is no part of it.

(The WRITER *pours more gin into the glass jar. The* MAN *who looks like Abe Lincoln in the movies comes in, his hands clasped behind him, his head bent down in thought. The* WRITER *studies him doubtfully.* ABE *looks up, nods to* DINAH, *glances at* FOLGER, *takes the offered glass.)*

WRITER: We were speaking of the winter flight of birds. *(He sips, to encourage* ABE *to sip, but* ABE *doesn't.)*

DINAH: I was saying how clever I think it is of them to go so swiftly—directly to where they go. *(She sips, but* ABE *doesn't.)* Excepting perhaps *owls,* which tend to *stay,* and for that, I suppose, are considered wise. *(She glances quickly for help, smiling enormously at the awkwardness.)*

FOLGER: As a matter of fact, we were *not* speaking of the winter flight of birds. We were drinking. *(He sips.)* (ABE *nods, sips, and* DINAH *sighs with relief.)*

DINAH *(of* FOLGER*)*: His brilliance appalls me. He knows so much for a man who knows nothing. Absolutely nothing. *(She turns quickly to* ABE, *smiles, nods.* ABE *nods in return.)*

ABE: Madam. At one time it fell to my lot to consider the right of right, which put me to walking. Barefoot, late at night, in a strange, spacious place, almost forgotten. As I walked, it further fell to my lot to consider the right of *wrong,* and the night wore on, the feet grew cold, and somebody thought, perhaps myself rather than another, although I cannot ever be sure, "There is no end." And so I went to my bed and knew I was dead.

DINAH *(sweetly, courteously)*: Your life is so interesting. Please don't stop.

ABE: Not *my* life. I *am* rehearsing from a play I hope will some day be written. My name is Bob, although for years I've been called Abe. Not a writer myself, I must hope some day to meet one.

WRITER: Look no further.

ABE: Have I the honor of speaking to a Lincoln writer?

WRITER: The pleasure, I hope, of speaking to a *writer,* presently disengaged from the awful intensity of it, happily come upon evening and friends, but alas, *not* a Lincoln writer.

ABE: I seek a Lincoln writer.

WRITER: You will surely find him. In the meantime, you were rehearsing. You had come to, "There is no end." Quite a place for pause.

ABE: I spoke as Abe, not as actor. How shall I speak now?

DINAH *(cheerfully, sweetly)*: As Abe *or* actor. It's surely six of one and half a dozen of another.

FOLGER *(quickly)*: Six of one, half a dozen of another? I must remember that. A state of *sameness,* differently put.

DINAH: Mister Folger is devoted to numbers.

FOLGER: Actually I despise them, but they persist in my thoughts. I am counting everything.

ABE: I worked in a theatre in a small town somewhere once, and on the same bill was a man who called himself The Mathematical Marvel.

FOLGER: Was he *cheerful?*

ABE: No, but he *was* swift.

FOLGER: It's not the same.

ABE: And he had an excellent sense of timing.

FOLGER: As a matter of fact, it's impossible *not* to count everything. How many worlds are there?

ABE: One.

FOLGER *(to* ABE*)*: Wrong.

WRITER *(begins to pour for everybody)*: Right or wrong, it's nice to speak about it in the evening. *(To* ABE.*)* I must say I was quite impressed by the manner in which you delivered the speech about the barefoot walking. *(To* DINAH.*)* Surely by now your sorrows have lost a little of their edge. *(To* FOLGER, *pouring.)* Of course you must count everything.

FOLGER: And *dis*count nothing.

DINAH: Oh, how *glib.*

FOLGER: I wish to drink and be humbly stupid.

DINAH: Alas, for you, then, poor Fred. Even your wishes are ambitious and pompous. *Be* stupid like the rest of us, neither humbly nor proudly so. Stupidly stupid, as it were, and therefore charmingly so, however unintentionally. It is evening and cool at last. The apricots are on the trees. The freckles are on the apricots.

FOLGER: I thank you for your swift, soothing speech. Speak on.

DINAH: I would rather listen to Honest Abe.

ABE: I am a teller of jokes, they say.

DINAH: Oh, then, tell one, please.

ABE: As a boy in Illinois I came one day upon a pig stuck in the mud, and a little old woman of the hills who asked me to get the pig out of the mud for her.

DINAH: And *did* you?

WRITER *(steps forward)*: Even in the evening, even in the time of friends and idle talk, art will not rest, and drunk with sorrow or joy or nothing at all, will nag a little more, say this, say that, and wait. And soon Friends One, Two and Three have had their fill of drink and talk and one another, and march off to where they were, to what they were *about.* (DINAH, FOLGER *and* ABE *go. The* SECRETARY *comes in.)*

WRITER: What are *you* doing here at this hour of the evening?

SECRETARY: I am here on *my own* time. *(The* WRITER *pours a drink for her, holds it out.)*

SECRETARY: I don't drink. I was at home with my mother who was dressing—that's *all* she does—and I said so. She in turn said I might take a hint from her, so I did.

WRITER: You dressed?

SECRETARY: Yes, and as Jerry's dead, and I *am* employed here . . .

WRITER *(mumbling)*: I never had a secretary in my life.

SECRETARY: It seemed to me that you might just wish—

WRITER *(mumbling)*: No such thing.

SECRETARY: And if that happened to be so, as it would have been if it were Jerry of a pleasant summer evening, then here suddenly I would be, waiting and ready. The New Play, Mr. Panafran, and I can only say it's part of my work.

WRITER: No thanks. The play's no good.

SECRETARY: Mr. Panafran, I wish you'd let the world judge your work.

WRITER: Is that from Jerry, too?

SECRETARY: *Of course.* All that I am today, I . . .

WRITER: Don't say it.

SECRETARY: Jerry said, "If fifty million people like my work, I owe it to them to give them more of it."

WRITER: What did he owe his mother, poor woman?

SECRETARY: He was kind to her. A telephone call on the first of every month. And a carbon copy of every one of his scenarios. Write your play, Mr. Panafran, and let the world judge it.

WRITER: Only *I* can judge what I write.

SECRETARY: I thought you were on your way to something quite exciting when you jumped up from the sofa this afternoon and asked me to write down *And.* It's right here in shorthand. *And.* Shall we go to work, then?

WRITER: I hope you won't mind, no. *(He goes. She goes.)*

(Scene Four: The PROFESSOR OF EVERYTHING *has a pitch pipe for a singing lesson with the* WRITER.*)*

PROFESSOR: Now, please. *(He blows pitch pipe, then demonstrates in a falsetto voice, on a rising scale.)* Ah ha ha ha ha, ah ha ha ha ha, ah ha ha ha ha. Ready?

WRITER *(hung-over but courteous)*: Not quite.

PROFESSOR *(he blows pitch pipe again)*: One, two, three—*now*. Ah ha ha ha ha? *(The* WRITER *does not join him. He stops, blows pitch pipe again.)*

PROFESSOR: You must put your heart *into* it. Ah ha ha ha ha? Ready?

WRITER: What do you say we forget it for the time being?

PROFESSOR: Forget *singing?* Oh, no, we *must* sing! Ah ha ha ha ha? *(Blows pitch pipe quickly.)* One, two, three—now.

WRITER: Listen, Professor . . .

PROFESSOR: No, no no, no no—ah ha ha ha ha?

WRITER: I'm not up to a lesson this morning.

PROFESSOR: But I am charging for one hour and I have worked only three minutes.

WRITER: That's O.K., Professor. Send me your bill and I'll send you a check.

PROFESSOR: I have been to Milano, you understand, and I have *memoirs* to write. Perhaps you would be kind enough to give me writing lessons in exchange for singing lessons.

WRITER: Yes, we might be able to do that, but not this morning.

PROFESSOR: But this is *Friday*—singing lesson day. A lesson every Friday, but not *once* have you *sung!*

WRITER: Professor, I don't really want to sing.

PROFESSOR: Oh, no, don't say that!

WRITER: It's just that when you came to the door six weeks ago and asked if I wanted to take singing lessons, three dollars an hour, I *was* impressed by your appearance . . .

PROFESSOR: A teacher of singing must present a good appearance at the front door.

WRITER: Yes, of course. And by the manner in which you held out the pitch pipe.

PROFESSOR *(he holds it out dynamically)*: Like *this*. It is the only way to do it.

WRITER: Yes, and being a writer, one who is interested in everybody—a *little* interested, at any rate—and always happy to have an excuse by which to postpone going to work, I accepted your offer.

PROFESSOR: And paid me in cash!—for which I thank you. Although from the first, you have not permitted me to give you one *full* lesson.

WRITER: Professor, the fact is *you* can't sing.

PROFESSOR: I am a *teacher.*

WRITER: And you can't *teach,* either. I know you need the work, and . . .

PROFESSOR: The money.

WRITER: Yes.

PROFESSOR: But I *have* been to Milano.

WRITER: Of course.

PROFESSOR: It is true that I did not *enter* the Opera House, but I *saw* it. *(Pause, then suddenly and shyly.)* You do not have the cash this time?

WRITER: I spent all my cash last night.

PROFESSOR: Ah ha ha ha ha. What did you buy?

WRITER: Dinner for an actress.

PROFESSOR: Oh, they *must* eat! And *only* where the food is expensive. I know. I've *taught* acting.

WRITER: I can write a check of course.

PROFESSOR: No no. No need. I have . . . *(He examines contents of his pocket: nothing.)*

WRITER: Well, *do* you have, Professor?

PROFESSOR: Today? No—I do not.

WRITER: Your other students, they will pay you something?

PROFESSOR: Today?

WRITER: Listen, Professor, if you don't *have* any other students, if you're hungry, go in there . . . *(He points.)* . . . and get yourself some food.

(The PROFESSOR *goes, and soon a refrigerator door is heard to open. The* WRITER *sits, writing a check. The refrigerator door is shut—he jumps. It is opened. He jumps. It is shut, and so on. The* PROFESSOR *returns eating a sandwich.)*

PROFESSOR *(bites into sandwich)*: If you do not feel well enough for a singing lesson, perhaps another lesson—spelling, conversation . . .

WRITER: I don't think so, Professor. *(Tears check out of the book, holds it out.)* I'm sorry I've got no cash.

PROFESSOR *(takes another bite of the sandwich, accepts the check, looks at it)*: Ten dollars? The lesson is *three* dollars.

WRITER: I'm paying a little in advance.

PROFESSOR: A lesson in Latin?

WRITER: I don't think so.

PROFESSOR: Painting?

WRITER: You teach painting, too?

PROFESSOR: Perhaps you have heard of Picasso.

WRITER: Yes, I have.

PROFESSOR: I have not only *heard* of Picasso, I have seen one of his paintings. In a magazine. In this kind of painting you want for the woman extra eyes, and for the man sorrow in the face.

WRITER: O.K., there's three dollars in the check for the painting lesson.

PROFESSOR: Composition?

WRITER: *Musical* composition?

PROFESSOR: Yes, of course. I teach only things of culture.

WRITER: O.K., Professor, I'll take a crack at that, too, then.

PROFESSOR: You have heard of Mozart?

WRITER: Yes, Professor, I've heard of Mozart.

PROFESSOR: I have heard this concerto for piano on the radio. In this kind of musical composition you need a man like Mozart, who has sadness, but sometimes also joy. Shershall forty-four, Longo thirty-three.

WRITER: I got it. There's three dollars in the check for that, too. Thank you very much, Professor.

PROFESSOR: Not yet. We have still left over one dollar.

WRITER: I don't think we need to bother about the dollar, Professor.

PROFESSOR: I have a suitable subject and lesson for a dollar, too—but *not* cultural.

WRITER: Well, O.K., if you say so.

PROFESSOR: You have seen a small boy flying a kite?

WRITER: Yes, I have.

PROFESSOR: To make a kite, then. You make a cross of two sticks. You put paper in front of the cross. You tie string around the cross. You paste paper around the string, and let the paste dry. Then more string in front, which you tie together where it crosses, and then you tie one end of a whole *ball* of string to the place where the string crosses, and you *fly* the kite.

WRITER: I got it.

PROFESSOR: But don't forget to tie on the tail, too.

WRITER: O.K. Thanks a lot, Professor.

PROFESSOR: I come again next Friday?

WRITER: Yes, I think so.

PROFESSOR: What subject shall we teach and learn?

WRITER: Oh, I leave that to you, Professor. I find that you teach one thing as well as another.

PROFESSOR: Thank you. I *try.*

WRITER: I don't really want any of the food in the kitchen, so on your way out, please help yourself.

PROFESSOR: Are you sure?

WRITER: All I want is the jar of instant coffee.

PROFESSOR: You are my best student. You learn very quickly.

(The PROFESSOR *goes. The* WRITER *shakes his head, trying to clear it. Kitchen sounds are heard. The* PROFESSOR *returns with a small jar.)*

PROFESSOR: What is *this?*

WRITER: Caviar.

PROFESSOR: I have never eaten caviar.
WRITER: There isn't very much in the jar, but there's enough for a *taste.*
PROFESSOR: You are sure you do not want it?
WRITER: No, Professor, I don't want it.
PROFESSOR: Thank you.

(He goes. The refrigerator door is opened and shut several times again, and the PROFESSOR *is heard "ah ha ha ha haing" happily. The* SECRETARY *comes in, removes her coat, puts her handbag on the table, glances at the* WRITER, *goes straight to the kitchen, comes back.)*

SECRETARY: Who *is* that man out there?
WRITER: My teacher.
SECRETARY: He's taking everything out of the kitchen.
PROFESSOR *(returns with two big bags full of stuff)*: I didn't take the instant coffee.
WRITER: Would you like a cup *now?*
PROFESSOR: Oh, no, it makes me nervous. Thank you. *(He bows to the* WRITER.*)* Good morning. *(The* WRITER *nods. The* PROFESSOR *bows to the* SECRETARY.*)* Good morning. *(The* SECRETARY *bows. The* PROFESSOR *goes.)*
SECRETARY: Well, who *is* he, for heaven's sake?
WRITER: I've been taking singing lessons from him.
SECRETARY: *Singing?*
WRITER: Yes, singing.
SECRETARY: I can't understand what kind of a writer you are. *(Pause.)* Well, I'd better get your coffee and cigarettes.

(She hurries off. The WRITER *sits with his head in his hands a moment, then stands slowly, shakes his head three times quickly, pulls himself up to his full height, smiles and steps forward.)*

WRITER: A writer is free to write *anything.* He is free to do so in any culture, any nation, and any time. He is free. He is very nearly the only man left who *is* free. *(The* SECRETARY *returns with a cup of coffee and a package of cigarettes.)*

SECRETARY *(swiftly)*: Can't you at least give me time to get my book?
WRITER *(takes the cup of coffee)*: Thank you. *(He takes a sip, half-enthusiastically.)*
SECRETARY *(with book and pencil)*: Time to work, now.
WRITER *(smiles)*: O.K.
SECRETARY: The New Play.
WRITER: O.K., The New Play.
SECRETARY: Are you still drunk?

WRITER: No doubt, but the morning's wearing away, and so I'll stretch out now and go back to sleep. *(He smiles, steps forward.)*

SECRETARY *(stands quickly; angry)*: But you haven't done any work! *(The* WRITER *goes. The* SECRETARY *stands, watching.)*

(Scene Five: There is an enormous screen of a television set on the stage. The SECRETARY *is lying on the sofa. The* WRITER *is seated at the table behind the sofa. On the table is a deck of cards. He takes a card off the top, looks at it, puts it down.)*

SECRETARY: My mother wasn't from the South, she was from the North. All the same, she believed she was irresistible to all men. My father wasn't from the East, he was from the West, but in his old clothes he looked a little like a cowboy—*off* his horse of course. He hardly ever spoke. My mother hardly ever stopped. When she wasn't speaking at home, she was speaking at one or another of the eleven or twelve clubs she belonged to.

(She stops. The WRITER *glances over at her, waits a moment. The* SECRETARY *blows her nose. The* WRITER *gets up, goes to the big television set, turns on a knob, there are waves of light, and then* FOLGER *appears.)*

FOLGER: Spend your money. Buy anything. Drive carefully. Watch out for cancer. Don't be afraid. Take out insurance. Rent something. Get your hat blocked. Eat potatoes. Read books. Marry somebody. Don't neglect your teeth. Vote for somebody. Believe in something. Don't be ashamed to go mad. Go to church. And now back to our story, *A Man and a Woman,* brought to you by *Everything. (*FOLGER *goes:* ABE *arrives, stands to one side.* DINAH *arrives.)*

DINAH: So then I said, "Well, why should *I* be the one?" They said, "Because you're George's wife, and George's name carries a lot of weight." I said, "Don't tell *me* how much weight George's name carries. I happen to be an authority on the subject, and I say his name carries no more weight than anybody else's." So then they said, "That's not so!" George, are you *listening* to me? *(*ABE *nods.)*

DINAH: So then I said, "Don't tell me what's so, and what isn't so. I *know.* Do it yourselves. I've done more than my share already, and *you* can begin to do a little for a change. Why should I be expected to do everything just because I happen to be married to George? If you really expect matters to improve, you simply must improve them yourselves." *(*ABE *turns a little. He is holding a rolled newspaper. He tightens the paper.)*

DINAH: So then they said, "It isn't as if we expected you to do anything that you haven't always *insisted* on doing." So I said, "Don't tell me what it isn't as if. . . (ABE *whacks her on top of the head with the rolled newspaper. She goes right on talking.)*

DINAH: I know better than you ever could what it isn't as if, and what it *is* as if, and I tell you it's as if you expect me to do everything, as always, and I want you to know once and for all I *won't.*" So then nobody said anything, and finally I said, "All right, I'll do it again." *(The* WRITER *goes and stands very near the television set.)*

DINAH: Well, then every one of them rushed up to embrace me, hypocrites that they are. *(The* WRITER *reaches for the knob.* DINAH *looks down at him.)*

DINAH: Don't you dare turn me off! This is very important.

(The WRITER *remains fixed but doesn't turn the dial.* DINAH *continues to speak.)*

DINAH: I said, "If you are so sure that only I can do *all* of the work, then of course I *will* try my best to do it, although I will absolutely not tolerate chocolate frosting on *all* of the cakes any more. We've had enough of chocolate frosting. (ABE, *standing behind DINAH, winds up and is about to whack her again when he decides not to.)*

DINAH: There are other kinds of frosting, and I think the sooner we agree to have them the better off we are going to be, and the better off. . . "

(The WRITER *turns the knob of the television set, and the screen is instantly dark. He goes back to the table and sits down.)*

SECRETARY: As a little girl my mother was terribly spoiled, and so there was always a very cruel streak in her—toward everybody, except any man who happened to be near by, and then she was all cooing sweetness and charm, although to me it was sickening, because it was really so pathetic and silly. She gloried in her figure inside her clothes, and she pitched her voice to what she believed was an exciting and irresistible pitch. She always said her laughter was like pretty little white birds suddenly taking to flight, and it disgusted my father.

WRITER *(gets up, goes forward)*: Just in case she plans to talk forever, I'm going for a walk. *(He goes.)*

SECRETARY: One day when my mother thought she was alone on the front porch, the postman came with two bills for my father, and my mother invited him to stop a moment. Well, my mother *wasn't* alone. I was just around the edge of the porch by the lilac tree, and I saw everything that happened. First, she insisted that he take off his postman's bag, and then she said it was silly for him to wear such a heavy coat on such a hot day, and then she wondered if he wouldn't like to go into the house for a little lemonade. *Well,* I ran around to the back of the house, to find a nice place to hide, and so I was there when they came in, and I'll never forget what happened.

(Scene Six: The WRITER *is stirring a big jar full of gin and ice. There is a potted plant on one side of the stage: a good-looking little tree. On the other is a modern-style bird-cage with a couple of small birds in it. The* SECRETARY *comes in with a tray of little things to eat, which she places on the table. She leans over happily, kisses the* WRITER *on the cheek, and smiles.)*

SECRETARY: Shall I bring in the children to say good night, or would you rather put them to bed yourself?

WRITER *(aside)*: What'd she say?

SECRETARY *(claps hands)*: Wake up. *(The* WRITER *looks at her, a little befuddled.)* They're watching *Annie Oakley* on T.V., but it's almost over. Immediately afterwards they're to go straight to bed. I don't like kids wandering around at a party. All our friends let their kids do that, and you know it's no fun at all for anybody, least of all the kids. They *like* to be rushed to bed. I must say I wish you'd wake up. You're still thinking about the play.

WRITER: Of course I am.

SECRETARY: Well, stop worrying about it. I'm sure it's your best. Have a nice big drink, and then have another. Everybody else at every party gets drunk in no time at all. I've never seen *you* drunk. Some of the best writing in the world was done by men in their fifties. You'll feel much better just as soon as our friends arrive. You need people a lot more than you imagine. Everybody senses you feel he's an idiot. It's nothing you *say,* necessarily. It's something everybody *feels,* though. I know I do, and I know the children do, too. It's only the little girl who doesn't. But then of course you really *do* make the little girl feel grand—*all* the time. She really knows how much you love *her*—how much more than you love anybody else in the whole world. It's quite a compliment to a woman, and she *is* a woman. Now, I hope you won't fly off the handle, I've asked Jerry's brother to the party. He wants you to write a story for a movie. He has an idea. What's wrong with letting him tell you his idea? If you like it, fine. If not, fine. He wants to talk business, pure and simple. He needs what you can write, and you need money. You *will* be nice to him, won't you? I'm not saying stop writing your *real* writing. I'm saying do a little for money, too. Try not to look scornful when you listen to him. Even if the idea is bad, try to see something in it that's good. Let him feel as if *he* were creating something. People like to feel they're a force behind the making of something good. I know he'll pay you well. Well, perhaps I'd better put the children to bed, after all. *(She goes. The* WRITER *smiles, steps forward.)*

WRITER: The New Play—is this the end of the new play? *(He goes.)*

The End

Questions

1. Do you think the scenes with the characters other than just the Writer and the Secretary are to be thought of as real or imaginary? Explain.
2. Why do you suppose Saroyan referred to the two main characters by label rather than by name?
3. Why do you think the play is divided into so many scenes? Do you think this is effective?
4. How do the Writer's and the Secretary's views of life differ? Which view do you think is more valid?
5. Is the ending logical within the framework of the play? Can you point to any clues that could predict what happens?
6. In a sentence or two trace the story line of the play. Besides the idea that life and theatre are similar, can you find any other ideas expressed by the author?

EUGÈNE IONESCO

The Chairs

EUGÈNE IONESCO was born in 1912, and spent his childhood moving between his native Rumania and Paris, eventually becoming a French citizen. In the early 1930's, he taught school, and in 1948 wrote his first play, *The Bald Soprano*.

The Bald Soprano was a reaction against the absurdity of the dialogue in a primer he was using to learn English. The characters are dehumanized, the plot leads nowhere, and much of the language means nothing in itself. The purpose is to show the absurdity of everyday life. From the completion of this first play, Ionesco's style of playwriting progressed through various changes.

Part of the Theater of the Absurd movement, Ionesco defined *absurd* as that which has no purpose. By the time he wrote *The Chairs*, there is an indication of a more humanized character in the moments of lucidity between the Old Man and the Old Woman.

THE CHAIRS was first produced in 1952. Even though they are somewhat mechanical, the Old Man and the Old Woman are more individualized than the characters in Ionesco's earlier plays.

Ionesco still uses nonsensical language. Words suggest other words because of sound and regardless of meaning. As in earlier plays, there is a mechanical aspect to the action. One example is the Old Woman's rushing from door to door and bringing in chair after chair.

The presence of the chairs also suggests that, even when people are present (and Ionesco specifies that there should be sounds of murmuring even if the guests are invisible), there is an absence of humanity and an overabundance of objects.

The Chairs: A Tragic Farce Eugène Ionesco

Characters:

OLD MAN, *aged 95*
OLD WOMAN, *aged 94*
THE ORATOR, *aged 45 to 50*
And many other characters

Setting

Circular walls with a recess upstage center. A large, very sparsely furnished room. To the right, going upstage from the proscenium, three doors. Then a window with a stool in front of it; then another door. In the center of the back wall of the recess, a large double door, and two other doors facing each other and bracketing the main door: these last two doors, or at least one of them, are almost hidden from the audience. To the left, going upstage from the proscenium, there are three doors, a window with a stool in front of it, opposite the window on the right, then a blackboard and a dais. See the plan below. Downstage are two chairs, side by side. A gas lamp hangs from the ceiling.

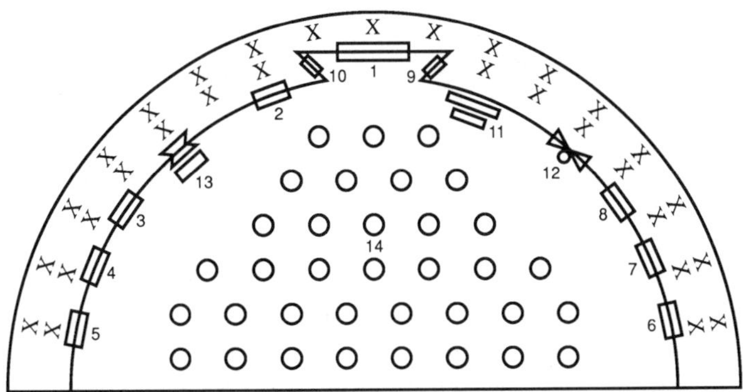

1: Main double door. 2, 3, 4, 5: Slide doors on the right. 6, 7, 8: Slide doors on the left. 9, 10: Two doors hidden in the recess. 11: Dais and blackboard. 12, 13: Windows, with stools, left and right. 14: Empty chairs. XXX Corridor, in wings.

(The curtain rises. Half-light. The OLD MAN *is up on the stool, leaning out the window on the left. The* OLD WOMAN *lights the gas lamp. Green light. She goes over to the* OLD MAN *and takes him by the sleeve.)*

OLD WOMAN: Come my darling, close the window. There's a bad smell from that stagnant water, and besides the mosquitoes are coming in.
OLD MAN: Leave me alone!
OLD WOMAN: Come, come, my darling, come sit down. You shouldn't

lean out, you might fall into the water. You know what happened to François I. You must be careful.

OLD MAN: Still more examples from history! Sweetheart, I'm tired of French history. I want to see—the boats on the water making blots in the sunlight.

OLD WOMAN: You can't see them, there's no sunlight, it's nighttime, my darling.

OLD MAN:There are still shadows. *(He leans out very far.)*

OLD WOMAN *(pulling him in with all her strength)*: Oh!. . . you're frightening me, my darling. . . come sit down, you won't be able to see them come, anyway. There's no use trying. It's dark. . . *(The* OLD MAN *reluctantly lets himself be pulled in.)*

OLD MAN: I wanted to see—you know how much I love to see the water.

OLD WOMAN: How can you, my darling. . . It makes me dizzy. Ah! this house, this island, I can't get used to it. Water all around us. . . water under the windows, stretching as far as the horizon.

(The OLD WOMAN *drags the* OLD MAN *down and they move towards the two chairs downstage; the* OLD MAN *seats himself quite naturally on the lap of the* OLD WOMAN.*)*

OLD MAN: It's six o'clock in the evening. . . it is dark already. It wasn't like this before. Surely you remember, there was still daylight at nine o'clock in the evening, at ten o'clock at midnight.

OLD WOMAN: Come to think of it, that's very true. What a remarkable memory you have!

OLD MAN: Things have certainly changed.

OLD WOMAN: Why is that, do you think?

OLD MAN: I don't know, Semiramis, sweetheart. . . Perhaps it's because the further one goes, the deeper one sinks. It's because the earth keeps turning around, around, around, around,. . .

OLD WOMAN: Around, around, my little pet. *(Silence.)* Ah! yes, you've certainly a fine intellect. You are very gifted, my darling. You could have been head president, head king, or even head doctor or head general, if you had wanted to, if only you'd had a little ambition in life. . .

OLD MAN: What good would that have done us? We'd not have lived any better. . . and besides, we have a position here, I am a general, in any case, of the house, since I am the general factotum.

OLD WOMAN *(caressing the* OLD MAN *as one caresses a child)*: My darling, my pet.

OLD MAN: I'm very bored.

OLD WOMAN: You were more cheerful when you were looking at the water . . . Let's amuse ourselves by making believe, the way you did the other evening.

OLD MAN: Make believe yourself, it's your turn.

OLD WOMAN: It's your turn.

OLD MAN: Your turn.

OLD WOMAN: Your turn.

OLD MAN: Your turn.

OLD WOMAN: Your turn.

OLD MAN: Drink your tea, Semiramis. *(Of course there is no tea.)*

OLD WOMAN: Come on now, imitate the month of February.

OLD MAN: I don't like the months of the year.

OLD WOMAN: Those are the only ones we have, up till now. Come on, just to please me . . .

OLD MAN: All right, here's the month of February. *(He scratches his head like Stan Laurel.)*

OLD WOMAN *(laughing, applauding)*: That's just right. Thank you, thank you, you're as cute as can be, my darling. *(She hugs him.)* Oh, you are so gifted, you could have been at least a head general, if you had wanted to . . .

OLD MAN: I am a general, general factotum. *(Silence.)*

OLD WOMAN: Tell me the story, you know *the* story: "Then at last we arrived . . ."

OLD MAN: Again? . . . I'm sick of it . . . "Then at last we arrived"? That again . . . you always ask for the same thing! . . . "Then at last we arrived . . ." But it's monotonous . . . For all of the seventy-five years that we've been married, every single evening, absolutely every blessed evening, you've made me tell the same story, you've made me imitate the same people, the same months . . . always the same . . . let's talk about something else . . .

OLD WOMAN: My darling, I'm not tired of it . . . it's your life, it fascinates me.

OLD MAN: You know it by heart.

OLD WOMAN: It's as if suddenly I'd forgotten everything . . . it's as though my mind were a clean slate every evening . . . Yes, my darling, I do it on purpose, I take a dose of salts . . . I become new again, for you, my darling, every evening . . . Come on, begin again, please.

OLD MAN: Well, if you want me to.

OLD WOMAN: Come on then, tell your story . . . It's also mine; what is yours is mine! Then at last we arrived . . .

OLD MAN: Then at last we arrived . . . my sweetheart . . .

OLD WOMAN: Then at last we arrived . . . my darling . . .

OLD MAN: Then at last we arrived at a big fence. We were soaked through, frozen to the bone, for hours, for days, for nights, for weeks . . .

OLD WOMAN: For months . . .

OLD MAN: . . . In the rain . . . Our ears, our feet, our knees, our noses, our teeth were chattering. . . that was eighty years ago. . . They wouldn't let us in. . . they might at least have opened the gate of the garden . . . *(Silence.)*

OLD WOMAN: In the garden the grass was wet.

OLD MAN: There was a path which led to a little square and in the center, a village church. . . Where was this village? Do you recall?

OLD WOMAN: No, my darling, I've forgotten.

OLD MAN: How did we reach it? Where is the road? This place was called Paris, I think. . .

OLD WOMAN: Paris never existed, my little one.

OLD MAN: That city must have existed because it collapsed. . . It was the city of light, but it has been extinguished, extinguished, for four hundred thousand years. . . Nothing remains of it today, except a song.

OLD WOMAN: A real song? That's odd. What song?

OLD MAN: A lullaby, an allegory: "Paris will always be Paris."

OLD WOMAN: And the way to it was through the garden? Was it far?

OLD MAN *(dreaming, lost)*: The song?. . . the rain?. . .

OLD WOMAN: You are very gifted. If you had had a little ambition in life you could have been head king, head journalist, head comedian, head general. . . All that's gone down the drain, alas. . . down the old black drain. . . down the old drain, I tell you. *(Silence.)*

OLD MAN: Then at last we arrived. . .

OLD WOMAN: Ah! yes, go on. . . tell me. . .

OLD MAN *(while the* OLD WOMAN *begins to laugh softly, senilely, then progressively in great bursts, the* OLD MAN *laughs, too, as he continues)*: Then at last we arrived, we laughed until we cried, the story was so idiotic. . . the idiot arrived full speed, bare-bellied, the idiot was pot-bellied. . . he arrived with a trunk chock full of rice; the rice spilled out on the ground. . . the idiot on the ground to, belly to ground. . . then at last we laughed, we laughed, we laughed, the idiotic belly, bare.with rice on the ground, the trunk, the story of sick from rice belly to ground, bare-bellied, all with rice, at last we laughed, the idiot at last arrived all bare, we laughed. . .

OLD WOMAN *(laughing)*: At last we laughed like idiots, at last arrived all bare, we laughed, the trunk, the trunk full of rice, the rice on the belly, on the ground. . .

OLD MAN AND OLD WOMAN *(laughing together)*: At last we laughed. Ah!. . . laughed. . . arrived. . . arrived. . . Ah!. . . Ah!. . . rived. . . arrived. . . arrived. . . the idiotic bare belly. . . arrived with the rice. . . arrived with the rice. . . *(This is all we hear.)* At last we. . . bare-bellied. . . arrived. . . the trunk. . . *(Then the* OLD MAN *and* OLD WOMAN *calm down little by little.)* We lau. . . Ah!. . . aughed. . . Ah!. . . arrived. . . Ah!. . . arrived. . . aughed. . . aughed.

OLD WOMAN: So that's the way it was, your wonderful Paris.

OLD MAN: Who could put it better?

OLD WOMAN: Oh! my darling, you are so really fine. Oh! so really, you know, so really, so really, you could have been anything in life, a lot more than general factotum.

OLD MAN: Let's be modest. . . we should be content with the little. . .

OLD WOMAN: Perhaps you've spoiled your career?

OLD MAN *(weeping suddenly)*: I've spoiled it? I've spilled it? Ah! where are you, Mamma, Mamma, where are you, Mamma?. . . hi, hi, hi, I'm an orphan. *(He moans)*. . . . an orphan, dworfan.

OLD WOMAN: Here I am, what are you afraid of?

OLD MAN: So, Semiramis, my sweetheart, you're not my mamma. . . orphan, dworfan, who will protect me?

OLD WOMAN: But I'm here, my darling!

OLD MAN: It's not the same thing. . . I want my mamma, na, you, you're not my mamma, you. . .

OLD WOMAN *(caressing him)*: You're breaking my heart, don't cry, my little one.

OLD MAN: Hi, hi, let me go, hi, hi, I'm all spoiled, I'm wet all over, my career is spilled, it's spoiled.

OLD WOMAN: Calm down.

(Long silence. They remain immobile for a time, completely rigid on their chairs.)

OLD MAN *(as in a dream)*: At the end of the garden there was. . . there was . . . there was. . . there was. . . was what, my dear?

OLD WOMAN: The city of Paris!

OLD MAN: At the end, at the end of the end of the city of Paris, there was, there was, was what?

OLD WOMAN: My darling, was what, my darling, was who?

OLD MAN: The place and the weather were beautiful. . .

OLD WOMAN: The weather was so beautiful, are you sure?

OLD MAN: I don't recall the place. . .

OLD WOMAN: Don't tax your mind then. . .

OLD MAN: It's too far away, I can no longer. . . recall it. . . where was this?

OLD WOMAN: But what?

OLD MAN: What I. . . what I. . . where was this? And who?

OLD WOMAN: No matter where it is—I will follow you anywhere, I'll follow you, my darling.

OLD MAN: Ah! I have so much difficulty expressing myself. . . but I must tell it all.

OLD WOMAN: It's a sacred duty. You've no right to keep your message from the world. You must reveal it to mankind, they're waiting for it . . . the universe waits only for you.

OLD MAN: Yes, yes, I will speak.

OLD WOMAN: Have you really decided? You must.

OLD MAN: Drink your tea.

OLD WOMAN: You could have been head orator, if you'd had more will power in life . . . I'm proud, I'm happy that you have at last decided to speak to every country, to Europe, to every continent!

OLD MAN: Unfortunately, I have so much difficulty expressing myself, it isn't easy for me.

OLD WOMAN: It's easy once you begin, like life and death . . . it's enough to have your mind made up. It's in speaking that ideas come to us, words, and then we, in our own words, we find perhaps everything, the city too, the garden, and then we are orphans no longer.

OLD MAN: It's not I who's going to speak, I've hired a professional orator, he'll speak in my name, you'll see.

OLD WOMAN: Then, it really is for this evening? And have you invited everyone, all the characters, all the property owners, and all the intellectuals?

OLD MAN: Yes, all the owners and all the intellectuals. *(Silence.)*

OLD WOMAN: The janitors? the bishops? the chemists? the tinsmiths? the violinists? the delegates? the presidents? the police? the merchants? the buildings? the pen holders? the chromosomes?

OLD MAN: Yes, yes, and the post-office employees, the innkeepers, and the artists, everybody who is a little intellectual, a little proprietary!

OLD WOMAN: And the bankers?

OLD MAN: Yes, invited.

OLD WOMAN: The proletarians? the functionaries? the militaries? the revolutionaries? the reactionaries? the alienists and their alienated?

OLD MAN: Of course, all of them, all of them, all of them, since actually everyone is either intellectual or proprietary.

OLD WOMAN: Don't get upset, my darling, I don't mean to annoy you, you are so very absent-minded, like all great geniuses. This meeting is important, they must all be here this evening. Can you count on them? Have they promised?

OLD MAN: Drink your tea, Semiramis. *(Silence.)*

OLD WOMAN: The papacy, the papayas, and the papers?

OLD MAN: I've invited them. *(Silence.)* I'm going to communicate the message to them . . . All my life, I've felt that I was suffocating; and now, they will know all, thanks to you and to the Orator, you are the only ones who have understood me.

OLD WOMAN: I'm so proud of you . . .

OLD MAN: The meeting will take place in a few minutes.

OLD WOMAN: It's true then, they're going to come, this evening? You won't feel like crying any more, the intellectuals and the proprietors will take the place of papas and mammas? *(Silence.)* Couldn't you put off this meeting? It won't be too tiring for us?

(More violent agitation. For several moments the OLD MAN *has been turning around the* OLD WOMAN *with the short, hesitant steps of an old man or of a child. He takes a step or two towards one of the doors, then returns and walks around her again.)*

OLD MAN: You really think this might tire us?

OLD WOMAN: You have a slight cold.

OLD MAN: How can I call it off?

OLD WOMAN: Invite them for another evening. You could telephone.

OLD MAN: No, my God, I can't do that, it's too late. They've probably already embarked!

OLD WOMAN: You should have been more careful. *(We hear the sound of a boat gliding through the water.)*

OLD MAN: I think someone is coming already . . . *(The gliding sound of a boat is heard more clearly.)* . . . Yes, they're coming! . . . *(The* OLD WOMAN *gets up also and walks with a hobble.)*

OLD WOMAN: Perhaps it's the Orator.

OLD MAN: He won't come so soon. This must be somebody else. *(We hear the doorbell ring.)* Ah!

OLD WOMAN: Ah!

(Nervously, the OLD MAN *and the* OLD WOMAN *move towards the concealed door in the recess to the right. As they move upstage, they say:)*

OLD MAN: Come on . . .

OLD WOMAN: My hair must look a sight . . . wait a moment . . .

(She arranges her hair and her dress as she hobbles along, pulling up her thick red stockings.)

OLD MAN: You should have gotten ready before . . . you had plenty of time.

OLD WOMAN: I'm so badly dressed . . . I'm wearing an old gown and it's all rumpled . . .

OLD MAN: All you had to do was to press it . . . hurry up! You're making our guests wait.

(The OLD MAN, *followed by the* OLD WOMAN *still grumbling, reaches the door in the recess; we don't see them for a moment; we hear them open the door, then close it again after having shown someone in.)*

VOICE OF OLD MAN: Good evening, madam, won't you please come in. We're delighted to see you. This is my wife.

VOICE OF OLD WOMAN: Good evening, madam, I am very happy to make your acquaintance. Take care, don't ruin your hat. You might take out the hatpin, that will be more comfortable. Oh! no, no one will sit on it.

VOICE OF OLD MAN: Put your fur down there. Let me help you. No, nothing will happen to it.

VOICE OF OLD WOMAN: Oh! what a pretty suit . . . and such darling colors in your blouse . . . Won't you have some cookies . . . Oh, you're not fat at all . . . no . . . plump . . . Just leave your umbrella there.

VOICE OF OLD MAN: Follow me, please.

OLD MAN *(back view)*: I have only a modest position . . .

(The OLD MAN *and* OLD WOMAN *re-enter together, leaving space between them for their guest. She is invisible. The* OLD MAN *and* OLD WOMAN *advance, downstage, facing the audience and speaking to the invisible Lady, who walks between them.)*

OLD MAN *(to the invisible Lady)*: You've had good weather?

OLD WOMAN *(to the Lady)*: You're not too tired? . . . Yes, a little.

OLD MAN *(to the Lady)*: At the edge of the water . . .

OLD WOMAN *(to the Lady)*: It's kind of you to say so.

OLD MAN *(to the Lady)*: Let me get you a chair. *(*OLD MAN *goes to the left, he exits by door No. 6.)*

OLD WOMAN *(to the Lady)*: Take this one, for the moment, please. *(She indicates one of the two chairs and seats herself on the other, to the right of the invisible Lady.)* It seems rather warm in here, doesn't it? *(She smiles at the Lady.)* What a charming fan you have! My husband . . . *(The* OLD MAN *re-enters through door No. 7, carrying a chair.)* . . . gave me one very like it, that must have been seventy-three years ago . . . and I still have it . . . *(The* OLD MAN *places the chair to the left of the invisible Lady.)* . . . it was for my birthday! . . .

(The OLD MAN *sits on the chair that he has just brought on-stage, so that the invisible Lady is between the old couple. The* OLD MAN *turns his face towards the Lady, smiles at her, nods his head, softly rubs his hands together, with the air of following what she says. The* OLD WOMAN *does the same business.)*

OLD MAN: No, madam, life is never cheap.

OLD WOMAN *(to the Lady)*: You are so right . . . *(The Lady speaks.)* As you say, it is about time all that changed . . . *(Changing her tone:)* Perhaps my husband can do something about it . . . he's going to tell you about it.

OLD MAN *(to the* OLD WOMAN*)*: Hush, hush, Semiramis, the time hasn't come to talk about that yet. *(To the Lady:)* Excuse me, madam, for having aroused your curiosity. *(The Lady reacts.)* Dear madam, don't insist . . .

(The OLD MAN *and* OLD WOMAN *smile. They even laugh. They appear to be very amused by the story the invisible Lady tells them. A pause, a moment of silence in the conversation. Their faces lose all expression.)*

OLD MAN *(to the invisible Lady)*: Yes, you're quite right . . .
OLD WOMAN: Yes, yes, yes . . . Oh! surely not.
OLD MAN: Yes, yes, yes. Not at all.
OLD WOMAN: Yes?
OLD MAN: No!?
OLD WOMAN: It's certainly true.
OLD MAN *(laughing)*: It isn't possible.
OLD WOMAN *(laughing)*: Oh! well. *(To the* OLD MAN.*)* she's charming.
OLD MAN *(to the* OLD WOMAN*)*: Madam has made a conquest. *(To the invisible Lady:)* my congratulations! . . .
OLD WOMAN *(to the invisible Lady)*: You're not like the young people today . . .
OLD MAN *(bending over painfully in order to recover an invisible object that the invisible Lady has dropped)*: Let me . . . don't disturb yourself . . . I'll get it . . . Oh! you're quicker than I . . . *(He straightens up again.)*
OLD WOMAN *(to the* OLD MAN*)*: She's younger than you!
OLD MAN *(to the invisible Lady)*: Old age is a heavy burden. I can only wish you an eternal youth.
OLD WOMAN *(to the invisible Lady)*: He's sincere, he speaks from the heart. *(To the* OLD MAN.*)* My darling!

(Several moments of silence. The OLD MAN *and* OLD WOMAN, *heads turned in profile, look at the invisible Lady, smiling politely; they then turn their heads towards the audience, then look again at the invisible Lady, answering her smile with their smiles, and her questions with their replies.)*

OLD WOMAN: It's very kind of you to take such an interest in us.
OLD MAN: We live a retired life.
OLD WOMAN: My husband's not really misanthropic, he just loves solitude.
OLD MAN: We have the radio, I get in some fishing, and then there's fairly regular boat service.
OLD WOMAN: On Sundays there are two boats in the morning, one in the evening, not to mention privately chartered trips.
OLD MAN *(to the invisible Lady)*: When the weather's clear, there is a moon.
OLD WOMAN *(to the invisible Lady)*: He's always concerned with his duties as general factotum . . . they keep him busy . . . On the other hand, at his age, he might very well take it easy.

OLD MAN *(to the invisible Lady)*: I'll have plenty of time to take it easy in my grave.

OLD WOMAN *(to the* OLD MAN*)*: Don't say that, my little darling. . . *(To the invisible Lady:)* Our family, what's left of it, my husband's friends, still came to see us, from time to time, ten years ago. . .

OLD MAN *(to the invisible Lady)*: In the winter, a good book, beside the radiator, and the memories of a lifetime.

OLD WOMAN *(to the invisible Lady)*: A modest life but a full one. . . he devotes two hours every day to work on his message. *The doorbell rings. After a short pause, we hear the noise of a boat leaving.)*

OLD WOMAN *(to the* OLD MAN*)*: Someone has come. Go quickly.

OLD MAN *(to the invisible Lady)*: Please excuse me, madam. Just a moment! *(To the* OLD WOMAN*:)* Hurry and bring some chairs! *(Loud ringing of the doorbell.)*

OLD MAN *(hastening, all bent over, towards door No. 2 to the right, while the* OLD WOMAN *goes towards the concealed door on the left, hurrying with difficulty, hobbling along)*: It must be someone important. *(He hurries, opens door No. 2, and the invisible Colonel enters. Perhaps it would be useful for us to hear discreetly several trumpet notes, several phrases, like "Hail the Chief." When he opens the door and sees the invisible Colonel, the* OLD MAN *stiffens into a respectful position of attention.)* Ah! . . . Colonel! *(He lifts his hand vaguely towards his forehead, so as to roughly sketch a salute.)* Good evening, my dear Colonel. . . This is a very great honor for me. . . I. . . I . . . I was not expecting it. . . although. . . indeed. . . in short, I am most proud to welcome you, a hero of your eminence, into my humble dwelling. . . *(He presses the invisible hand that the invisible Colonel gives him, bending forward ceremoniously, then straightening up again.)* Without false modesty, nevertheless, I permit myself to confess to you that I do not feel unworthy of the honor of your visit! Proud, yes. . . unworthy, no! . . . *(The* OLD WOMAN *appears with a chair, entering from the right.)*

OLD WOMAN: Oh!, What a handsome uniform! What beautiful medals! Who is it, my darling?

OLD MAN *(to the* OLD WOMAN*)*: Can't you see that it's the Colonel?

OLD WOMAN *(to the* OLD MAN*)*: Ah!

OLD MAN *(to the* OLD WOMAN*)*: Count his stripes! *(To the Colonel.)* This is my wife, Semiramis. *(To the* OLD WOMAN.*)* Come here so that I can introduce you to the Colonel. *(The* OLD WOMAN *approaches, dragging the chair by one hand, and makes a curtsey, without letting go of the chair. To the Colonel:)* My wife. *(To the* OLD WOMAN.*)* The Colonel.

OLD WOMAN: How do you do, Colonel. Welcome. You're an old comrade of my husband's, he's a general. . .

OLD MAN *(annoyed)*: factotum, factotum. . .

(The invisible Colonel kisses the hand of the OLD WOMAN. *This is apparent from the gesture she makes as she raises her hand toward his lips. Overcome with emotion, the* OLD WOMAN *lets go of the chair.)*

OLD WOMAN: Oh! He's most polite . . . you can see that he's really superior, a superior being! . . . *(She takes hold of the chair again. To the Colonel.)* This chair is for you . . .

OLD MAN *(to the invisible Colonel)*: This way, if you please . . . *(They move downstage, the* OLD WOMAN *dragging the chair. To the Colonel.)* Yes, one guest has come already. We're expecting a great many more people! . . . *(The* OLD WOMAN *places the chair to the right.)*

OLD WOMAN *(to the Colonel)*: Sit here, please. *(The* OLD MAN *introduces the two invisible guests to each other.)*

OLD MAN: A young lady we know . . .

OLD WOMAN: A very dear friend . . .

OLD MAN *(same business)*: The Colonel . . . a famous soldier.

OLD WOMAN *(indicating the chair she has just brought in to the Colonel)*: Do take this chair . . .

OLD MAN *(to the* OLD WOMAN*)*: No, no, can't you see that the Colonel wishes to sit beside the Lady! . . .

(The Colonel seats himself invisibly on the third chair from the left; the invisible Lady is supposedly sitting on the second chair; seated next to each other they engage in an inaudible conversation; the OLD WOMAN *and* OLD MAN *continue to stand behind their chairs, on both sides of their invisible guests; the* OLD MAN *to the left of the Lady, the* OLD WOMAN *to the right of the Colonel.)*

OLD WOMAN *(listening to the conversation of the two guests)*: Oh! Oh! That's going too far.

OLD MAN *(same business)*: Perhaps. *(The* OLD MAN *and the* OLD WOMAN *make signs to each other over the heads of their guests, while they follow the inaudible conversation which takes a turn that seems to displease them. Abruptly.)* Yes, Colonel, they are not here yet, but they'll be here. And the Orator will speak in my behalf, he will explain the meaning of my message . . . Take care, Colonel, this Lady's husband may arrive at any moment.

OLD WOMAN *(to the* OLD MAN*)*: Who is this gentleman?

OLD MAN *(to the* OLD WOMAN*)*: I've told you, it's the Colonel. *(Some embarrassing things take place, invisibly.)*

OLD WOMAN *(to the* OLD MAN*)*: I knew it. I knew it.

OLD MAN: Then why are you asking?

OLD WOMAN: For my information. Colonel, no cigarette butts on the floor!

OLD MAN *(to Colonel)*: Colonel, Colonel, it's slipped my mind—in the last war did you win or lose?

OLD WOMAN *(to the invisible Lady)*: But my dear, don't let it happen!

OLD MAN: Look at me, look at me, do I look like a bad soldier? One time, Colonel, under fire . . .

OLD WOMAN: He's going too far! It's embarrassing! *(She seizes the invisible sleeve of the Colonel.)* Listen to him! My darling, why don't you stop him!

OLD MAN *(continuing quickly)*: And all on my own, I killed 209 of them; we called them that because they jumped so high to escape, however there weren't so many of them as there were flies; of course it is less amusing, Colonel, but thanks to my strength of character, I have . . . Oh! no, I must, please.

OLD WOMAN *(to Colonel)*: My husband never lies; it may be true that we are old, nevertheless we're respectable.

OLD MAN *(violently, to the Colonel)*: A hero must be a gentleman too, if he hopes to be a complete hero!

OLD WOMAN *(to the Colonel)*: I've known you for many years, but I'd never have believed you were capable of this. *(To the Lady, while we hear the sound of boats.)* I'd never have believed him capable of this. We have our dignity, our self-respect.

OLD MAN *(in a quavering voice)*: I'm still capable of bearing arms. *(Doorbell rings.)* Excuse me, I must go to the door. *(He stumbles and knocks over the chair of the invisible Lady.)* Oh! pardon.

OLD WOMAN *(rushing forward)*: You didn't hurt yourself? *(The* OLD MAN *and* OLD WOMAN *help the invisible Lady onto her feet.)* You've got all dirty, there's some dust. *(She helps brush the Lady. The doorbell rings again.)*

OLD MAN: Forgive me, forgive me. *(To the* OLD WOMAN.*)* Go bring a chair.

OLD WOMAN *(to the two invisible guests)*: Excuse me for a moment.

(While the OLD MAN *goes to open door No. 3, the* OLD WOMAN *exits through door No. 5 to look for a chair, and she re-enters by door No. 8.)*

OLD MAN *(moving towards the door)*: He was trying to get my goat. I'm almost angry. *(He opens the door.)* Oh! madam, you're here! I can scarcely believe my eyes, and yet, nevertheless . . . I didn't really dare to hope . . . really it's . . . Oh! madam, madam . . . I have thought about you, all my life, all my life, madam, they always called you La Belle . . . it's your husband . . . someone told me, certainly . . . you haven't changed a bit . . . Oh! yes, yes, your nose *has* grown longer, maybe it's a little swollen . . . I didn't notice it when I first saw you, but I see it now . . . a lot longer . . . ah! how unfortunate! You certainly didn't do it on purpose . . . how did it happen? . . . little by little . . . excuse me, sir and dear friend, you'll permit me to call you "dear friend," I knew your wife long before you . . . she was the same, but with a completely different nose . . . I congratulate you, sir, you seem to love each other very much. *(The* OLD WOMAN *re-enters through door No. 8 with a chair.)* Semiramis, two guests have arrived, we need one more chair . . . *(The* OLD WOMAN *puts the chair behind the four others, then exits by door No. 8 and re-enters by door No. 5, after a few moments, with another chair that she places beside the one she has just brought in. By this time, the* OLD MAN *and the two guests have moved near the* OLD WOMAN.*)* Come this way, please, more guests have arrived. I'm going to introduce you . . . now then, madam . . . Oh! Belle, Belle, Miss Belle, that's what they used to call you . . . now you're all bent over . . . Oh! sir, she is still Belle to me, even so; under her glasses, she still has pretty eyes; her hair is white, but under the white one can see brown, and blue, I'm sure of that . . . come nearer, nearer . . . what is this, sir, a gift, for my wife? *(To the* OLD WOMAN, *who has just come on with the chair.)* Semiramis, this is Belle, you know, Belle . . . *(To the Colonel and the invisible Lady.)* This is Miss, pardon, Mrs. Belle, don't smile . . . and her husband . . . *(To the* OLD WOMAN.*)* A childhood friend, I've often spoken of her to you . . . and her husband. *(Again to the Colonel and to the invisible Lady:)* And her husband . . .

OLD WOMAN *(making a little curtsey)*: He certainly makes good introductions. He has fine manners. Good evening, madam, good evening, sir. *(She indicates the two first guests to the newly arrived couple:)* Our friends, yes . . .

OLD MAN *(to the* OLD WOMAN*)*: He's brought you a present. *(The* OLD WOMAN *takes the present.)*

OLD WOMAN: Is it a flower, sir? or a cradle? a pear tree? or a crow?

OLD MAN *(to the* OLD WOMAN*)*: No, no, can't you see that it's a painting?

OLD WOMAN: Oh! how pretty! Thank you, sir . . . *(To the invisible Lady.)* Would you like to see it, dear friend?

OLD MAN *(to the invisible Colonel)*: Would you like to see it?

OLD WOMAN *(to Belle's husband)*: Doctor, Doctor, I feel squeamish, I have hot flashes, I feel sick, I've aches and pains, I haven't any feeling in my feet, I've caught cold in my eyes, I've a cold in my fingers, I'm suffering from liver trouble, Doctor, Doctor! . . .

OLD MAN *(to the* OLD WOMAN*)*: This gentleman is not a doctor, he's a photo-engraver.

OLD WOMAN *(to the first invisible Lady)*: If you've finished looking at it, you might hang it up. *(To the* OLD MAN*:)* That doesn't matter, he's charming even so, he's dazzling. *(To the Photo-engraver:)* Without meaning to flatter you . . .

(The OLD MAN *and the* OLD WOMAN *now move behind the chairs, close to each other, almost touching, but back to back; they talk: the* OLD MAN *to Belle, the* OLD

WOMAN *to the Photo-engraver; from time to time their replies, as shown by the way they turn their heads, are addressed to one or the other of the first two guests.)*

OLD MAN *(to Belle)*: I am very touched... You're still the same, in spite of everything... I've loved you, a hundred years ago... But there's been such a change... No, you haven't changed a bit... I loved you, I love you...

OLD WOMAN *(to the Photo-engraver)*: Oh! Sir, sir, sir...

OLD MAN *(to the Colonel)*: I'm in complete agreement with you on that point.

OLD WOMAN *(to the Photo-engraver)*: Oh! certainly, sir, certainly... *(To the first Lady)*: Thanks for hanging it up... Forgive me if I've inconvenienced you.

(The light grows stronger. It should grow stronger and stronger as the invisible guests continue to arrive.)

OLD MAN *(almost whimpering to Belle)*: Where are the snows of yester year?

OLD WOMAN *(to the Photo-engraver)*: Oh! Sir, sir, sir... Oh! sir...

OLD MAN *(pointing out the first lady to Belle)*: She's a young friend... she's very sweet...

OLD WOMAN *(pointing the Colonel out to the Photo-engraver)*: Yes, he's a mounted staff colonel... a comrade of my husband... a subaltern, my husband's a general...

OLD MAN *(to Belle)*: Your ears were not always so pointed!... My Belle, do you remember?

OLD WOMAN *(to the Photo-engraver, simpering grotesquely; she develops this manner more and more in this scene; she shows her thick red stockings, raises her many petticoats, shows an underskirt full of holes... this business, entirely different from her manner heretofore as well as from that she will have subsequently, and which must reveal the hidden personality of the* OLD WOMAN, *ceases abruptly)*: So you think I'm too old for that, do you?

OLD MAN *(to Belle, very romantically)*: When we were young, the moon was a living star, Ah! yes, yes, if only we had dared, but we were only children. Wouldn't you like to recapture those bygone days... is it still possible? Is it still possible? Ah! no, no, it is no longer possible. Those days have flown away as fast as a train. Time has left the marks of his wheels on our skin. So you believe surgeons can perform miracles? *(To the Colonel)*: I am a soldier, and you, too, we soldiers are always young, the generals are like gods... *(To Belle)*: It ought to be that way ... Alas! Alas! We have lost everything. We could have been so happy, I'm sure of it, we could have been, we could have been; perhaps the flowers are budding again beneath the snow!...

OLD WOMAN *(to Photo-engraver)*: Flatterer! Rascal! Ah! Ah! I look younger than my years? You're a little savage! You're exciting.

OLD MAN *(to Belle)*: Will you be my Isolde and let me be your Tristan? Beauty is more than skin deep, it's in the heart... Do you understand? We could have had the pleasure of sharing, joy, beauty, eternity... an eternity... Why didn't we dare? We weren't brave enough... Everything is lost, lost, lost.

OLD WOMAN *(to Photo-engraver)*: Oh no, Oh! no, Oh! la la, you give me the shivers. You too, are you ticklish? To tickle or be tickled? I'm a little embarrassed... *(She laughs.)* Do you like my petticoat? Or do you like this skirt better?

OLD MAN *(to Belle)*: A general factotum has a poor life!

OLD WOMAN *(turning her head towards the first invisible Lady)*: In order to make crepes de Chine? A leaf of beef, an hour of flour, a little gastric sugar. *(To the Photo-engraver)*: You've got clever fingers, ah... all the sa-a-a-me!... Oh-oh-oh-oh.

OLD MAN *(to Belle)*: My worthy helpmeet, Semiramis, has taken the place of my mother. *(He turns towards the Colonel)*: Colonel, as I've often observed to you, one must take the truth as one finds it. *(He turns back towards Belle.)*

OLD WOMAN *(to Photo-engraver)*: Do you really really believe that one could have children at any age? Any age children?

OLD MAN *(to Belle)*: It's this alone that has saved me: the inner life, peace of mind, austerity, my scientific investigations, philosophy, my message...

OLD WOMAN *(to Photo-engraver)*: I've never yet betrayed my husband, the general... not so hard, you're going to make me fall... I'm only his poor mamma! *(She sobs.)* A great, great *(She pushes him back.)*, great ... mamma. My conscience causes these tears to flow. For me the branch of the apple tree is broken. Try to find somebody else. I no longer want to gather rosebuds...

OLD MAN *(to Belle)*:... All the preoccupations of a superior order...

(The OLD MAN *and* OLD WOMAN *lead Belle and the Photo-engraver up alongside the two other invisible guests, and seat them.)*

OLD MAN AND OLD WOMAN *(to the Photo-engraver and Belle):* Sit down, please sit down.

(The OLD MAN *and* OLD WOMAN *sit down too, he to the left, she to the right, with the four empty chairs between them. A long mute scene, punctuated at intervals with "no," "yes," "yes." The* OLD MAN *and* OLD WOMAN *listen to the conversation of the invisible guests.)*

OLD WOMAN *(to the Photo-engraver)*: We had one son . . . of course, he's still alive . . . he's gone away . . . it's a common story . . . or, rather, unusual . . . he abandoned his parents . . . he had a heart of gold . . . that was a long time ago . . . We loved him so much . . . he slammed the door . . . My husband and I tried to hold him back with all our might . . . he was seven years old, the age of reason, I called after him: "My son, my child, my son, my child." . . . He didn't even look back . . .

OLD MAN: Alas, no . . . no, we've never had a child . . . I'd hoped for a son . . . Semiramis, too . . . we did everything . . . and my poor Semiramis is so maternal, too. Perhaps it was better that way . . . As for me I was an ungrateful son myself . . . Ah! . . . grief, regret, remorse, that's all we have . . . that's all we have left . . .

OLD WOMAN: He said to me: "You kill birds! Why do you kill birds?" . . . But we don't kill birds . . . we've never harmed so much as a fly . . . His eyes were full of big tears. He wouldn't let us dry them. He wouldn't let me come near him. He said: "Yes, you kill all the birds, all the birds." . . . He showed us his little fists . . . "You're lying, you've betrayed me! The streets are full of dead birds, of dying baby birds." It's the song of the birds! . . . "No, it's their death rattle. The sky is red with blood." . . . No, my child, it's blue. He cried again: "You've betrayed me, I adored you, I believed you to be good . . . the streets are full of dead birds, you've torn out their eyes . . . Papa, mamma, you're wicked! . . . I refuse to stay with you." . . . I threw myself at his feet . . . His father was weeping. We couldn't hold him back. As he went we could still hear him calling: "It's you who are responsible" . . . What does that mean, "responsible"?

OLD MAN: I let my mother die all alone in a ditch. She called after me, moaning feebly: "My child, my beloved son, don't leave me to die all alone . . . Stay with me. I don't have much time left." Don't worry, Mamma, I told her, I'll be back in a moment . . . I was in a hurry . . . I was going to the ball, to dance. I will be back in a minute. But when I returned, she was already dead, and they had buried her deep . . . I broke open the grave, I searched for her . . . I couldn't find her . . . I know, I know, sons, always, abandon their mothers, and they more or less kill their fathers . . . Life is like that . . . but I, I suffer from it . . . and the others, they don't . . .

OLD WOMAN: He cried: "Papa, Mamma, I'll never set eyes on you again."

OLD MAN: I suffer from it, yes, the others don't . . .

OLD WOMAN: Don't speak of him to my husband. He loved his parents so much. He never left them for a single moment. He cared for them, coddled them . . . And they died in his arms, saying to him: "You have been a perfect son. God will be good to you."

OLD MAN: I can still see her stretched out in the ditch, she was holding lily of the valley in her hand, she cried: "Don't forget me, don't forget me" . . . her eyes were full of big tears, and she called me by my baby name: "Little Chick," and said, "Little Chick, don't leave me here all alone."

OLD WOMAN *(to the Photo-engraver)*: He has never written to us. From time to time, a friend tells us that he's been seen here or there, that he is well, that he is a good husband . . .

OLD MAN *(to Belle)*: When I got back, she had been buried a long time. *(To the first invisible Lady.)* Oh, yes. Oh! yes, madam, we have a movie theatre in the house, a restaurant, bathrooms . . .

OLD WOMAN *(to the Colonel)*: Yes, Colonel, it is because he . . .

OLD MAN: Basically that's it. *(Desultory conversation, getting bogged down.)*

OLD WOMAN: If only!

OLD MAN: Thus, I've not . . . I, it . . . certainly . . .

OLD WOMAN *(dislocated dialogue, exhaustion)*: All in all.

OLD MAN: To ours and to theirs.

OLD WOMAN: So that.

OLD MAN: From me to him.

OLD WOMAN: Him, or her?

OLD MAN: Them.

OLD WOMAN: Curl-papers . . . After all.

OLD MAN: It's not that.

OLD WOMAN: Why?

OLD MAN: Yes.

OLD WOMAN: I.

OLD MAN: All in all.

OLD WOMAN: All in all.

OLD MAN *(to the first invisible Lady)*: What was that, madam?

(A long silence, the OLD MAN *and* OLD WOMAN *remain rigid on their chairs. Then the doorbell rings.)*

OLD MAN *(with increasing nervousness)*: Someone has come. People. Still more people.

OLD WOMAN: I thought I heard some boats.

OLD MAN: I'll go to the door. Go bring some chairs. Excuse me, gentlemen, ladies. *(He goes towards door No. 7.)*

OLD WOMAN *(to the invisible guests who have already arrived)*: Get up for a moment, please. The Orator will be here soon. We must ready the room for the meeting. *(The* OLD WOMAN *arranges the chairs, turning their backs towards the audience.)* Lend me a hand, please. Thanks.

OLD MAN *(opening door No. 7)*: Good evening, ladies, good evening, gentlemen. Please come in.

(The three or four invisible persons who have arrived are very tall, and the OLD MAN *has to stand on his toes in order to shake hands with them. The* OLD WOMAN, *after placing the chairs as indicated above, goes over to the* OLD MAN.*)*

OLD MAN *(making introductions)*: My wife . . . Mr. . . . Mrs. . . . my wife . . . Mr. . . . Mrs. . . . my wife . . .

OLD WOMAN: Who are all these people, my darling?

OLD MAN *(to* OLD WOMAN*)*: Go find some chairs, dear.

OLD WOMAN: I can't do everything! . . .

(She exits, grumbling, by door No. 6 and re-enters by door No. 7, while the OLD MAN, *with the newly arrived guests, moves downstage.)*

OLD MAN: Don't drop your movie camera. *(More introductions.)* The Colonel . . . the Lady . . . Mrs. Belle . . . the Photo-engraver . . . These are the newspaper men, they have come to hear the Orator too, who should be here any minute now . . . Don't be impatient . . . You'll not be bored . . . all together now . . . *(The* OLD WOMAN *re-enters through door No. 7 with two chairs.)* Come along, bring the chairs more quickly . . . we're still short one.

(The OLD WOMAN *goes to find another chair, still grumbling, exiting by door No. 3, and re-entering by door No. 8.)*

OLD WOMAN: All right, and so . . . I'm doing as well as I can . . . I'm not a machine, you know . . . Who are all these people? *(She exits.)*

OLD MAN: Sit down, sit down, the ladies with the ladies, and the gentlemen with the gentlemen, or vice versa, if you prefer . . . We don't have any more nice chairs . . . we have to make do with what we have . . . I'm sorry . . . take the one in the middle . . . does anyone need a fountain pen? Telephone Maillot, you'll get Monique . . . Claude is an angel. I don't have a radio . . . I take all the newspapers . . . that depends on a number of things; I manage these buildings, but I have no help . . . we have to economize . . . no interviews, please, for the moment . . . later, we'll see . . . you'll soon have a place to sit . . . what can she be doing? *(The OLD WOMAN enters by door No. 8 with a chair.)* Faster, Semiramis . . .

OLD WOMAN: I'm doing my best . . . Who are all these people?

OLD MAN: I'll explain it all to you later.

OLD WOMAN: And that woman? That woman, my darling?

OLD MAN: Don't get upset . . . *(To the Colonel:)* Colonel, journalism is a profession too, like a fighting man's . . . *(To the* OLD WOMAN*:)* Take care of the ladies, my dear . . . *(The doorbell rings. The* OLD MAN *hurries towards door No. 8.)* Wait a moment . . . *(To the* OLD WOMAN*:)* Bring chairs!

OLD WOMAN: Gentlemen, ladies, excuse me . . .

(She exits by door No. 3, re-entering by door No. 2; the OLD MAN *goes to open concealed door No. 9, and disappears at the moment the* OLD WOMAN *re-enters by door No. 2.)*

OLD MAN *(out of sight)*: Come in . . . come in . . . come in . . . come in . . . *(He reappears, leading in a number of invisible people, including one very small child he holds by the hand.)* One doesn't bring little children to a scientific lecture . . . the poor thing is going to be bored . . . if he begins to cry or to peepee on the ladies' dresses, that'll be a fine state of affairs! *(He conducts them to stage center; the* OLD WOMAN *comes on with two chairs.)* I wish to introduce you to my wife, Semiramis; and these are their children.

OLD WOMAN: Ladies, gentlemen . . . Oh! aren't they sweet!

OLD MAN: That one is the smallest.

OLD WOMAN: Oh, he's so cute . . . so cute . . . so cute!

OLD MAN: Not enough chairs.

OLD WOMAN: Oh! dear, oh dear, oh dear . . .

(She exits, looking for another chair, using now door No. 2 as exit and door No. 3 on the right to re-enter.)

OLD MAN: Hold the little boy on your lap . . . The twins can sit together in the same chair. Be careful, they're not very strong . . . they go with the house, they belong to the landlord. Yes, my children, he'd make trouble for us, he's a bad man . . . he wants us to buy them from him, these worthless chairs. *(The* OLD WOMAN *returns as quickly as she can with a chair.)* You don't all know each other . . . you're seeing each other for the first time . . . you knew each other by name . . . *(To the* OLD WOMAN*:)* Semiramis, help me make the introductions . . .

OLD WOMAN: Who are all these people? . . . May I introduce you, excuse me . . . May I introduce you . . . but who are they?

OLD MAN: May I introduce you . . . Allow me to introduce you . . . permit me to introduce you . . . Mr., Mrs., Miss . . . Mr. . . . Mrs. . . . Mrs. . . . Mr.

OLD WOMAN *(to* OLD MAN*)*: Did you put on your sweater? *(To the invisible guests:)* Mr., Mrs., Mr. . . . *(Doorbell rings again.)*

OLD MAN: More people! *(Another ring of doorbell)*.

OLD WOMAN: More people!

(The doorbell rings again, then several more times, and more times again; the OLD MAN *is beside himself; the chairs, turned towards the dais, with their backs to the audience, form regular rows, each one longer as in a theatre; the* OLD MAN *is winded, he mops his brow, goes from one door to another, seats invisible people, while the* OLD WOMAN, *hobbling along, unable to move any faster, goes as rapidly as she can, from one door to another, hunting for chairs and carrying them in. There are*

now many invisible people on stage; both the OLD MAN *and* OLD WOMAN *take care not to bump into people and to thread their way between the rows of chairs. The movement could go like this: the* OLD MAN *goes to door No. 4, the* OLD WOMAN *exits by door No. 3, returns by door No. 2; the* OLD MAN *goes to open door No. 7, the* OLD WOMAN *exits by door No. 8, re-enters by door No. 6 with chairs, etc., in this manner making their way around the stage, using all the doors.)*

OLD WOMAN: Beg pardon . . . excuse me . . . what . . . oh,yes . . . beg pardon . . . excuse me . . .

OLD MAN: Gentlemen . . . come in . . . ladies . . . enter . . . it is Mrs. . . . let me . . . yes . . .

OLD WOMAN *(with more chairs)*: Oh dear . . . Oh dear . . . there are too many . . . There really are too, too . . . too many, oh dear, oh dear, oh dear . . .

(We hear from outside, louder and louder and approaching nearer and nearer, the sounds of boats moving through the water; all the noises come directly from the wings. The OLD WOMAN *and the* OLD MAN *continue the business outlined above; they open the doors, they carry in chairs. The doorbell continues to ring.)*

OLD MAN: This table is in our way. *(He moves a table, or he sketches the business of moving it, without slowing down his rhythm, aided by the* OLD WOMAN.*)* There's scarcely a place left here, excuse us . . .

OLD WOMAN *(making a gesture of clearing the table, to the* OLD MAN*)*: Are you wearing your sweater?

(Doorbell rings.)

OLD MAN: More people! More chairs! More people! More chairs! Come in, come in, ladies and gentlemen . . . Semiramis, faster . . . We'll give you a hand soon . . .

OLD WOMAN: Beg pardon . . . beg pardon . . . good evening, Mrs. . . . Mrs. . . . Mr. . . . Mr. . . . yes, yes, the chairs . . .

(The doorbell rings louder and louder and we hear the noises of boats striking the quay very close by, and more and more frequently. The OLD MAN *flounders among the chairs; he has scarcely enough time to go from one door to another, so rapidly do the ringings of the doorbell succeed each other.)*

OLD MAN: Yes, right away . . . are you wearing your sweater? Yes, yes . . . immediately, patience, yes, yes . . . patience . . .

OLD WOMAN: Your sweater? My sweater? . . . Beg pardon, beg pardon.

OLD MAN: This way, ladies and gentlemen, I request you . . . I re you . . . pardon . . . quest . . . enter, enter . . . going to show . . . there, the seats . . . dear friend . . . not there . . . take care . . . you, my friend!

(Then a long moment without words. We hear waves, boats, the continuous ringing

of the doorbell. The movement culminates in intensity at this point. The doors are now opening and shutting all together ceaselessly. Only the main door in the center of the recess remains closed. The OLD MAN *and* OLD WOMAN *come and go, without saying a word, from one door to another; they appear to be gliding on roller skates. The* OLD MAN *receives the people, accompanies them, but doesn't take them very far, he only indicates seats to them after having taken one or two steps with them; he hasn't enough time. The* OLD WOMAN *carries in chairs. The* OLD MAN *and the* OLD WOMAN *meet each other and bump into each other, once or twice, without interrupting their rhythm. Then, the* OLD MAN *takes a position upstage center, and turns from left to right, from right to left, etc., towards all the doors and indicates the seats with his arms. His arms move very rapidly. Then, finally the* OLD WOMAN *stops, with a chair in one hand, which she places, takes up again, replaces, looks as though she, too, wants to go from one door to another, from right to left, from left to right, moving her head and neck very rapidly. This must not interrupt the rhythm; the* OLD MAN *and* OLD WOMAN *must still give the impression of not stopping, even while remaining almost in one place; their hands, their chests, their heads, their eyes are agitated, perhaps moving in little circles. Finally, there is a progressive slowing down of movement, at first slight: the ringings of the doorbell are less loud, less frequent; the doors open less and less rapidly; the gestures of the* OLD MAN *and* OLD WOMAN *slacken continuously. At the moment when the doors stop opening and closing altogether, and the ringings cease to be heard, we have the impression that the stage is packed with people.)*

OLD MAN: I'm going to find a place for you . . . patience . . . Semiramis, for the love of . . .

OLD WOMAN *(with a large gesture, her hands empty)*: There are no more chairs, my darling. *(Then, abruptly, she begins to sell invisible programs in a full hall, with the doors closed.)* Programs, get your programs here, the program of the evening, buy your program!

OLD MAN: Relax, ladies and gentlemen, we'll take care of you . . . Each in his turn, in the order of your arrival . . . You'll have a seat. I'll take care of you.

OLD WOMAN: Buy your programs! Wait a moment, madam, I cannot take care of everyone at the same time, I haven't got thirty-three hands, you know, I'm not a cow . . . Mister, please be kind enough to pass the program to the lady next to you, thank you . . . my change, my change . . .

OLD MAN: I've told you that I'd find a place for you! Don't get excited! Over here, it's over here, there, take care . . . oh, dear friend . . . dear friends . . .

OLD WOMAN: . . . Programs . . . get your grams . . . grams . . .

OLD MAN: Yes, my dear, she's over there, further down, she's selling programs . . . no trade is unworthy . . . that's her . . . do you see her? . . .

you have a seat in the second row . . . to the right . . . no, to the left . . . that's it!

OLD WOMAN: . . . gram . . . gram . . . program . . . get your program.

OLD MAN: What do you expect me to do? I'm doing my best! *(To invisible seated people:)* Push over a little, if you will please . . . there's still a little room, that will do for you, won't it, Mrs. . . . come here. *(He mounts the dais, forced by the pushing of the crowd.)* Ladies, gentlemen, please excuse us, there are no more seats available . . .

OLD WOMAN *(who is now on the opposite side of the stage, across from the* OLD MAN, *between door No. 3 and the window)*: Get your programs . . . who wants a program? Eskimo pies, caramels . . . fruit drops . . . *(Unable to move, the* OLD WOMAN, *hemmed in by the crowd, scatters her programs and candies anywhere, above the invisible heads.)* Here are some! There they are!

OLD MAN *(standing on the dais, very animated; he is jostled as he descends from the dais, remounts it, steps down again, hits someone in the face, is struck by an elbow, says)*: Pardon . . . please excuse us . . . take care . . . *(Pushed, he staggers, has trouble regaining his equilibrium, clutches at shoulders.)*

OLD WOMAN: Why are there so many people? Programs, get your program here, Eskimo pies.

OLD MAN: Ladies, young ladies, gentlemen, a moment of silence, I beg you . . . silence . . . it's very important . . . those people who've no seats are asked to clear the aisles . . . that's it . . . don't stand between the chairs.

OLD WOMAN *(to the* OLD MAN, *almost screaming)*: Who are all these people, my darling? What are they doing here?

OLD MAN: Clear the aisles, ladies and gentlemen. Those who do not have seats must, for the convenience of all, stand against the wall, there, along the right or left . . . you'll be able to hear everything, you'll see everything, don't worry, you won't miss a thing, all seats are equally good!

(There is a great hullabaloo. Pushed by the crowd, the OLD MAN *makes almost a complete turn around the stage and ends up at the window on the right, near to the stool. The* OLD WOMAN *makes the same movement in reverse and ends up at the window on the left, near the stool there.)*

OLD MAN *(making this movement)*: Don't push, don't push.

OLD WOMAN *(same business)*: Don't push, don't push.

OLD MAN *(same business)*: Don't push, don't push.

OLD WOMAN *(same business)*: Don't push, ladies and gentlemen, don't push.

OLD MAN *(same business)*: Relax . . . take it easy . . . be quiet . . . what's going on here?

OLD WOMAN *(same business)*: There's no need to act like savages, in any case.

(At last they reach their final positions. Each is near a window. The OLD MAN *to the left, by the window which is beside the dais. The* OLD WOMAN *on the right. They don't move from these positions until the end.)*

OLD WOMAN *(calling to the* OLD MAN*)*: My darling. . . I can't see you, anymore. . . where are you? Who are they? What do all these people want? Who is that man over there?

OLD MAN: Where are you? Where are you, Semiramis?

OLD WOMAN: My darling, where are you?

OLD MAN: Here, beside the window. . . Can you hear me?

OLD WOMAN: Yes, I hear your voice!. . . there are so many. . . but I can make out yours. . .

OLD MAN: And you, where are you?

OLD WOMAN: I'm beside the window too!. . . My dear, I'm frightened, there are too many people. . . we are very far from each other. . . at our age we have to be careful. . . we might get lost. . . We must stay close together, one never knows, my darling, my darling. . .

OLD MAN: Ah!. . . I just caught sight of you. . . Oh!. . . We'll find each other, never fear. . . I'm with friends. *(To the friends:)* I'm happy to shake your hands. . . But of course, I believe in progress, uninterrupted progress, with some jolts, nevertheless. . .

OLD WOMAN: That's fine, thanks. . . What foul weather! Yes, it's been nice! *(Aside:)* I'm afraid, even so. . . What am I doing here?. . . *(She screams:)* My darling, My darling!

(The OLD MAN *and* OLD WOMAN *individually speak to guests near them.)*

OLD MAN: In order to prevent the exploitation of man by man, we need money, money, and still more money!

OLD WOMAN: My darling! *(Then, hemmed in by friends:)* Yes, my husband is here, he's organizing everything. . . over there. . . Oh! you'll never get there. . . you'd have to go across, he's with friends. . .

OLD MAN: Certainly not. . . as I've always said. . . pure logic does not exist . . . all we've got is an imitation.

OLD WOMAN: But you know, there are people who are happy. In the morning they eat breakfast on the plane, at noon they lunch in the pullman, and in the evening they dine aboard the liner. At night they sleep in the trucks that roll, roll, roll. . .

OLD MAN: Talk about the dignity of man! At least let's try to save face. Dignity is only skin deep.

OLD WOMAN: Don't slink away into the shadows. . . *(She bursts out laughing in conversation.)*

OLD MAN: Your compatriots ask of me.

OLD WOMAN: Certainly. . . tell me everything.

OLD MAN: I've invited you. . . in order to explain to you. . . that the individual and the person are one and the same.

OLD WOMAN: He has a borrowed look about him. He owes us a lot of money.

OLD MAN: I am not myself. I am another. I am the one in the other.

OLD WOMAN: My children, take care not to trust one another.

OLD MAN: Sometimes I awaken in the midst of absolute silence. It's a perfect circle. There's nothing lacking. But one must be careful, all the same. Its shape might disappear. There are holes through which it can escape.

OLD WOMAN: Ghosts, you know, phantoms, mere nothings. . . The duties my husband fulfills are very important sublime.

OLD MAN: Excuse me. . . that's not at all my opinion! At the proper time, I'll communicate my views on this subject to you. . . I have nothing to say for the present!. . . We're waiting for the Orator, he'll tell you, he'll speak in my behalf, and explain everything that we hold most dear. . . he'll explain everything to you. . . when?. . . when the moment has come. . . the moment will come soon. . .

OLD WOMAN *(on her side to her friends)*: The sooner, the better. . . That's understood. . . *(Aside:)* They're never going to leave us alone. Let them go, why don't they go?. . . My poor darling, where is he? I can't see him any more. . .

OLD MAN *(same business)*: Don't be so impatient. You'll hear my message. In just a moment.

OLD WOMAN *(Aside)*: Ah!. . . I hear his voice!. . . *(To her friends:)* Do you know, my husband has never been understood. But at last his hour has come.

OLD MAN: Listen to me, I've had a rich experience of life. In all walks of life, at every level of thought. . . I'm not an egotist: humanity must profit by what I've learned.

OLD WOMAN: Ow! You stepped on my foot. . . I've got chilblains!

OLD MAN: I've perfected a real system. *(Aside:)* The Orator ought to be here. *(Aloud:)* I've suffered enormously.

OLD WOMAN: We have suffered so much. *(Aside:)* The Orator ought to be here. It's certainly time.

OLD MAN: Suffered much, learned much.

OLD WOMAN *(like an echo)*: Suffered much, learned much.

OLD MAN: You'll see for yourselves, my system is perfect.

OLD WOMAN *(like an echo)*: You'll see for yourselves, his system is perfect.

OLD MAN: If only my instructions are carried out.

OLD WOMAN *(echo)*: If only his instructions are carried out.

OLD MAN: We'll save the world!. . .

OLD WOMAN *(echo)*: Saving his own soul by saving the world! . . .
OLD MAN: One truth for all!
OLD WOMAN *(echo)*: One truth for all!
OLD MAN: Follow me! . . .
OLD WOMAN *(echo)*: Follow him! . . .
OLD MAN: For I have absolute certainty! . . .
OLD WOMAN *(echo)*: He has absolute certainty!
OLD MAN: Never . . .
OLD WOMAN *(echo)*: Ever and ever . . . *(Suddenly we hear noises in the wings, fanfares.)*
OLD WOMAN: What's going on?

(The noises increase, then the main door opens wide, with a great crash; through the open door we see nothing but a very powerful light which floods onto the stage through the main door and the windows, which at the entrance of the Emperor are brightly lighted.)

OLD MAN: I don't know . . . I can scarcely believe . . . is it possible . . . but yes . . . but yes . . . incredible . . . and still it's true . . . yes . . . if . . . yes . . . it is the Emperor! His Majesty the Emperor!

(The light reaches its maximum intensity, through the open door and through the windows; but the light is cold, empty; more noises which cease abruptly.)

OLD MAN: Stand up! . . . It's His Majesty the Emperor! The Emperor in my house, in our house . . . Semiramis . . . do you realize what this means?
OLD WOMAN *(not understanding)*: The Emperor . . . the Emperor? My darling! *(Then suddenly she understands.)* Ah, yes, the Emperor! Your Majesty! Your Majesty! *(She wildly makes countless grotesque curtsies.)* In our house! In our house!
OLD MAN *(weeping with emotion)*: Your Majesty! . . . Oh! Your Majesty . . . Your little, Your great Majesty! . . . Oh! what a sublime honor . . . it's all a marvelous dream.
OLD WOMAN *(like an echo)*: A marvelous dream . . . arvelous . . .
OLD MAN *(to the invisible crowd)*: Ladies, gentlemen, stand up, our beloved sovereign, the Emperor, is among us! Hurrah! Hurrah!

(He stands up on the stool; he stands on his toes in order to see the Emperor; the OLD WOMAN *does the same on her side.)*

OLD WOMAN: Hurrah! Hurrah! *(Stamping of feet.)*
OLD MAN: Your Majesty! . . . I'm over here! . . . Your Majesty! Can you hear me? Can you see me? Please tell his Majesty that I'm here! Your Majesty! Your Majesty!!! I'm here, your most faithful servant! . . .
OLD WOMAN *(still echoing)*: Your most faithful servant, Your Majesty!

OLD MAN: Your servant, your slave, your dog, arf, arf, your dog, Your Majesty! . . .

OLD WOMAN *(barking loudly like a dog)*: Arf. . . arf. . . arf. . .

OLD MAN *(wringing his hands)*: Can you see me?. . . Answer, Sire!. . . Ah, I can see you, I've just caught sight of Your Majesty's august face. . . your divine forehead. . . I've seen you, yes, in spite of the screen of courtiers. . .

OLD WOMAN: In spite of the courtiers. . . we're here, Your Majesty!

OLD MAN: Your Majesty! Your Majesty! Ladies, gentlemen, don't keep him—His Majesty standing. . . you see, Your Majesty, I'm truly the only one who cares for you, for your health, I'm the most faithful of all your subjects. . .

OLD WOMAN *(echoing)*: Your Majesty's most faithful subjects!

OLD MAN: Let me through, now, ladies and gentlemen. . . how can I make my way through such a crowd?. . . I must go to present my most humble respects to His Majesty, the Emperor. . . let me pass. . .

OLD WOMAN *(echo)*: Let him pass. . . let him pass. . . pass. . . ass. . .

OLD MAN: Let me pass, please, let me pass. *(Desperate:)* Ah! Will I ever be able to reach him?

OLD WOMAN *(echo)*: Reach him. . . reach him. . .

OLD MAN: Nevertheless, my heart and my whole being are at his feet, the crowd of courtiers surrounds him, ah! ah! they want to prevent me from approaching him. . . They know very well that. . . oh! I understand, I understand. . . Court intrigues, I know all about it. . . They hope to separate me from Your Majesty!

OLD WOMAN: Calm yourself, my darling. . . His Majesty sees you, he's looking at you. . . His Majesty has given me a wink. . . His Majesty is on our side! . . .

OLD MAN: They must give the Emperor the best seat. . . near the dais. . . so that he can hear everything the Orator is going to say.

OLD WOMAN *(hoisting herself up on the stool, on her toes, lifting her chin as high as she can, in order to see better)*: At last they're taking care of the Emperor.

OLD MAN: Thank heaven for that! *(To the Emperor:)* Sire. . . Your Majesty may rely on him. It's my friend, it's my representative who is at Your Majesty's side. *(On his toes, standing on the stool:)* Gentlemen, ladies, young ladies, little children, I implore you.

OLD WOMAN *(echoing)*: Plore. . . plore. . .

OLD MAN: . . . I want to see. . . move aside. . . I want. . . the celestial gaze, the noble face, the crown, the radiance of His Majesty. . . Sire, deign to turn your illustrious face in my direction, toward your humble servant. . . so humble. . . Oh! I caught sight of him clearly that time . . . I caught sight. . .

OLD WOMAN *(echo)*: He caught sight that time... he caught sight... caught... sight...

OLD MAN: I'm at the height of joy... I've no more words to express my boundless gratitude... in my humble dwelling, Oh! Majesty! Oh! radiance!... here... here... in the dwelling where I am, true enough, a general... but within the hierarchy of your army, I'm only a simple general factotum[1]...

OLD WOMAN *(echo)*: General factotum...

OLD MAN: I'm proud of it... proud and humble, at the same time... as I should be... alas! certainly, I am a general, I might have been at the imperial court, I have only a little court here to take care of... Your Majesty... I... Your Majesty, I have difficulty expressing myself... I might have had... many things, not a few possessions if I'd known, if I'd wanted, if I... if we... Your Majesty, forgive my emotion...

OLD WOMAN: Speak in the third person!

OLD MAN *(sniveling)*: May Your Majesty deign to forgive me! You are here at last... We had given up hope... you might not even have come ... Oh! Savior, in my life, I have been humiliated...

OLD WOMAN *(echo, sobbing)*: ... miliated... miliated...

OLD MAN: I've suffered much in my life... I might have been something, if I could have been sure of the support of Your Majesty... I have no other support... if you hadn't come, everything would have been too late... you are, Sire, my last recourse...

OLD WOMAN *(echo)*: Last recourse... Sire... ast recourse... ire... recourse...

OLD MAN: I've brought bad luck to my friends, to all those who have helped me... Lightning struck the hand which was held out toward me...

OLD WOMAN *(echo)*: ... hand that was held out... held out... out...

OLD MAN: They've always had good reasons for hating me, bad reasons for loving me...

OLD WOMAN: That's not true, my darling, not true. *I* love you, I'm your little mother...

OLD MAN: All my enemies have been rewarded and my friends have betrayed me...

OLD WOMAN *(echo)*: Friends... betrayed... betrayed...

OLD MAN: They've treated me badly. They've persecuted me. If I complained, it was always they who were in the right... Sometimes I've tried to revenge myself... I was never able to, never able to revenge myself... I have too much pity... I refused to strike the enemy to the ground, I have always been too good.

1. A handyman or servant.

OLD WOMAN *(echo)*: He was too good, good, good, good, good...

OLD MAN: It is my pity that has defeated me.

OLD WOMAN *(echo)*: My pity...pity...pity...

OLD MAN: But they never pitied me. I gave them a pin prick, and they repaid me with club blows, with knife blows, with cannon blows, they've crushed my bones...

OLD WOMAN *(echo)*: ...My bones...my bones...my bones...

OLD MAN: They've supplanted me, they've robbed me, they've assassinated me...I've been the collector of injustice, the lightning rod of catastrophes...

OLD WOMAN *(echo)*: Lightning rod...catastrophe...lightning rod...

OLD MAN: In order to forget, Your Majesty, I wanted to go in for sports ...for mountain climbing...they pulled my feet and made me slip ...I wanted to climb stairways, they rotted the steps...I fell down ...I wanted to travel, they refused me a passport...I wanted to cross the river, they burnt my bridges...

OLD WOMAN *(echo)*: Burnt my bridges.

OLD MAN: I wanted to cross the Pyrenees, and there were no more Pyrenees.

OLD WOMAN *(echo)*: No more Pyrenees...He could have been, he too, Your Majesty, like so many others, a head editor, a head actor, a head doctor, Your Majesty, a head king...

OLD MAN: Furthermore, no one has ever shown me due consideration... no one has ever sent me invitations...However, I, hear me, I say this to you, I alone could have saved humanity, who is so sick. Your Majesty realizes this as do I...or, at the least, I could have spared it the evils from which it has suffered so much this last quarter of a century, had I had the opportunity to communicate my message; I do not despair of saving it, there is still time, I have a plan...alas, I express myself with difficulty...

OLD WOMAN *(above the invisible heads)*: The Orator will be here, he'll speak for you. His Majesty is here, thus you'll be heard, you've no reason to despair, you hold all the trumps, everything has changed, everything has changed...

OLD MAN: I hope Your Majesty will excuse me...I know you have many other worries...I've been humiliated...Ladies and gentlemen, move aside just a little bit, don't hide His Majesty's nose from me altogether, I want to see the diamonds of the imperial crown glittering ...But if Your Majesty has deigned to come to our miserable home, it is because you have condescended to take into consideration my wretched self. What an extraordinary reward. Your Majesty, if corporeally I raise myself on my toes, this is not through pride, this is only in order to gaze upon you!...morally, I throw myself at your knees.

OLD WOMAN *(sobbing)*: At your knees, Sire, we throw ourselves at your knees, at your feet, at your toes...

OLD MAN: I've had scabies. My employer fired me because I did not bow to his baby, to his horse. I've been kicked in the ass, but all this, Sire, no longer has any importance...since...since...Sir...Your Majesty...look...I am here...here...

OLD WOMAN *(echo)*: Here...here...here...here...here...here...

OLD MAN: Since Your Majesty is here...since Your Majesty will take my message into consideration...But the Orator should be here...he's making His Majesty wait...

OLD WOMAN: If your Majesty will forgive him. He's surely coming. He will be here in a moment. They've telephoned us.

OLD MAN: His Majesty is so kind. His Majesty wouldn't depart just like that, without having listened to everything, heard everything.

OLD WOMAN *(echo)*: Heard everything...heard... listened to everything ...

OLD MAN: It is he who will speak in my name...I, I cannot...I lack the talent...he has all the papers, all the documents...

OLD WOMAN *(echo)*: He has all the documents...

OLD MAN: A little patience, Sire, I beg of you...he should be coming.

OLD WOMAN: He should be coming in a moment.

OLD MAN *(so that the Emperor will not grow impatient)*: Your Majesty, hear me, a long time ago I had the revelation...I was forty years old...I say this also to you, ladies and gentlemen...one evening, after supper, as was our custom, before going to bed, I seated myself on my father's knees...my mustaches were longer than his and more pointed...I had more hair on my chest...my hair was graying already, but his was still brown...There were some guests, grownups, sitting at table, who began to laugh, laugh.

OLD WOMAN *(echo)*: Laugh...laugh...

OLD MAN: I'm not joking, I told them, I love my papa very much. Someone replied: It is midnight, a child shouldn't stay up so late. If you don't go beddy-bye, then you're no longer a kid. But I'd still not have believed them if they hadn't addressed me as an adult.

OLD WOMAN *(echo)*: An adult.

OLD MAN: Instead of as a child...

OLD WOMAN *(echo)*: A child.

OLD MAN: Nevertheless, I thought to myself, I'm not married. Hence, I'm still a child. They married me off right then, expressly to prove the contrary to me...Fortunately, my wife has been both father and mother to me...

OLD WOMAN: The Orator should be here, Your Majesty...

OLD MAN: The Orator will come.

OLD WOMAN: He will come.

OLD MAN: He will come.
OLD WOMAN: He will come.
OLD MAN: He will come.
OLD WOMAN: He will come.
OLD MAN: He will come, he will come.
OLD WOMAN: He will come, he will come.
OLD MAN: He will come.
OLD WOMAN: He is coming.
OLD MAN: He is coming.
OLD WOMAN: He is coming, he is here.
OLD MAN: He is coming, he is here.
OLD WOMAN: He is coming, he is here.
OLD MAN AND OLD WOMAN: He is here . . .
OLD WOMAN: Here he is!

(Silence; all movement stops. Petrified, the two old people stare at door No. 5; this immobility lasts rather long—about thirty seconds; very slowly, very slowly the door opens wide, silently; then the ORATOR *appears. He is a real person. He's a typical painter or poet of the nineteenth century; he wears a large black felt hat with a wide brim, loosely tied bow tie, artist's blouse, mustache and goatee, very histrionic in manner, conceited; just as the invisible people must be as real as possible, the* ORATOR *must appear unreal. He goes along the wall to the right, gliding, softly, to upstage center, in front of the main door, without turning his head to right or left; he passes close by the* OLD WOMAN *without appearing to notice her, not even when the* OLD WOMAN *touches his arm in order to assure herself that he exists. It is at this moment that the* OLD WOMAN *says: "Here he is!")*

OLD MAN: Here he is!
OLD WOMAN *(following the* ORATOR *with her eyes and continuing to stare at him)*: It's really he, he exists. In flesh and blood.
OLD MAN *(following him with his eyes)*: He exists. It's really he. This is not a dream!
OLD WOMAN: This is not a dream, I told you so.

(The OLD MAN *clasps his hands, lifts his eyes to heaven; he exults silently. The* ORATOR, *having reached upstage center, lifts his hat, bends forward in silence, saluting the invisible Emperor with his hat with a Musketeer's flourish and somewhat like an automaton. At this moment:)*

OLD MAN: Your Majesty . . . May I present to you, the Orator . . .
OLD WOMAN: It is he!

(Then the ORATOR *puts his hat back on his head and mounts the dais from which he looks down on the invisible crowd on the stage and at the chairs; he freezes in a solemn pose.)*

OLD MAN *(to the invisible crowd)*: You may ask him for autographs. *(Automatically, silently, the* ORATOR *signs and distributes numberless autographs. The* OLD MAN *during this time lifts his eyes again to heaven, clasping his hands, and exultantly says:)* No man, in his lifetime, could hope for more...

OLD WOMAN *(echo)*: No man could hope for more.

OLD MAN *(to the invisible crowd)*: And now, with the permission of Your Majesty, I will address myself to all of you, ladies, young ladies, gentlemen, little children, dear colleagues, dear compatriots, Your Honor the President, dear comrades in arms...

OLD WOMAN *(echo)*: And little children...dren...dren...

OLD MAN: I address myself to all of you, without distinction of age, sex, civil status, social rank, or business, to thank you, with all my heart.

OLD WOMAN *(echo)*: To thank you...

OLD MAN: As well as the Orator...cordially, for having come in such large numbers...silence, gentlemen!...

OLD WOMAN *(echo)*: ...Silence, gentlemen...

OLD MAN: I address my thanks also to those who have made possible the meeting this evening, to the organizers...

OLD WOMAN: Bravo!

(Meanwhile, the ORATOR *on the dais remains solemn, immobile, except for his hand, which signs autographs automatically.)*

OLD MAN: To the owners of this building, to the architect, to the masons who were kind enough to erect these walls!...

OLD WOMAN *(echo)*: ...walls...

OLD MAN: To all those who've dug the foundations...Silence, ladies and gentlemen...

OLD WOMAN: ...'adies and gentlemen...

OLD MAN: Last but not least I address my warmest thanks to the cabinetmakers who have made these chairs on which you have been able to sit, to the master carpenter...

OLD WOMAN *(echo)*: ...penter...

OLD MAN: ...Who made the armchair in which Your Majesty is sinking so softly, which does not prevent you, nevertheless, from maintaining a firm and manly attitude...Thanks again to all the technicians, machinists, electrocutioners...

OLD WOMAN *(echoing)*: ...cutioners... cutioners...

OLD MAN: ...To the paper manufacturers and the printers, proofreaders, editors to whom we owe the programs, so charmingly decorated, to the universal solidarity of all men, thanks, thanks, to our country, to the State *(He turns toward where the Emperor is sitting:)* whose helm Your Majesty directs with the skill of a true pilot...thanks to the usher...

OLD WOMAN *(echo)*: . . . usher . . . rusher . . .

OLD MAN *(pointing to the* OLD WOMAN*)*: Hawker of Eskimo pies and programs . . .

OLD WOMAN *(echo)*: . . . grams . . .

OLD MAN: . . . My wife, my helpmeet . . . Semiramis! . . .

OLD WOMAN *(echo)*: . . . ife . . . meet . . . mis . . . *(Aside:)* The darling, he never forgets to give me credit.

OLD MAN: Thanks to all those who have given me their precious and expert, financial or moral support, thereby contributing to the overwhelming success of this evening's gathering . . . thanks again, thanks above all to our beloved sovereign, His Majesty the Emperor . . .

OLD WOMAN *(echo)*: . . . jesty the Emperor . . .

OLD MAN *(in a total silence)*: . . . A little silence . . . Your Majesty . . .

OLD WOMAN *(echo)*: . . . jesty . . . jesty . . .

OLD MAN: Your Majesty, my wife and myself have nothing more to ask of life. Our existence can come to an end in this apotheosis[2] . . . thanks be to heaven who has granted us such long and peaceful years . . . My life has been filled to overflowing. My mission is accomplished. I will not have lived in vain, since my message will be revealed to the world . . . *(Gesture towards the* ORATOR, *who does not perceive it; the* ORATOR *waves off requests for autographs, very dignified and firm.)* To the world, or rather to what is left of it! *(Wide gesture toward the invisible crowd.)* To you, ladies and gentlemen, and dear comrades, who are all that is left from humanity, but with such leftovers one can still make a very good soup . . . Orator, friend . . . *(The* ORATOR *looks in another direction.)* If I have been long unrecognized, underestimated by my contemporaries, it is because it had to be . . . *(The* OLD WOMAN *sobs.)* What matters all that now when I am leaving to you, to you, my dear Orator and friend *(The* ORATOR *rejects a new request for an autograph, then takes an indifferent pose, looking in all directions.)* . . . the responsibility of radiating upon posterity the light of my mind . . . thus making known to the universe my philosophy. Neglect none of the details of my private life, some laughable, some painful or heartwarming, of my tastes, my amusing gluttony . . . tell everything . . . speak of my helpmeet . . . *(The* OLD WOMAN *redoubles her sobs.)* . . . of the way she prepared those marvelous little Turkish pies, of her potted rabbit à la Normandabbit . . . speak of Berry, my native province . . . I count on you, great master and Orator . . . as for me and my faithful helpmeet, after our long years of labor in behalf of the progress of humanity during which we fought the good fight, nothing remains for us but

2. Elevation to divine status.

to withdraw . . . immediately, in order to make the supreme sacrifice which no one demands of us but which we will carry out even so . . .

OLD WOMAN *(sobbing)*: Yes, yes, let's die in full glory . . . let's die in order to become a legend . . . At least, they'll name a street after us . . .

OLD MAN *(to* OLD WOMAN*)*: O my faithful helpmeet! . . . you who have believed in me, unfailingly, during a whole century, who have never left me, never . . . alas, today, at this supreme moment, the crowd pitilessly separates us . . .

Above all I had hoped
that together we might lie
with all our bones together
within the selfsame skin
within the same sepulchre
and that the same worms
might share our old flesh
that we might rot together . . .

OLD WOMAN: . . . Rot together . . .

OLD MAN: Alas! . . . alas! . . .

OLD WOMAN: Alas! . . . alas! . . .

OLD MAN: . . . Our corpses will fall far from each other, and we will rot in an aquatic solitude . . . Don't pity us over much.

OLD WOMAN: What will be, will be!

OLD MAN: We shall not be forgotten. The eternal Emperor will remember us, always.

OLD WOMAN *(echo)*: Always.

OLD MAN: We will leave some traces, for we are people and not cities.

OLD MAN AND OLD WOMAN *(together)*: We will have a street named after us.

OLD MAN: Let us be united in time and in eternity, even if we are not together in space, as we were in adversity: let us die at the same moment . . . *(To the* ORATOR, *who is impassive, immobile:)* One last time . . . I place my trust in you . . . I count on you. You will tell all . . . bequeath my message . . . *(To the Emperor:)* If Your Majesty will excuse me . . . Farewell to all. Farewell, Semiramis.

OLD WOMAN: Farewell to all! . . . Farewell, my darling!

OLD MAN: Long live the Emperor!

(He throws confetti and paper streamers on the invisible Emperor; we hear fanfares; bright lights like fireworks.)

OLD WOMAN: Long live the Emperor!

(Confetti and streamers thrown in the direction of the Emperor, then on the immobile and impassive ORATOR, *and on the empty chairs.)*

OLD MAN *(same business)*: Long live the Emperor!

OLD WOMAN *(same business)*: Long live the Emperor!

(The OLD WOMAN *and* OLD MAN *at the same moment throw themselves out the windows, shouting "Long Live the Emperor." Sudden silence; no more fireworks; we hear an "Ah" from both sides of the stage, the sea-green noises of bodies falling into the water. The light coming through the main door and the windows has disappeared; there remains only a weak light as at the beginning of the play; the darkened windows remain wide open, their curtains floating on the wind.*

ORATOR *(he has remained immobile and impassive during the scene of the double suicide, and now, after several moments, he decides to speak. He faces the rows of empty chairs; he makes the invisible crowd understand that he is deaf and dumb; he makes the signs of a deafmute; desperate efforts to make himself understood; then he coughs, groans, utters the gutteral sounds of a mute)*: He, mme, mm, mm, Ju, gou, hou, hou. Heu, heu, gu gou, gueue.

(Helpless, he lets his arms fall down alongside his body; suddenly, his face lights up, he has an idea, he turns toward the blackboard, he takes a piece of chalk out of his pocket, and writes, in large capitals:

ANGELFOOD

then:

NNAA NNM NWNWNW V

He turns around again, towards the invisible crowd on the stage, and points with his finger to what he's written on the blackboard.)

ORATOR: Mmm, Mmm, Gueue, Gou, Gu. Mmm, Mmm, Mmm, Mmm.

(Then, not satisfied, with abrupt gestures he wipes out the chalk letters, and replaces them with others, among which we can make out, still in large capitals:

ΛADIEU ΛDIEU APΛ

Again, the ORATOR *turns around to face the crowd; he smiles, questions, with an air of hoping that he's been understood, of having said something; he indicates to the empty chairs what he's just written. He remains immobile for a few seconds, rather satisfied and a little solemn; but then, faced with the absence of the hoped for reaction, little by little his smile disappears, his face darkens; he waits another moment; suddenly he bows petulantly, brusquely, descends from the dais; he goes toward the main door upstage center, gliding like a ghost; before exiting through this door, he bows ceremoniously again to the rows of empty chairs, to the invisible Emperor. The stage remains empty with only the chairs, the dais, the floor covered with streamers and confetti. The main door is wide open onto darkness.*

We hear for the first time the human noises of the invisible crowd; these are bursts of laughter, murmurs, shh's, ironical coughs; weak at the beginning, these noises grow louder, then, again, progressively they become weaker. All this should last *long enough for the audience—the real and visible audience—to leave with this ending firmly impressed on its mind. The curtain falls very slowly.)* *

April–June, 1951

* In the original production the curtain fell on the mumblings of the mute ORATOR. The blackboard was not used.

Questions

1. What is the play's central idea?
2. Generally in plays, each of the characters has a basic need that he or she tries to meet. What is the Old Woman's basic need? The Old Man's?
3. Why do the two main characters jump out the window into the water?
4. In many of his plays, Ionesco uses words because of their progression of sounds. Can you find instances of this device in *The Chairs*?
5. Can you point out any instances of mechanical behavior on the part of the two main characters?
6. Why do so many people come to hear the message? What is the significance of the Emperor's attendance at the meeting?
7. The play deals with the idea that people cannot communicate effectively with each other. How many illustrations of this idea can you find in *The Chairs*?